Soviet Policy toward Western Europe

Soviet Policy toward Western Europe

Implications for the Atlantic Alliance

Edited by HERBERT J. ELLISON

UNIVERSITY OF WASHINGTON PRESS

Seattle and London

Library of Congress Cataloging in Publication Data
Main entry under title:

Soviet policy toward Western Europe.

Papers presented at a conference sponsored by the
Center for Contemporary Chinese and Soviet Studies of
the University of Washington, held in Seattle, Wash.,
in April 1982.

Includes index.

1. Europe—Foreign relations—Soviet Union—Addresses,
essays, lectures. 2. Soviet Union—Foreign relations—
Europe—Addresses, essays, lectures. 3. Europe—Foreign
relations—1945- —Addresses, essays, lectures.
4. Europe—Foreign economic relations—Soviet Union—
Addresses, essays, lectures. 5. Soviet Union—Foreign
economic relations—Europe—Addresses, essays, lectures.
I. Ellison, Herbert J. II. University of Washington.
            Center for Contemporary Chinese and Soviet Studies.
D1065.S65S69   1983   327.4704   83-47977
                ISBN 0-295-96035-3
                ISBN 0-295-96036-1 (pbk.)

44, 193

Contents

Acknowledgments

The present volume is part of a series of conferences and publications on Soviet foreign policy in the 1980s sponsored by the Center for Contemporary Chinese and Soviet Studies of the School of International Studies. The first volume—published as *The Sino-Soviet Conflict: A Global Perspective*—appeared in 1982, and other volumes will be forthcoming. The purpose of the series is to elucidate major changes in international politics resulting from the emergence of the Soviet Union as a global power.

I am deeply indebted to many people—in addition to the authors—who have contributed to this effort. Professor William Griffith not only provided a chapter but also gave invaluable help in planning the conference topics. The session chairmen (Professor Gary Bertsch, Dr. James Huntley, Professor Joel Migdal, Professor Peter Sugar, Professor Judith Thornton, and Professor Donald Treadgold) played a very important role in guiding the discussion of the papers at the conference in Seattle in April 1982. And the commentators (Professor Lawrence Caldwell, Professor Gregory Grossman, Professor Stanley Hoffmann, Professor John Keeler, Professor John Reshetar, Professor Michael Sodaro, Professor Angela Stent, and Dr. Heinz Timmermann) contributed much to the final revision of the material in the present chapters.

I am grateful for the help of many colleagues and staff of the School of International Studies, especially the Director, Professor Kenneth B. Pyle, who has given firm and generous support to this ambitious project from its inception, and to Ms. Beverly Weiss, who made conference arrangements. I am grateful too for the excellent editorial work provided by Ms. Leila Charbonneau.

I should also like to thank the following individuals and organizations whose generous donations to the Center have made this studies series financially

Acknowledgments

possible: The Boeing Company; Mr. Edward E. Carlson; John Deere Foundation; Mr. and Mrs. George P. Duecy; Mr. Stanley D. Golub; Mrs. Maxwell Hamilton; Senator Henry M. Jackson; Kaiser Family Foundation; Mr. Henry Kotkins, Sr.; Dr. Haakon Ragde; Rainier National Bank; Mr. and Mrs. Walter E. Schoenfeld; John L. Scott, Inc.; United Airlines Foundation; and United Technologies Corporation. The Boeing Company very generously provided a separate grant for the present conference and volume.

HERBERT J. ELLISON, Chairman
Center for Contemporary Chinese and Soviet Studies
School of International Studies
University of Washington

Introduction

There is no more important question of contemporary international affairs than that of the Soviet relationship with Western Europe. That relationship has undergone major changes since the late 1960s, and it is those changes, and their implications for European and world politics, that the present volume examines. To introduce the subject requires comment both on the broad history of the relationship, particularly since World War II, and on the more specific circumstances that have rapidly and extensively altered it during the last fifteen years.

A remarkable continuity is to be found in the broad outlines of Soviet policy toward Europe since the Bolshevik Revolution, both in goals and instruments. In the beginning, the main goal was the spread of communist revolution, and Germany was the chief target. Germany was the most developed of the European industrial states, and because of its large industrial proletariat, it appeared to the Russian leaders to be ripe for revolution. A communist Germany would be Soviet Russia's ally and provide the power for revolution throughout Europe; a capitalist Germany might join other capitalist states against Russian communism.

In the first years after he came to power, Lenin had three main instruments with which to pursue his goal of a communist Germany and a communist Europe: the revolutionary left wing of the German and other socialist movements, the diplomacy and diplomatic missions of Soviet Russia, and the Red Army. After the German revolution of November 1918, all three came into action, but the post-Kaiser German state and society proved far sturdier than the Russian state after the abdication of Nicholas II, and leftist insurrections were crushed, a result that Soviet diplomacy, envoys, and advice could scarcely alter. Meanwhile the Red Army, already grown to an impressive half million in size by November 1918, had still to reckon with internal military opposition and Allied intervention, and was far from German territory.

Lenin had demonstrated the possibilities for combining Russian military force with local Bolshevik insurrection in the invasion of the Ukraine in January 1918, and variations on that combination would work to extend his control to most of the non-Russian borderlands of the former Russian Empire. Following the German revolution of November 1918, the Red Army advanced rapidly westward through Estonia, Latvia, and Lithuania in late 1918 and early 1919, and soviet governments were proclaimed in all three states. Meanwhile communist insurrection in Germany early in 1919 proclaimed soviet governments in Bavaria, the Ruhr, and several large cities. The First Congress of the Communist International (Comintern), meeting in Moscow in March 1919, viewed these developments, together with the news that the communist leader Béla Kun had taken power in Hungary, as evidence that the long-awaited European revolution had arrived. But all these efforts met failure, as did the Soviet invasion of Poland the following year. For the time being, the limits of European communism had been established. As it recovered from the exertions of revolution and civil war, the Soviet government had to accept indefinite postponement of European revolution and concentrate on building a more conventional structure of diplomatic relations with the European states.

The years between the two world wars were extremely important ones in the history of Soviet policy toward Western Europe. They were years when the Soviet leadership faced frequent difficulties in reconciling the interests and activities of the foreign communist parties with the diplomatic and security requirements of the Soviet state. Conflict between the two efforts was often unavoidable; it is a mistake, however, to see Soviet caution about revolutionary initiatives of the German Communist Party, for example, as abandonment of revolution. Throughout these years Soviet leaders devoted much attention and money to the training, financing, and direction of the European communist movement. But they had to reckon with the weakness of the Soviet state vis-à-vis the capitalist powers, and above all to avoid a coalition against the Soviet Union. The solution to that problem was provided by the Treaty of Rapallo with Germany in 1922. As the pariah of World War I, Germany was a logical ally, and the tendency of the Versailles powers to keep Germany at arm's length served the Soviet purpose. The fruits of Soviet-German cooperation were reciprocal agreements for training of military forces (Germany was able to bypass the Versailles restrictions by training military forces on Soviet territory), and extensive economic agreements which helped to modernize the Soviet economy. Yet even as these agreements functioned there were periodic conflicts with the German government over Soviet support of revolutionary activity in Germany.

The Soviets regarded Great Britain as their chief opponent, and chronic tension marked Anglo-Soviet relations throughout the 1920s. Yet Soviet diplomacy sought to establish diplomatic relations with all states, including Britain (1924), and also to encourage hostility between Germany and the Versailles victors. It aimed to break down the barriers between the USSR and the East European protégés of the Versailles victors, especially the Little Entente states — Czechoslovakia, Romania, and Yugoslavia. The Soviets also signed a series of nonaggression treaties with East European states.

Soviet policy toward Germany changed abruptly when it became clear after the signing of the German-Polish nonaggression treaty of January 1934 that Hitler was not interested in German-Soviet cooperation and was probably intent on expansion eastward. The establishment of diplomatic relations with the United States in 1933, and the efforts in 1934 and 1935 to work out effective diplomatic and military collaboration with France and Czechoslovakia, were part of the desperate efforts of the Soviets to lay the framework for cooperation against Germany. That effort foundered largely because of the Western leaders' illusions about the limits of Hitler's ambition, their fears about Soviet purposes, and a widespread pacifism in their societies. When Hitler agreed in 1939 to give the Soviets what the Western powers had denied them—a territorial position in the Baltic states and Poland—the opportunity was seized and the Nazi-Soviet Pact followed.

Viewed overall, then, the main objective of Soviet diplomacy in the interwar years was to avoid isolation and to maintain and maximize the division between the victors and vanquished of World War I. The link with Germany was central, and was given up reluctantly only when it became untenable, but was reestablished in 1939 when it seemed possible both to restore cooperation with Germany and to gain territorially in the bargain. Aside from calculations of gain, the point is well made by Max Beloff that the Soviets were incapable of understanding a political movement (German Nazism) that was "at once revolutionary and nonproletarian." They therefore missed the revolutionary implications of Hitler's Nazism and its dangers for themselves. Such were the consequences of a dogma that denied any significant distinction between fascism and parliamentary democracy.

The Soviets were also busy between the wars in the organization and leadership of the European communist movement. The major European parties were founded in the early years after the Bolshevik revolution. At the time of the First Comintern Congress in 1919 the organization and program of these parties were still in flux, but it was clear that Lenin aimed to make them organizational and ideological models of the Soviet party. By the Second Comintern Congress in 1920 the Soviet domination of the international apparatus (the Congress, the executive committee in Moscow) and its operatives was complete. Against strong resistance from many European communists, Lenin, and after him Stalin, established a firm control of the policies and leadership of the foreign parties, using the organizational, financial, and other levers in the hands of the Soviet leadership to dominate their affairs.

Concerning the policies of the European communist parties, Lenin was right in insisting in 1921 that the revolutionary opportunities of the wartime era had waned and that the main task was to broaden the base of communist power by building parliamentary structures, penetrating labor unions, and building mass front organizations that could extend party influence. United front meant cooperation with socialist parties and with the labor movements they led. It also meant every effort to penetrate the socialist parties and their labor organizations in order to be able to influence them in future political situations.

In 1928 the Sixth Comintern Congress announced that revolutionary opportunities had returned and abandoned the united front policy in favor of a new policy of "class against class." Depression-era Germany provided the main opportunity, but there the determination of the Comintern to have the German party treat the socialists as the major enemy helped greatly to crush that party and the Weimar Republic it sustained, and aided the Nazi victory. With Hitler's victory, the line became popular front, a variation of united front focused on diplomatic objectives—namely, broad coalitions of communists and other parties of the center and left in support of a policy favorable to cooperation between the Entente powers and the Soviet Union against Germany, Italy, and Japan.

The popular front movement achieved success in the Blum government in France, and provided the basis of the communist and Soviet support of the Loyalist government against Franco in Spain. But the former was short-lived, and the latter was defeated by Franco's military forces. Nevertheless, it demonstrated the capacity of the Soviets to use their control of the European communist parties as an arm of Soviet diplomacy.

In general, the condition of the communist parties was a sad one on the eve of the Second World War. The Spanish, Italian, and German parties had been crushed by fascist dictatorships, and other governments had repressed most of the parties in Eastern Europe as well. Meanwhile the parties in the democratic states were rent by internal conflict born of the Soviet domination of party affairs. Stalin required absolute obedience of the foreign parties to Moscow's will, and those party leaders who survived the turbulence of the 1930s were guaranteed financial support from the Comintern to keep the core of the organization alive for better times. Less fortunate were those communist leaders who sought refuge against persecution in Moscow and fell victim in frightening numbers to Stalin's purges.

The coming of the World War II meant that for the second time in the twentieth century war would be the instrument of a transformation of the European state structure, and of the Russian role in that structure. As the tide of war turned in Russia's favor, it was apparent that the communist parties and the Axis-occupied states of Europe had employed a common strategy of building broad-based resistance organizations—political and military—in preparation for a postwar drive for power. The strongest movements were in Italy, France, Yugoslavia, Albania, and Greece. When the war ended, Soviet military presence throughout Eastern Europe added further strength to the communist cause.

The postwar policy sought rapid consolidation in Eastern Europe by the Soviets themselves and by local communists with varying degrees of Soviet direction and support, and within four years of the war's end communist power was established in eight countries of Central and Eastern Europe. Simultaneously, the Soviets were engaged in remodeling the political structure of Eastern Europe to ensure long-range control. One of the elements of this change was the removal of twelve million Germans and the conversion of East Germany into a communist-ruled Soviet satellite, a policy aimed at providing protection against German resurgence and leverage on the future of German politics. Poland was now surrounded by either Soviet or Soviet-controlled territory, and the Soviets had direct territorial access, for the first time, to Hungary and Czechoslovakia. The restructuring of boundaries and the new Soviet geopolitical position provided a much expanded Soviet influence in Europe.

The central question that preoccupied the Western leadership at the end of World War II was the possibility of Russian hegemony on the European continent—with all the possibilities for political and social influence such hegemony implied. Within the zone of Allied military control the communist parties provided the main Soviet leverage. But the military power they had acquired in wartime resistance movements was dismantled in France and Italy before 1945, and crushed in Greece soon after, and both the French and Italian parties were removed from government in 1947. During the next few years the division of Europe was rapidly stabilized, and in the West the process of economic recovery got rapidly under way protected by American power and aided by the Marshall Plan, the new programs of European economic integration, and the expanding global system of trade.

On the Soviet side, meanwhile, it was clear that both the substance and the style of postwar expansion into Eastern Europe and the forced introduction of communist rule in many countries had carried costs. They encouraged the movement toward American-West European cooperation (political, economic, and military), the formation of the NATO Alliance, and the integration of West Germany into that alliance as its most important European element militarily and economically. And Stalin's imperious dealings with the new East European communist leaders brought a break with Tito in 1948 and created a burdensome legacy of internal dissatisfaction with Soviet influence and communist power.

A new phase of Soviet postwar European policy, following the death of Stalin in 1953, focused primarily on the problems created by the late Stalin era. One aim was to reduce and divide the Western alliance, playing on the tensions within the alliance—"the internal struggles and contradictions" as Georgi Malenkov called them—meanwhile giving assurance of Soviet peaceful intentions to secure a "relaxation of tensions" and "peaceful coexistence." Implementation of the policy was complicated not only by accumulated Western mistrust but also by the eruption of anti-Soviet and anticommunist resistance in East Germany, Czechoslovakia, Hungary, and Poland.

The turbulence in Eastern Europe from 1953 to 1956 had an important resonance in the communist parties of Western Europe, particularly in Italy. Just as the East European leaders—notably the Hungarian and Polish—looked to independent Yugoslavia as an alternative model of communist rule, so too did the Italian party leaders, who felt that the Soviet break with Tito in 1948 was the result of Soviet tyrannizing of the communist movement, and that the eruption of revolution in Hungary in 1956 was the direct consequence of that policy. The Italian leader Palmiro Togliatti argued for a policy of "poly-centrism" as a recognition of a variety of centers of communist activity and leadership, and juxtaposed this with the Soviet-dominated movement which had been the pattern of the past. The increasing independent-mindedness of communist leaderships, in both Eastern and Western Europe, created a new pattern of problems for the Soviet leadership and obliged them to confront a newly forceful resistance to their policies. The independence was greatly aided by the Sino-Soviet conflict. Neither East (except Albania) nor West European communist leaders favored Maoism, but they were eager to use the conflict to weaken Soviet control in Europe. But in Eastern Europe the Soviets set the limits of autonomy for fellow communist states with their action in Czechoslovakia in 1968.

As America became more heavily involved in Vietnam in the late 1960s, and its policy interests appeared to shift to Asia, the European states—feeling a new economic and political strength and detached or negative in their attitudes toward the U.S. Vietnam policy—pursued increasingly independent policies toward the USSR. Not even the Soviet invasion of Czechoslovakia (though it challenged the central premise of Western participation in the "relaxation of tensions") seemed to interrupt the trend.

Contemporary Soviet policy toward Western Europe unfolds against a background of vital relationships—between Europe and the Soviet Union, Europe and the United States, and the Soviet Union and the United States—that have been radically transformed since the late 1960s. Among the most important changes are those in the military-strategic balance between the United States and the USSR. The American strategic weapons superiority, which lasted into the 1960s, has given way to a rough parity of American-Soviet weapons strength, ending an American advantage which had counterbalanced Soviet conventional weapons superiority in Europe. The simultaneous expansion of the Soviet armory of intermediate-range nuclear weapons directed at Europe, and the thorough modernization and expansion of Warsaw Pact conventional military forces, created a new vulnerability of Europe to pressure from the east. That vulnerability was further increased by the massive expansion of the Soviet Navy in the seas and sea lanes vital to European security. Combined with new sea and airlift capabilities, an aggressive diplomatic and political penetration of the Middle East and Africa, such policies altered the basic structure and balance of the Soviet–West European strategic relationship.

The 1970s also witnessed a severe weakening of the global economy that the Western powers and Japan had built in the postwar era: the end of the gold-based dollar and the stable international trading system it had sustained; the end of cheap energy in the wake of two oil crises; trade deficits, inflation, unemployment, and declining economic growth rates. The financial crisis created by heavy indebtedness, especially in Eastern Europe and Latin America, and the growing trade conflicts between Europe, the United States, and Japan, added to the tension in the early 1980s. For Europeans the problems seemed to be aggravated by major American policies, especially during the Vietnam War, and by the reduction of presidential foreign policy initiative and assertive American leadership following it. A new phase of European-American policy conflict appeared in the late 1970s in the debate over policy responses to the growing Soviet military power, Soviet policy in Afghanistan and in Poland, and the related question of the future of Western policies of détente in Europe.

In Western discussion it has become almost a cliché to say that the 1970s and 1980s have brought the most severe threat to West European security in the period since the founding of NATO; yet for the first time the response (at least the early response) seemed to be more one of conflict—of American–West European disagreement—than of cooperation and closer alliance.

The focus of the present volume is contemporary, with the main concentration on the period since the late 1960s. The end of the 1960s brought two superficially contradictory events: the Soviet invasion of Czechoslovakia, which tried to set limits to the liberalization of communist regimes in the Soviet zone of Eastern Europe; and a vigorous new German Ostpolitik, which was soon followed by significant Soviet-American détente in the 1970s. The events were in fact quite consistent from the Soviet viewpoint. Firm Soviet control in Eastern Europe was a prerequisite of détente with Western Europe.

To deal with all aspects of Soviet policy toward Western Europe in the last fifteen years is too large an order, particularly if one attempts to include the complex Soviet bilateral relations with all states—or even the major states—of Western Europe. We have therefore chosen a more manageable approach. The opening chapter, by William Griffith, provides both a broad historical overview of the Russian-European relationship and a more intensive examination of that relationship for the period of our concentration. There then follow two chapters—one on Germany by Gerhard Wettig, and one on France by Robert Legvold—that examine both countries' relations with the Soviet Union. For the period under review these two countries are the most important from the Soviet viewpoint, and both authors treat their subjects in a broad context of West European–Soviet relations.

The ensuing four chapters deal with functional aspects of Soviet policy toward Western Europe. Joan Urban treats the relationship between the Soviets and the West European communist parties, a subject that covers highly important new developments. As parliamentary parties, the West European communists have faced new problems and opportunities within their own countries. And they have been much affected by Soviet policy in Eastern Europe, from the Czech invasion to the events in Poland since the summer of 1980. There are also important interconnections between the European communist parties and the Chinese party which have had indirect, but important, repercussions in Europe.

Trond Gilberg's chapter on the Soviets and the noncommunist left deals with one of the most important questions of recent Soviet policy. He provides historical background on the patterns of Soviet (and European communist) relations with the left, and then offers a closer examination of those relations in the 1970s and 1980s. It is clear that a new kind of popular front policy has emerged in the 1970s and 1980s, one that seeks to build the broadest possible cooperation of the left (chiefly the main socialist parties) with the Soviet policy of détente and peace. In Soviet parlance "peace" has meant opposition to any increment in Western armaments in response to the large increments in Soviet military power in Europe. The chapter also discusses the problems created for Soviet policy by the different views of Soviet purposes within the main socialist parties and the Socialist International, by the challenge of anti-Soviet left-wing socialists, and by differences with major European communist parties.

The John Hardt–Kate Tomlinson chapter treats the immensely important question of Soviet economic policy toward Western Europe. The enormous expansion of trade and credit in the economic relations between Eastern and Western Europe is one of the most important developments in that relationship during recent years. It has helped to meet pressing Soviet needs – for technology, consumer goods, and capital – and has provided new levers of influence for Soviet policy makers. It has also created elements of interdependence between Eastern and Western Europe which provide both opportunities and hazards for the Soviets. For these and other reasons it is an increasingly important and complex element of Soviet policy.

The chapter on Soviet military policy by Benjamin Lambeth provides a review of the trends of Soviet military analysis and policy and relates these trends to the vital policy debates currently under way on the East-West military balance in Europe. No other issue is more important in the current phase of Soviet policy toward Western Europe, and none has created more protracted or bitter controversy, or controversy more divisive for American relations with Western Europe.

The fascinating chapter by Michael Sodaro on Soviet studies of the Western alliance provides an important perspective on all aspects of Soviet policy. The Soviet view of the Western alliance is given far too little attention by those who think and write about Soviet policy toward Western Europe, and yet it is basic to Soviet policy. The careful examination of this issue casts a great deal of light on many issues raised elsewhere in the volume.

Finally, Pierre Hassner of the University of Paris has imaginatively and knowledgeably surveyed the whole pattern of Soviet–West European relations in recent years to assess the implications for the Atlantic Alliance. One would be hard pressed to find a more skillful job of examining the complexities of the West European–Soviet relationship, and it also manages to see this relationship in the context of the complex system that simultaneously ties both parties to Eastern Europe and to the United States.

HERBERT J. ELLISON

Soviet Policy toward Western Europe

Chapter 1

The Soviets and Western Europe: An Overview

William E. Griffith

HISTORICAL BACKGROUND

First, as the Guide Michelin puts it, *un peu d'histoire*. The historical background of Soviet foreign policy, especially toward Western Europe, is much more important than that of United States foreign policy toward the same region, for several reasons. The first and most important is that the historical memory of Soviet leaders and their subjects is much more traumatic and therefore influential. A cursory glance at the history of Russia makes clear why: the long Mongol and Tatar occupation of Russia; the subsequent expansion of the Grand Duchy of Muscovy, and then of the Russian Empire, to the west, south, and east, into an intercontinental, multinational empire; and the historicism of Marxism-Leninism—its conscious, permanent attempt to apply the lessons of the past to the present and future.

The second point is best put as a question: Is Russia in and of Europe? Or is it an outpost, a cultural dependency of it? Or is it much more different than similar? It will be more illuminating for us to begin with the differences. Russia is vast. It is, even today, far from Western Europe except by air. In the seventeenth century it expanded to become an Asian power as well, but this expansion was different from the way the West European colonial powers expanded (except, in part, the French in Algeria): Siberia was as empty a land as the United States, Canada, or Australia, and Russians settled it as Europeans did these other three countries. It became an extension, in effect, of European Russia. Other regions that Russia conquered—the Ukraine, the Baltic states, the Caucasus, and what is now Central Asia—were already settled, often at a higher level of civilization than Russia. Thus Russia became a multinational continental empire, like Poland in Lithuania and the Ukraine, and Hungary in Slovakia and Romania, not a seaborne one like Germany in the Baltic states, or France, Britain, Spain, and Portugal overseas.

3

Mongol and Tatar rule deprived Russia of the Renaissance and Reformation. Its traditions remained Byzantine and Orthodox, not Catholic and Latin; autocratic, not really feudal; and militarized by its insecurity and its conquests.

Because Russia's initial conquests in Europe came before modern nationalism had grown up there, Russia was all the less inclined thereafter, once nationalism did rise (for example, in the Ukraine and Poland), to make any concessions to it. Russian nationalism was first forged in the fight against the Tatars—just as Castilian and later Spanish national feeling was first formed in the long struggle to drive the Moors from the Iberian Peninsula. In both cases, national liberation, unification, and multinational expansion followed one upon the other. Finally, Russia justified its conquest of the Ukraine and Belorussia from Poland as their "national and Orthodox" liberation from their Polish Catholic rulers.

But the analogy is far from perfect. Russia's conquests westward, most of all of Polish territory, were in areas of higher economic and cultural development—rare in the history of multinational empires. Nor did Russia's exploitation of them make its level of development higher than those of Poland and the Baltic states. (One has only to visit Warsaw, or for that matter Riga, to realize how far ahead they still are of Moscow and Leningrad.) To be colonized and ruled by culturally superior countries is one thing, as the continuing prestige of France in *l'Afrique francophone* shows. It is quite another to be ruled by those whom one despises—and with much reason—as one's cultural inferiors.

Of all Russia's conquests in Europe, the most fateful was that of the Polish territories. Poland has itself been a multinational empire. It had strong ties with Western Europe, for it was Roman Catholic; it had often been ruled by Saxon kings; it had many ethnic German settlers and historic cultural ties with France. The three partitions of Poland took place at the end of the eighteenth century, just when modern nationalism was sparked by the French Revolution. These Russian conquests had been made possible by the almost simultaneous decline of Sweden and the Ottoman Empire as well as the Polish Commonwealth. But the Russian absorption of so much of Poland and of even more after the defeat of Napoleon, and its ruthless, bloody repression of the Polish risings of 1830 and 1863 and of the Hungarian revolution of 1848, made European liberals see Tsar Nicholas I as the "gendarme of Europe" and the Russian Empire as the enemy of nationalism, liberalism, and selfdetermination in Europe.

The overwhelming majority of Russians, including even many liberals, deeply resented this European revulsion against their country. Pushkin, Russia's greatest poet, whom Nicholas I was barely prevented from consigning to a lunatic asylum and "pardoned" to two years of exile in Moldavia, bitterly denounced the European "enemies of Russia" who condemned the suppression of the 1830 Polish rising. The great liberal populist Alexander Herzen was politically destroyed in Russia by his opposition to Tsar Alexander II's crushing of the Polish rising of 1863.

Nor is this surprising. Once Russia became a multinational empire, and, through the Polish partitions and victory over Napoleon, a major European power, what we now call "self-determination" for the non-Great Russian inhabitants of the Russian Empire meant the end of Russia as a great power.

Thus Great Russian nationalism and European nationalism and liberalism became permanent enemies. Moreover, the Russian image of "security," because of the memory of the Mongol, Polish, and Swedish invasions, the near-defeat Russia suffered in the Napoleonic invasion, its defeat in the Crimean War, its increasing technological backwardness, and its fear of the rising power of imperial Germany, made the Russian elite even more determined to hang onto the empire and helped its rulers turn Russia into a militarized police state.

Three other, extra-European factors strengthened this attitude. First, Siberia had been nearly empty land, and if Russia were to have a strong Asian policy, it must be kept and settled. Second, Russia wanted to inherit some of the spoils of the two decrepit, declining empires: Ottoman and Chinese. Third, the Great Russians became more nationalistic.

Great Russian nationalism was significantly different from, and therefore more hostile to, West European nationalisms. First, it was Orthodox and intolerant of Catholicism and Protestantism. Second, it was Slavophile and therefore anti-German and anti-Austrian. Third, it was linked with a domestic policy of repression and of unquestioning support of tsarist autocracy.

Throughout modern Russian and Soviet history the interrelationship of repression at home and expansionism abroad was interacting and self-reinforcing. The Polish rebellions played a major role in this, but the interaction began much earlier. The grand dukes of Muscovy believed repression necessary in order to concentrate all their resources on escaping from Tatar rule. The more the Russian Empire became multinational, and particularly the more it annexed European areas at a higher level of development, the more suspicious the tsars became of the "European infections" that came from them. The more that "liberalism" rose in Europe, the more determined the tsars became to keep it out of Russia.

The first example was the Decembrist revolt in 1825. Tsar Nicholas I overestimated its danger and the European ideological infection that it represented, but his draconic punishment of its leaders, his establishment of the Third Section of the Imperial Chancery, his secret police, and the consequences for political dissidence in the Russian Empire proved lasting and corrosive. Russia became a military and police state. The greater the repression, the smaller, more extreme, and conspiratorial resistance to tsarist rule became. Moreover, since the tsars were less inhumane than the Bolsheviks, their opponents were often allowed to go into exile in Western Europe. Bakunin and Nechaev in Geneva and Lenin in Germany, Austria, and Switzerland were only three of the many examples. In London Herzen's *Kolokol (The Bell)* was long the principal Russian dissident publication. Thus, and with much reason, the tsars came to identify dissent with "Europe."

The attitude of the tsars and most of the elite toward Europe thus became ambivalent. Because Russia grew increasingly backward technologically, especially in military technology, there was never any significant anti-European attitude in Russia in the economic and technological sectors. Baltic Germans played a significant role in them, and the rush forward of Russian industrialization in the early twentieth century owed much to economic ties with Europe and imports of technology from there.

In the cultural sector, the tsarist attitude was also ambivalent. Ever since the eighteenth century the tsarist elite had embraced European, especially French, culture. French was the language of the court. Diplomatic dispatches were written in French until the 1880s. Russian thought was profoundly influenced by German philosophy. Educated Russians traveled extensively in Western and Central Europe. Thus the Russian elite became in many respects "Europeanized," while the masses remained backward, largely illiterate peasants. However, as Western Europe became more democratized and, in contrast, Slavophilism and Great Russian nationalism arose in the tsarist empire, the cultural contrast between Russia and the West increased.

Politically, the gap between Russia and Europe was great indeed. True, the *Dreikaiserbund* of Russia, Prussia (and later the German Empire), and Austria, although based primarily on their common determination to keep Poland partitioned, also had an ideological component: common hostility to the enemies of aristocratic-based authoritarianism. However, Russian nationalism and imperialism eventually led the tsars to compromise this ideological attitude. Russia's competition with Austria-Hungary for the spoils of the Ottoman Empire led to covert tsarist support of several "national liberation movements" in the Balkans. Russia's defeat in the Russo-Japanese War led to temporary liberalization in the tsarist empire and toleration of dissident political movements, including even the Bolsheviks.

Russian Marxism was a special case of Western influence in Russia. Marxism entered Russia from Western and Central Europe, through publications, travel, and, particularly, radical Russian political exiles in Western Europe. Yet Russian Marxism—especially Russian Bolshevism—was far from entirely "European." The fact that effective resistance to the tsars within Russia had to be conspiratorial drove it to elitism and violence. Russia's backwardness seemed to many radical Russians a challenge and opportunity quite foreign to Western Europe. Trotsky's theory of permanent revolution was in part based on the weakness, as he saw it, of Russian capitalism. Bakunin believed that the European *Lumpenproletariat* and the Russian peasant masses were the best base for revolution. And Lenin, though a Marxist, believed that an elitist, vanguard party representing the true interests of the working class would have to be conspiratorial and undemocratic. Not that Russia was unique in this respect, but tsarist repression predisposed most extreme dissidence to these practices and made Lenin's victory easier.

Lenin's conspiratorial elitism and his pessimism about the working class, both in part remnants of his populist-terrorist past, helped to separate him from West European social democracy. World War I and his triumph in Russia confirmed the split and further intensified Russian ambivalence toward Western Europe. Lenin was an internationalist. He expected that the Bolshevik revolution would spread to Western Europe and that the German, not the Russian, communist party would become the leading one. Even when it did not, and "socialism" was established only in the Soviet Union, Lenin was not consciously a Great Russian nationalist. But inevitably the Soviet Bolshevik party did become the leading party, and Stalin reduced the other European parties to complete vassalage by purge and terror.

Soviet "Europeanism" was therefore not an attitude of one Europeanized elite toward others but that of an increasingly *non*-Europeanized Bolshevik elite toward European communists out of power and often persecuted. Remnants of Europeanism and internationalism were overshadowed by the hatred of Stalin and his associates, and of Lenin before him, for European "bourgeois capitalist" society. Thus Russia's Bolshevik rulers became, and have remained, much *less* European than the tsars.

Russia was increasingly outstripped, as the nineteenth century gave way to the twentieth, by Germany, especially in military arts and technology. Tsar Alexander III blundered disastrously by doing nothing to prevent Bismarck's unification of Germany. But Germany's opponents, France and Austria-Hungary, were anathema to the tsar—France for its republicanism and Austria-Hungary as a competitor of Russia's for the territories of the declining Ottoman Empire. Above all, Bismarck's diplomatic skill kept the tsar on his side. Bismarck's Germany carried out a policy of "saturation." But the imperialism of his successors and Russia's competition with Germany's ally Austria-Hungary for the Balkans, together with the massive blunders of all the European powers, brought world war.[1]

LENIN AND STALIN

World War I left Russia defeated and temporarily dismembered, and Lenin faced Allied intervention. How much this gave the Bolsheviks complexes of insecurity, encirclement, and inveterate foreign hostility is difficult to estimate. Probably not as much as they claimed, but certainly it helped dispose of Lenin's promises of self-determination for the non-Great Russian peoples. The Allied

1. In writing the above, I have drawn particularly on Hugh Seton-Watson, *The Russian Empire, 1801–1917* (New York: Oxford University Press, 1967); Richard Pipes, *Russia under the Old Regime* (New York: Charles Scribner's Sons, 1974); and Dimitri K. Simes, "The Military and Militarism in Soviet Society," *International Security*, 6, no. 3 (Winter 1981–82): 123–43.

interventions, as George Kennan and Richard Ullman have well demonstrated, were worse than crimes, they were blunders.[2]

Once Lenin consolidated his power, and despite his failures in Poland, Hungary, and Germany, the Bolsheviks expanded the nature and extent of Soviet foreign policy. They acted like a great power, gradually reemerging on the European and world scene, and also as the center of the international communist movement – directing, supporting, financing, training, and sometimes arming communist parties in Western Europe. These latter activities were especially important where mass communist parties existed: Italy (until Mussolini), Germany (until Hitler), and France. And in Spain, where the party was not so large, Stalin's support – almost alone of all powers – of the Loyalists in the Spanish Civil War enabled him to use the Spanish Communist Party to gain great influence over them.

Stalin was, as George Kennan once said, "a tyrant drenched in the blood of every crime." He built "socialism in one country." He concentrated on industrialization, agricultural collectivization, and, later, mass bloody terror. He became less ideological, more Great Russian nationalist, and more pathologically suspicious, but he never faltered in his determination to disrupt, divide, and expand his influence throughout the world.

The basic Soviet aims in Europe have not changed since 1917. They have been, first and minimally, to restore and maintain the territorial integrity of the Russian Empire. Most of this, including the most important part, the Ukraine, was accomplished in the early 1920s. The rest, the Baltic states, Bessarabia, and much of interwar eastern Poland, Stalin reconquered in World War II, and conquered in addition some territories never a part of the Russian Empire: eastern Galicia, northern Bukovina, Sub- and Carpatho-Ukraine, and the northern part of East Prussia. The second aim has been to get and keep control over Eastern Europe, notably Poland, to prevent it from allying with the West (as in the interwar Petit Entente) or falling under German influence. The third has been to neutralize and, maximally, get control of all or part of Germany. This was a part of the fourth, maximal objective: to prevent the unity of Western Europe, especially on an anti-Soviet basis. Stalin achieved the first three – he recreated 1914 in Poland and 1865 in Germany – but not wholly the fourth. But he did not achieve the predominance in Western Europe that Soviet power would have given him except for the continuing U.S. presence there.

Lenin's first task in foreign policy was to escape from the isolation to which the victorious European powers, having failed to crush him, tried to confine him. Not surprisingly, he turned to Berlin, which had the same motives, and

2. George F. Kennan, *Russia Leaves the War* (New York: Atheneum, 1967); Richard Ullman, *Intervention and the War* (Princeton: Princeton University Press, 1971), *Britain and the Russian Civil War: November 1918–February 1920* (Princeton: Princeton University Press, 1968), and *Anglo-Soviet Accord* (Princeton: Princeton University Press, 1973).

the Soviet-German Treaty of Rapallo in 1922 marked the escape of both countries from isolation.

Stalin's attitude toward Germany was always ambivalent. He shared the traditional Russian ambivalence toward it; he greatly respected its military potential; he saw Great Britain (wrongly) as his main and most dangerous enemy; and he hoped to profit from Germany, as Germany hoped to profit from him, in two major respects: mutual secret arming, and reannexation of Russian territory lost to Poland. The Germans and Russians rearmed each other: The Reichswehr secretly rearmed in Russia and helped train the Red Army there. Stalin also gained from this some influence, although less than he had hoped for, on German foreign policy.

No German party, and none of the Bolsheviks, had accepted the 1920 Polish boundaries. Germany was determined to get back Pomerania, East Prussia, the Polish Corridor, and Upper Silesia. Russia was determined to get back what had become the Polish eastern territories. (Stalin's maximum ambition was total control over Poland; Weimar Germany's was not.) Soviet and German hostility to Poland culminated in its fourth partition in 1939.

Stalin had hopes, also, in France, but even in the popular front period there he gained little. In Britain he gained even less: the British Communist Party never got a mass base, and the colonial possessions of France and Britain predisposed them against the anticolonialist Soviets. But Stalin presented little danger to British and French colonialism because he refused to cooperate with such noncommunist anticolonial nationalists as Gandhi and Nehru in India. Nor did Stalin's plans for communist revolution in interwar China, which would have destroyed British influence there, have any success; rather, they destroyed the mass base of the Chinese Communist Party, aided Japanese penetration, and were part of the background of the Sino-Soviet split.

Stalin's greatest miscalculation was his underestimation of Hitler, for it brought Russia to the brink of defeat in World War II and cost it some twenty million dead. Stalin also overestimated France and underestimated Britain. During World War II he never faltered in his refusal to compromise on his territorial aims—indeed, the same ones he had so unwisely had Molotov expose to Hitler in December 1940: control of much of Eastern Europe, Constantinople, and the Turkish and Danish straits. Stalin profited from Roosevelt's naïveté and repaid American aid, without which he would probably have been defeated, by blocking American objectives. But then, gratitude has never been prominent in international politics.

Churchill was primarily interested in retaining British influence in the Mediterranean, the road to India. Roosevelt, like most Americans, was mainly interested in winning the war, and naïvely thought, as many of them did, that the United Nations would end the balance-of-power curse in international politics. Roosevelt and Churchill would probably have had to make a separate peace with the German opposition to Hitler (as Metternich and Castlereagh combined with Talleyrand against Alexander I) to have blocked Stalin from Eastern Europe. But even if they had wanted to, which they did not, their peoples would not have tolerated it.

By the time, immediately before his death, Roosevelt began to realize what Stalin was up to, it was too late. Stalin had conquered more territory in Europe than had any previous Russian ruler. He had acquired predominant influence over Eastern Europe. He had pushed Poland westward, giving it most of East Prussia and all of Pomerania and Silesia, and thus tied it to an alliance with Russia against the possibility of a resurgent Germany. By also getting the Soviet zone of Germany, Stalin guaranteed that Germany would be either sovietized, "Finlandized," or partitioned.

Whether or not Stalin, like the United States, underestimated the weakness of Western Europe at the end of World War II, or simply overestimated American resistance to his policies, we do not know. Unlike Bismarck, he did not embrace a policy of "saturation." Whether or not he expected to get hegemony over all of Western Europe, he did hope to increase his influence over the western zones of Germany; if successful, it would have meant much the same thing. The peace plans drawn up, in all probability at Soviet direction, by the German communist leadership in Moscow in 1944, and the policies carried out by them and by their superiors, the Soviet Military Administration, in the Soviet zone of Germany in the two years immediately after the end of the war, make this quite clear. The German communist leaders and their Soviet masters did not intend that communists and social democrats should merge only in the Soviet zone. They tried to accomplish this in the western sectors of Berlin and in the three western zones. The postwar quadripartite conferences of the United States, the USSR, Great Britain, and France demonstrated that Stalin at least wanted a part in controlling the coal and steel industries of the Ruhr, and that he failed to get it. He wanted it primarily to prevent the economic revival, and later—he feared—the military revival, of Western Germany and therefore of Western Europe, thus further increasing Western power.

The cold war did not begin in Europe, but in Iran and Korea. But its first major crisis was in Europe: the first Berlin blockade. It was a measure of Stalin's ambition and risk taking (for the United States still had a nuclear monopoly) that he began the blockade. It was a measure of his caution that he gave it up. It was a measure of his miscalculation, as his permission to North Korea to begin the Korean War was another, that he so underestimated the United States.

In 1947, with American encouragement, the communists were thrown out of the French and Italian governments—a significant loss of Soviet influence. The first Berlin blockade brought NATO, the indefinite stationing of four American divisions in Europe, and the establishment of the Federal Republic of Germany (and thereafter of the German Democratic Republic), and pushed the cold war to a height that lasted until Stalin's death in 1953.

Stalin's principal conclusion from these developments was military: the necessity of continued, massive buildup of Soviet military power. This policy was not new with him: imperial Russia was a highly militarized society. Lenin had done his best to improve Soviet military power, including the assistance from the Reichswehr. Stalin's near defeat by Hitler, and America's 1945 acquisition of the atom bomb, must have driven him much farther in this respect. He gave maximum priority to Soviet acquisition of nuclear capability.

Stalin's background, ideology, and experiences predisposed him to regard the West as his inveterate enemy. Mao Zedong's victory in 1949, although Stalin was somewhat ambivalent about it, must have seemed to him to help his and hurt the West's interests. When Stalin died, in March 1953, he left a Soviet Union much more powerful than when he took power, with much more territory and influence, and at the head of an international communist movement that seemed firmly under Russia's control. That it cost some twenty-five million lives, of which millions were sacrificed to Stalin's pathological mania, is another matter. Judgments of Stalin, even among Great Russian nationalists, will long differ.

KHRUSHCHEV

Stalin had tried to push the United States (and Britain and France) out of West Berlin, in order to stabilize East Germany and (inevitably) destabilize West Germany. He had also tried to prevent the consolidation of West Germany and to influence France and Britain against it. All these efforts failed. Khrushchev initially followed the same policies: he remained generally hostile to West Germany while occasionally trying to woo it, cultivated Gaullist France and the British Labour Party, staged another Berlin crisis (1958–62) for the same purpose as the first, and also failed. Since the 1962 Cuban missile crisis was intended by him in part to settle the pending Berlin crisis in his favor, and since West Germany continued its economic and technological rise and raised and developed the most powerful land army in Western Europe, one might conclude that Khrushchev failed to influence Western Europe to Moscow's benefit.

However, in three other respects Khrushchev (like his successor Brezhnev) scored successes: the continued Soviet military buildup toward parity with the United States, the successful containment of unrest in Eastern Europe, and the gains in the Third World. The last became especially, albeit indirectly, important for Soviet policy in Western Europe when in the 1970s the West European economies became increasingly dependent on the oil of the Middle East, as Soviet influence in Egypt, Syria, and Iraq increased rapidly. Indeed, having failed to increase Soviet influence in Western Europe directly, Khrushchev and Brezhnev until the late 1970s seemed to have returned to the slogan attributed to Lenin that the "road to Paris goes through Calcutta and Peking."[3]

3. Adam B. Ulam, *Expansion and Coexistence*, 2d ed. (New York: Praeger, 1974) and *The Bolsheviks* (New York: Macmillan, 1965); William E. Griffith, *The Ostpolitik of the Federal*

But—and this was the other great Soviet loss—no longer could it go through Peking. For in large part as a result of Khrushchev's blunders, but in the last analysis probably unavoidably, in 1959 Sino-Soviet relations collapsed and alliance gave way to hostility. In general, West Europeans, and many Americans, have failed to realize the significance of this epochal event for European politics, and for Soviet policy toward them. No such mistake would have been made in the nineteenth century, when the West European powers had global responsibilities: Britain and Russia several times almost came to blows over Afghanistan; and Russia, like Britain and France, had Asian as well as European policies. In fact, the impact of the Sino-Soviet split, including in Western Europe, played a significant role in détente politics.[4]

Soviet Détente Policy

What has Soviet policy been, globally and in Europe? To begin with, it was the Soviet Union that initiated détente, and its first definition of it has remained the same to this day. It is, in sum, to combine the lowering of the risk of nuclear war with the United States (or any other power), by accident or miscalculation, with extension of Soviet power and influence, notably in the Third World and, if possible, elsewhere (such as in Europe), by the use of the expanded Soviet military capability and the troops of its allies (such as Cuba) and through the political demobilization which détente produces in the West and Japan.

Détente, or, as the Soviets call it, "peaceful coexistence," was not new with Khrushchev: Lenin had also been for it. Khrushchev added several new emphases: (1) higher priority for the avoidance of general war, while intensifying support for Third World guerrilla wars ("national liberation movements"); (2) search for cooperation with noncommunist radical anti-Western Third World leaders (Brezhnev became disillusioned with this and had largely returned to cooperation with communists); and (3) priority for transfer of grain, technology, and other products from the West and Japan in order to increase Soviet economic (and military) growth.

Soviet détente policy with the West had three areas of operation: (1) the nuclear relationship with the United States, which did not become an issue in West European politics until the late 1970s; (2) Soviet-Western political struggle in the Third World, interrelated with Sino-Soviet and, later, Sino-American relations; and (3) Soviet policy in Western Europe.

Republic of Germany (Cambridge, Mass.: M.I.T. Press, 1978), pp. 1–106; Vojtech Mastny, *Russia's Road to the Cold War* (New York: Columbia University Press, 1979).

4. William E. Griffith, *Albania and the Sino-Soviet Rift* (Cambridge, Mass.: M.I.T. Press, 1963), *The Sino-Soviet Rift* (Cambridge, Mass.: M.I.T. Press, 1964), and *Sino-Soviet Relations, 1964–1965* (Cambridge, Mass.: M.I.T. Press, 1967).

Khrushchev hoped through détente to lower the risk of war, consolidate his position in Eastern Europe, notably in East Germany, launch a politicomilitary offensive in the Third World, and improve his position in Western Europe. And he wanted to do all three while lowering the risk of effective U.S. countermoves. His first major move in the Third World—the Soviet involvement in Egypt—occurred only a few weeks after the first East-West summit conference, at Geneva in 1955.[5]

Khrushchev's West European policy began with France. At first he did not get far with Paris. But when General de Gaulle returned to power as a result of the Algerian War, in which the USSR provided much of the National Liberation Front's (FLN) arms supply, Khrushchev tried to cultivate him and profit from his increasingly independent course. But, again, he made little progress. De Gaulle had no illusions about the Soviet Union. He had several aims: to set up a confederated Europe, under French leadership, which would cooperate with, but not be subordinate to, the United States; to exercise more influence in Eastern Europe; and to balance between Washington and Moscow, tilting toward whichever was weaker, and thereby increase French independence and influence. De Gaulle's immediate support of Kennedy in the 1962 Cuban missile crisis must have convinced Khrushchev that when the chips were down France remained a sure ally of the United States. Thereafter, however, de Gaulle, realizing that Khrushchev had lost in that crisis, agreed to the institutionalized cooperation with Moscow which later became a pattern in Soviet dealings with Western Europe.[6]

BREZHNEV

The years 1968 (with the Soviet invasion of Czechoslovakia) and 1969 marked a major watershed with respect to Eastern Europe and Soviet relations with the West European communist parties, with China and Vietnam, and with West Germany. Indeed, in these years began the unfolding of Brezhnev's policy toward Western Europe, which the invasion of Czechoslovakia made possible and the Sino-Soviet split and the SPD/FDP (Social Democratic Party and Free Democratic Party) government in Bonn made desirable—for the former made Moscow want to keep its western flank quiet and the latter made Bonn ready to accept it.

In order to understand this "great turn" in global and European politics, we must turn briefly to Brezhnev's style of governance: organized, controlled, depoliticized stability at home and gradual expansion abroad. The former required the repression of the dissident movement combined with what Moscow called *delovitost'* ("businesslike behavior"): the organized, institutionalized stability of "mature socialism" instead of Khrushchev's "harebrained scheming."

5. William E. Griffith, *The Super-powers and Regional Tensions: The USSR, the United States, and Europe* (Lexington, Mass.: Lexington Books, 1981), pp. 1–30.

6. See the summary in my *Ostpolitik of the Federal Republic of Germany*, passim, and the literature cited there.

Abroad, it meant politicization, not stability: expansion by military force in the Third World, and expansion in Europe by a process that Brzezinski and I once called "peaceful engagement"–gradual, controlled changed in Moscow's favor in the West European "island of détente" under the guise of recognizing the European status quo.

Soviet détente policy thus was initially based on the assumption that the "change in the correlation of forces in favor of the camp of socialism" (that is, primarily the Soviet military buildup to parity with the United States) would compel the United States to accept détente as "irreversible" and would gradually compel it to accept Moscow's definition of its implementation: at Helsinki in 1975 through the Final Act of the Conference on Security and Cooperation in Europe (CSCE); through the "struggle for peace"; and through a network of East-West ties and institutions in Europe whereby the U.S. presence there would be gradually reduced and the Soviet Union would gradually acquire a *droit de regard* in relation to the West European states–that is, Western Europe would gradually drift closer to "Finlandization."

Brezhnev's European policy was indeed *reculer pour mieux sauter*. Initially this meant that the Soviet Union would settle for the status quo, especially in the two Germanies, including U.S. military presence in Europe. It also meant trying to seal off Eastern Europe from the destabilizing effects of détente–for example, in East Germany by *Abgrenzung* ("demarcation") vis-à-vis the Federal Republic. Finally, it meant accepting the economic aspects of the European Community (EC) while continuing to oppose its political and military aspects or potentialities.

Moscow had hoped in the early 1970s to carry out this policy within the context of continued global détente with the United States. But the Soviet military buildup increasingly alarmed an American society that was going conservative; and the Soviet use of this to win influence in Angola, Ethiopia, and Afghanistan convinced Washington, especially the Reagan administration, that Soviet expansion must be strongly resisted. By the end of the 1970s, therefore, Moscow had to retreat to a less ambitious policy to continue its détente policy in Western Europe and thereby to help worsen U.S.-West European relations.[7]

The 1968 Prague Spring was a belated revival of the traditional democratic, leftist Czech political culture and of the Slovak push for autonomy. It so departed from the Soviet model; it so threatened to infect East Germany, Poland, and even the western Ukraine; and it had such attraction for reformist communists in Western Europe that Brezhnev finally felt compelled to crush it. For the West European communist parties, the Prague Spring was an example of democratic, decentralized socialism without terror, with ties to the Soviet Communist Party, with decentralization and economic reform, and still not social

7. I have relied for the above primarily on John Van Oudenaren, "Political Change and Detente in Europe: Soviet Policy, 1969–1976" (Ph.D. dissertation, M.I.T., 1982).

democratic. This was particularly true among communist intellectuals and in the Italian and Spanish communist parties. The Italian Communist Party (PCI) had benefited from a long tradition of autonomist thought, close ties with the Yugoslav communists, the towering intellectual heritage of its first leader, Antonio Gramsci, and the skillful, Machiavellian hand of his successor, Palmiro Togliatti, who as early as 1956 had publicly, albeit briefly, shown his doubts about Soviet policy. By 1968 Santiago Carrillo, the head of the Spanish Communist Party (PCE), was also ready to differ with Moscow. Only the French Communist Party (PCF) still remained faithful to Moscow's line.

The August 20–21, 1968, Soviet invasion of Czechoslovakia precipitated the first public defiance by West European communists of Soviet foreign policy. Practically all of them—including the Italian, Spanish, and even French communist parties—condemned the invasion. Along with many other communist parties throughout the world, they had been engaged in preparations, under Soviet chairmanship, for another international communist conference in Moscow. When it finally met, in 1969, it further documented the decline in Soviet influence in West European communist parties, for many of them endorsed only part of the declaration, made reservations to it, or rejected it entirely, and most of them refused to condemn the Chinese.

This drifting away from Soviet leadership continued apace in the 1970s. One of its high points, at which the French party also followed the Eurocommunist line, was the East Berlin European communist conference in June 1976. The Yugoslavs participated in this, for the first time since 1957; the rule of "consensus" (i.e., unanimity) was adopted at their insistence; and the final declaration did not include the principal Soviet ideological formulations at issue. Until 1982, the CPSU had seemed to accept, *nolens volens*, domestic autonomy for West European communist parties in return for support of, or at least minimal differences with, Soviet foreign policy—what Togliatti had called "unity in diversity." But the Soviet invasion of Afghanistan seriously strained, and the December 1981 declaration of martial law in Poland finally ruptured, this tacit partial agreement to disagree.[8]

8. See the chapter by Joan Barth Urban in this volume and her "Soviet Policies and Conduct toward the PCI," paper presented to the annual convention of the American Association for the Advancement of Slavic Studies, September 1981 (to be published in *Studies in Comparative Communism*); her "The West European Communist Challenge to Soviet Foreign Policy" in Roger E. Kanet, ed., *Soviet Foreign Policy in the 1980s* (New York: Praeger, 1982); Donald L. M. Blackmer, "Notes on the Foreign Policy of the Italian Communist Policy," paper presented to a conference on the foreign policy of Eurocommunism, Airlie House, May 1977; and my "The Diplomacy of Eurocommunism" in Rudolf L. Tőkés, ed., *Eurocommunism and Détente* (New York: New York University Press, for the Council on Foreign Relations, 1978), pp. 385–436; my *Super-powers and Regional Tensions*, chap. 5, "The USSR, the United States and the West European Left," pp. 75–82; and my *The European Left* (Lexington, Mass.: Lexington Books, 1979).

Soviet Westpolitik and West German Ostpolitik

The major event in Soviet–West German relations in 1968–69 was the coming to power in Bonn in 1969 of the SPD/FDP coalition, headed by Willy Brandt as chancellor and Walter Scheel as foreign minister, and the launching of their Ostpolitik, which led to the German treaties. I have written elsewhere of these developments in detail, and shall therefore make only a few main points here.

First, for Moscow, the Soviet invasion of Czechoslovakia was a precondition for détente with West Germany, for only after Moscow's hold over Eastern Europe had been reconsolidated could it afford such a move. Second, because Moscow resumed its approaches to Bonn in early 1969, when a Christian Democratic Union (CDU) chancellor was still leading a Grand Coalition with the Christian Social Union (CSU) and SPD, these approaches did not in Moscow's view depend on the SPD being in power in Bonn. Third, Moscow stepped up its detente policy toward Bonn when the new Brandt-Scheel government made clear that it was ready to give de facto recognition to the Oder-Neisse line and East Germany. Fourth, the Soviets were prepared to give, in return, further guarantees, to the three Western allies and thereby indirectly to the West Germans, of stability in West Berlin and access to and from it, and of visits by West Germans and West Berliners to East Germany. The Soviets made some concessions, particularly on Berlin. The West Germans made others, but—as Brandt said—lost only what Hitler had lost before. Was Soviet Westpolitik (and West German Ostpolitik), then, a stabilizing, balanced compromise—for the Soviet Union, for West Germany, and for the United States? Or did it lay the necessary foundations for Moscow to gain influence in West Germany?[9]

The Aftermath of Ostpolitik

This was in 1982 one of the two principal questions about Soviet policy in Europe. The other, Soviet relations with the West European communist parties, will be treated below. Both issues, Ostpolitik and Eurocommunism, are intensely controversial, and likely to remain so. What have been the objectives of Soviet Westpolitik since 1968, and how successfully have they been implemented?

The first, minimal political objective has been to restabilize the status quo in Eastern Europe, consolidate Soviet hegemony over it, and have this hegemony recognized by West Germany and then by the United States and Western Europe. Moscow wanted the former to be accomplished within the context of East-West détente by the German treaties and the latter by the Final Act of the CSCE. It was

9. See my *Ostpolitik of the Federal Republic of Germany*, passim; Angela Stent, *From Embargo to Ostpolitik: The Political Economy of West German-Soviet Relations, 1955–1980* (New York: Cambridge University Press, 1981), and her "The USSR and Germany," *Problems of Communism*, 30, no. 5 (September–October 1981): 1–24; and Arnulf Baring, *Machtwechsel: Die Ära Brandt-Scheel* (Stuttgart: Deutsche Verlags-Anstalt, 1982), pp. 197–360.

to be accompanied by the limitation of West European, especially West German, and U.S. military expenditures through the SALT and MBFR (mutual and balanced force reduction) negotiations. Finally, Moscow hoped that this would contain Western—particularly West German—influence, which in Eastern Europe was potentially increased by détente, toward more liberalization and autonomy from Moscow. In any case, the Soviets could rely on their decisive insurance policy against destabilization in Eastern Europe: the threat, and if necessary the implementation, of military intervention.

The second Soviet objective was economic, especially technological, and therefore partly military: to increase the transfer of high-level technology from Western Europe, particularly West Germany, to the Soviet Union and Eastern Europe, in part in return for Soviet delivery of raw materials, notably petroleum and natural gas. Moscow hoped that this would enable it to slow down, if not reverse, its increasing technological backwardness and declining economic growth and thus tie Western Europe to it economically so that its influence over West European policies would increase.

Moscow had the same economic objectives regarding the United States and Japan. But it failed to achieve them, because of its worsening relations with the United States, the domestic American political opposition to détente (in general and on the issue of Soviet Jewish emigration) which effectively blocked major Soviet-U.S. trade, and Japanese resentment of the continued Soviet occupation of the four southern Kurile Islands.

The third Soviet objective was military: to increase its military advantage in Europe by massive tank and air deployment on the central front and by massive SS-20 nuclear missile deployment, primarily targeted on Western Europe and not compensated for by equivalent Western deployments. This would mean the attainment of Soviet military superiority in, and over, Western Europe (tacitly accepted by the West), which would lead, as military superiority historically always has, to greater Soviet political influence there.

Soviet military doctrine and strategy are those of deterrence, but the Soviets do take into account the possibility of nuclear war and the necessity, therefore, to be able to fight and win it while denying the same option to the United States. They also believe, correctly, that their attainment of strategic nuclear parity, Eurostrategic superiority, and a major sea- and airlift capability enable them to profit politically in Western Europe, from the intimidating effect of military strength, and militarily in the Third World.

The Soviet Union had decided, after its 1968 invasion of Czechoslovakia, that it had reconsolidated its control over Eastern Europe. Its global military buildup was proceeding so rapidly that it could take more advantage of opportunities in the Third World. However, Moscow realized that Western Europe could not be revolutionized nor the Common Market broken up, nor could the United States be expelled from Western Europe in the near future. Finally, it was increasingly probable that Moscow could come to favorable terms with Bonn.

The Soviet leadership therefore adopted a strategy of complex efforts for gradual, evolutionary change in its favor in Western Europe, within the context of continued détente there, while simultaneously expanding Soviet influence, primarily by military means, in the Third World.

Moscow called this a strategy for peace and cooperation in Europe. Peace through disarmament was its principal propaganda theme. Soviet detente policy in Europe has certainly been against nuclear war and therefore for peace. It has also pushed for a massive increase in bilateral and multilateral negotiations, commissions, and institutions.

This meant three changes in Soviet strategy in Europe: abandon attempts to isolate and demonize West Germany, boycott the European Economic Community (EEC or Common Market), and denounce the Socialist International and its member parties. The Soviets had opposed the EEC because they saw it as an instrument of American policy and predominance in Western Europe and a precursor of an anti-Soviet, and politically and militarily united, Western Europe. But as the EEC became a reality, Moscow began to see it as an organization with which trade would be profitable, which was a potential rival for the United States, and which they hoped to influence not to move toward political or military union (which Moscow continued to oppose) but toward more economic ties with the Soviet Union and Eastern Europe.[10] Moscow tried, with not much success, to use the Socialist International in its peace campaigns and in the Third World.

Soviet strategy in Western Europe has five other goals (all directed against current Western policies): to maintain the Soviet sphere of influence in Eastern Europe from whatever infection détente and more multilateral ties might create; to downgrade West European NATO ties; to distract attention from the massive Soviet nuclear and conventional buildup in Europe (in tanks and SS–20s); to increase Soviet cultivation, particularly through the CPSU, of West European peace activists, left-wing social democrats, and left-wing Catholics in favor of Soviet aims; and thereby to work for the gradual growth of differences between Western Europe and the United States and the decline of U.S. influence in Western Europe.[11]

Moscow's strategy has been aided by the development in West Germany of a widely based prodétente consensus. Its causes were geographic, historic, military, economic, and nationalist. First, West Germany was on the frontier of the Soviet Army and thus the most likely West European state to be destroyed first and most thoroughly in a war. Second, Germany historically had more

10. Robert Legvold, "The Soviet Union and Western Europe," in William E. Griffith, ed., The Soviet Empire: Expansion and Detente (Lexington, Mass.: Lexington Books, 1976), pp. 217–57, at pp. 225–26.
11. Van Oudenaren, "Political Change and Detente in Europe."

extensive relations with the East, and was more ambivalent about the West, than any other Western or Central European state. Third, West Germany is especially dependent on U.S. military protection, because, despite its economic and technological power and its excellent and large conventional army, it is, and is likely to remain, nonnuclear. Moreover, it cannot physically defend West Berlin (only the United States can and will), thus it is vulnerable to major Soviet and East German pressures. Economically, Bonn's trade with the East is quite small, but it is very important for certain industries and therefore for any West German government. And the widely popular conviction that West Germany is part of a divided German nation (millions of West Germans have relatives in East Germany), along with the more general desire, as Willy Brandt put it, for "die Erhaltung der Substanz der Nation" ("the maintenance of the substance of the nation"), makes some relations with East Germany seem essential to most West Germans.

Thus West Germany fears and needs the Soviet Union, which alone can modify East Germany's *Abgrenzung* policy as Bonn wishes. West Germany needs arms control and must oppose superpower confrontation. This makes West Germany's Ostpolitik vulnerable to pressure by Soviet Westpolitik, below the threshold of decisively endangering Bonn's American military protection.[12]

These have been the principal Soviet aims and strategies in Western Europe. Moscow has recently made other gains outside Europe—especially in the Third World—which have had an important impact on its relations with Western Europe. Moscow has also had losses in the Third World: in Egypt, Indonesia, Iraq, Algeria, Guinea, Ghana, and elsewhere. But its gains since 1975 in Angola, Ethiopia, Afghanistan, and Indochina have been impressive and have had important reverberations in Western Europe and on West European–American relations, essentially to Moscow's benefit. For the first time since World War II, these Soviet gains have neither strengthened NATO nor led to an increase in anti-Soviet policies or rearmament in Western Europe. On the contrary, for the first time they have produced serious strains between the United States and Western Europe. They have also contributed indirectly but importantly to the recent rise of a major peace movement in Western Europe, whose principal objective is to prevent the United States from modernizing its theater nuclear forces (TNF) there to compensate for the Soviet SS–20 buildup.

The United States, the West European states, and the Soviet Union all feel that their minimal objectives are defensive. Because the Soviet Union is a young, expanding empire, it is more interested in political and military expansion

---

12. See Gerhard Wettig's chapter in this volume, my "U.S.–West German Relations: Deterioration or Crisis?" *Orbis*, Spring 1982, and especially Günther Schmid, *Sicherheitspolitik und Friedensbewegung*, Akademiebeiträge zur Lehrerbildung, vol. II (Munich: Olzog, 1982). For background, see my *Ostpolitik of the Federal Republic of Germany* and *The Super-powers and Regional Tensions*.

than the Western powers and Japan, who concentrate on international economic expansion, largely through multinational corporations. The United States and the West European powers are status quo powers politically and militarily. (The Soviet Union argues, from time to time, that West Germany is an expansionist power with respect to East Germany. Since about 1977 it has claimed that the United States is "expansionist," and since 1980 that the United States is trying to reacquire strategic nuclear superiority.)

The Soviet Union, as it has recently for the first time publicly declared, sees itself (with considerable reason) encircled by the quasi alliance between the United States and China, in which, it believes, Japan has become a limited junior partner.[13] One of the principal Soviet defensive objectives in Western Europe, therefore, is to keep it, especially West Germany, from joining this encirclement. The Soviet Union *is* faced with nuclear encirclement: all potential and actual nuclear powers are in different degrees anti-Soviet. Moscow therefore feels that its security requires parity with *all* of its nuclear opponents—the United States, Great Britain, France, and China—and therefore superiority over the United States alone.

Four logical consequences follow. First, because the United States will not accept Soviet superiority, the Soviet Union has to assume that it must accept intercontinental strategic parity with the United States. Second, it must carry on the kind of détente policies with London and Paris that will prevent them from joining what Moscow perceives to be the Sino-U.S. encirclement of the Soviet Union, and it also must limit the growth of their nuclear forces. (Such growth is unlikely anyway, because of the rising costs of nuclear weapons systems.) Third, Moscow must try to erode the ties, and therefore the likelihood of nuclear coordination, between the United States and Western Europe and the United States and China. (This is probably one of the reasons why since 1964 the Soviet Union has intermittently and unsuccessfully tried to get a partial détente with China on the state level.) Fourth, Moscow can hope to have strategic superiority only over Western Europe (i.e., over the U.S. intermediate-range nuclear weapons).

The Soviet Union is thus trying, with varying success, to keep several balls in the air at once: détente, especially in Western Europe, and increased trade with Western Europe; expansion in the Third World; and erosion of West European–U.S. ties. Logically, these might be thought contradictory, indeed incompatible. The Soviets have done fairly well in overcoming the contradiction.

There are two principal reasons why the Soviets have done fairly well. Neither one is the effectiveness of Soviet foreign policy. The first is the determination of most West European governments, for their own reasons, to maintain Western Europe as an "island of détente" amid what seems to them to be a

13. *The Threat to Europe* (Moscow: Progress Publishers, 1981), p. 8.

Soviet-American "second cold war." The second is the strongly anti-Soviet cast of the Reagan administration and of American public opinion, and, in contrast, the less anti-Soviet atmosphere in Western Europe.

Western Europe, in the view of its citizens and governments (except, perhaps, Margaret Thatcher), has profited from détente: by an increased feeling of security from the danger of nuclear or conventional war, by the profits of East-West trade, and by cultural exchange between East and West. Many West Europeans feel that the 1980–81 Polish developments could not have occurred without détente. Détente, they also feel, has enabled them to have greater autonomy in relation to the United States.

In the United States, détente has lost much of the wide popularity it enjoyed in the early 1970s. As early as 1976 this tendency had gone so far that President Ford banished the word détente from his campaign. SALT remained popular, but the nationalist reaction to the U.S. defeat in Vietnam, rising public concern about the Soviet military buildup and the Soviet gains in Angola, Ethiopia, and Afghanistan, and the domestic trend toward conservatism, fueled by inflation and the cultural counterrevolution against the leftism and bohemianism of the 1960s, all eroded public support for détente. Reagan's nomination and election and the defeat of the liberal Democrats eroded it further.

The Soviet Union would have preferred to maintain its desired version of détente. Moscow continued to try to reactivate the SALT negotiations. By 1982 Moscow had turned to its optimum objective for Western Europe: to make so attractive Western Europe's own goal of keeping itself an island of détente that it would gradually loosen its ties with the United States and thus accept a Soviet *droit de regard* over its foreign policies, a lack of concern about Soviet gains outside Europe, and thereby a slow slide toward "self-Finlandization."

MOSCOW AND THE WEST EUROPEAN PEACE MOVEMENT

The Soviet Union had one other aspect of West European public opinion in its favor: the revival of the fear of nuclear war as expressed in the West European "peace movement." The success of the movement had several causes: the worsening economic situation and the psychological anxieties it produced; the organizational involvement in the movement of pacifist and left-wing Protestants (the movement has made little progress in the European Latin and Catholic countries); the reaction against what most West Europeans saw as the belligerent anti-Soviet rhetoric of the Reagan administration; the drastic loss of confidence in U.S. leadership, arising out of its Vietnam defeat and/the Watergate scandal; the "un-European" style of a succession of mediocre presidents; and in West Germany a search for national identity, the development of a pacifist, ecological, postmaterialist counterculture among a minority of educated youth, and a greater concern for East Germany.

The Soviet Union did not start and does not control the West European peace movement. But Moscow has skillfully exploited it, by providing arguments and, via West European communist parties, some organizational and financial support. This Soviet effort has been coordinated and directed by the relatively new International Information Department of the CPSU Central Committee, headed by Leonid Zamiatin and his first deputy Valentin Falin, formerly Soviet ambassador in Bonn. They, Vadim Zagladin, first deputy head of the CPSU International Department, and others have also carried on effective personal lobbying, notably in the Benelux countries and West Germany, against INF (intermediate-range nuclear forces) deployment. This new flexibility and sophistication of Soviet propaganda was also reflected in the publication of two pamphlets in Moscow—primarily directed at Western Europe—which for the first time refer to the nuclear encirclement of the Soviet Union and deny that the Soviet Union is trying to achieve a nuclear war-fighting capability (see note 4 of Benjamin Lambeth's chapter in this volume).

Finally, recent U.S. nuclear technological developments have contributed psychologically to the West European peace movement. They are also potentially so unfavorable to the Soviet strategic position that Moscow has strong defensive motives in trying to block them. Why is this so?

The West European peace movement, notably in West Germany and Great Britain, has concluded (1) that a major nuclear weapons escalation is under way, which is true qualitatively, primarily because of improvements in missile accuracy, for example, of SS–20s, Pershing II and cruise missiles, and MARVs (maneuverable reentry vehicles); (2) that this makes a nuclear war more likely, which is not true: it makes only land-based nuclear weapons more vulnerable; (3) that the United States is trying to recover nuclear superiority, which is not true: the Reagan administration supports nuclear parity, and its current strategic programs do not even meet the Minuteman accuracy problem; (4) that the United States and the Soviet Union want to fight a nuclear war in Europe while preserving themselves as nuclear sanctuaries, which is not true, if only because it would not be possible; and (5) that the United States is a greater danger to world peace than the Soviet Union, which is a matter of opinion: mine, like that of most West Europeans, is that it is not.

The NATO dual-track decision of December 12, 1979, will result in the deployment of 572 new U.S.-made Pershing II and cruise missiles in Europe between December 1983 and December 1985, subject to European approval, unless the Soviet Union agrees to an arms-reduction treaty (108 Pershing II missiles will be deployed in West Germany and 464 cruise missiles throughout Western Europe). The Soviet Union finds new U.S. nuclear weapons deployments unfavorable for three main reasons. First, they will greatly increase the Soviet military technological gap. Second, they make it possible for the United States to deploy modernized theater nuclear forces in Western Europe—Pershing II and ground-launched cruise missiles (GLCMs)—that for the first time can reach

Soviet targets, have greater accuracy than the Soviet SS–20s, and give the Soviet Union a warning time of only around ten minutes; the Soviets claim that because these forces will in part be based in West Germany, they may be the first step to West German acquisition of these military technologies. Third, the Soviets also maintain that, contrary to the NATO view and that of almost all independent Western experts, the USSR does not have Eurostrategic nuclear superiority (despite the deployment of its SS–20s) but that there is rough Eurostrategic parity between them and the West when one includes the U.S. forward-based systems (FBS) and the British and French nuclear forces and subtracts the SS–20s deployed against China. They therefore insist that the NATO decision is in fact part of the U.S. intention to reacquire nuclear superiority.

In Great Britain, where some cruise missiles would be stationed, the peace movement is centered in the left wing of the Labour Party. Most of it advocates unilateral British nuclear disarmament. In West Germany it is centered in the Protestant Church, the left wing of the Social Democratic Party, and the ecological party (the Greens or Alternatives). One part of the movement also wants, as in Britain, a neutral Western Europe between the two powers; and another – smaller – part wants a neutral united Germany (i.e., they are German nationalists or, as they call themselves, Patriots). The West German peace movement has been encouraged by the development of a small, similar, frustrated peace movement in East Germany.

The Soviet Union is probably ambivalent about both of these German peace movements, as is shown, for example, by East Berlin's initial tolerance and limited encouragement of the East German movement. (The Socialist Unity Party soon turned against it.) Moscow is aware of its (minority) German nationalist aspects, but presumably considers its opposition to INF deployment more important.

Russia has always been ambivalent about Germany. Since 1953 Moscow has preferred to come to some global arrangement with the United States. But when, as in 1982, this did not seem likely, Moscow turned to Western Europe, particularly West Germany, in the hope of profiting from Bonn's desire for détente, East-West trade, and the continuation of the "human ties" with East Germany and the stability of West Berlin.

How is Moscow likely to do in relations with Bonn? Basically, I think, not well. Popular fear of the Russians, desire to retain prosperity and freedom, rejection of the East German system, and conviction of the necessity of American nuclear protection, along with its identification with the unpopular ecological movement, are likely to continue to deprive the West German peace movement of a mass base or the electoral support of more than about 6 percent of the West German voters. But what the Soviets can hope to achieve there, and elsewhere in Western Europe, is (1) to encourage, though not control, the rising desire for more autonomy from American leadership and for the maintenance of Europe as an island of détente, and (2) to help establish West European "peace" cadres and institutions that may win later.

In late 1981 two events occurred that showed that Soviet hopes of this sort could suffer significant blows. The first, less important, event was President Reagan's November 1981 speech proposing INF negotiations with the Soviet Union on the basis of the so-called zero option (i.e., Soviet dismantling of their deployed SS-20s in return for NATO's reversal of its INF deployment decision). This was a proposal made originally *inter alia* by Willy Brandt, whose desire to integrate the peace movement into the SPD put him somewhere between it and Chancellor Schmidt. The second event was the December 13, 1981, proclamation of martial law in Poland. During 1982 this event worked partly to the Soviets' advantage, because of the differences it produced between the United States and Western Europe over what sanctions, if any, should be imposed on the Soviet Union because of it. At the same time, however, martial law administered a blow to the peace movement. In early 1982 some in the peace movement were already elaborating theories why the U.S. response to the Polish events, and the events themselves, made for an even greater danger to peace than before; but a split began to divide the (minority) communists and the (majority) Protestants and ecologists on the Polish issue.[14] Subsequent developments unfavorable both to the Soviets and to the peace movement were the coming to power in Bonn in October 1982 of a CDU/CSU-FDP coalition, and the CDU/CSU success in the March 1983 elections, which made INF deployment even more likely.

14. The discussion above is primarily based on conversations in West Germany while I was a visiting professor at the University of Munich, May–July 1981, and on a brief visit to Bonn and Munich in December 1981, sponsored by *Reader's Digest*, of which I am a roving editor. See also Pierre Hassner, "Arms Control and the Politics of Pacifism in Protestant Europe," Woodrow Wilson Center International Security Studies Program, no. 31, October 27, 1981; Philip Windsor, *Germany and the Western Alliance: Lessons from the 1980 Crises*, Adelphi Paper no. 170 (London: International Institute for Strategic Studies, Autumn 1981); and (for a SPD center-left analysis of INF, Eckhard Lübkemeier, "PD5g und LRTNF-Modernisierung: Militärstrategische und sicherheitspolitische Implikationen der erweiterten Abschreckung für die Bundesrepublik Deutschland," Forschungsinstitut der Friedrich-Ebert-Stiftung, Bonn, September 1981 (mimeographed). The foreign policy of the peace movement is best set forth in Peter Bender, *Das Ende des ideologischen Zeitalters* (Berlin: Severin and Siedler, 1981) and the critical review of it by Christian Kind, "Deutsche Distanzierungen," *Neue Zürcher Zeitung*, August 30–31, 1981. For recent books sympathetic to the peace movement in Germany, see Dieter S. Lutz, *Weltkrieg wider Willen?* (Reinbek bei Hamburg: Rowolt, 1981), and on its view of the USSR, Ulrich Albrecht, Alain Joze, and Mary Kaldor, "Gegen den Alarmismus!" in Freimut Duve, ed., *Aufrüsten um abzurüsten?* (Reinbek bei Hamburg: Rowolt, 1981). pp. 107–45. For criticism, see Josef Joffe, "Die sieben Irrtümer der Friedensbewegung," *Der Monat*, no. 282, 1982. For a Soviet view, see O. N. Melikian, "Zapadnaia Evropa 80-kh godov: Dvizhenie antivoennogo soprotivleniia," *Rabochii klass i sovremennyi mir*, no. 3, 1982, pp. 89–97.

THE SOVIET-EUROCOMMUNIST CONFLICT

Meanwhile, while Soviet hopes of gains through the peace movements continued in Britain and West Germany, developments in the Latin communist parties were going against Moscow. In January 1982 the Italian communist reaction to the Polish declaration of martial law and suppression of Solidarity precipitated such a violent Soviet denunciation that CPSU-PCI relations were de facto, though not formally, ruptured.

The West European communist parties have historically been foreign policy and ideological assets to Moscow. The USSR hoped through them to have more influence on Latin Europe than Soviet state power alone would warrant. And until 1968, despite the continuing, semisubmerged autonomist and Western Marxist PCI traditions of Gramsci and Togliatti, this remained the case. But in Moscow's scale of priorities, this aim was far below the maintenance of Soviet control over Eastern Europe and the USSR's insistence that it be recognized as the unique custodian of communist ideological orthodoxy. Moscow wanted the West European communist parties to support Soviet foreign policy, its claim to be the communist ideological and organizational Vatican, and therefore its sole right to define the "general laws" of socialist construction.

Moscow's turn in Western Europe in the 1970s to controlled, depoliticized change from above antagonized the PCF, for example, by its support of Valéry Giscard d'Estaing. But the endemic instability in Eastern Europe, and Moscow's consequent periodic reestablishment of its control by military force there, was the principal external cause of tension in relations between the CPSU and the West European communist parties.

This became the clearest with the PCI: Togliatti's brief polycentric heterodoxy in 1956 because of the Polish and Hungarian events; his Yalta memorandum's criticism in 1964 of Soviet repression at home and intolerance toward the Chinese; the public criticism by the PCI, PCF, and PCE of the Soviet invasion of Czechoslovakia in 1968; the PCI's and PCE's support of pluralism and rejection of Moscow's "general laws" in the 1970s; the PCI's support of a coalition with the Christian Democrats in its *compromesso storico*; and the CPSU-PCI crisis of 1982 over Jaruzelski's suppression of Solidarity. Eurocommunist criticism was supported by the Yugoslav and Romanian communists, because they also rejected Soviet hegemony.

PCI defiance of the CPSU began with criticism of Soviet procedure in international and European communist conferences, including Moscow's exclusion of the Yugoslav and Chinese parties and its insistence that the majority (which it dominated) define the minority. Later, within and outside the conference context, the PCI rejected certain key elements of Soviet ideology: "general laws of the construction of socialism," "proletarian internationalism" (i.e., Soviet hegemony), for which the PCI substituted "new internationalism," and the "dictatorship of the proletariat," for which the PCI substituted its *terza via* ("third way") somewhere between Marxism-Leninism (Soviet style) and social democracy. Moscow replied with strong but initially only implicit ideological polemics.

The third phase of the PCI criticism, and for the Soviets the most unacceptable, was against Soviet foreign policy in Afghanistan, Poland, and Indochina and Soviet military policy in the Third World, along with the Soviet suppression of the dissident movement. Moreover, the PCI abandoned its support of Moscow's anti-NATO policy and refused to participate in a Soviet sponsored anti-INF rally in Paris in 1980. The PCI and the PCE also resumed party relations with the Chinese, just when Sino-Soviet relations worsened after the Soviet invasion of Afghanistan.

The French Communist Party, outraged by Brezhnev's support of Giscard, in 1975–78 moved toward Eurocommunism. But, again for domestic reasons—its determination of 1978 not to be the minority party in a socialist-dominated left coalition—the PCF returned to the pro-Soviet camp. The defeat of the left in the 1978 elections, which the PCF's break with the French Socialist Party (PS) largely caused, made it all the more subject to Soviet pressure. The PCI and the PCE, in contrast, had ample domestic political reasons to move, as they did, farther away from Moscow. Having returned to the opposition in 1979 without having been able to enter the coalition, the PCI had to try to pick up votes on its right and take some of the wind out of the sails of its current main enemy, the Socialist leader Bettino Craxi. The PCE was rent with factional struggle. Carrillo was challenged by pro-Soviet and ethnic minority groups on his left and revisionists on his right, and was therefore so much weaker than the Spanish socialists that he needed to strengthen his "Spanish" credentials. Thus for the PCI and the PCE the Polish events provided an excellent occasion to distance themselves much further from the Soviet Union.

The PCI and PCE had so praised the Polish "renewal" (odnowa) that they had no alternative but to denounce its suppression and the Soviet role in it. Even so, the PCI used it as the occasion for a far stronger attack on Soviet domestic and foreign policy than it had yet made, and for an explicit assertion that the global leadership of the left, forfeited by Moscow, must now be assumed by the West European workers' movement. This inevitably brought a violent Soviet response. To understand why, one must first understand the breadth and depth of the PCI move.

Its principal theses were the following: (1) The declaration of martial law in Poland, and all its consequences, should be completely reversed, and the Soviet pressure on the Polish "renewal" should cease. (2) The Polish events, and others as well, including Moscow's imports of U.S. grain and repression of dissidents, demonstrated that the historic role of the Soviet Union and its East European allies was "exhausted," just as the Second International's had been before it, because the Soviet model of socialism was unexportable to Western Europe and was itself in crisis in Eastern Europe. (3) Therefore, the West European workers' movement must develop a *terza via* between "exhausted" Soviet Marxism-Leninism and social democracy, which would have global validity and appeal. (4) This "new internationalism" must stress East-West détente and include socialist, social democratic, and Third World democratic, progressive, and revolutionary forces, not only communist parties. (In contrast, Moscow wrongly conducts an almost wholly military policy in the Third World.) It will be the "third phase" in the history of socialism. (Marxism and the October Revolution and its aftermath were the first two.) The PCI added that it did not want a break with the CPSU or any other communist party. (5) Moscow's support of national liberation movements in the Third World was too military (including use of Cuban troops) as opposed to political and economic, in nature, and in the Horn of Africa—a traditional area of Italian concern—it was too pro-Ethiopian, while it should be neutral between Ethiopia and Somalia and support Eritrean independence. (The PCI also was neutral on INF deployment.) (6) The PCI implied that it wanted to help build (and lead?) a "Euroneutralist" group in Western Europe, including all those fighting for peace, workers' self-management, women's liberation, youth culture, and ecology, along with, presumably, the left wings of the PS, PSOE (Spanish Socialist Party), and SPD and Andreas Papandreou's PASOK (Panhellenic Socialist Union), as well as the PCI and the PCE. The foreign policy aim of this bloc should be to establish an independent Europe between the two superpowers, and thus to overcome both blocs and struggle effectively for peace and arms control. It should also transcend—as, the PCI maintained, social democracy will not—the capitalist system. (The drifting away of Western Europe from U.S. dominance helped, the PCI probably believed, to make this aim more plausible.)

The Soviet responses to these PCI declarations accused the PCI leadership of a long catalogue of sins: preaching a "new way very much akin" to opportunism and revisionism; wrongly stating that Western Europe, not the USSR, is the main force for peace—"the old social democratic idea of 'Euro-centrism'"; trying to "appease" NATO and slandering the Soviet Union, *inter alia* by Enrico Berlinguer; the "false" accusation that the USSR is limiting détente in order to defend its sphere of influence; giving "moral-political support to the leaders of China"; advocating freedom of action for such antisocialist forces as Solidarity in Poland, "repeating almost word for word the fabrications of Reagan, Weinberger, Haig, Brzezinski, and other imperialist politicians," and thus being guilty of "crude interference in Poland's internal affairs"; declaring Marxism-Leninism "bankrupt," the communist movement "obsolete" and the socialist community "degenerated"; calling into question (by "Comrades" Giorgio Napolitano and Petro Ingrao) the existence of socialism in the Soviet Union; carrying out a "gradual departure from the Marxist-Leninist revolutionary platform" (the main point) and having "openly come out against world socialism," a course that "means direct aid to imperialism" at a time when the latter is stepping up its attacks on socialism; giving priority to "allegiance to the bourgeois-parliamentary political system" and "the rationalization . . . and the modernization of Italian state monopoly capitalism" over socialization of capitalist property; and doing all this "without any preliminary exchange of opinions with the CPSU or the PZPR [Polish United Workers' Party]" and not even replying to a CPSU letter of January 1982 before the PCI Central Committee plenum that same month. The CPSU also began mobilizing support from pro-Soviet parties against the PCI and financing the previously unimportant neo-Stalinist opposition in Italy to the PCI's policies.

In late 1982 it was too early to see how far this CPSU-PCI crisis would go and what its European and global reverberations would be. Since the Polish situation seemed likely to worsen still further, it was difficult to see how it could be papered over or repaired. The PCI and the CPSU both declared that they did not want a break in party relations, but these were essentially tactical declarations. Whether an explicit break would come remained unclear. It is also possible, given the precedent of the Soviet break — and subsequent attempt to restore party relations — with the Japanese Communist Party, that Moscow or the PCI will make such an attempt in the future. The chances that it would succeed did not, in late 1982, seem very good. In any case, many of the West European communist parties either supported the PCI or remained neutral in the controversy.

Moscow was trying, as it did in Spain in the 1970s, to encourage opposition within the PCI to its own leadership. However, that only one Central Committee member, Armando Cossutta, long known as pro-Soviet, publicly criticized the PCI's move indicated that Moscow would probably not have too much success.

Ironically, however, to the extent that the PCI was successful with its Euroleft bloc, and that it might return to the *compromesso storico*, cooperate with some of the DC (Christian Democrats) against the PSI (Italian Socialist Party) and thus improve its position in Italian politics, while continuing to oppose, for example, INF deployment, the PCI-CPSU break might also work against U.S. foreign policy in Europe. But that would hardly compensate for this latest Soviet defeat in Latin communism, which may well become the third great schism in the (*ci-devant!*) "international communist and workers' movement." Whether it does or not, the Soviet reaction to the PCI declarations further lowered Soviet prestige in Western Europe. It also once more demonstrated that Moscow, like any other great power, gives priority to the security of its borders, its empire, and its ideological hegemony (with respect to Poland) over gains farther away.[15]

15. For background, see note 8 above. For the recent CPSU-PCI exchange of polemics, see the statement by the PCI Direzione in *l'Unità*, December 30, 1981; the criticism of it by Armando Cossutta, ibid., January 6, 1982 (FBIS/WEU/Jan. 13, 1982/L2–4); the speech by Berlinguer at a PCI CC plenum, ibid., January 12, 1982 (FBIS/WEU/Jan. 21, 1982/L1–20); the speech there by Cossutta, ibid., January 13, 1982 (FBIS/WEU/Jan. 22, 1982/L1–3); and other speeches at the same plenum by Pajetta (ibid., Jan. 13, 1982) and Segre (ibid., Jan. 14, 1982); the final plenum speech by Berlinguer, ibid., Jan. 15, 1982 (only Cossutta voted against the plenum resolution; one other abstained); "Against the Interests of

CONCLUSION

Russia's central preoccupation in foreign policy has historically been with Europe. In the nuclear age, it switched to the United States and its role in Europe. The Russian aim has been to maintain control over Eastern Europe, notably Poland and at least part of Germany, and to get hegemony, if possible, over Western Europe. The Russian Empire's peak was in 1815, and the combination of the other powers against it at the Congress of Vienna and then its increasing technological and military inferiority to Western Europe, along with the rise of Germany, twice led to near disaster, which in 1917 and 1941–43, Russia barely escaped.

The nuclear age, Europe's political suicide in the two world wars, and the Soviet Union's acquisition of nuclear weapons froze European boundaries. The power and will of the Soviet leadership maintained control, by military force if need be, over most of Eastern Europe, notably Poland and East Germany. The growth of Soviet naval and airlift capability and the availability of Cuban troops ensured by the mid-1970s that the USSR could exploit more successfully the instability of the Third World. Its massive nuclear and conventional buildup, the American setbacks of Vietnam and Watergate, and the continued military weakness and disunity of Western Europe enabled Moscow at the end of the 1970s to begin, for the first time since 1939, to exploit successfully differences in the Western alliance and simultaneously to reestablish its influence over Poland. The latter was not surprising: it repeated the pattern of post-World War II East European history, and indeed most of modern Russian history. That the USSR was able, even if with only partial success, to do the former as well was the result more of Western disunity than of Soviet skill. Whether Moscow will continue to succeed in disrupting the alliance will largely be determined by the degree of determination and skill with which the United States and the principal West European states compromise their differences about how to deal with this Soviet attempt.

But these differences were not as great as they often appeared, and in 1983 both sides seemed to be tackling them. However, mutual understanding and readiness to compromise would be difficult, because the two elites had drifted apart and significant, if secondary, differences of national interest had emerged.

Peace and Socialism," *Pravda*, January 24, 1982 (FBIS/SOV/Jan. 25, 1982/G1–8 and corrections, ibid. January 27, 1982/G3); the PCI reply, *l'Unità*, Jan. 25, 1982; "On the Slippery Path: About Recent Statements by the Leadership of the Italian Communist Party," *Kommunist*, no. 2, 1982, reprinted in *Novoe vremia* (and *New Times*), January 29, 1982 (FBIS/SOV/Jan. 28, 1982/G1–11); "On the Form and the Substance of the Polemic Unleashed by the PCI Leadership," *Pravda*, February 13, 1982 (FBIS/SOV/Feb. 16, 1982/G1–3); and "Once Again Concerning the Positions of the PCI Leadership," *Kommunist*, no. 4, 1982; S. Vasil'tsov, A. Galkin, and T. Timofeev, "Ital'ianskie problemy," *Rabochii klass i sovremennyi mir*, no. 3, 1982, pp. 98–107.

Even so, the Soviet Union has many problems of its own: low economic growth, rising infant and male mortality, stagnant agricultural production, and, by the late 1990s, a shortage of Great Russian labor along with high population growth in the Islamic Central Asian republics. To what extent Moscow will succeed in its attempt at a preemptive breakout from its nuclear encirclement, in Western Europe as well as Indochina and the Middle East, cannot, like the future itself, be foreseen. As Hegel reminded us, "The owl of Minerva flies only at dusk."

Chapter 2

Germany, Europe, and the Soviets

Gerhard Wettig

In the Soviet perception, the Federal Republic of Germany is the crucial political factor in Western Europe. Both NATO and the European Community (EC) are seen as groupings that would not be viable without West German participation. After France left the military organization of NATO, the Soviet leaders felt that the Atlantic Alliance would have neither a sufficient territorial base nor a sufficient conventional defense force on the European continent if the Federal Republic declined to participate in the joint Western effort. At the same time, West Germany was regarded as the only possible base for the military presence of the United States in Europe. For these reasons, Moscow has always concluded that NATO would cease to exist on the mainland of Europe if the West Germans could be induced to turn their back on the Western alliance.[1] In a similar way, the EC could be deprived of an indispensable heartland and of a force carrying decisive political and economic weight if the Federal Republic were no longer a member.

The Soviet leaders have tried to break West Germany out of the Western community again and again, whenever there seemed to be some chance of success. In 1966, they hoped to lure first the Social Democratic Party, then still in opposition, and later the emerging Grand Coalition government, formed by Social Democrats and allegedly "Gaullist" Christian Democrats, out of the

---

1. See, for example, "Opasnye tendentsii," *Novoe vremia*, no. 6, 1967, p. 4; V. Kriukov, "Germanskii vopros i sovremennost'," *Mezhdunarodnaia zhizn'*, no. 2, 1967, p. 19; "V interesakh prochnogo mira," *Mezhdunarodnaia zhizn'*, no. 6, 1967, pp. 5–6.

pro-Atlantic consensus.[2] After that attempt failed, they tried to apply concerted pressure against the West Germans. A political campaign was waged against the Federal Republic under the label of "revanchism," which was presented as the main danger to "European security." The West Germans were allegedly threatening their fellow Europeans both in East and West with crisis- and war-provoking territorial ambitions in West Berlin, East Germany, Poland, and the USSR. Such a West German undertaking, which was said to parallel U.S. "imperialist" designs, had to be stopped—according to Soviet and pro-Soviet spokesman—by East and West Europeans alike, if they did not want to be involved in an all-devastating European war that would suit the exclusive purposes of the "West German revanchists," the "American imperialists," and their accomplices in NATO. That campaign was designed to isolate the government of the Federal Republic both domestically and among its NATO allies and thereby gradually to render it incapable of sustaining its allegiance to the Western alliance.[3]

It was only after the Soviet invasion of Czechoslovakia in 1968 that the Soviet argument lost its impact on Western public opinion and the Federal Republic felt the political pressures receding. Early in 1969, the Soviet leadership changed its political strategy once more: Bonn suddenly found itself in the role of a partner whose cooperation was being sought by the Soviet Union. The new constellation made détente in Central Europe possible, and the Soviets hoped that the ties of the Federal Republic to the West might be gradually weakened. Such expectations, however, did not mature.[4] When, at the end of the 1970s, East-West relations in Europe began to grow more tense again, the Kremlin still stood with regard to the Federal Republic where it had been in the early 1960s: West Germany was as unequivocally embedded in NATO as it had ever been; neither carrots nor sticks had effected any change.

Soviet Attempts to Influence the West Germans since 1979

The central issue that came to divide East and West was whether NATO was to restore the military balance in Europe after the Soviet Union and its allies had gained considerable military advantage there over the West. This was of particular interest to the West European NATO members, most notably the Federal Republic. Nevertheless, the Soviet leaders, who, as always, felt that West Germany was the decisive political factor on the European side

2. Gerhard Wettig, *Community and Conflict in the Socialist Camp: The Soviet Union, East Germany and the German Problem, 1965–1972* (London: C. Hurst; New York: St. Martin's, 1975), pp. 20–47.

3. Cf. Gerhard Wettig, "Entwicklungsphasen der sowjetischen Westpolitik," in *Moderne Welt: Jahrbuch für Ost-West-Fragen*, vol. 1976: *Elemente des Wandels in der östlichen Welt*, ed. Boris Meissner, pp. 224–27.

4. Ibid, pp. 227–51.

of NATO,[5] were determined to concentrate their efforts against Western armament of the Federal Republic. As early as the beginning of 1979 (long before the
NATO decision of December 12, 1979), they set the political stage. They established the International Information Department in the CPSU party apparatus
and staffed it with experts on German affairs. Leonid Zamiatin headed that
new center for foreign propaganda; Valentin Falin became his first deputy;
other "Germanologists"—such as Nikolai Portugalov—figured prominently in
the work of the department.

Shortly afterward, both the International Information Department people and
other prominent Moscow experts on Germany—most notably Vadim Zagladin,
Boris Ponomarev's deputy in the CPSU International Department (who is, in
fact, the party functionary responsible for relations with the West)—began
systematically to give detailed and lengthy interviews to the West German media
that seemed most suitable for disseminating Soviet views to the West German
public, who continue to receive information on the Soviet standpoint through
widely distributed domestic media. These efforts often bring the Soviet argument
to the people more readily and extensively than any other opinion.

The Soviet leaders have done their best to popularize their views in West
Germany. Indeed, one of the reasons they have been able to impress quite a few
West Germans with a position that is essentially contrary to the best interests
of the Federal Republic is their inventiveness in gearing political proposals, and
other moves regarding NATO, to propagandistic needs. Despite the fact that
Moscow wants to preserve, increase, and cement those elements of military advantage in relation to the West that are apt to jeopardize the security particularly
of a country as exposed as the Federal Republic, the relevant statements have
been worded in such a way that the average West German is inclined to feel
sympathetic to them. The Soviet leaders have declared themselves to be the
partisans of an allegedly existing "military equilibrium" in Europe and elsewhere
that was threatened by a U.S. drive for military superiority. It was in the best
interests of all Europeans—particularly those who, like the West Germans,
would be right in the center of any future European war—to stop that drive,
since its main rationale was to provide for the possibility of a limited nuclear
war in Europe.

Soviet propaganda linked that prospect, which could not but frighten any
West German, to NATO's willingness to endorse an arms buildup, as implied
in the double-track decision of December 12, 1979. Moscow tried to persuade its
West German audience that the United States intended to prepare for the destruction of the Soviet intercontinental-strategic capability from West European and West German soil. The Americans thus wanted to eliminate the
USSR militarily in the course of an exclusively European war, which would

5. See V. Shaposhnikov, "O nekotorykh problemakh sovremennogo antivoennogo
dvizheniia," *Mirovaia ekonomika i mezhdunarodnye otnosheniia*, no. 12, 1981, p. 23.

also mean the physical extermination of the European NATO countries. In contrast to that alleged U.S. policy, Moscow posed as the defender of both equilibrium and disarmament.

Brezhnev's proposals and announcements of October 6, 1979, July 1, 1980, February 23, 1981, June 30, 1981, March 16, 1982, and May 18, 1982, reveal their strong pro-Soviet and anti-NATO bias only in expert analysis.[6] The public at large, however, got an image of seeming Soviet willingness to negotiate and compromise, even to accept unilateral sacrifice and exercise unilateral restraint. The deliberate vaguenesses and hidden reservations that form part of all the "concessions" offered by the USSR so far tend to escape the uneducated public. At the same time, the man in the street is often unaware of the quantitative and qualitative imbalances that make Soviet attempts at "freeze" arrangements unacceptable to NATO. The extent to which the Soviet leaders base their negotiating postures on considerations of propaganda in West Germany becomes visible also when one looks at personalities. One of the most distinguished and perceptive German specialists in the Soviet diplomatic service, Yuli Kvitsinsky (who had previously served in Bonn), was chosen as his country's chief negotiator for the Geneva talks on intermediate-range arms limitation which began on November 30, 1981, between the United States and the Soviet Union.

Two Lines of Soviet Policy toward Bonn

The Soviet interest in influencing the Federal Republic's attitudes toward NATO policies in no way means that the USSR feels bound to policies of friendly cooperation with Bonn. One can only conclude that the Soviet leaders would see their options of influencing West German behavior too restricted by that, since the basic incompatibility of mutual security allows only for a very limited Soviet–West Germany commonality in that crucial field. Therefore, Moscow tries to use two contradictory policy lines on the Federal Republic of Germany—often at the same time.

On the one hand, the Soviet leaders seek to draw the West Germans into some kind of cooperative relations. Bonn is asked to unite its efforts with those of the USSR in order to stem rising East-West tensions or to initiate talks on the mutual security of both alliances. On the other hand, the Soviet leaders

6. For October 6, 1979: text in *Pravda*, October 7, 1979. July 1, 1980: see the protocol notes on Brezhnev's conversations with Chancellor Schmidt in *Die Welt*, July 4, 1980. February 23, 1981: text in *Pravda*, February 24, 1981. June 30, 1981: see reports on the Brezhnev-Brandt talks in "Bonbons auspacken, Peitsche zeigen," *Der Spiegel*, July 6, 1981, pp. 17–19; Brandt's "Spiegel" interview in *Der Spiegel*, July 6, 1981, pp. 24–26; Uwe Engelbrecht and Thomas Meyer, "Brandt: Gespräche nicht unterschätzen," *Kölner Stadt-Anzeiger*, July 3, 1981. March 16, 1982: text in *Pravda*, March 17, 1982. May 18, 1982: text in *Pravda*, May 19, 1982.

exert pressure on the government of the Federal Republic by mobilizing opposition against official West German policies both inside and outside the country. Most notably, they have never hesitated to inspire and promote campaigns aimed at counteracting West German defense efforts and West German NATO support. That line of Soviet behavior has become particularly pronounced in the course of the political contest over NATO's double-track decision of December 12, 1979.

Soviet propaganda has not refrained from employing any falsification that seems useful. The argument that has the strongest impact on West German public opinion is that the United States is seeking nuclear war against the Soviet Union that is to be contained in the European theater. Soviet representatives and sympathizers impress their West German audiences by saying that this is the very rationale of the NATO decision of December 12. In fact, however, the thesis of alleged American plans for nuclear warfare exclusively in Europe has been part of the Soviet propaganda instructions to the West European communists since 1970,[7] and therefore has nothing to do with the Western plans for compensatory Eurostrategic armament, the initial stages of which did not begin until late 1977. What is more, the idea that nuclear war, should it break out between the two superpowers, was to be limited to the territory of the European allies originates with the USSR, not with the United States. In the fall of 1972 Soviet representatives, including Brezhnev himself, urged it upon Secretary of State Kissinger, who rejected it.[8]

BASIC SOVIET PERCEPTIONS IN THE FIELD OF SECURITY

Soviet policies regarding Western Europe are largely determined by security interests. They can best be described by using a model of three different military "levels" in East-West relations. The "highest" military level is the correlation of the intercontinental-strategic forces that both the United States and the USSR possess and with which the superpowers can hit one another from their own territories and from the seas. Below that level are the strategic levels of continental (or intermediate) range—particularly the continental-strategic level in Europe, but also in the Middle and Far East. The "lowest" levels are the potential battlefield theaters with the forces assigned to them. They have both a ("tactical") nuclear and a conventional dimension.

The Soviet leaders insist on "equal security" (sometimes also "undiminished security") and strongly disagree with NATO's demands for "military parity." At first glance, both postulates seem to imply much the same thing. However, there are decisive differences. The Soviet representatives protest violently against the Western idea that there should be a balance of military forces the

7. V. V. Zagladin, chief ed., *Mezhdunarodnoe kommunisticheskoe dvizhenie* (Moscow: Izdatel'stvo politicheskoi literatury, 1970), p. 114.

8. Henry A. Kissinger, *Years of Upheaval* (Boston: Little, Brown, 1982), pp. 276–79.

equality of which would have to be measured by objective criteria mutually agreed upon. The USSR insists on a kind of military sufficiency and equivalence that can be determined only by those who are responsible for the country's security. At the same time, "equal security" implies the notion that "equality" applies exclusively to the two superpowers. That means in practice that the West European allies of the United States are not entitled to demand "equal security" for themselves. U.S.-USSR arrangements on mutual security would leave them out.[9] These theoretical claims correspond to an armament policy by which the Soviet Union, if only for reasons of utter impossibility to gain an exploitable measure of superiority, acknowledges intercontinental-strategic parity with the United States but strives for continental-strategic and battlefield-theater superiority in various regions, particularly Europe.

Regional superiority seems indispensable for Soviet security. The leaders of the USSR see their security primarily not in terms of deterrence (maximum hope of preventing war) but in terms of defense (maximum chance for military success in case war should break out). Therefore, their security perceptions have to be seen against the background of the warfare contingency. This has far-reaching practical implications. Since war, if only possible through Western fault, has to be regarded as the contingency to be provided for, the Soviet leaders cannot conceivably be satisfied with more-or-less equal war-waging opportunities in the regions bordering the USSR. They must ensure their maximum capability to survive, repel, and defeat the opponent's aggression, which in their outlook can be the only way into war between East and West.

The Soviet rationale for the war scenario, which has to be taken seriously, is the idea that the USSR must prevail over any war-initiating enemy, for the "imperialist" powers of the West can never be sufficiently trusted to refrain from aggressive policies and employment of military means. Accordingly, the USSR can achieve security only if it commands a margin of military superiority along its periphery and thereby discourages U.S. nuclear involvement from the beginning and has the capability of liquidating U.S. forward-based positions during an early phase of the war.

---

9. This view found clear expression in Soviet behavior during the SALT I and SALT II negotiations, when the Soviet leaders and representatives argued that U.S. intercontinental and continental (the forward-based systems, or FBS) capabilities should equal Soviet intercontinental systems alone, since that was what the two negotiating parties could muster against one another. Therefore, the best possible solution was said to be elimination of the American FBS altogether, while at the same time the continental-strategic weapons of the USSR would not be subject to any limitation. Such an arrangement would have provided for strategic equality between the two superpowers, but left the European NATO countries without adequate counterweight to the medium-range systems of the Soviet Union.

The Soviet assumption that war cannot happen without Western instigation and therefore will be a defensive one does not imply defensive military strategies to be used in the theaters around the USSR, particularly Europe. On the contrary, the Soviet military doctrine (which has been put into practice in the course of dozens of Warsaw Pact maneuvers) strongly emphasizes initiative, attack, and surprise to be employed in the regional theaters. A blitzkrieg type of war is designed to push the military conflagration as far away from Soviet territory and from the politically unreliable areas of Warsaw Pact allies as possible. War, if ever it should break out, must be fought on Western soil. In Europe, the goal is clearly to throw the United States into the Atlantic so as not to allow the other superpower to continue military activities on the Eurasian landmass (which, in the course of subsequent military mobilization in the United States, could result in a successful attack on the USSR). The Soviet strategy of quick military attack against Western Europe implies that, in case of need, nuclear weapons must be used, even if NATO should decide not to employ them.[10]

In the Soviet view, the intended capability to deprive the United States of its European and other military bridgeheads along the periphery of the USSR is an essential requirement of "equal security": the United States is not to have its military foot near the Soviet borders as long as the Soviet Union has no similar military strongholds on the American continent. In this context, the Soviet argument ignores the fact that the United States, if thrown out of Europe and Asia, would be left with a "Fortress (North) America" alone, while the USSR would gain access to worldwide domination.

"Equal security" with the United States, as demanded and sought by the Soviet Union, largely denies security to the West Europeans and other allies of the United States. In case of war, their territory would be destroyed and overrun by Eastern forces, if the Soviet concept worked out as intended. There would be no security whatsoever for them. Such a situation is unacceptable to countries such as the Federal Republic of Germany. If the allies of the United States perceived themselves to be unprotected, they might feel compelled to avoid any serious political conflict with the USSR so as not to risk transformation into a military contest, which their opponent, unlike themselves, could easily afford. The result would be that they would have to seek accommodation with Moscow on Soviet conditions. NATO, which would be deprived of its potential to couple West European security with that of the United States, would then not fail to break apart.[11]

10. Cf. Marshal Ogarkov, "Militärstrategie," in *Sowjetische Militärenzyklopädie*, vol. 7 (East Berlin, 1979), pp. 555–65; Joseph D. Douglass, Jr., and Amoretta M. Hoeber, *Conventional War and Escalation: The Soviet View*, ed. National Strategy Information Center (New York: Crane, Russak, 1981).

11. Such a long-term goal has been openly acknowledged by Vadim Zagladin in *Der Spiegel*, June 8, 1981, p. 119.

Soviet security policies are based on a defensive logic. But since that logic demands "successful defense" if war should break out, it entails claims to superior military capabilities in bordering regions and therefore implies offensive military and political effects in the relevant regions. The Federal Republic of Germany, as the Western country most exposed to the USSR, clearly perceives the latent threat in the military posture of the Soviet Union. This is why West Germany perceives its basic security interests to be antagonistic to those of the USSR and opts for NATO as a security community that confronts the Soviet Union with a united policy of war- and threat-preventing deterrence. It is this united front that Moscow seeks to weaken, hopefully also to break up, when it tries to bring its influence to bear on Bonn.

Soviet Ways of Influencing West German Policies

It seems inconceivable that the Soviet leaders can gain any West German support for a policy that has definite anti–West German implications. Nevertheless, it is the Federal Republic of Germany that plays a crucial role in Soviet policy considerations. In Soviet appeals to the West Germans, anticonfrontationist arguments are used to convince the Germans that both their anti-Soviet and their pro-NATO security perceptions are wrong and run counter to their genuine self-interest.

As has already been stated, one of the ways to do that is to try to mobilize an uninformed West German public against the policy line followed by the government. Since almost every West German is fully aware that any war in Europe, whether nuclear or conventional, would be suicidal to himself and his countrymen, Soviet propaganda can easily exploit a latent fear of war. It is no coincidence that the anti-NATO campaigns of the USSR are always under the heading of a "struggle for peace." The main propaganda weapon Moscow uses is the allegation that the United States is preparing for war in Europe. Since 1980 the Soviet approach has gained increasing credibility with parts of the West German audience, for Reaganite rhetoric on the need for a war strategy seemed to imply that it was the capability to make war that motivated Washington to put emphasis on armament.

The impact of Soviet appeals to West Germany, however, is not limited to the public. The awareness that war in Europe would be suicidal extends to the federal government. Bonn must necessarily seek any possible way to minimize the risk of war between East and West. This results in a clear West German interest in establishing a permanently stabilizing and mutually reassuring East-West agreement on security so as to increase continuity, reliability, and calculability in East-West relations and thereby reduce the likelihood of war breaking out in some future crisis. Whenever the Soviet leaders feel that Western reactions to confrontationist moves on their side become too tense to be comfortable, they exploit the Bonn interest in dialogue and tension reduction, by urging the

West German government to counteract the "dangerous tendencies" of its NATO allies and pursue a policy of talking with one another in East-West relations.[12]

That kind of appeal applies not only to the area of agreement on mutual security. The Soviet leaders realize that the Federal Republic has a much wider interest in East-West détente. West Germany badly needs a certain amount of general tension attenuation for various reasons. Within the context of NATO, Bonn is responsible for the continued economic, social, and political viability of West Berlin as an isolated enclave within East German territory. Such a task cannot be fulfilled without active Soviet and East German cooperation.[13] Both the USSR and the GDR have occasionally warned Bonn that its policies must not become confrontationist, if such cooperation is to continue.[14]

There is also a strong West German interest in preserving the personal ties of family and friendship between the people of the two Germanies, which are being threatened by increasing restrictions in consequence of the GDR's seclusionist policies.[15] To stem the tide of East Berlin's seclusionist trend is possible only by securing some measure of cooperation with the other side.[16] At the same time, the federal government shares the general West European interest in keeping and promoting the cultural, social, and economic bonds between both parts of Europe. It is not only common history and common heritage that motivates this. One is also aware that the East Europeans are keen to preserve the traditions linking them to Western Europe and assuaging their forced affiliation to the Soviet orbit.

West Germany, of course, also feels an overriding need to preempt crisis- and war-producing situations of political tension and acute confrontation through policies of moderation and dialogue in general and modus vivendi agreements at potential trouble spots in particular. Such interest, it is true, is common to all Western countries (and to those in the East as well). The Federal Republic,

12. Characteristic is the attitude of the Federal Republic to SALT II. The resulting agreement contained, as Bonn was quite aware, several arrangements that were detrimental to West German security interests. Nevertheless, Bonn decided to support SALT II strongly in private and in public. From the West German perspective, the SALT II treaty was a most important token of cooperation between the United States and the USSR in avoiding war, which was seen as infinitely more relevant than most of the military detail.

13. Only left wingers outside government occasionally plead for more than very limited political cooperation with the GDR and the USSR. The problem has been discussed by Gerhard Wettig, "Eine neue politische Orientierung für Berlin?" *Recht und Politik*, no. 4, 1981, pp. 157–60.

14. See, for example, the Soviet press declaration of May 22, 1976 (*Pravda*, May 22, 1976).

15. See the protocol notes on Brezhnev's conversations with Chancellor Schmidt in *Die Welt*, July 4, 1980.

16. For a discussion of the problem see titles in note 6 above (for February 23 and June 30, 1981).

however, which in case of military conflict would be right in the center of devastating warfare, is most sensitive to the need to reinforce NATO deterrence by reducing acute political controversies between East and West in Europe.

If one considers all the factors listed above (of which the Soviet leaders are well aware), it is not surprising that Moscow can count on West German willingness to reduce tensions and seek understanding in European East-West relations, whenever it chooses to enunciate appeals to that effect. The Soviets, therefore, feel that they always have a good chance to succeed when they seek to use the Federal Republic as a moderating influence against "hardliners" in the Western camp. This in itself is a means of provoking discord in the Atlantic Alliance during periods when harshly anti-Soviet attitudes prevail.

The Soviet leaders try to manipulate West German interests even further. Not only the public but also the government of the Federal Republic is exposed to arguments that the basically antagonistic relationship as perceived by the West Germans is more or less a matter of self-deception. After all, it is maintained, the Soviet Union is only seeking security for itself and peace for all mankind. It threatens no other country and wants to negotiate all kinds of agreements on mutual security—quite in contrast to what "imperialist circles" in NATO and the United States have in mind. Shouldn't the West Germans, for this reason, opt for cooperation with the USSR in making the forces of "reason," "understanding," and "peace" prevail in Europe? Shouldn't the West Germans at least refrain from antagonizing the Soviet Union by adhering to "extremist" NATO policies?

The latter question has been put to Bonn by Moscow again and again in regard to the dual-track decision of December 12, 1979. The implicit meaning of such inquiries is whether the Federal Republic can really afford to have the Pershing II and cruise missiles deployed on its territory against strong Soviet opposition, given that the West Germans badly need cooperation with the USSR and her allies on issues such as West Berlin, intra-German relations, and the preservation of peace in Europe. This is a Soviet form of linkage politics that makes unconditional adherence to any NATO line extremely difficult for Bonn.

Soviet Purposes in Exerting Influence on the Federal Republic

Whenever the West German—and to a considerable extent the West European—response to Soviet policies is different from the line taken by the United States, Moscow can hope to influence the Atlantic community contrary to the common Atlantic interest. Various purposes are conceivable in this context. The Soviet leadership can try to drive as many wedges into NATO as possible, in order to provide for a breakdown of the Western alliance, if that should prove possible. It is that priority that was favored in the late 1960s prior to the conflict over reformist Czechoslovakia.[17] Another potential line of action is to aim at

17. Cf. Wolfgang Berner, "Das Karlsbader Aktionsprogram," Europa-Archiv, no. 11, 1967, pp. 393–400.

dividing up NATO, but with the more moderate purpose of weakening it, not dissolving it altogether. Western observers who see Soviet policies in that light feel that Moscow has an interest in keeping Europe stable through some kind of limited NATO–Warsaw Pact condominium. A third Soviet option would be to use the Federal Republic and other West European NATO members as a lever to make the United States attenuate her anti-Soviet attitudes and become more responsive to Soviet wishes. Such motives seem to have been behind much of Soviet wooing of Bonn in the immediate post-Afghanistan period.

The evidence of Soviet foreign policy since World War II suggests that the three purposes cannot be seen as mutually exclusive. One can trace all of them in the record of Soviet behavior toward West Germany, often more or less simultaneously. It seems to be characteristic of Soviet decision makers that they are reluctant to make choices among their policy options, even if their options seem to be logically contradictory. From a Western perspective, they often want to have their cake and eat it too. Western observers are sometimes struck by the extent of what seems to amount to a kind of political greediness: Moscow tenaciously pursues options seen as conflicting with one another.[18]

Frequently the underlying motive seems to be an unresolved conflict of priorities. However, there are often instances when one cannot deny the good common sense in Moscow's behavior. The Soviet leaders will rarely reject any options until the situation has developed to a point where the relative merits of different alternatives are fully visible. The reluctance of the Soviet decision makers to commit themselves to one course of action at the expense of another often spares them the loss of options, when subsequently Western actions that have been decided upon fail to be implemented forcefully. The Soviet wait-and-see attitude then proves wise.

The Soviet way of dealing with foreign policy issues is fundamentally different from the strategic approach common in the West. Obviously, the Soviet leaders do not design strategic master plans in advance. They are much more opportunistic. That is to say, they are keen to sense opportunities, expected or unexpected, which will allow them to reach their security and power goals without too much effort or risk. To express it in the quasi-military language that has formed Bolshevik thinking since Lenin's days, the USSR tends to probe the Western front all along its length. Wherever a weak spot is detected, the probe is intensified with a view to finding out how far it is possible to go in order to have a reasonable chance of success without undue risk. Even when at some point the decision is made to step in, there is still a reservation that the action might have to be reversed if unforeseen difficulties and risks should

18. A classical example is the Soviet attitude to the European Community; see Eberhard Schulz, *Moskau und die europäische Integration* (Munich and Vienna: Oldenbourg, 1975).

arise.[19] Accordingly, Soviet policies imply lengthy time spans during which the course to be taken remains undecided and during which it would be most unwise to forgo any policy options.

The Soviet choice whether to use leverage on the Federal Republic for the purpose of breaking up NATO, of only weakening it, or of counteracting undesired U.S. policies has to be viewed against this background. Moscow has occasionally favored one of these options over the others, but it has never committed itself to just one course of action that—though it might be justified for the moment—was almost certain to be proven wrong sooner or later. At present, the Soviet leaders obviously nourish hope that the West European peace movement, particularly the "friends of peace" in West Germany, will greatly help them against NATO, possibly even to the extent that they might be able to pressure Bonn and other West European governments into arrangements against their free will and to do irreparable harm to both the deterrence posture and the political cohesion of the Western alliance.[20] But such an outcome, if desirable, is far from certain. Therefore, Moscow also prepares for the contingency that security issues such as the ones raised by Soviet SS–20 deployment and the NATO dual-track decision might finally have to be settled in negotiations with Western governments that command full freedom of political action.[21]

Moscow and the Two Triangles with West Germany

At present, it is the Federal Republic's interest in European détente that the Soviet leaders are most interested in exploiting. This has not always been the case. In fact, Gaullist France was the first NATO country to offer a specific détente relationship to the USSR and her allies. President de Gaulle's overtures to the East in the mid-1960s even implied a deliberate policy of weakening NATO and thereby triggered Soviet hopes at the time that NATO might soon be broken up. France has remained the honorary number one détente partner

19. A typical example of this kind of cautious probing is the Soviet handling of the Angolan civil war in 1975–76. A similar action—but with an opposite outcome—was taken with regard to the political developments in Portugal. See Gerhard Wettig, "Entspannungs- und Klassenpolitik: Das sowjetische Verhalten gegenüber Portugal," *Beiträge zur Konfliktforschung*, no. 1, 1976, pp. 77–136.

20. Cf. V. Zagladin, "Oktiabr', mir, zhiznennye interesy chelovechestva," *Mirovaia ekonomika i mezhdunarodnye otnosheniia*, no. 11, 1981, pp. 3–4, 10–11, 15–16; G. Vorontsov, "SShA i Zapadnaia Evropa v usloviiakh obostreniia mezhdunarodnoi obstanovki," *Mirovaia ekonomika i mezhdunarodnye otnosheniia*, no. 11, 1981, p. 36; Shaposhnikov, "O nekotorykh problemakh sovremennogo antivoennogo dvizheniia," pp. 19–29.

21. Accordingly, the Soviet negotiators at the Madrid CSCE follow-up meeting and at the Geneva medium-range missile talks have adopted a wait-and-see attitude so far, hoping that the peace movement in Western Europe might largely do the job for them, but at the same time have been anxious to keep diplomatic channels open to future agreement in case they should be needed.

of Moscow almost to this day. Even when, in 1969–70, West Germany was becoming the crucial factor of Soviet détente relations with Western Europe, France was still being wooed as the country most responsible for the success of East-West détente. As late as 1980, it was on the initiative of France's Giscard d'Estaing that the diplomatic East-West dialogue in Europe—which had broken off after the December 1979 decision of NATO and Soviet invasion of Afghanistan two weeks later—was resumed, much to the relief of the Soviet leadership.

In dealing with both France and West Germany, the Soviet leaders have to reckon with a paradoxical relationship between the policies of the two countries: the "harder" (more intransigent) toward the USSR that West German policies are, the more forthcoming France's behavior is likely to be. De Gaulle's conciliatory moves toward the East, which were accompanied by severe restrictions on France's participation in NATO, rested on the premise that the Federal Republic would certainly not follow suit; that is, the détente relationship with the USSR and Eastern Europe would make France a unique—hence privileged—partner and thereby enhance the world power status the French president was seeking. When Bonn joined détente in 1969–70, Paris could no longer enjoy exclusiveness, and this made détente less attractive. The negative trend toward détente has become more pronounced since François Mitterrand took power. The new French leader is impressed by the deep political inroads the USSR is making in Western Europe, particularly among the West German public, and feels a strong need to counteract that by a hard policy of his own.

A similar phenomenon applies in security policies. When de Gaulle withdrew from the military organization of NATO, he felt certain that he could afford to do so, since West Germany's close adherence to the Western alliance would sufficiently compensate for the loss and allow the NATO military organization to continue its activities and thereby provide a functioning forward security shield for France. As long as the Federal Republic could be safely counted on to give the necessary support to NATO, the French could afford to take a more national stance and employ their military potential largely for purposes of independence and grandeur enhancement. In the meantime, the situation has changed psychologically. The peace movement, which has gained considerable ground in West Germany, makes the French government feel uncertain about the furture military role of the Federal Republic. Under these circumstances, there seems to be a strong French interest in strengthening the elements of commonality in the Western alliance, so as not to jeopardize the protective shield that NATO provides for France.

In the beginning, the Soviet leaders seem to have had little awareness of the subtleties in the West German–French relationship. One indication of this is the enthusiasm with which they hailed de Gaulle's withdrawal from the military organization of NATO as the starting point of a development that would lead to a gradual NATO breakup. They also seem to have had little understanding of France's diminishing commitment to détente once the West Germans joined in. In the meantime, the Soviet leaders appear to have learned a bit more on the subject. They may also have realized that there is little they can do to make the competition between the two West European capitals work in their favor—at least, if one leaves out the more limited aspect of economic East-West exchange. The practical conclusion they derive from that is that—at least for the time being—priority is to be accorded to relations with the Federal Republic, if only implicitly.

A policy triangle that the Soviet leaders hope to make use of in relation to Bonn is the one connecting them with the two Germanies. Since the Federal Republic highly desires cooperation with the GDR in matters of West Berlin and intra-German personal contacts, Moscow (which still has considerable control over the relevant East German policies) can easily offer to promote or to bar West German efforts. In fact, Soviet leaders repeatedly have pressed in East Berlin for minimum concessions or at least for some show of conciliatory attitude in regard to Bonn's wishes—for example, during the Gromyko-Bahr talks in early 1970, through back-channel activities concerning the Basic Treaty between the two Germanies, or in the context of Brezhnev's Bonn visit in November 1981. Contrariwise, they have been quite blunt in calling the East German leadership to task when it seemed to get involved in intra-German cooperation too deeply, as was the case after the understanding between Bonn and East Berlin of December 1974.[22]

The Soviet leaders can, and usually do, employ both sticks and carrots. The threat that the GDR could deny cooperation has either been veiled in Soviet statements or expressed more openly in East German statements alone. Thus Moscow has carefully avoided the blame of employing direct political threats against the Federal Republic. Soviet talk about potential incentives if the West Germans prove forthcoming in crucial East-West issues has been more clearly pronounced, but has still been cautious. The Soviet leaders seem to feel that such linkages, if voiced too strongly, might prove counterproductive—for example, by giving propaganda ammunition to domestic opponents of the federal government. At the same time, there would be harm to the prestige of the GDR if the USSR prejudiced its future policy decisions openly.

There are also inherent limitations to the incentives Moscow can offer to Bonn. Both sides understand that nothing can be agreed upon that would offer German unification. The Soviet leadership—like practically all European governments—feels strongly that Germany has to remain divided. What may be talked about is some measure of token national satisfaction for the West Germans through limited intra-German cooperation and limited family contacts across the intra-German borders.

22. See the literature mentioned in note 18 of Fred Oldenburg and Gerhard Wettig, "The Special Status of the GDR in East-West Relations," *East Central Europe*, 4, no. 2 (Fall 1979): 173–86.

Even in that respect, the Soviet attitude, despite the rhetoric occasionally used by Soviet diplomats, tends to be very restrictive indeed. To preserve domestic stability in the GDR against any possible encroachment is the number one priority of Soviet policy. The East German leaders have always felt themselves threatened from within. West German attempts to enhance their domestic stature and self-confidence by some degree of economic patronage have so far been futile. Consequently, the GDR policy of hostile seclusion against the Federal Republic, though reduced somewhat in 1972, strongly reemerged soon afterward and has repeatedly reduced possibilities for intra-German contacts below the pre-1972 level. The drastic increase of the compulsory currency exchange rate, which the East German authorities introduced under the pretext of the Polish situation in October 1980, is only one of a long series of seclusionist measures taken since early 1973. The Soviet leaders have publicly supported these and other restrictions against human movement across the intra-German border.[23] Despite such setbacks and disappointments, the West German goverment feels it must keep political channels to Moscow open. In Bonn's perspective, the intra-German situation would become much worse if the Federal Republic ceased to be responsive to Soviet and East German needs altogether.

SOVIET–WEST GERMAN RELATIONS IN A PHASE OF INCREASING EAST-WEST TENSION

The pecularities of the Soviet–West German relationship have shown themselves clearly on the historical record. As long as Presidents Nixon and Ford held office, American-Soviet conflicts remained within reasonable limits. Although the hopes of a harmonious worldwide delimitation of conflicts awakened by the Moscow declaration of May 1972 and the agreement for the prevention of a nuclear war of June 1973 had not been fulfilled,[24] neither the confrontation during the Yom Kippur War of October 1973, nor the Soviet attempts to exploit America's domestic weakness during the Cuban-Soviet intervention in Angola in 1975–76, nor Kissinger's Middle East diplomacy with the aim of elbowing out the USSR brought the situation to an open break. It was not until after President Carter took office that relations between the two world powers appeared to be threatened by significant deterioration.

It was above all the new U.S. policies on human rights that caused irritation in Moscow. The American administration apparently took the view that the Soviet leadership was obliged by its endorsement of the principle of human rights in the Final Act of the CSCE (1975) to respect human rights and the basic freedoms as they are understood in the Western democracies. For this reason,

23. See, for example, Iu. Voronov, "Fakty protiv domyslov," *Pravda*, October 13, 1980; V. Lapskii, "Ugroza dlia razriadki," *Izvestiia*, November 2, 1980.

24. Text of May 1972 declaration: *Europa-Archiv*, no. 12, 1972, pp. D 289–91; of June 1973 agreement: *Europa-Archiv*, no. 15, 1973, pp. D 418–19.

the USSR was expected to recognize inalienable rights and freedoms of the individual in his dealings with the state, and to make this a guideline for its domestic policies. This was diametrically opposed to the Soviet viewpoint, which maintains that the collective legal rights represented by the leadership must enjoy absolute priority over the rights of the individual and that, accordingly, the citizen can at best hope for only arbitrary legal concessions from the executive powers, in keeping with governmental practices up to that time. If the Soviet leaders had acceded to the American demands, they would have been depriving their own regime of its raison d'être and ability to function.

That was something that no one had ever dreamed of in Moscow. Soviet agreement to the Final Act of the CSCE had been based on a tacit agreement to disagree on whether the term "human rights" should be understood in its Western-democratic or its Soviet-communist connotations. Thus, from the Soviet point of view, the provisions on human rights in the CSCE meant nothing more than that the leadership of the state should in the future regard the wishes of the citizens with good will in its decision making. To Moscow, Carter's demands amounted to a completely unfounded impudence, the purpose of which could only be to put the Soviet Union in the wrong in the eyes of an ill-informed public. The leaders in the Kremlin interpreted this as a sign that the United States was no longer interested in détente.

The Soviet reading met with some measure of understanding in Bonn. The West German government endeavored to preserve and extend the consensus reached at the CSCE. All attempts to go beyond the CSCE consensus and to force upon the Soviet government concessions that were a priori unacceptable could not, as the West Germans saw it, bring the implementation of human rights any closer. It was feared in Bonn that the leaders of the USSR and its allies, already in trouble as a result of the activities of proponents of human rights and of the expectations of relaxation harbored by large sections of the population, could revert to an intensification of repressive measures if others took advantage of its difficulties to launch polemical attacks. The makers of West German policy pleaded, as did other West European governments, in favor of a pragmatically cautious approach: Western diplomacy should dispense with propagandistic efforts in public and urge that any breaches of human rights that came to light be eliminated at the conference table behind closed doors.

At the Belgrade follow-up meeting to the CSCE in 1977–78, the USSR and other countries of the Warsaw Pact involved in violations of human rights found themselves up against a twofold political strategy on the part of the West, the two aspects of which could only imperfectly be harmonized by attempts to coordinate them within NATO. The Americans preferred a denunciatory approach, while the West Europeans in general attempted to bring their influence to bear on the Eastern leaders in a businesslike, cooperative manner. The result was—even if frequently curbed and only sporadically pursued—an anti-Soviet offensive involving large-scale publicity. Moscow's answer was to refuse to engage in any continued cooperation with the countries of the West in détente policy and, both during and after the follow-up conference, to step up the repression of human rights activists on its own territory.[25]

The critical development of East-West relations went into its second stage when the USSR intervened militarily in Afghanistan in late December 1979. This breach of international law also violated the principle of nonintervention, which according to the CSCE is also binding on relations with nonsignatory nations, and left a deep impression on the administration and public opinion in the United States. President Carter admitted that he would have to revise his ideas on the nature of Soviet foreign policy. American indignation was aggravated further by the fact that the Soviet Union had adopted a shady position in the humiliating Teheran hostage affair and had openly proclaimed its willingness to come to terms with the brutal Khomeini regime.

In the West European capitals, especially Bonn, the surprise and indignation were somewhat less pronounced. On the one hand, the Europeans had, in light of earlier cases of intervention – the military involvement in the GDR in 1953, in Hungary in 1956, and in Czechoslovakia in 1968, and the acts of armed intervention in Angola in 1975-76 and in Ethiopia in 1978 – never precluded the possibility of such behavior on the part of the Soviet Union. On the other hand, they were aware that, from the Soviet point of view, certain elements of the situation in Afghanistan practically compelled the Soviet Union to take military action.[26]

This does not mean that the governments of the Federal Republic of Germany and the other countries of the European Community in any way condoned this Soviet step. They were, however, prepared to give the Soviet leadership credit in the form of a certain understanding of its motives. Above all, they were convinced that there would be no prospect of reversing the Soviet occupation of the country on the Hindu Kush by using polemics, pressure, and sanctions, but only by adopting an approach of patient diplomacy coupled with the expression of willingness to cooperate subject to certain conditions.

It was for this reason that the Federal Republic of Germany felt unable to comply with U.S. appeals for it to discontinue economic and other forms of cooperation with the Soviet Union. The feeling in Bonn was that détente, having broken down in the Middle East, must not be jeopardized in Europe. It was a matter of preserving the regions where peace and stability prevailed in order to be able to use them as a basis for resisting the spread of discord that had broken out elsewhere. This amounted to taking a political burden off the

25. Gerhard Wettig, "Die Menschenrechtsproblematik auf der Belgrader KSZE-Folgekonferenz," in *Aus Politik und Zeitgeschichte: Beilage zur Wochenzeitung "Das Parlament,"* B 27/78, July 8, 1978, pp. 25-43.

26. Cf. Heinrich Vogel, ed., *Die sowjetische Intervention in Afghanistan* (Baden-Baden: Nomos, 1980).

Soviet Union in a tense situation. But it was not without its advantages for NATO: if the peace had been disturbed in the European theater, the alliance would have found itself confronted with problems for which it would hardly have been possible to find solutions. Nevertheless, the impression growing in Moscow that the Western side was divided and incapable of resolute action was, of course, a source of concern to the North Atlantic Alliance.

The differences of opinion within NATO repeated themselves in late 1981 and early 1982 in the wake of the declaration of martial law in Poland. The Reagan administration assessed this measure on the part of the Polish Military Council as an act forced upon it by the Soviet leadership and thus as no more than a quasi-military intervention by the USSR glossed over for the benefit of outside observers. In contrast, Bonn took the stand as the spokesman for those countries of Western Europe that assumed a primarily Polish causality and thus did not attribute any direct responsibility to the Soviet leadership.

These diverging appraisals held on either side of the Atlantic led to different practical consequences. In Washington's view, the point was to use economic sanctions (which did not, however, include a ban on the grain deliveries that are of such great importance to Moscow) to impress on the Soviet leaders the error of their ways. The West German government, on the other hand, along with the governments of its partner countries in the European Community, was of the opinion that it was more important to help the Polish Military Council to consolidate the economy in order to give it both an incentive and an opportunity to relax the domestic political restrictions and to enter into a dialogue with the church and the labor union.

In all three cases of critical deterioration in East-West relations, the West German government demonstrated a consistent approach: to check the aggravation and then to relax tensions in Europe by preserving existing patterns of cooperative relations, believing that the best chance of bringing influence to bear on the actions of the other side was to carry on a political dialogue backed up by positive economic incentives.

The lack of inclination in Bonn and the other West European capitals to join in the imposition of sanctions can further be attributed to a pronounced reluctance on the part of the European NATO members to resort to a policy of ineffectual "castigation." The measures imposed by President Carter after the Soviet intervention in Afghanistan, for example, were assessed by the West Europeans from the very beginning as no more than irrational acts of moral retaliation by which there was nothing to be gained. They might perhaps, in the light of the West's powerlessness to change anything regarding this breach of international law by the USSR, have served some function as a domestic-policy safety valve, but for the rest they appeared likely to place a further burden on East-West relations. They would only make it more difficult to resolve future problems. The governments of the Federal Republic of Germany and the other West European countries felt that they were right and justified in refusing to participate in the American policy of imposing sanctions, because the United States had, in each case, made its decisions to this effect unilaterally without due consideration of the needs and interests of its European allies.

Of course, since the leading Western power was taking a completely different course, it was impossible for the political line followed by the Federal Republic and the other West European countries to develop its full potential. The result of the transatlantic differences was that the NATO countries obstructed each other's efforts and were not able to apply either their cooperation or their sanctions effectively against the USSR. Thus it was possible for the Soviet Union to profit from the West European countries' willingness to cooperate, which relieved it from American pressure, while using the American go-it-alone attitude as an excuse for not meeting the expectations that the Europeans intended should go hand in hand with their conciliatory measures. As an additional political bonus, Moscow was even able to benefit from the visible disunion in the Western camp.

SOVIET–WEST GERMAN ANTAGONISM IN THE FIELD OF SECURITY

The Soviet Union has acquired elements of superiority in the European theater. Therefore, NATO can no longer be certain that its defenses will stand the test of war under any circumstances.[27] The Soviet arms buildup is being perceived as all the more threatening by the West, for Soviet military doctrine provides for an immediate offensive against Western Europe in case of war. Deployment, armament, and other elements of the Warsaw Pact military posture clearly reflect that basic operational orientation.[28]

In order to offset the military threat from the East, Western deterrence strategy calls for lowering the nuclear threshold. The deficit in conventional defensive capability can only be compensated for by resorting to the employment of short- and medium-range nuclear weapons at an earlier stage than had been envisaged in the past. The Soviet Union is at present attempting to deprive NATO of precisely this option. Its Eurostrategic arms buildup, in particular the rapidly progressing deployment of the modern SS–20 weapons system, is aimed at gaining a Euronuclear superiority that would make Soviet territory invulnerable from

27. Gerhard Wettig, *Umstrittene Sicherheit: Friedenswahrung und Rüstungsbegrenzung in Europa* (West Berlin: Berlin Verlag, 1982), pp. 51–101.

28. Cf. Günter Poser, *Militärmacht Sowjetunion 1980* (Munich: Oldenbourg, 1980), pp. 38–40; Eberhard Schulz, "Charakteristika sowjetischer Westpolitik," in Josef Füllenbach and Eberhard Schulz, eds., *Entspannung am Ende?* (Munich and Vienna: Oldenbourg, 1980), pp. 239–42; Stephan Tiedtke, "Militärische Planung und MBFR-Politik der Sowjetunion," *Osteuropa*, 30, no. 4 (April 1980): 301–19; Hans-Jürgen Hartung, "Angriff-Hauptkampfart der Roten Armee," *Wehrforschung*, no. 3, 1971, p. 88; interview with General I. G. Pavlovsky in *Soviet Military Review*, no. 9, 1976, pp. 2–7.

the West while exposing Western Europe to the threat of a disarming first strike.[29] The Atlantic Alliance would then have no potential for step-by-step nuclear escalation in Europe to point to in response to a threat of Soviet attack.

The threat to the Federal Republic as a result of these developments is even greater than it is to the other countries of Western Europe. It is thus no coincidence that West German Chancellor Schmidt was the first to speak of the need for Eurostrategic arms buildup within NATO.[30] During the subsequent consultations in the NATO organs, the West German delegates insisted, despite persistent opposition from the Carter administration, that remedial measures of this nature were indispensable. It was not until the West Europeans had explained to the Americans time and again that global-strategic parity between the United States and the USSR as part of the official doctrine of graduated deterrence was not enough to guarantee the military balance in Europe that the Atlantic Alliance reached agreement on Eurostrategic armament in the spring of 1979.[31]

The detailed plans drawn up in pursuance of this agreement called for NATO to catch up qualitatively with the USSR in the Eurostrategic sector in order to make credible both its capability to launch retaliatory strikes against Soviet territory and to direct crippling strikes against attacking Warsaw Pact troops. At the same time, however, NATO decided not to deploy weapons that would indicate to Moscow an intended preemptive first strike against the USSR. For this reason, the planned Western systems remained quantitatively far below parity and were designed to cover the limited ranges of 1,800 to 2,500 kilometers.[32]

---

29. The SS–20 is—in contrast to all Eurostrategic carriers in the West—a mobile weapon system capable of carrying three MIRVs and is reloadable. Its accuracy with a CEP (circular error probable) of less than 300 meters has increased by a factor of three to six compared with previous Soviet missiles; the penetrating power of its warheads makes the SS–20 capable of destroying even armored pinpoint targets. It thus conceivably opens up the option of using the weapon to deliver a preemptive first strike against now vulnerable NATO targets in Western Europe. By contrast, Warsaw Pact targets, particularly those in the USSR, are becoming increasingly invulnerable from the West. In light of the increasing perfection of the East's air defense systems, American nuclear bombers in Western Europe have less and less chance of reaching their targets. It is, above all, the qualitative gap by which the present NATO systems lag behind the Soviet weapons that is bringing the day closer and closer when U.S. "forward-based systems" will have hardly any combat value left and the SS–20 will be able to threaten the countries of Western Europe in a completely unilateral manner.

30. Public discussion was prompted by Chancellor Schmidt's statement at the London Institute for Strategic Studies, October 28, 1977, published in *Survival*, January-February 1978, pp. 2–10.

31. See *Aspekte der Friedenspolitik*, ed. Presse- und Informationsamt der Bundesregierung, Bonn, June 1981, pp. 51–52.

32. Ibid., pp. 59–60; Lothar Ruehl, "Der Beschluß der NATO zur Einführung nuklearer Mittelstreckenwaffen," *Europa-Archiv*, no. 4, 1980, pp. 101–6.

As long as Eurostrategic arming remained without concrete form, the Soviet leadership let it be known that it was not impressed. It simply ignored repeated emphatic warnings by Schmidt in the course of 1978–79 that the buildup of SS–20s, if it continued, would be answered in kind by the West.[33] Even when the Western armament plans began to take shape, Moscow still saw no reason to cooperate. The Eurostrategic moratorium brought into the discussion by Schmidt, and which would have allowed the USSR to keep the SS–20 already deployed while denying NATO the right to build up the envisaged counter-capacity, was rejected by the Soviet leadership after some discussion as not favorable enough. Instead, Brezhnev categorically called on the Atlantic Alliance on October 6, 1979, to drop its plans. Then the USSR might also be prepared to enter into discussions on limitation and even reduction of its Eurostrategic weapons.[34]

According to this offer, it would, for all practical purpose, have been at the discretion of the Soviet leadership to decide the scope of the proposed reduction, and whether it would include the decisive SS–20 system at all. Furthermore, subsequent statements by Soviet commentators tend to indicate that the offer of "reduction" was taken to mean merely the redeployment of the SS–20s beyond the Urals (from where they could still reach Western Europe). This proposal revealed no signs of appreciation for the West Europeans' and West Germans' feelings about the constant threat presented by the Soviet Eurostrategic weapons. For this reason, the governments of the NATO countries saw no grounds for departing from their rearmament program.

The Roots of the East-West Conflict over Security

The Soviet buildup of SS–20 missiles is to be seen in connection with Moscow's campaign against the United States' "forward-based systems" in Western Europe. In the 1950s the two world powers had had only nuclear-warhead delivery systems of medium range at their disposal, which were stationed on both sides along the borders of the Soviet sphere of power, most of them in the European theater. This gave the United States the advantage that it could launch a nuclear attack on the USSR without its own territory being in danger of a Soviet counterattack. If there had been a nuclear exchange, the Soviet leadership would have been able to deliver its nuclear destructive potential only into West European target areas.

This situation changed when both world powers developed carrier systems of global range. The American administration drew its consequences from this by withdrawing the medium-range missiles directed at the USSR from Europe and stationing the new long-range missiles it built to replace them on the North American continent and on the high seas. All that remained in Western Europe

33. See, for example, *Aspekte der Friedenspolitik*, p. 16.
34. Text: *Pravda*, October 7, 1979.

was about 150 F–111 medium-range bombers. On the other side, however, the Soviet leadership reduced neither its 700 medium-range missiles directed at Western Europe nor its medium-range nuclear bombers. NATO accepted this asymmetry as tolerable as long as the F–111 bombers were thought capable of inflicting unacceptable damage on the USSR and thus making the risk of a nuclear escalation in Europe credible to the Soviet leadership.

Moscow, however, declared itself to be offensively threatened. During the negotiations on SALT I and SALT II, the Soviet delegates demanded the removal of the American "forward-based systems." The "strategic balance" that was the subject of the discussions should be defined in strictly bilateral terms. Not only those nuclear weapons stationed on the territories of the United States and the Soviet Union and on the high seas were to be counted; the short-range nuclear-warhead carrier systems of the United States and its allies deployed around the USSR should also be included, because they too could reach Soviet territory. The Soviet negotiators, on the other hand, could see no reason for subjecting their own country's medium-range missile systems to similar restrictions, since, it was argued, these could not threaten American territory. The American delegates rejected this approach as a basis for negotiations, because a Soviet right to threaten Western Europe unilaterally was unacceptable to NATO.

Nevertheless, the Americans did meet the Soviet wishes halfway. At SALT I they accepted a noncircumvention clause that was to serve as a guarantee to the USSR that they would not seek to undermine the balance of power established in the agreements on the global strategic systems by expanding their Eurostrategic capacities.[35] Brezhnev was similarly assured during his meeting with President Ford in November 1974.[36] Ever since, Moscow has claimed that the United States had committed itself to an unconditional renunciation of any expansion of its "forward-based systems."[37]

Another reason why this interpretation appears consistent in Soviet eyes is that the American delegates conceded to further unilateral restrictions of their country's medium-range weapons during the following SALT II negotiations. For example, they accepted that the American cruise missiles under development for deployment on land and at sea should have a range of under 600 kilometers, whereas the Soviet Backfire bomber with a range of about 5,000 kilometers and the USSR's comparable missile systems were excluded from the

35. See the nonofficial protocol notes as published in *Die Welt*, July 1980. Official Soviet statement: "Radi bezopasnosti narodov," *Pravda*, July 15, 1980.
36. Chancellor Schmidt in a "Spiegel" interview in *Der Spiegel*, July 7, 1980, pp. 28–29; TASS from Moscow, July 7, 1980, protocol notes as published in *Die Welt*, July 7, 1980.
37. This is particularly noticeable in the protocol notes published in *Die Welt*, July 7, 1980.

terms of reference of the negotiations.[38] Although the limitations imposed on the cruise missile were scheduled to run out in 1981, in the Soviet view they nevertheless constituted a permanent agreement, only the detailed modalities of which required future clarification.[39]

The course of SALT II left a permanent impression on the expectations of the Soviet leaders as regards questions of security in Europe. It appeared to them that the American administration had declared itself to agree in principle with the Soviet demand that the USSR should no longer be exposed to any effective nuclear threat to its territory proceeding from the European periphery: according to the arrangement reached in SALT II, apparently, no new medium-range weapons systems were to be introduced in response to future military requirements; at the same time, Washington seemed to be prepared to commit itself to a unilateral renunciation of any expansion of Eurostrategic capacities. On this basis, it is only logical that the Soviet leadership should have come to the conclusion that the buildup of a superior continental strategic potential in relation to the West European countries would contradict neither the letter nor the spirit of the SALT II treaty.

The Soviet leadership demanded that neither the USSR nor the United States (which had successfully opposed such a possibility in the case of the Cuban crisis) must be exposed to an additional nuclear threat from forward-based strategic weapons systems. No allowance was made for the security of the countries of Western Europe in this conception. Moscow expects them to put up with a unilateral and thus uncountered nuclear strategic threat from the Soviet Union. Soviet officials have expounded on occasion that the West Europeans laid claim to protection from the U.S. global-strategic deterrence shield anyway.[40]

THE ISSUE IMPLIED IN THE CONFLICT OVER MEDIUM-RANGE SYSTEMS IN EUROPE

This boils down to the preposterous demand that the United States' West European allies should be satisfied with a lesser degree of security than the two world powers. Within the framework of their mutual relationship, the United States and the USSR countered each other's threats on the same geographical basis that they originate on–at the global level. The West European countries, on the other hand, and by contrast with the USSR, should possess no possibility

---

38. "SALT and the NATO Allies: A Staff Report to the Subcommittee on European Affairs on the Committee on Foreign Relations," U.S. Senate, Washington, D.C., October 1979, pp. 14–15, 32–34.

39. See A. Arbatov, "Trebovanie vremeni," *Sovetskaia Rossiia*, June 20, 1980; Leonid Zamiatin, "Miru nuzhna voennaia razriadka," *Literaturnaia gazeta*, December 26, 1979.

40. See V. Falin, "Budushchee Evropy: V mirnom sotrudnichestve," *Izvestiia*, November 22, 1979.

of counterthreat to deter any adversary at the European level, but must rely exclusively on the effectiveness of deterrent capacities existing elsewhere (namely at the global level).

Since President de Gaulle first cast doubt on the assurance that the United States afforded the West European nations a reliable guarantee of deterrence even despite the autodeterrent aspects of a global strategic nuclear exchange and its effects on the United States itself, such a global-strategic arrangement, which only reconfirms the fears of the West European partners, has threatened to tear NATO apart from within. The Soviet leadership may itself harbor doubts that adequate deterrence protection exists for Western Europe under some circumstances. This is all the more possible since the NATO concept of a graduated deterrent ("flexible response" or "countervailing strategy") makes no provision for the Americans' responding to a possible Soviet threat of attack against Western Europe with a counterthreat of "all or nothing" to confront Moscow with the choice between abandoning the path to war or being party to all-out catastrophe.

As the directive (PD–59) issued by President Carter in the summer of 1980 again made clear, Washington considers a step-by-step escalation of countermeasures essential in case the other world power should start to use military force. In this way, the Soviet leaders are to be given repeated opportunities at successive levels to rethink and discontinue their strategy of threat. Only if this attempt to bring the other side to reason in a protracted process of stage-by-stage escalation were to break down completely would the global strategic nuclear exchange between the two world powers become inevitable.[41] The implementation of this deterrence concept presupposes the existence of a military instrumentarium that permits the continuous graduation of NATO reactions from conventional conflict on the European battlefield up to worldwide nuclear war. Thus the means must be available to employ nuclear weapons in Europe at an intermediate stage.

If the Soviet leadership were to succeed in depriving the Western deterrence policy of this component, then the countries of Western Europe–particularly the Federal Republic of Germany, which is in the most exposed position–would be bound to feel insecure. Despite the vociferous adherents of the new peace movement, the vast majority of the West German population regards the Eurostrategic armament of NATO as an indispensable guarantee of security.[42] Of course, Soviet politicians would not be displeased if the calls for the West to revoke its armament decision would entail a divisive and confidence-destroying effect in the Western camp. The more the coherence of

41. Walter Slocombe, "The Countervailing Strategy," *International Security*, Spring 1981, pp. 24–25.
42. For more details see Dieter Just and Peter Caspar Mülhens, "Zur Wechselbeziehung von Politik und Demoskopie," *Aus Politik und Zeitgeschichte: Beilage zur Wochenzeitung "Das Parlament,"* B 32/81, August 8, 1981, pp. 63–68.

the Atlantic Alliance is diminished and the more the presence of American forces in West Germany is undermined, the stronger would grow the USSR's capability to bring imperious influence to bear on Western Europe.

SOVIET PUBLIC ARGUMENT ON SECURITY

If, up to the mid-1970s, the Soviet leaders had again and again presented the "continuous shift in the balance of power in favor of socialism" as the decisive criterion for success in foreign policy in their public statements, they have since 1977–78 never grown tired of assuring the West Europeans that they are not striving for superiority and that they are content to pursue an armaments program designed to satisfy defensive requirements only.[43] But this change in argumentation has not been accompanied by any change in practical actions. The military capacities of the USSR and its allies, which previously had been portrayed as instruments to restrain Western "imperialism," are now depicted in Moscow's interpretation as elements of military equilibrium. Not infrequently, inconsistencies find their way into this presentation. For example, in May 1978, when there were thirty-five SS-20 launchers stationed in the European part of the USSR, the Soviet politicians claimed they had established Eurostrategic equilibrium. By the end of 1981, this number had grown to 210. But this did not prevent Moscow officials from continuing to proclaim the existence of a Eurostrategic equilibrium.

Nor does the way in which the Soviet commentators argue corroborate their claim to equilibrium. When they talk of arms buildups and displays of power, they invariably refer only to the NATO countries—and use these terms as a moral reproach. Only the NATO countries are called upon to forgo arms buildups. In the process, a picture emerges of a permanent Western lead of immense proportions in an arms race with which the USSR then has to catch up out of bitter necessity. In reality—particularly in Europe—the arms lead is unmistakably on the Soviet side.[44] The premise that NATO must at last reduce its military prowess is the central theme of all Soviet pleadings in favor of "military détente." If, for once, the Western side is able to point convincingly to large-scale military expenditure on the part of the Warsaw Pact, Moscow's propaganda falls back on its last resort, the assertion that that USSR is by its very nature a peace-loving nation and is thus incapable of threatening anybody. For that reason any forces directed against it must be regarded as offensive.

43. West German–Soviet declaration of May 6, 1978, published in *Europa-Archiv*, no. 18, 1978, pp. D 513–16.

44. Western estimates put the USSR's expenditure on arms at about 12–13 percent of its gross national product. By contrast, the United States spent only 5.8 percent on its armed forces in 1979. It is estimated that in absolute terms Soviet military expenditure was about 50 percent higher than that of the Americans in 1979 (*Aspekte der Friedenspolitik*, p. 43).

For some years the Soviet side has endeavored to back up its theory that a military balance exists in Europe primarily by using military arguments. This is accompanied by the attempt to relegate to oblivion all previously propagated theories that could be used to point to the USSR as being in a favorable military position or to portray a balance of power in favor of the Warsaw Pact as being desirable. Accordingly, the references, familiar until the mid-1970s, to changing power relationships as an essential precondition for the achievement of foreign policy successes,[45] or that, because of shifts in the balance of power, the Federal Republic of Germany could no longer count on adequate American protection, have been dropped. To all appearances, however, these terminological shifts are essentially verbal adaptations to those conceptions of parity that public opinion in Western Europe has accustomed itself to applying in its approaches to the assessment of questions of security policy.[46]

The Soviet leadership has failed to change the real military factors to match the expressed sentiments. The elements of threat to Western Europe have not been reduced but in many cases intensified. The existence of a politically significant military prowess in the European theater continues in Moscow's eyes to be a decisive prerequisite for successful foreign policy dealings. And these efforts can be assumed to be primarily aimed at making the West Europeans inclined to entertain Soviet wishes while at the same time dissuading them from bringing undesired influence to bear on the USSR's East Central European forefield, which is already showing signs of domestic political instability.

The Soviet estimate that it is essential to persuade the West Germans more than anybody else to take sides against rearmament in Europe is reflected in public statements regarding the Federal Republic. Although the Soviet leaders fully realize that Chancellor Schmidt was the decisive initiator of the resolution to rearm (and that his successor continues to advocate the implementation of that resolution), they nevertheless approached him with a conciliatory mien. The West German government finds itself the target of wooing from Moscow while the responsibility for rearmament plans is attributed to the Americans. In Soviet propaganda, too, the discretion toward Bonn is striking. While there is no form of denunciatory polemics too harsh to be used against the United States, West German politics continues to get off lightly. In general, the West German government is portrayed more as a victim of sinister American machinations than as a voluntary advocate of NATO policies. In Soviet appeals to the new peace movement, too, the fight against the rearmament concept takes priority over vilification of its proponents in Bonn.

---

45. See Günter Wagenlehner, "Militärische Überlegenheit, Gewalt und Krieg in den Aussagen der sowjetischen Führung," *Beiträge zur Konfliktforschung*, no. 4, 1981, pp. 5–35.

46. See text of Gromyko's press conference in Bonn on November 23, 1979, *Izvestiia*, November 25, 1979.

SOVIET EUROSTRATEGIC POLICIES SINCE 1980

This does not mean that the Kremlin has committed itself to a wholesale policy of dangling carrots in front of the West German government. It is also capable of using the stick if it appears to promise better results. Two and a half weeks before the NATO resolution of December 12, 1979, Foreign Minister Andrei Gromyko during a visit to Bonn attempted to put pressure on the West German government by making a promise of negotiations on Eurostrategic arms limitation conditional upon the Western alliance's refraining from passing the envisaged resolution.[47] He called on the West German side to lend weight to this line within the Atlantic Alliance. Otherwise the chance for coming to an agreement with Moscow would be lost. Accordingly, after NATO had passed the decision, the Soviet leaders for a time refused to respond to any Western suggestions of diplomatic talks.

The longer they tried, however, the more the makers of Soviet policy were forced to realize that this approach was getting them nowhere. Notwithstanding the opposition that was forming in West Germany and other West European countries against rearmament, it was considered highly doubtful in Moscow whether a political breakthrough could be achieved in this way. At the same time, the international political isolation into which they had maneuvered themselves with their intervention in Afghanistan was resting heavily on the shoulders of the Soviet leaders. Negotiations with the West on the Eurostrategic problem appeared desirable—all the more so since the breakdown of the dialogue with Washington and the failure of the U.S. Senate to ratify the SALT II treaty seemed to have made relations with the United States subject to uncontrollable risks. For this reason, Brezhnev arranged for Schmidt to pay a visit to Moscow in mid-1980 and used this opportunity to convey to his guest the news that the Soviet Union was willing to enter into bilateral talks with the Americans on the limitation of medium-range nuclear weapons.

Although the Soviet side adhered to its proposal of the previous fall in principle, it nevertheless came up with one alternative. It would thus not be possible to restrict talks to medium-range missiles, but would be necessary to include—in an "intrinsic and indissoluble correlation"—the U.S. "forward-based systems." At the same time, the Soviet leaders refused to give the West German chancellor the clarification he had requested to the effect that these talks would also deal with the corresponding medium-range weapons deployed by the USSR.[48] The subsequent resolution by the supreme organs of the Soviet party and state

47. Nonofficial protocol notes in *Die Welt*, July 7, 1980.

48. Decision of the highest authorities of party and state in the USSR, in *Pravda*, July 6, 1980; "V interesakh mira i dobrososedstva," *Pravda*, July 8, 1980; "Radi bezopasnosti narodov," *Pravda*, July 15, 1980; RTL interview with Vadim Zagladin in *Zhurnalist*, no. 9, 1980, p. 10.

and the ensuing official comments indicate that this was not intended.[49] According to their model, Soviet capabilities would have been allowed to remain unilaterally outside the "strategic equation," without Moscow having committed itself to the principle of military parity in any way.

Although the West German government was prepared to pave the way in Washington for negotiations, it was not willing to accept the ideas the Soviet side had put forward as to the scope of the talks. What Moscow was offering the West was only attractive to those circles in West Germany that were opposed to Eurostrategic armament anyway. There were no sympathies to be gained among wider sections of the West German population by these one-sided proposals. This prevailed upon the Soviet leadership to modify its position yet again in mid-1981.

In informal talks with West German government party politicians Egon Bahr and Willy Brandt, top-level Soviet officials as high as Brezhnev himself intimated that there was a chance the Soviet Union might make concessions to Western wishes. It would be possible to count missiles against missiles and aircraft against aircraft and to treat the two equations separately on a staggered time basis.[50] The USSR was even inclined to give consideration to a "zero option" (such as enjoys widespread popularity in West German public opinion). In that case, all Eurostrategic systems on both sides would disappear. On closer inspection, of course, these proposals reveal two catches: on the Western side more nuclear warhead delivery systems of shorter range were to be covered than on the Soviet side; when the Soviet side spoke of "reductions," what they actually meant was withdrawal to behind the Urals.[51] A comparison of data later entered by the Soviet side confirmed this tendency to equate the unequal to NATO's disadvantage.

Thus the Soviet leaders were unable to make any great impression in Bonn by virtue of the actual substance of their proposal. Moscow concentrated all the more on making an impression on West German public opinion. Brandt's remark on his return from Moscow that Brezhnev was deeply concerned about the spread of tensions and was positively trembling out of fear for peace was given large-scale media coverage.[52] The West German government was unpleasantly affected by these developments. In its opinion, Brezhnev's appeal to the emotions did nothing to help overcome the conflict on the Eurostrategic question.

49. "Ungebetener Rat," *Der Spiegel*, June 29, 1981, p. 20; "Bonbons auspacken, Peitsche zeigen," *Der Spiegel*, July 6, 1981, pp. 17–21; "Bonn: Eine Null-Lösung der SPD," *Parlamentarisch-Politischer Pressedienst*, July 10, 1981, p. 2.

50. "Bonbons auspacken, Peitsche zeigen," pp. 17–19; Willy Brandt in "Spiegel" interview, *Der Spiegel*, July 6, 1981, pp. 24–26; Engelbrecht and Meyer, "Brandt: Gespräche nicht unterschätzen," *Kölner Stadt-Anzeiger*, July 3, 1981.

51. Data as presented by Brezhnev in *Der Spiegel*, November 2, 1981, pp. 45–47; data as presented by Zamiatin in *General-Anzeiger*, November 25, 1981.

52. See "Spiegel" interview with Brandt, *Der Spiegel*, July 6, 1981, pp. 23–29.

Nevertheless, Bonn continued to make energetic efforts to get U.S.-Soviet negotiations on this question under way. Brezhnev's visit to Bonn in early November 1981 was intended to serve predominantly symbolic functions. Both sides meant the visit to signify that they continued to adhere to the prospect of political balance in Europe. In addition, the exchange of views between the top men of the Soviet Union and the Federal Republic of Germany provided an opportunity for articulating and understanding more clearly the divergent conceptions of the respective sides. For example, the Soviet side appears to have harbored illusionary expectations with regard to some West German positions. Otherwise, how are we to explain Moscow's disappointment when, at the outset of the U.S.-Soviet negotiations for a limitation of Eurostrategic arms in late November 1981, the West German government endorsed the American position without reservation.

CONCLUSIONS

The Soviet leaders have always found an understanding partner in the West German government whenever they have pursued a policy of attempting to contain disagreeably high tensions and incentives for a continued arms race in Europe. Bonn has never ceased, even when it did not particularly suit the Soviet policy makers, in its endeavors to pave the way for the widest possible political dialogue between the countries of the West and those of the East.

However, Soviet hopes that the West German government could adapt its policies substantially to the conceptions propagated by Moscow have remained unfulfilled. The USSR's military policies are much too antagonistic and, above all, allow too little for the interests of the countries of Western Europe for the responsible representatives of the Federal Republic to be able to take any liking to the leading Eastern power's security policies. The West German state continues, in its own appraisal, to be dependent on the protection in the form of deterrent capabilities afforded by the United States and NATO. Thus the Eurostrategic armament of the Western alliance is of even greater importance to West Germany than it is to the United States itself. If the leaders in Bonn at the same time stress the desirability of cooperation to reduce tensions and limit armaments in Europe, then this is only a secondary, complementary line.

This unequivocally pro-Atlantic orientation on the part of the government in Bonn is complicated by a domestic situation in which the activities of opponents of rearmament play a prominent role. This relatively small but vociferous section of the West German public, which allows itself to be guided by fears of war and other emotions, provides fertile soil for Soviet propaganda. The fact that Western Europe would be completely and unilaterally defenseless against the Soviet Union, with all the consequences that such a situation would entail, should their opposition be successful, does not seem to bother many of the pacifists.

For their part, the makers of Soviet policy are trying to exploit this situation as far as possible with a view to bringing influence to bear on the West German government. But this creates a dilemma for them. To all appearances they are not fully convinced that the new peace movement can succeed in its objectives. For this reason, they consider it expedient to maintain unperturbed contacts with the West German government to ensure that the latter does not become disaffected but remains open to the East's conciliatory approaches. It seems doubtful whether this double-dealing game can be continued indefinitely.

Chapter 3

France and Soviet Policy

Robert Legvold

In October 1964, Leonid Brezhnev and a few others deposed Nikita Khrushchev and appointed themselves to nearly the longest tenure in Soviet history. Four months earlier, at the Republican Party convention in San Francisco, Ronald Reagan had nominated Barry Goldwater as his party's candidate for president, and he did it so well that leadership of Republican conservatives was his soon after Lyndon Johnson's crushing triumph in the November election. A few months later, in the summer of 1965, François Mitterrand assumed dominance of the French Socialist Party (PS), and, with the formal blessing of the French Communist Party (PCF), launched the first of his three quests for the presidency of the Fifth Republic. And, for the first of three occasions, his opponent had Soviet sympathy and support.[1] His opponent, of course, was Charles de Gaulle, who, to complete this brief prehistory, had Soviet sympathy and support because he also at this moment was setting off on a fresh course—in his case, an opening to the Soviet Union that would dictate the shape of Franco-Soviet relations for the decade and a half to come.

The year 1965, not de Gaulle's return to power in 1958, marks the start of contemporary Franco-Soviet relations. By then the French leader had lost hope of rallying Europe or, separately, West Germany to his struggle against a Western alliance dominated by U.S. power, and was readying his unilateral declaration of independence, France's withdrawal from NATO. By then Soviet leaders had come to believe in his revolt, a change from Khrushchev, who was never very

---

1. The evidence is circumstantial, but in each of the presidential elections—December 1965, May 1974, and May 1980—the Soviets did something to indicate their preference for

impressed with de Gaulle's original schemes for revising the alliance or his obstruction within the Common Market, including his opposition to British entry. By 1965, however, de Gaulle's early steps toward actually leaving the NATO military organization and his growing dissent on a range of issues, from the proposed multilateral nuclear force to U.S. policy in Vietnam, convinced Khrushchev's successors that France under de Gaulle indeed meant to follow an independent course. Once persuaded of his challenge to NATO. Soviet leaders viewed the whole of de Gaulle's foreign policy more enthusiastically, especially his attachment to independence in the other European arena of concern to them, the Common Market. Thus, ironically, Gaullism as an influence on developments within NATO and the Common Market captured the Soviet imagination at about the time that Mitterrand and Reagan began their long, improbable journeys to power.

Now, nearly two decades later, Mitterrand and Reagan are in power. As any Soviet will complain, Reagan's arrival has significantly affected U.S.-Soviet relations. But has Mitterrand's arrival made a significant or enduring difference to Franco-Soviet relations? Are relations between France and the Soviet Union to be understood as a continuation of what de Gaulle and his heirs fashioned, or has an important threshold been crossed? At a moment when East-West relations are in turmoil and alliances in both East and West are increasingly

---

the other side. In 1965 it was an implied endorsement in a *Pravda* editorial and a TASS communiqué that seemed to encourage voters of the left to vote for the incumbent. See François Fejtö, *The French Communist Party and the Crisis of International Communism* (Cambridge, Mass.: M.I.T. Press, 1967), p. 200. On the same subject, see also Ronald Tiersky, *French Communism, 1920–1972* (New York: Columbia University Press, 1974), p. 243, and François Mitterrand, *Ma part de vérité* (Paris: Fayard, 1969), pp. 52–56. In 1974, the press in general and the PCF in particular thought that a visit to Giscard d'Estaing by the Soviet ambassador to France during the first and second rounds of the elections amounted to an endorsement. And, again, in 1981 observers made much of an article in *Pravda*, March 13, 1981, that seemingly favored Giscard over Mitterrand. The article was filed by *Pravda's* Paris correspondent, Yuri Kharlanov, and therefore was less authoritative than senior commentary from someone in Moscow. Although critical of economic trends under Giscard, Kharlanov noted that "in France" the French president had won "personal authority as a consistent, careful political figure, particularly in the international arena, where France's position in recent years has strengthened." This is all he said about foreign policy under Giscard. In contrast, what he said about Mitterrand was critical. He wrote of the Socialist Party's tactical vacillations, its general shift to the right, its "Atlantic orientation," and its refusal to join the French and European left in the struggle for détente, in arms control, and against NATO's "dangerous plans." G. Dadiants, *Sotsialisticheskaia industriia's* observer in Paris, on the eve of the first round of the election, provided another warm account of Giscard's foreign policy, but without criticizing Mitterrand's positions on international affairs. See *Sotsialisticheskaia industriia*, April 25, 1981.

troubled, what place does a socialist France occupy in Soviet calculations? And how much is the Soviet strategy toward France changing to reflect Soviet assessments of change within either France or the larger European context?

From the start, relations between France and the Soviet Union have had a highly instrumental quality for both. More than usual, the leaders of each have prized the relationship less for what they could get from one another than for the results it might deliver in their relations with others. De Gaulle turned to the Soviet Union in the mid–1960s in part to affect West German docility to U.S. policy, in part to intrude on the clubbiness of the superpowers, and in particular to ease the reintegration of Europe's two halves. The last he would pursue in his own camp by offering the Soviet Union the more consoling relationship of "détente, entente, and cooperation."

The Soviets, in turn, saw France under de Gaulle as their best means for circumscribing and eroding the Atlantic partnership, for isolating and pressuring the Germans toward a settlement, and for impeding West European integration—their three core objectives in Europe. From the beginning, Gaullist France interested the Soviet Union less for itself than for what it was a part of: a part of the Atlantic Alliance, a part of the European Economic Community (EEC, or Common Market), and a partner of the Federal Republic of Germany. Later the Soviet Union would be interested in the French Communist Party as a part of Eurocommunism, and still later, the French socialists as a part of the Socialist International. For twenty years, the way de Gaulle and his successors have played their part in these different settings has shaped the terms of reference of Soviet policy toward France.

THE STAGES OF FRENCH-SOVIET RELATIONS

De Gaulle created the standard against which to measure the evolution of Franco-Soviet relations. His vision of France and its role abroad was the most grandiose and fundamental. From it, the retreats of those who followed are to be charted, although some of these were foreshadowed by his own late misgivings. Pursuit of his vision gave Franco-Soviet relations their greatest possibilities, which were then clouded and attenuated by his successors, but again only after he himself showed the way.

Yet the retreats I am about to sketch fall far short of a repudiation, unless a repudiation of Gaullist foreign policy is in the cards under the new Mitterrand government; and that, to anticipate the analysis to come, seems unlikely. De Gaulle's successors adjusted his priorities, compromised his aspirations, and softened his tactics, but they never turned their backs on the essence of his design: French autonomy within the Western alliance, French national interest within the Common Market, French partnership with the Germans in Western Europe, and Franco-Soviet détente between a divided Europe. For the Soviets the continuity in French foreign policy has been as important as the strayings.

The French, Pierre Hassner once wrote, play "triangular games" with the Federal Republic of Germany and the United States. In these games, either the Soviet Union is assigned the role of "counterweight" to the other two or France assigns itself the role of mediator or balance between the Soviet Union and the others.[2] If the point has merit, de Gaulle was its most perfect reflection. He told Konrad Adenauer in one of their early meetings that "as long as there was a threat of German *revanche*, he had to throw his weight on the Soviet side."[3] But, when in fact the problem was not German revanchism but Erhard's eagerness to preserve U.S.–West German defense collaboration at the expense of a Franco-German entente, de Gaulle also looked toward Moscow. With the Americans, he seized on the Soviet option apparently both to demonstrate his independence and to counteract the effects of superpower collusion.

As for the other half of Hassner's point, de Gaulle sought to make France the Soviet Union's *interlocuteur valable*–or interlocutor *privilégié*, as the Soviets would later flatter him–not only to give flexibility or leverage to his policy but also to erode or bridge the gulf between East and West. Thus he approached the Soviets when the Germans could not, in no small part to represent their case or, at least, to open the door of East-West relations a crack without betraying their case.[4] Between the Americans and the Soviets, he also took it upon himself to mediate, though not literally so. He, in contrast to Harold Wilson, for example, had little interest in serving as a go-between on specific problems like Vietnam. Rather, he assumed that the French could help break down the tensions of East-West relations and cushion the confrontation between superpowers. As Hassner notes, the Europeans' great fear is that the superpowers are either "too close to collision or too close to collusion," and none has had it more than de Gaulle, nor has anyone done so much about it as he.[5]

De Gaulle did all this, if we are to believe him, to achieve two overriding objectives: first, to give back to France control over its own destiny; second, to restore his nation's self-respect, lost after June 1940 and left unrecovered by the Fourth Republic. He sought in the first instance to draw France away from entangling commitments, whether military or economic, threatening to create "a vacuum of will and a confusion of purposes that would benefit the most powerful manipulator or, at best, deprive the nation of control over policies and

2. See Pierre Hassner, "West European Perceptions of the USSR," *Daedalus*, 108, no. 1 (Winter 1979): 124.

3. This is Stanley Hoffmann's rendering from Adenauer's memoirs, *Erinnerungen*, vol. 2, p. 429, in his "De Gaulle's Foreign Policy: The Stage and the Play, the Power and the Glory," *Decline or Renewal? France since the 1930s* (New York: Viking Press, 1974), p. 314.

4. De Gaulle, of course, had firm views on the postwar change in German frontiers and German access to nuclear weapons; the first he expected them to accept, the second, to abjure. But he made his arguments with the Germans, never alongside the Soviets.

5. Hassner, "West European Perceptions of the USSR," p. 123.

resources."[6] Having failed in 1958 to reorder the leadership of NATO in a way strengthening the French role, he withdrew France from its military organization in 1966. Within the European Economic Community, he fought for a political collaboration enhancing the French voice in Europe and harder still against projects of integration submerging that voice; and he fought against British entry for fear that it would enhance an American voice already too dominant in Europe.

But, as Stanley Hoffmann reminds us, de Gaulle's vision for France both sustained and depended on his vision for Europe, and, indeed, the world at large.[7] Three slogans embodied the essence of his ideas. The first, *l'Europe européenne*, stood for the emancipation of Europe from the yoke of Atlanticism and the American ascendancy which it guaranteed. The Second, *l'Europe des patries*, hailed a Europe of strong, self-confident nation-states, ready to cooperate, even collaborate, but leery of self-sacrificing supranational schemes and jealous of the prerogatives their bureaucratic partisans were thought ready to usurp.[8] And the third, Europe from the Atlantic to the Urals, represented the rejoining of Europe cleaved into unnatural halves by the war and the conferences that followed. It was in such a Europe that France would flourish and it was toward such a Europe that it would lead.

For de Gaulle the three concepts were intertwined: Western Europe liberated from American hegemony would make it easier for the Soviet Union to relinquish its own dominance of Eastern Europe. Western Europe pulling together, following a French lead, and benefiting from an (unequal) Franco-West German partnership would soon free itself from American hegemony and push the East toward a "pan-European reconciliation."[9] And a pan-European reconciliation would transform the Old Continent into a third force giving reinforcement and freedom to the policies of its members.

Not surprisingly, the Soviet leadership viewed all this from its own perspective. "De Gaulle," Brezhnev is reported to have said, "is our enemy and we are well aware of it."[10] But because of him the position of the Americans in Europe is weakening, "and this weakening will continue." "He is a sly old fox," who "is aiming for mastery in Europe for himself and in opposition to us." His schemes, however, "have no chance of succeeding because other, more powerful, West

6. Hoffmann, "De Gaulle's Foreign Policy," p. 284.

7. Ibid., pp. 287–90 and 297–99.

8. De Gaulle denied using the phrase, but he was hardly offended by the notion. See Charles de Gaulle, *Discours et messages*, vol. 4 (Paris: Plon, 1970), p. 427.

9. To use Hoffmann's phrase in "De Gaulle's Foreign Policy," p. 297.

10. Erwin Weit, *Dans l'ombre de Gomulka* (Paris: Robert Laffont, 1971), p. 118. Weit was Gomulka's German interpreter. He was reporting a conversation between Brezhnev, Gomulka, and Ulbricht in April 1967 at the Seventh Congress of the GDR's Socialist Unity Party (SED).

European countries will never allow them to succeed." Meanwhile, "the balance sheet, comrades . . . is it not favorable?"

Whether Brezhnev ever put his feelings quite so baldly, surely the incident corresponds roughly to the way Soviet leaders looked upon their relationship with de Gaulle's France. Thus they could be grateful that he arrived in Moscow in June 1966 alone, not as the vanguard figure of a West European entente, nor even as the senior partner in a Franco-German axis, the way he would have had it. De Gaulle's opening to them, they must have known, represented in some respects the failure of a grander strategy, and in that they could take comfort. What mattered to the Soviets was that de Gaulle pursue his vision, not that he succeed.

Soon after the current French socialist government assumed control in 1981, Soviet commentators began complaining of its disloyalty to the independent line of its predecessors. Mitterrand's people had taken a tough stance on the issue of modernizing NATO's long-range theater nuclear forces, prompting *Pravda* (July 30, 1981) to remind the French that they had "achieved greatest respect in the international arena not during their years of subordination to NATO's policy of arms race but only when they started pursuing a really independent policy of détente and cooperation with all states . . . and when they refused to follow the Pentagon's plans." Soviet speakers, however, had said much the same of Valéry Giscard d'Estaing's government. In early 1979, when Giscard selected Jean François-Poncet as his foreign minister, a man whom the Soviets regarded as too committed to European integration, they lashed out at "France's ruling quarters" not only for "dreaming of a united Europe that would become a new power center able to talk to the Soviet Union and the United States . . . on equal footing" and in which France "would play the leading role" but for permitting France once more to drift back to "Atlanticism."[11] Even that criticism was not new. The French Communist Party had been talking about "les orientations atlantiques de l'Elysée" for years, a charge that had occasionally found its way into the Soviet press.

The truth is that the Soviets had been worrying about the constancy of France's independent stand within the Atlantic Alliance and the Common Market almost from the start. Indeed, the charge that Mitterrand's government was "sliding back to Atlanticism" was first leveled ten years earlier against de Gaulle's immediate successor Georges Pompidou. One of the first things Pompidou had done was to fly to Washington and there celebrate "our oldest and our greatest friend and ally . . . the one to whom we are closest in our hearts."[12] More important, he had appealed to the Americans to keep a "substantial military

---

11. Leonid Ivanov, "France and West European Integration," *New Times*, no. 4, January 1979, pp. 8–9.

12. See Robert Legvold, "The Franco-Soviet Rapprochement after de Gaulle," *Survey*, 20, no. 4 (93) (Autumn 1974): 76.

presence in Europe," and he had quietly begun to restore French cooperation in various NATO training activities. Even before Pompidou's trip to the United States, the PCF had begun attacking the "pro-Atlantic tendencies" of the new leadership and accusing it of "working to reinforce its political and military alliance with the United States."[13]

Pompidou had also indicated a readiness to lift the French veto on British entry into the EEC and to breathe new life into the process of Common Market integration. He had been the moving spirit behind the EEC Hague Summit Conference in December 1969, marking the end of the twelve-year transition period of the 1958 Rome Treaty, providing at that point the most coherent and far-reaching discussion of the Community's future. Afterward, *Pravda's* senior commentator Yuri Zhukov noted (February 11, 1970) the chipping away at French resistance to a "United States of Western Europe," and grumbled that during the "previous period" French "ruling circles" would have shown more courage. Since the Hague summit, he said, the French evidently "occupy another position in favor of the political integration of 'little Europe.'"

Zhukov, however, was probably wrong about the "ruling circles" in the "previous period." In the year before the referendum of April 1969 leading to de Gaulle's exit, two events had badly shaken the underpinnings of Gaullist policy. First, the "revolution" of May 1968 in an instant called into question the political and economic stability of the Fifth Republic, the premise of all that de Gaulle had set out to do. Second, the Warsaw Pact invasion of Czechoslovakia three months later dramatized how long and impeded the road to Europe's liberation would be.

Neither event destroyed de Gaulle's convictions. He remained dedicated to French independence within an emancipated and reunified Europe, but his sense of urgency and confidence weakened and his priorities changed. By February 1969 he had raised with the British ambassador to France the old idea of a West European entente, this time with British participation.[14] And, while reaffirming his policy of détente, entente, and cooperation with the East, he also increased French cooperation with NATO's MARIMED (Mediterranean Sea maneuvers) operation and joined in criticizing the Soviet Union's growing intrusion into the Mediterranean. Rudely the first and most exuberant stage in Franco-Soviet relations had drawn to a close.

The second stage extended from 1969 to Mitterrand's victory in 1981. It began with a seminal event elsewhere. Willy Brandt's election in September 1969 and the launching of the SPD/FDP's new Ostpolitik altered beyond recognition the European political field of play. Overnight the German problem, the crux of

13. *L'Humanité,* December 11, 1969.
14. For the details and an analysis of this initiative with Ambassador Christopher Soames, see Edward A. Kolodziej, *French International Policy under De Gaulle and Pompidou: The Politics of Grandeur* (Ithaca and London: Cornell University Press, 1974), pp. 401–3.

postwar European politics, was set aside. Overnight the Soviet Union had another, more impressive *interlocuteur valable*.[15]

But these were not the only changes affecting the setting within which Franco-Soviet relations unfolded. NATO's twentieth anniversary had passed in 1969, and with it the hopes Soviet leaders had nursed only a few years earlier of the beginning of the end for NATO. A year or so later, the Soviet Union made its peace with the existence of the European Economic Community. "The Soviet Union," Brezhnev announced to the Fifteenth Trade Union Congress in March 1972, "by no means ignores the existing situation in Western Europe, including the existence of an economic grouping of capitalist countries such as the Common Market" (*Pravda*, March 21, 1972). It was, he said, ready to deal with the EEC, provided it was sensitive to the interests of Comecon. Thus, by the early 1970s, the Soviet Union no longer counted on France to challenge the continuation of the Common Market, no longer expected it to contribute to the doom of NATO, and no longer needed it to isolate and harass the West Germans.

Gaullism as the Soviets preferred it faltered in the 1970s, but then so did the Soviet Union's sense of both opportunity and imperative in Western Europe. The rigid, stark objectives of the late 1950s and 1960s melded into the more moderate and diffuse concerns of détente. This created a different framework for Franco-Soviet relations. In an ideal world, doubtless the Soviet leadership would have liked for the French to cause more trouble within NATO and the Common Market, but in the world of the 1970s the imperfect Gaullism of Pompidou and Giscard sufficed. French foreign policy was now judged mostly by the requirements of détente.

The Soviet Union needed France less as an intermediary with the Western camp or as a European dissident riding *cavalier seul*. Instead, what it wanted from France was leadership in détente, setting a good example, and defending the process from the faint-hearted and the critical. When in the early stages of détente the Soviets were eager to move from the German accords to a European security conference without undue delay and without too close a coupling to MBFR (mutual and balanced force reduction), they counted on the French to push in the same direction. When, during the conference at Helsinki in 1972–75, trouble flared over Basket III issues (on humanitarian and related fields), they counted on the French to help pacify matters. When the Ford administration began to debunk the idea of détente, they counted on the French to defend it. When the new Carter administration mixed carrot and stick, arms control with human rights campaigns, they counted on the French to follow a purer and steadier course. When the Americans applied sanctions and disrupted the dialogue after the Soviet invasion of Afghanistan, they counted on the French

15. Here I am stressing the special impact of Brandt's election on a process that in fact began several years earlier with the formation of the Grand Coalition (Kiesinger-Brandt) in 1966.

to resist sanctions and maintain the dialogue. And, when détente vanished in U.S.-Soviet relations in the harsh climate of the Reagan administration, they counted on the French, no less than the West Germans, to keep it alive in Europe. For the most part, they were not disappointed. Throughout this second stage, the French did put a premium on fostering, and later saving, detente. From Michel Debré's doughty, insensitive dismissal of the 1968 Czech invasion as an *accident de parcours*, a traffic incident on the long road of East-West relations, through Giscard's whirlwind weekend with Brezhnev in Wilanow Palace five months after the Soviet invasion of Afghanistan, the French remained as devoted to improved East-West relations as any government, including Helmut Schmidt's.

Their devotion, however, came to mean the most to the Soviet leadership in the late 1970s when the United States–Soviet relationship began to disintegrate, endangering the whole edifice of detente. Six months into the Carter administration, Giscard obliged Brezhnev on a visit to Paris by concluding a formal Joint Declaration on Détente, praising détente as a "favorable development" and expressing pleasure that "a growing number of states has adopted this policy and that the trend toward détente has become general."[16] The document is unique in Soviet relations with Western powers. A year later, again in Paris, with U.S.-Soviet relations staggered by the Soviet-Cuban intervention in the Horn of Africa and the SALT negotiations marking time, Andrei Gromyko raised his glass to his French hosts for practicing "a policy of détente without zig-zags," adding that his visit had "confirmed France's privileged relations with the Soviet Union," and, said he, "I want to stress the word privileged."[17]

But unquestionably French efforts mattered most in the wake of the Soviet invasion of Afghanistan. By then the prospect was real that U.S.-Soviet relations would be deeply and enduringly ruptured, threatening as well cooperation between Eastern and Western Europe. Giscard did the minimum to maintain the semblance of a coherent Western response to Soviet aggression — half-heartedly endorsing the Olympic boycott, giving Gromyko a "chilly" reception in April, joining Schmidt in a statement warning that detente would not survive another blow like Afghanistan (then softening the warning a day or two later). "Giscard d'Estaing looked through his fingers on that one," a senior Soviet official reportedly said later when Mitterrand came to office with a harsher view of what the Soviet invasion of Afghanistan represented.[18]

Most important, Giscard rushed to defend the importance of maintaining an East-West dialogue, as the Americans gathered their forces to undermine contacts and disrupt the dialogue. "Dialogue is never more necessary," François-Poncet

16. "Joint Declaration on Détente by France and the Soviet Union," Rambouillet, June 22, 1977, in *French Embassy Press and Information Division*, no. 77/89 (1977).
17. *Le Monde*, October 26, 1978.
18. See Ned Temko's report in the *Christian Science Monitor*, August 4, 1981.

told the National Assembly in April, "than in a period of crisis."[19] The next week he received Gromyko in Paris; and the next month Giscard, to almost universal criticism at home, stole off to Warsaw for his meeting with Brezhnev.[20] In the months after Afghanistan, Soviet praise for all that was good in French policy grew nearly unctuous, while Soviet impatience with its less satisfactory aspects virtually disappeared.[21]

There were, of course, less satisfactory aspects to Giscard's policy. He was, as noted earlier, too open to cooperation within the Common Market for Soviet taste.[22] He continued to sanction increasing French involvement with NATO, tolerating participation in NATO's communications, sending forces to NATO maneuvers, and taking an interest in NATO planning. His refusal to join in significant forms of European arms control annoyed the Soviet leadership, but even more they criticized the evolution of French military doctrine. Their unhappiness on both counts is something to which I will return later, because it relates to Soviet perspectives on the French role within the Atlantic Alliance.

After 1976, the Soviet press began censuring the French for their "policy of parachutists," a reference to the military assistance provided Zaire and the Central African Republic, and for conniving to form military alliances among Africans to resist change.[23] (The French, in turn, had complained on several occasions, most notably during Foreign Minister Louis de Guiringaud's visit to Moscow in June 1977, of Soviet troublemaking in Africa.) The Soviets were also distressed by France's apparent willingness to sell military items to the Chinese. In spring 1979, the French received, along with several other West European governments, a letter from Brezhnev firmly warning against arms sales to China.

Added to these more serious grievances, the Soviet leadership must also have resented Giscard's badgering them on the Soviet role in the North-South dialogue for a new international economic order and his exhortations to do

19. See *Le Monde*, April 18, 1980.

20. Though not the sudden affair that many thought (the origins of the meeting went back to February or March), according to some who were close to the decision, Giscard precipitated the trip, over the opposition of his foreign minister, when Armand Hammer, returning from a conversation with Brezhnev, persuaded him that the moment was one of great peril.

21. For a particularly good illustration, see V. Kravtsov, "France and the Soviet Union: Dependable Partners," *International Affairs*, no. 8, August 1980, pp. 12–18.

22. For example, Soviet commentators criticized Giscard's government for supporting direct elections to the European Parliament, for accepting the admission of Greece, Portugal, and Spain to the EEC, and for taking the initiative, along with the Germans, in creating the European Monetary System. See Ivanov, "France and West European Integration," pp. 8–9.

23. See, for example, V. Sidenko, "African Ambitions of the Socialist International," *New Times*, no. 3, January 1978, pp. 18–20, and TASS in *Pravda*, May 29, 1978.

more to aid the developing countries.[24] And they evidently were piqued by his post-Helsinki stress on "ideological détente." In Moscow a few months after the Helsinki agreement, Giscard had called for "détente in ideological rivalry so that competition between economic and social systems should not result in excessive tensions."[25] Brezhnev retorted: "International détente in no way puts an end to the struggle of ideas," and left the French leader to cool his heels for a day in the midst of the visit.

Finally there were the recurrent flashes of Soviet anger over the "anti-Soviet" sentiments of the French press and, more seriously, over the invidious comments of French officials. When the French minister of the interior, Michel Poniatowski, publicly warned the French socialists against collaborating with the PCF because Moscow continued to mastermind subversion through local communist parties, TASS rebuked him for "irresponsible and hostile remarks . . . in flagrant contradiction to official French policy," and the Soviet Foreign Ministry called in the French ambassador to read him the commentary.[26]

On balance, however, the Soviet Union valued its relationship with France throughout this period, regarding French policy as largely complementary to its own policy in Western Europe. In one final respect the French pleased the Soviet Union, and that was in their readiness, even eagerness, to trade. From the start of Giscard's presidency the French had pressed for an expansion of economic cooperation, celebrating the doubling of trade over the 1970–74 period and calling for another doubling in the next five-year period, then at the 1977 summit for a tripling. Said Giscard to Brezhnev at that meeting: "Last year, we drew up a balance sheet for the previous decade. It is impressive: trade increased eightfold, spectacular industrial achievements were carried out" by each in the other's country; "there was striking growth in our scientific and technical cooperation, in particular in high-technology sectors such as nuclear physics and space exploration."[27] How happy a contrast for Soviet leaders to the attitude Jimmy Carter and his successor would soon adopt.

With Mitterrand's election the question is whether Franco-Soviet relations are entering a third stage. Generally the new French president has taken a stronger stand on a variety of East-West issues from the modernization of theater nuclear forces to the Soviet occupation of Afghanistan. He has been far blunter in portraying the Soviet military threat to Western Europe. He or his subordinates have shown concern over the transfer of high technology to the Soviet Union, and they have taken steps to regulate it. And he has manifested

24. This was a theme he harped on particularly at the June 1977 summit in Rambouillet. See his press conference, *Le Monde*, June 24, 1977.
25. See the *New York Times*, October 17, 1975.
26. See the *Washington Post*, August 3, 1975.
27. *French Embassy Press and Information Division*, no. 77/91 (June 1977).

relatively little interest in "privileged" Franco-Soviet relations. As a matter of fact, according to his advisers, he intends to purge his direct dealings with the Soviets of the atmospherics and phony amity marking high-level encounters under Giscard.[28] Claude Arnaud, France's new ambassador to the Soviet Union, when presenting his credentials, talked of a dialogue that is to be "clear, realistic, and constructive."[29] In general, Mitterrand's people like to say that where the last regime was anticommunist at home and soft on the Soviet Union, they are the reverse.[30]

But it remains unclear how profoundly these shifts in style and emphasis are affecting the basic thrust of French policy toward the Soviet Union. From all appearances, the Soviet leaders have wisely decided to see more of the new government before determining how much of a difference it is likely to make. Thinking Soviet observers are doubtless asking three questions. First, what is Mitterrand's basic attitude toward the Soviet Union? Second, how is the re-mainder of Mitterrand's foreign policy to be weighed against its Soviet dimension? What, from a Soviet perspective, are the comparative advantages and disadvantages of the different parts of his foreign policy? Third, what are the constraints under which French policy operates or will operate? Apart from Mitterrand's intentions, in short, what are likely to be his possibilities?

Generally, on the question of Mitterrand's basic attitude toward the Soviet Union, opinion among non-Soviet observers has taken one of two forms. Some have been inclined to see Mitterrand's harder line toward the Soviet Union as largely tactical—that is, an offset for the radical domestic course he wishes to follow, or a counterbalance to his commitment to progressive change in the Third World, or perhaps merely a means of disciplining his communist allies at home. For them Mitterrand's deeper thoughts on the Soviet Union are either beside the point or, as someone who has taken a relatively benign view of Soviet intentions in the past, rather suspect.

Others, a growing number, including close observers of Mitterrand, are satisfied that his tougher stance on Soviet issues reflects a hardheaded and skeptical view of the Soviet Union. Having dealt firsthand with communists for more than twenty years, Mitterrand, they say, "has no illusions about the nature of the Soviet regime and the power of its ideology, which he seeks to combat by proposing an alternative road to socialism."[31] As a result, his alarm

28. Interviews in Paris, November 1981.

29. See Le Monde, January 21, 1982.

30. One of Mitterrand's closest advisers used the formula in my presence. Dominique Moïsi makes the same point in "Mitterrand's Foreign Policy: The Limits of Continuity," Foreign Affairs, Winter 1981–82, p. 348.

31. Ibid., p. 350. See also Samuel F. Wells, Jr., "The Mitterrand Challenge," Foreign Policy, Fall 1981, p. 61, who quotes a senior French military officer: "Mitterrand after all understands the communists. He has lived with them for a long time."

over the growth of Soviet military power in Europe, they say, is to be taken at face value. He meant it when he said to *Stern* (July 9, 1981): "I believe the Soviet Union has supremacy in Europe, and I consider it a real danger." He is sincere when he endorses efforts to restore the theater nuclear balance as a precondition for arms control or, as some would say of him, as an alternative to arms control. And his foreign minister, Claude Cheysson, they contend, speaks for Mitterrand when asserting that for the last ten years the Soviet Union's main strategic objective has clearly been to "separate the defense of Europe from that of *l'ensemble atlantique*."[32] Even Cheysson's Reagan-like comments on the nature of Soviet "totalitarianism" in Eastern Europe, they say, reflect a generally shared outlook.[33]

The truth seems to me more complex, and apparently it does to Soviet observers as well. Mitterrand and his colleagues evidently do believe that the military balance favors the Soviet Union too much, and their desire to see NATO and the United States react is genuine. But they have reached this conclusion relatively recently—roughly since 1978 with the breakup of the left in France and the buildup of the theater nuclear forces (TNF) issue in Germany—and not necessarily because of a long and deep mistrust of Soviet policy. If anything, for much of the last decade, the socialists largely ignored the challenge posed by Soviet policy, or perhaps even soft-pedaled it.[34] Their image of the Soviet Union seemed to be of a vast, ineffective society, excessively attracted to the building of military power, but driven by largely conservative and defensive concerns. As late as 1978, Mitterrand wrote in *L'abeille et l'architecte*: "Despite the *complexe d'expansion* present in every empire, compelled to go farther in order to preserve what it has, I believe in the Soviet commitment to peace."[35] On his first visit to Moscow in April 1975, he recounted how moved he was by Brezhnev's memories of World War II and persuaded of his dedication to détente, and then assured the Soviet leader that when in power "we will not do less than the present team. We will seek good and solid agreements; we will seek to reinforce and maintain what exists."[36]

32. *Le Monde*, January 12, 1982.

33. Although Soviet observers must have noticed the rebuke administered to Cheysson by one of the senior people at the Élysée when he carried the point a step beyond, telling a television audience that Western governments should seize the "horrible occasion of Poland" to "demonstrate the true nature of totalitarianism in Eastern Europe." For Cheysson's comment, see *Le Monde*, December 2, 1981; for Pierre Beregovoy's adjustment, see *Le Monde*, January 14, 1982.

34. See Michael M. Harrison, *The Reluctant Ally: France and Atlantic Security* (Baltimore: Johns Hopkins University Press, 1981), pp. 207-11, for a similar and more detailed view.

35. François Mitterrand, *L'abeille et l'architecte* (Paris: Flammarion, 1978), p. 202.

36. See *Le Monde*, April 30, 1975. He remembers this part of his trip somewhat differently in *L'abeille et l'architecte*, pp. 26-30.

74   ROBERT LEGVOLD

Moreover, one wonders how completely Mitterrand's long-standing foreign policy idealism has been supplanted—how permanently he has freed himself from an old French radical-socialist fascination with a moderate collective security system tracing back to the interwar period and which he espoused only yesterday. And one wonders what his special sympathy for Castro's Cuba says about his general hostility to orthodox communism or to many aspects of Soviet foreign policy. After all, Mitterrand has not been merely charmed by the romantic side to Cuba's involvement in Third World revolution. The figure within the regime of whom he is the most enamored is Carlos Rafael Rodríguez, a shrewd, hardheaded man whose commitment to Marxism-Leninism goes back to the 1930s and whose style inspires the greatest confidence in Moscow.[37] In short, one can believe in Mitterrand's present mistrust of the Soviet Union's military efforts and still suspect the depth and durability of his hard line toward Moscow.

In any case, Soviet commentators have conspicuously chosen not to assume the worst and lead the charge against Mitterrand. On the contrary, they have gone out of their way to avoid criticizing him. They take their swipes only at this or that misguided impression, not at his basic orientation toward the Soviet Union. They condemn him for sharing the "absurd hypothesis" that the Soviet Union has some massive advantage through its modern theater nuclear forces, not for being anti-Soviet, anti-détente, or a devotee of the cold war.[38] Even when protesting the shift in French attitude on theater nuclear forces, they tend to look for something good to say about Mitterrand himself. In one sentence, a Soviet writer will condemn French officials for supporting the NATO line on theater nuclear forces, and in the next note: "François Mitterrand has often expressed his deep concern about present international tension, the arms race, and the growth of the nuclear arsenal in Europe. He labeled as problem number one for peace in Europe the question of medium-range missiles, repeatedly supporting the maximum possible arms control which does not endanger either side's security."[39] Pravda's editor, Viktor Afanas'ev, describes him as an "erudite, experienced, intelligent, and flexible politician" (October 16, 1981; my emphasis). Mitterrand, in short, is classed with Helmut Schmidt in the Soviet pantheon of contemporary Western leaders, not with Ronald Reagan and Margaret Thatcher. In fact, given Soviet readiness to criticize Schmidt during his last year in office, Mitterrand, significantly, may be the least criticized of major Western leaders.

37. For Mitterrand's fascination with Rodríguez, see L'abeille et l'architecte. In April 1982, Rodríguez made an official visit to Paris, despite the awkwardness of coming at the height of the Falkland Islands crisis, and despite Mitterrand's general reluctance to meet with leaders of the Soviet Union or its allies in present international circumstances.
38. See, for example, Pravda, September 26, 1981.
39. I. Manfred, "Novyi etap antivoennoi bor'by v Zapadnoi Evrope: Frantsiia," Mirovaia ekonomika i mezhdunarodnye otnosheniia, no. 1, 1982, pp. 107–8.

It would, of course, be misleading to imply that Soviet leaders find nothing seriously bothering about the Mitterrand government. Certainly they do, and they have indicated the sources of their misgivings since before the May 1981 elections—stressing the socialists' so-called Atlantic orientation and their general "shift to the right."[40] But, for a second reason, Soviet leaders seem inclined to soften their criticism: whatever they dislike in Mitterrand's approach to their country, his overall policy has many sides, some of them rather attractive.

Even his Soviet policy has its merits from their perspective. Cold and critical as his rhetoric has been, his actions lead elsewhere. He has gone forward with the great gas pipeline deal, and on terms criticized as too liberal by both Giscard and the West Germans.[41] His foreign minister has said there can be no regular high-level French-Soviet dialogue as long as the Soviets prosecute their war in Afghanistan, but in fact less regular meetings at the summit have not been ruled out and they are likely to occur at any time. France has given strong formal support to NATO's dual-track decision on theater nuclear forces, but then reacted rather evenhandedly to U.S.-Soviet negotiations on the subject. Unlike the brusque dismissal of the Reagan administration, for example, the French response to Brezhnev's announcement of a unilateral moratorium on the deployment of long-range theater nuclear forces was more temperate. Pierre Beregovoy, the president's secretary general, called it an initiative "meriting careful attention," and, on the negotiations themselves, added that so far it seemed to him the "positions taken by neither superpower permit a solution to this agonizing problem."[42]

Other aspects of French foreign policy under Mitterrand no doubt intrigue the Soviet leadership even more. Various Western observers have commented on the new government's identification with Third World causes and the friction this was expected to create with the Reagan administration, and indeed the friction that French arms sales to Nicaragua, political relations with the Salvadorian left, and responsiveness on North-South economic issues have created. But the problem may be more subtle. For example, although the Soviets may not yet have noticed, the longer-run gulf in U.S. and French approaches to Third World instability is not merely over strategy but over fundamental priorities. The Americans, even before Reagan's election, were inclined to subordinate troubled change in the Third World to the East-West dimension

40. *Pravda*, March 13, 1981. The same concerns were raised on the eve of the elections; see *Pravda*, May 8, 1981.

41. Giscard in an interview with *Paris-Match*, published February 12, 1981, criticized the decision both for "imprudently" increasing French energy dependence on the Soviet Union and for doing so at a time when Polish events made it unseemly. See *Le Monde*, February 11, 1982. The West Germans were upset over the terms of the financing and its timing. See the *New York Times*, February 11, 1982.

42. See *Le Monde*, March 19, 1982.

and to focus on East-West problems as the first order of business. The French socialists do not merely resist this subordination, they are more inclined to put North-South issues at the head of their agenda.

Moreover, somewhere below the surface lurks another still more profound source of tension, if some French observers are right about Mitterrand and his party. Dominique Moïsi says of the socialists, especially of Mitterrand, that in their minds "Soviet military and American economic imperialisms are equally dangerous."[43] "Out of realism, one has to denounce Soviet military imperialism, but in ideological terms the emotional 'imperialism' which holds the Socialist Party together is American economic and cultural imperialism." If he is correct, sooner or later, old and deep-seated biases are likely to reextrude. There may even be an element of this in the statement of Prime Minister Pierre Mauroy condemning "the effects of Soviet policy in Poland as we condemn the influence of American policy in El Salvador."[44] The Soviets who read Moïsi or gather their insights more directly have every incentive to give Mitterrand more time.

Meanwhile they are carefully watching to see how leaderships with such different ideologies and programs get along. They assume, or at least maintain, that the Reaganites and the French socialists cannot remain at peace. Thus, while relatively little Soviet analysis focuses on rifts in French and American approaches to the outside world, enormous attention is given to reviewing the hostility of each to the domestic economic program of the other. As a recent representative *Izvestiia* piece puts it: The United States is "creating by every means economic difficulties for its competition," in particular, for France, "trying to put the Left majority in a difficult position" and "to torpedo the social reforms which it has undertaken."[45]

This last point touches on the third Soviet reason for avoiding hasty judgments on the new French government. Even if its policy is real, as most Soviet analysts seem to accept, and not tactical, the Soviets are the first to ask how grave the limits on its freedom of action are likely to be—to ask, as one Soviet diplomat said to me, what the "objective factors" will allow. Foremost they have in mind the domestic base for policy—both political and economic. In public and particularly in private Soviet observers seem confident that Mitterrand will find himself hemmed in by economic considerations. His program, they say, faces constant, determined opposition from political, business, and bureaucratic interests. "The bitter resistance put up by big business," one analyst contends, "makes logical the question of whether victory in the election is tantamount to real

43. Moïsi, "Mitterrand's Foreign Policy," p. 355.

44. Interview with *Stern*, quoted in *Le Monde*, January 28, 1982.

45. *Izvestiia*, March 19, 1982, or see *Pravda*, April 10, 1982. For a more detailed account of what Soviet analysts think the Reagan administration is doing, see Vitaly Semyonov, "The First 100 Days," *New Times*, no. 33, August 1981, pp. 14–15.

possession of power."[46] Although "the Right" has lost political power, he continues, "it retains all other levers"; it controls finances, production, the sphere
of exchange, the state apparatus, and the mass media. These political complications, Soviet commentators suggest, will compound the inherent weaknesses of
the French economy, and these, in turn, will limit what Mitterrand can do in
foreign policy.

The regime suffers from its own internal divisions, to which Soviet analysts
show a keen sensitivity. Beyond the fundamental gap dividing communists
from socialists, the socialists themselves from time to time have their warring
camps—Cereists, Rocardiens, and the center; or sometimes party versus government. Lately Soviet analysts have begun commenting publicly on these divisions, treating them as an impediment of the government's ability to do what it
wishes, both at home and abroad. On becoming the "First Party of France,"
writes one Soviet correspondent, the French Socialist Party "has retained and
even aggravated its old contradictions and chronic ailments."[47] Then there are
the divergences between the leadership of the prosocialist union and the government over the government's decision to go forward with the gas deal, and even
within the government between the Quai d'Orsay and the Élysée over this and
other issues. Soviet observers notice when the more strident or uncompromising
stands of the foreign minister get toned down by Beregovoy or Mitterrand himself, as has happened on several occasions.

Soviet observers do not pretend to know what effect all these economic and
political constraints will have on French policy. In some cases they expect the
effect to be good from the Soviet point of view. Constrained by limited resources,
French efforts to rally progressive forces to the West's side in Africa and Latin
America or to whittle away Soviet influence in countries such as India, Vietnam,
or Ethiopia are not likely to get far. (One is reminded of the Soviet Union's
Janus-faced stake in de Gaulle's foreign policy. The striving—in this case,
French dissent from the American approach to the Third World—counts for
much, but so does French failure.)

In other respects, Soviet observers are unsure of the effects. They hesitate to
say in what direction domestic failure will push French foreign policy. Will
Mitterrand's problems with the business community reinforce a harsher policy
toward the Soviet Union, or, on the contrary, encourage him to look for open-
ings to the East, particularly an expansion of trade? If they have answers, the
Soviets are keeping them to themselves. Will complications at home make
French foreign policy more vulnerable to pressure from Mitterrand's PCF allies?
Again, Soviet analysts are silent, although they are not above trying to gener-
ate an effect. After the opposition parties won all four seats in by-elections to
the National Assembly in January, the *New Times'* man in Paris noted that

46. Vitaly Semyonov, "The Scene Today," *New Times*, no. 51, December 1981, p. 21.
47. Vitaly Semyonov, "After the First Year," *New Times*, no. 20, May 1982, p. 24.

"some people" explain the outcome as the result of disaffected communist voters who withheld support from socialist candidates.[48] "Journalists," he goes on, "say this was the result of the fierce anti-communist campaign mounted in connection with the Polish events which have nothing in common with the national interests of France." "Regrettably" some in the leadership have been too quick to join the "anti-Polish chorus" and "this could not but undermine the unity of the Left voters."

At one level, therefore, the Soviets have good cause not to assume Franco-Soviet relations are now moving into a new, more confrontational third stage. The mixed nature of the answers to the three questions asked earlier—What is the Mitterrand government's basic attitude toward the Soviet Union? What are the comparative advantages of different aspects of its foreign policy? What are the constraints under which it operates?—explains Soviet willingness to withhold a quick and ultimate judgment of the new French government.

This is at one level. At another, however, if there has been an evolution in Soviet commentary during Mitterrand's first year, the evolution has been toward less good grace. In assessing both Mitterrand's revolution at home and the character of his foreign policy, Soviet writers have gradually put less stress on the positive. They began with surprising enthusiasm for the program promised by the left, treating its objectives with considerable respect and the obstacles it faced with much understanding. For the first six months of the new government, Soviet commentary was devoted almost entirely to recounting its initial legislative successes and lamenting the problems it faced because of the policy failures of previous governments (e.g., continuing inflation and high unemployment) or the hostile policies of others (e.g., high U.S. interest rates and other measures to put economic pressure on the new French government), or simply the hostility of unreconstructed bourgeois elements in France (e.g., the bureaucrats and businessmen mentioned earlier). Gradually, however, the emphasis has shifted to the shortcomings of the original program, the readiness of the socialists to compromise their objectives, and the growing influence of those least committed to significant change.

Similarly, at the outset, Soviet analysts went out of their way to find the positive in the new government's foreign policy. Some of what they wrote had a hortatory quality, as though they were coaxing Mitterrand and his people as much as reporting French policy as they saw it. Typical accounts would start by noting Mitterrand's impatient rebuff of Reagan officials who opposed communist participation in his government. Having made the point that Mitterrand would not let himself be pushed around by the Americans, these accounts would then make some reference to the more progressive nature of Mitterrand's policy toward the Third World, or perhaps an allusion to his recognition of the "legitimacy of revolutionary movements in Latin America," or a comment on

48. Vitaly Semyonov, "Warning Signal," *New Times*, no. 5, January 1982, p. 26.

French efforts to achieve a fair outcome in southern Africa. Often they noted earlier PS-PCF statements favoring the suppression of military blocs.

Not that Soviet writers overlooked the early, worrisome signs that Mitterrand would take a tougher position on East-West issues. Statements by Mitterrand, Cheysson, and Minister of Defense Charles Hernu on the shift in the European military balance, the need for theater nuclear force modernization, and the dangers in the Soviet invasion of Afghanistan were all noted, but the tendency was to downplay these aspects of policy, stressing instead parts of policy either compatible with Soviet approaches or incompatible with those of the United States.[49]

In the course of the year, Soviet commentators have put a little less emphasis on the helpful or hope-inspiring side of policy, and expressed more their reservations. "When they were in the opposition," goes one recent article, "the socialists gave their due to statements in favor of détente, ending the arms race, and establishing a system of collective security in Europe."[50] But now the socialists "cast aspersions" on the antiwar movement, support deployment of new U.S. nuclear missiles in Western Europe, and, despite their commitment to strive for the dissolution of military blocs, do "exactly the opposite." They talk of ending economic relations with the "apartheid regime in Pretoria," but "initial socialist scruples have been sacrificed on the altar of France's trade balance." They urge noninterference in the internal affairs of newly independent states, but they now give "open support to the separatists in Ethiopia who are waging a struggle against the country's lawful government."

Thus it would be incomplete merely to note the basic restraint in Soviet reactions to the Mitterrand government and ignore the increasingly critical trend of Soviet analysis. If wise students of France, such as Stanley Hoffmann, are right and Mitterrand's policy extends rather than breaks with the Gaullist tradition, or if the answers to the basic questions posed earlier remain as mixed, the Soviets are not likely to let their criticism of France grow too sharp. Nor are they likely to jeopardize the potential for closer and more active relations between the two countries. But if, as seems less likely, the socialists become politically vulnerable at home, or, more important, if they concede many of

49. This was evident in most Soviet commentary through fall of 1981, but particularly marked in two major articles: one, a long and generally glowing two-part essay by Viktor Afanas'ev, *Pravda*'s editor and a man who prides himself as being knowledgeable about France, in *Pravda*, October 16 and 17, 1981; the other by *Pravda*'s senior commentator, Yuri Zhukov, another man who regards himself as an expert on France, in *Pravda*, November 2, 1981.

50. Semyonov, "After the First Year," p. 26. This article is a good, if somewhat exaggerated, illustration of my point. Semyonov has all along been the most critical Soviet correspondent in Paris; indeed, the most critical author writing on France. But he has also been the most thorough and detailed in his analysis.

their positions on East-West relations to hard-line American leaders, pursue a policy in the Third World more threatening to the Soviet Union than troubling to the United States, and take up the cause of West European integration or Atlantic Alliance cohesion, the Soviet Union may begin writing the Mitterrand government off and move toward a more abrasive or confrontational policy.

FRANCE, THE SOVIET UNION, WESTERN EUROPE, AND THE WORLD BEYOND

Viewing Soviet policy toward France in such a self-contained fashion, however, is only a start. One is still left to question what difference the state of this policy makes and in what contexts it is relevant. Ultimately what matters is Soviet policy toward France as a part of Soviet policy in Western Europe.

That policy of the Soviet Union, most would agree, is at the intersection of three concerns: the fate of its East European empire, the course of its competition with the United States, and the content of change within Western Europe itself. The three mingle in complex ways that probably not even the Soviet leadership can fully sort out. As a result, none of the simple models of offensive and defensive Soviet designs used to explain Soviet policy in Europe work very well. One needs instead a framework by which the mind can hold in place crosscutting and often contradictory Soviet interests, derived from a maze of relationships, unfolding on both global and regional planes. For the task is to understand how the Soviets relate Europe to their larger global aspirations and Europe's two halves to their concerns within each.

It helps to start by seeing Western Europe as the pivot between the Soviet Union's imperial and global concerns—that is, as both a resource and a threat in the pursuit of Soviet objectives in Eastern Europe and in the world at large, particularly with or against the United States. In the latter case, Western Europe, primarily NATO's European members, represents for the Soviet Union the most important reserve of U.S. global strength but also its most important vulnerability. The Atlantic Alliance, after all, in Soviet eyes not merely brings U.S. power to Europe, if fortifies the U.S. hand everywhere, and when the alliance begins to creak or sag the whole edifice of American strength is weakened. The trouble is that whereas the *alliance* remains an increment of U.S. power, the *allies* are potentially an influence over U.S. behavior. At the moment the Soviets would like to see allied influence on behalf of détente grow, but it will not the greater is the divorce within the alliance. Thus, while in the long run Soviet leaders may wish for a widening rift between the United States and its NATO partners, for the moment they also have a stake in the West Germans' and others' restraining the cold war instincts of the Reagan administration.

Western Europe has a parallel relationship to Eastern Europe. It is both a source of fragility within the area (as a conduit of contaminating ideas, negative political pressures, and economic hazards) and a hedge against fragility (as a source of economic relief and political moderation—or, as some would say, timidity). Moreover, to the extent that the fragility of empire diverts the Soviet Union from cultivating its power in the world at large, Western Europe in contributing to that fragility has a second indirect effect on the global balance between the superpowers.

To control Western Europe's impact in both contexts, the Soviet Union, Pierre Hassner contends, may have been pursuing its own form of "pan-Europeanization" for much of the last decade, particularly in the last year or so.[51] This is not the "pan-European reconciliation" sought by de Gaulle, but on the contrary an effort to exploit East and West European interdependence to reinforce Soviet power in Eastern Europe and weaken U.S. power in Western Europe. Hassner wonders whether the Soviet Union, by preying on Western Europe's expanded relations with the other Europe, subtly reinforced by offers of help in securing access to vital supplies of Persian Gulf oil, may not be after an "organic relationship increasingly separating Western Europe from the United States."

Hassner, in fact, wonders about a whole set of relationships emerging in the last half of the 1970s. Looking at the Soviet Union's aggressiveness in the Third World, sustained in part by what he calls the "globalization" of the East European alliance (the role taken up by East Germans and Czechoslovaks in Africa and elsewhere), he asks whether the Soviet Union has not begun to think in triangular or quadrilateral terms, linking itself, Europe (East and West), and the Middle East. At issue is an implicit political-economic bargain: for Western Europe, Soviet oil and gas as well as Soviet-guaranteed Middle Eastern oil in exchange for West European credits and goods supplied to Eastern Europe.

The process of protecting (and "globalizing") one alliance while "pan-Europeanizing" the other, Hassner suspects, parallels Soviet efforts to weaken U.S. influence in Western Europe while strengthening its own by means of the theater nuclear forces issue. Thus, whether or not the Soviet Union intentionally developed the SS–20 to strain the Western alliance, the politics of theater nuclear weapons irresistibly turned it into that kind of instrument. The obviously intense Soviet eagerness to make worse a self-inflicted wound, NATO's divisive dual-track decision, adds to the image of a self-confident, offensive policy.

The picture is a plausible one, and so is that part of it devoted to Soviet objectives in Western Europe itself. If in fact the Soviet Union has systematically determined Western Europe's role within the Soviet empire and in the competition with the other superpower, more than likely it has a reasonably clear notion of what it seeks in the area itself. Perhaps the Soviet aim is, as some have suggested, to make itself the "regional security manager"—that is, to assume the role of guarantor of peace throughout the European continent, entitled to a *droit de regard* over the defense initiatives of everyone. Perhaps it is also a region

51. See Pierre Hassner, "Soviet Policy in Western Europe: The East European Factor," in Sarah M. Terry, ed., *Soviet Policy in Eastern Europe* (forthcoming).

pliable in the face of Soviet power and respectful of Soviet interests as Moscow chooses to define them. And, at their core, Soviet purposes may be as neat as Hassner has often suggested: a Berlin as separate from Germany as possible, a Germany as separate from Western Europe as possible, and a Western Europe as separate from the United States as possible.

Much of this I would not challenge. Soviet aspirations doubtless do run in these directions. But, in my judgment, there is more to the story. Because so many trends in Europe have mixed implications, because so many developments have two sides, most probably Soviet policy does as well. Soviet choices are frequently not easy: The withdrawal of U.S. military forces, yes, but if their retreat promotes a stronger Bundeswehr or European military integration? A resurgent left, yes, but a revisionist left in power or one dominated by a party like the French PS? Economic cooperation with the West Europeans, yes, but if it leads to the headaches of Poland, Romania, and now Hungary? Distressed Western economies, yes, but if, as seems inevitable, their recessions are imported into Eastern Europe? Turmoil over the issue of theater nuclear forces, yes, but how much if too much crystallizes the will to restructure NATO's dilapidated defense concept? Political instability in the Federal Republic, yes, but if it casts a numbing pall over relations between East and West or, worse, destabilizes the larger European setting?

These, like dozens of other minidilemmas, do not facilitate decisive, orderly, well-integrated policies. The overall Soviet instinct may be to do as much damage to Western cohesion and sense of well-being as possible. But when it comes to the narrow, practical choices it faces daily, the Soviet Union is left with fewer and less freewheeling options. Most of Soviet policy in Western Europe, it seems to me, has less to do with controlling events than with managing effects—often delicately balanced effects. It is concerned not with undoing NATO or tearing Western Europe from the United States, but with affecting concrete West European choices to help build a pipeline, to forgo nuclear deployments in Northern Europe, or to resist American pressure for economic sanctions against the Soviet Union.

The choices the Soviets seek obviously are intended to fit with larger Soviet purposes, many of which do not fit with Western interests, but not necessarily so dramatically or schematically as is often assumed. They have plenty of reasons to want the pipeline, short of plotting Western Europe's bondage through dependency on Soviet gas. They have a variety of reasons for wanting to exploit the West European peace movement in order to obstruct the deployment of new strategic nuclear missiles, including the military ramifications of the weapons systems NATO means to put into Europe. Surely these are not reasons that should reassure the allies, but they do not necessarily form the chain usually argued: "The Soviet Union works so hard to fan the peace movement in order to block TNF modernization (and to avoid arms control) in order to destroy extended deterrence in order to 'Finlandize' Western Europe."

If Soviet policy in Western Europe is really about managing effects or trends—rather than controlling events or dictating decisions—then Franco-German relations provide a good case in point. From a Soviet perspective, such a partnership is neither inherently all good nor all bad. It depends. Franco-German cooperation as de Gaulle conceived it, to underwrite his vision for Europe, stirred their hostility. But Franco-German (and British) cohesion has long been regarded as the key to a Europe that can stand up to the United States—and therefore desirable, provided it did not evolve into an effective political, economic, or military integration. Today the Soviet leadership continues to fear a Franco-German collaboration that gives force to foreign policy coordination among Common Market members. But, at the same time, Soviet establishmentarians openly endorse cooperation between the two as essential to détente and healthy for European stability. One of the most interesting and influential of them, Alexander Bovin, wrote in June 1980, "Without a common position between France and Germany on the great world problems, it is difficult to think of Europe as a continent of peace and cooperation."[52]

Beyond the mixed character of the tasks and opportunities facing the Soviet Union in Western Europe, a second change gives policy a more limited character. By and large the great challenges as well as the great hopes of the 1960s have passed for the Soviet leaders. No longer is policy much inspired by far-reaching concerns like the German problem, the survival of NATO, or the existence of the Common Market. Those concerns tended to produce simpler, cruder, and more ambitious policies—policies of "breakthrough," as Richard Löwenthal characterized Khrushchev's gambit in Berlin from 1958 to 1962. Now the Soviet leadership is more taken with this or that inflection of German Ostpolitik, with the EEC's approach to trade credits for the East or toward the Camp David settlement in the Middle East, and with the capacity of the United States to rally NATO allies to 3 percent real growth in defense spending.

This is not to say that were the current malaise within the Western alliance to deepen into a debilitating crisis, the Soviet leadership would not quickly revert to a more single-minded policy. For the moment, however, the Soviets have been slow to conclude—slower than many in the West—that such a crisis is likely. Instead they continue laboring with a more trivial range of problems, such as Spain's entry into NATO, the Socialist International's support for arms control, the opening created by the new Greek socialist government, the hardening occasioned by the new Norwegian government, and a host of other disparate, discontinuous issues.

Again, at this level, French policy raises a delicate, albeit undramatic, balance of advantages and disadvantages. For example, on the issue of European military cooperation: the Soviets have not much liked France's own military efforts or many of its joint military programs with others in Europe, and they

52. *Izvestiia*, June 9, 1980.

would not have been pleased had Giscard proposed to Helmut Schmidt a common review of their two countries' security problems in Europe, as he recently revealed that he meant to do if he had been reelected.[53] But set against these considerations were Giscard's remarkable comments in the spring of 1975 on the inappropriateness of European defense cooperation, because of "the fears—and I must say understandable fears—that proposals for the organization of a European defense arouse in the Soviet Union," for the Soviet Union sees in them a "certain threat or a certain European military pressure against it."[54] Or, similarly, as a general matter the Soviets have welcomed the emergence of a Euroleft, uniting communists and socialists, largely because of the fillip they hope it may provide détente. In this spirit, they looked rather benignly on the original contacts a few years ago between the Italian Communist Party and the French PS. But now—when the liaison is gathering momentum—cooperation between two parties whose course troubles Moscow as much as that of these two parties does suddenly looks quite different.

Finally, Soviet policy in Western Europe is constrained, and indeed is likely to be increasingly constrained, by the same fundamental reality constraining Western policies in the East. Each has entered a period when the problems within its own alliance system exceed the opportunities within the other—all the more significant when the other side's problems are not likely to translate easily into opportunity for one's own side. The game now ceases to be the pursuit of what Hassner used to call the "status quo plus"—the status quo in one's own camp, change in the other's. For the 1980s the essential contest will be to see which side does a better job of containing or managing debilitating change within its own camp. The place the Soviet Union assigns France in that contest leads to a final topic.

THE SOVIET UNION, FRANCE, AND THE ATLANTIC ALLIANCE

For most of the Fifth Republic's history, France's main value to the Soviet Union has been in complicating the existence of the Western alliance. Initially, the Soviet leadership entertained hopes that France under de Gaulle might be an important part of the alliance's disintegration. At a minimum, it was seen as a deep threat to NATO's cohesion, and therefore objectively as a critical help in weakening the bases of a recalcitrant West German policy, the Soviet Union's principal West European objective.

These, however, were merely Soviet hopes at their most untrammeled, and when French defiance fell short—and, equally important, Soviet needs on this score diminished—the Soviets settled for less. It would be enough if France would stay outside the NATO structure, assert an independent military course,

53. For *Paris-Match* as reported in *Le Monde*, February 12, 1982.
54. See his press luncheon, *Le Monde*, May 23, 1975.

create an alternative pull for West German foreign policy, and, from time to time, harass the Americans. Lately the Soviets have wanted the French to show their independence by also dissenting from the United States' increasingly cold war ways and by rallying to the defense of détente.

Always, however, some level of French defection from the U.S. partnership with Western Europe has remained for Moscow the touchstone of Soviet relations with France. In practice, this has meant "some level" of estrangement from the United States, whether reflected directly in bilateral U.S.-French relations or indirectly through the U.S.–French–West German triangle. The Soviets make no secret of this, though rarely are they as open as Gromyko was in Paris in February 1974 a few days after Foreign Minister Michel Jobert's angry joust with Henry Kissinger at the Washington energy conference. Said Gromyko in a public toast, "We applaud all countries which pursue an independent policy in the interests of world peace. If you hear from afar cheers for your policy of independence, be sure they come from us."[55]

The irony is that Gromyko's toast marked what most Soviet observers feel was a watershed in France's independent policy. Having fought and lost to the Americans on the energy issue, largely because the British and the Germans yielded to the Americans, the French themselves gradually fell into line.[56] By the fall 1974 meeting in Martinique, Giscard and his people were supposedly showing considerably more readiness to cooperate with the United States on economic and monetary questions. Their growing pliability, manifest in their approach to the series of economic summits that followed, paralleled in turn, according to Soviet accounts, France's partial reintegration into NATO. "France," Georgi Vorontsov writes, "obviously feels itself a part of the West and set limits on how far it is prepared to challenge the alliance or the United States."[57] But from the mid–1970s, this general proposition was beginning to translate into an active "reconciliation of France's basic positions with NATO." From then on, "both the French and the Americans began to avoid sharp confrontations in their mutual relations."

The relatively direct link the Soviets see between the state of U.S.-French relations and the state of France's attitude toward the Atlantic Alliance, however, is only one critical nexus. For, as the French role in the Western alliance remains, in the Soviet view, a function of Franco-American relations, Franco-Soviet relations have also been a function of U.S.-Soviet relations. As the first evolved in the 1970s, so did the second.

---

55. London *Times*, February 18, 1974.

56. The argument takes various forms, but one of the clearest expositions is in G. A. Vorontsov, *SShA i Zapadnaia Evropa: Novyi etap otnoshenii* (Moscow: Mezhdunarodyne otnosheniia, 1979), pp. 235–50.

57. Ibid., p. 243.

Through the first half of the decade, the issue emerged primarily in French sensitivity to developments in U.S.-Soviet relations. During the October War in the Middle East, for example, Jobert reacted furiously to U.S.-Soviet sum-mitry. He called Kissinger's emergency diplomacy with the Soviets a "veritable condominium" which had rendered Europe helpless.[58] Europe, he said, had been "treated like a nonperson, humiliated all along the line." The Soviet Union, in particular, had demeaned France by failing to consult as their agree-ment on consultation required. *Literaturnaia gazeta* (November 28, 1973) retorted to those who complained of Europe being bypassed and reduced to "political nothings": "Even in France, which was the first of the Western coun-tries to establish relations with the USSR based on trust, mutual understand-ing and mutually profitable cooperation, one can come across from time to time statements directly aimed at undermining those principles." Only a few months earlier, the French had been ruffled by the U.S.-Soviet agreement on the prevention of nuclear war, the centerpiece of the U.S.-Soviet summit of 1973. When Brezhnev, on his way back from Washington, stopped in Paris to reassure the French, Giscard went out of his way to let the Soviet leader know his displeasure over superpower deals to control others' nuclear decisions.

But these episodes in a long tradition of mistrusting superpower collusion were among the last in recent years, in no small part because of the subsequent deterioration in U.S.-Soviet relations. Simultaneously, in a reverse arc, Soviet sensitivity to Franco-Soviet relations as a function of U.S.-Soviet relations in-tensified. With the steady collapse of U.S.-Soviet détente after 1975, Soviet in-terest in the French paralleled directly Soviet troubles with the Americans. One noticed it first when Brezhnev went on French television in May 1977, two months after Secretary of State Cyrus Vance's abortive mission to Moscow, to praise Franco-Soviet relations and to complain of the United States' "non-constructive course in the strategic arms race."[59] Then in June, Brezhnev ar-rived in Paris for his first trip to Western Europe since late 1974, and spent much of his time trying to reach the Americans through the French. At one point while reading from his prepared notes, he stopped and asked who in the French delegation was in charge of "propaganda"; he wanted to make sure that the propagandist had "noticed" his reference to détente as "the only practical approach to avoid a confrontation in this nuclear age."[60] Later in the summit, Brezhnev stressed to Giscard how deeply concerned he was by the continuing failure of the United States and the Soviet Union to reach agreement on strategic arms limitations, and then he authorized French officials to convey to the press his distress.

58. See *Le Monde*, November 12, 1973.
59. See *Le Monde*, June 20, 1977.
60. *Washington Post*, June 23, 1977.

At the next low point in U.S.-Soviet relations, following the Soviet-Cuban intervention in the Ogaden war, Gromyko showed up in Paris, and once again in his comments and toasts contrasted the virtues of Franco-Soviet relations with the perils of U.S.-Soviet relations. Since then it has become standard for the Soviets to make Washington's wayward course the central issue of nearly every high-level encounter with the French, and the practice continues under Mitterrand.

Thus, at a general level, Soviet reactions to French foreign policy depend on two related concerns: the broad tone and texture of Franco-American relations, and the general drift of French attitudes toward NATO. On the first score the Soviets have worried about France drawing closer to the United States, particularly since 1974, but without slackening their own efforts to exploit the differences that remain. Under Mitterrand, the Soviets are not necessarily fearful of still closer Franco-American collusion. If anything, despite the Reagan administration's general satisfaction with France's tougher stance on East-West military issues, Soviet observers sense a growing gulf between France and the United States on most other issues. The trouble is that until now the Soviet Union's own opportunities with the French have diminished. On the second score, Mitterrand continues a trend begun by others, although in this instance the Soviets seem concerned that he may be ready to go further than they in reintegrating France into the alliance. The articles on the enthusiasm of the French Atlanticists for Mitterrand seem shriller than before; the annoyance is more intense that people such as Joseph Luns, secretary general of NATO, find much to praise in Mitterrand's foreign policy.

Beyond these critical relations, there is a second key dimension influencing Soviet judgments of France and the alliance: France's own military posture and the related issue of French policy on arms control. From a Soviet point of view, the two have evolved in opposite directions over the last decade. Whether this evolution will continue under Mitterrand is too early to tell.

Generally, on the issue of arms control, the French position has evolved favorably, as Moscow sees things. That is easily said largely because in the beginning the French position was so unsatisfactory. De Gaulle resisted nearly all the major arms control ventures of the 1960s, the partial test ban and the nonproliferation treaty, and his successors continued the tradition in their response to MBFR, expanded SALT, and even in some measure the theater nuclear force negotiations. Their refusal to take part stemmed only partly from a jealous regard for their own freedom of action; as the Soviets knew, the French did not much believe in these ventures even without their participation. The French were, in Michel Tatu's phrase, proponents of an "armed détente," a détente in which arms control came at the end, not the beginning, of the process.

From Pompidou's first meeting with Brezhnev in Pitsunda in January 1973, on the eve of the exploratory phase of the MBFR talks, Brezhnev and his colleagues have criticized, cajoled, and appealed to the French to get involved. Knowing French touchiness on this score, they have done so gingerly, but without missing an occasion to make their case. Gradually the French have moved, albeit least on the principal negotiations and not enough on any of them, but still in ways that are seen as useful and reassuring. First Giscard added his voice to Soviet proposals in the mid-1970s for a world disarmament conference; then, when in Moscow in October 1974, he gave a favorable hearing to proposals for negotiations to prohibit the development and deployment of weapons of mass destruction, and he acknowledged French responsibility for preventing the spread of nuclear weapons. In 1979 the French rejoined the Geneva disarmament talks. Before that, at the UN Special Session on Disarmament in the spring of 1978, Giscard had introduced a series of arms control ideas, including a conference on European disarmament from the Atlantic to the Urals. The Warsaw Treaty Organization later proposed a similar undertaking, and the merger of the two ideas, focused on extended confidence-building measures, produced the notion of a European Disarmament Conference, a major topic at the now-adjourned Madrid meeting.

Despite their tough position on theater nuclear force negotiations, the socialists in general and Mitterrand in particular have long held strong antinuclear, prodisarmament views, and therefore the Soviets have some basis for hoping the evolution of the French position will continue. The socialists have endorsed most of the key arms control efforts, from the Geneva general disarmament talks to MBFR, and their communist allies are faithful advocates of virtually every new arms control idea. Defense may yet turn out to be only one side of a coin that also carries a prominent arms control face.

In contrast, from a Soviet perspective, French military doctrine has evolved unfavorably. The Fifth Republic's defense posture has passed through essentially three stages. Of the three, the Soviets preferred the first, granted their irreducible unhappiness with facing another nuclear power whatever its strategic doctrine. Initially, under de Gaulle, the French adhered to a strategy of massive retaliation, theoretically directed against all fronts, East and West. If France's role was global, argued the French chief of staff, General Charles Ailleret, threats could come from any direction. In Moscow this looked better than the usual formula. Even the French version of massive retaliation had its virtues. For, while the Soviet leadership obviously disapproved the triggering role French nuclear forces might play in a general conflict—indeed, were designed to play—it valued more French dissent from the U.S. and NATO doctrine of "flexible response," a doctrine whose concepts were far more anathema to the Soviet Union.

Thus, for the Soviets, the first important retreat in French doctrine occurred in 1969, when Ailleret's successor, General Michel Fourquet, announced the adoption of a form of flexible response for France. Although still not accepting the NATO posture or the integration of French strategic forces into it, the new posture envisaged graduated stages of escalation in which French conventional forces in the Federal Republic of Germany would serve as a trip wire and tactical nuclear weapons as a warning shot preceding a nuclear assault. Soviet leaders did not like the adjustment, seeing it as a further reason to worry over France's cooperation with NATO.

Viewed from Moscow, however, the real break in French strategy came in 1976, when under Giscard, General Guy Méry announced that France now regarded territory to its east (in effect West Germany) as an integral part of the national sanctuary. No longer was this area merely the foyer of Soviet aggression, but now territory for which France intended to mount an effective "forward defense." Effective forward defense involved more potent conventional forces, and, with a certain confusion, a role for enhanced radiation weapons.

The Soviet leadership deeply disapproved of the whole idea, because it provided a de facto convergence of French and NATO strategy without a formal reintegration, and gave Giscard's flirtation with NATO a more profound content. When Brezhnev arrived in Paris for the June 1977 summit, he made a considerable fuss over what he called the "new directions" in French defense policy, including France's increased involvement with NATO and a "new doctrine of forward battle."[61] "This forward battle, who is it supposed to be against?" he asked, according to the carefully orchestrated public reporting of his principal press spokesman, Leonid Zamiatin. Soviet commentary picked up the theme, and continued to make an issue of the change for the remainder of Giscard's time in office.

In reality, the French under Giscard made relatively little headway toward implementing the new doctrine, and his administration left office without fully sorting out the French defense posture. The new government, after formally embracing most of what Giscard's people had set out, appears to be making scarcely more progress toward its implementation. Still, the Soviet side is unhappy with developing French defense preferences, and watchful of the progress they may achieve.

Finally, and ultimately, Soviet perspectives on France and the Atlantic Alliance depend on a third consideration: the strategies each follows toward the Soviet Union itself. Under Giscard (as under Schmidt and now Kohl), French (and German) strategies for dealing with the Soviet threat diverged increasingly from the U.S. approach. This was true even before Reagan's election. Some of the discrepancy between France and the United States, many people are inclined to argue, has been reduced under Mitterrand. To the degree that the French view the Soviet threat more gravely and seem ready to deal with it, the gulf has indeed been reduced. But the issue does not end there. Merely seeing the Soviet military threat as important does not insure a convergence of French and American strategy toward the Soviet Union. On the contrary, while Mitterrand has come to believe in the importance of maintaining a military balance with the Soviet Union, he also believes in pursuing a dialogue with the Soviet

61. *Le Monde*, June 20, 1977.

Union and in seeking ways to integrate it into the world community. As one French official put it, he believes in "keeping the door to the Soviet Union open but standing there with a pistol in your pocket." He believes that one can and should involve the Soviet Union in the great international challenges of the day, and that the Soviet Union at some point will have to be brought into crisis settlements involving regions like the Middle East and into international economic institutions. He does not believe, as the Reagan administration apparently does, that the Soviet Union should be treated as an outlaw nation and quarantined. In the Third World, he believes the West can and should compete with the Soviet Union, not confront it; that the West can win the "class struggle" in these areas; and that the real issue is the larger political contest, not a narrowly conceived military competition in every trouble spot. And, in particular, Mitterrand believes that a firm policy toward the Soviet Union should be nonprovocative—not a quality with which he would credit Reagan's policy. Soviet leaders may not like Mitterrand's approach to them, but they realize that it is different from the American approach, and, by that standard, better. Moreover, it remains, despite the current Franco-American enthusiasm, a basis of future U.S.-French discord.

Thus, when the Soviet Union looks at France in the context of the Atlantic Alliance, it sees countervailing tendencies at several levels, just as it does when it considers French policy as a whole. Under Giscard, these tendencies formed a kind of suspended equilibrium: France edged back toward the alliance, but firmly refused to step across the threshold; aligned its military posture with NATO, but made something of a mess of its implementation; eased the tension in Franco-American relations, but preserved an independent course in Franco-Soviet relations. Under Mitterrand the equilibrium is likely to persist.

If so, so will the continuity in Soviet policy toward France. I started this chapter by arguing that Franco-Soviet relations have long reflected the instrumental stake each leadership has in the policies of the other—a stake mostly determined by the larger European context (first a predétente Europe, when the target was a recalcitrant West Germany buttressed by NATO, and then a Europe during détente). Provided they are not fundamental, shifts in French (or Soviet) foreign policy will affect Franco-Soviet relations less than basic alterations in the European context. If there are no fundamental changes in Europe—East or West—or in the Atlantic Alliance, shifts in Soviet policy toward France are likely to be more superficial than real. The problem is in being sure that substantial changes will not occur within Europe or within the Atlantic Alliance.

Chapter 4

The Soviets and the West European Communist Parties

Joan Barth Urban

The CPSU has always needed ties with an international communist constituency in order to bolster the domestic legitimacy of the Soviet regime. Yet considerations of foreign policy have been paramount in shaping the character of those ties. These familiar axioms hold true for recent Soviet–West European communist relations as well as CPSU relations with foreign communist parties in an earlier era. In the final analysis, conformity to the USSR's foreign policy line remains to this day the touchstone of a nonruling communist party's political rectitude in Moscow's eyes.

This truism was once again brought home by the dramatic deterioration of CPSU relations with the Italian Communist Party (PCI) in January 1982. Confronted with a sweeping PCI indictment of the USSR's international behavior, the Soviet leaders retorted in classic Stalinist fashion that the leaders of the largest communist party in the capitalist West had become dupes of imperialism. This use of explicit two-camp imagery marked a departure from Moscow's efforts during the mid–1970s to reach a modus vivendi with its increasingly vocal Western communist critics. It was sparked, in turn, by the broadening of the PCI's criticism of Soviet international conduct from specific actions within the world communist movement (the break with China, the invasions of Czechoslovakia and Afghanistan) to Soviet foreign policy across the board. At the same time, the CPSU's harsh riposte to the PCI's global challenge was facilitated by what was perhaps Moscow's most controversial foreign policy initiative: its direct military support of radical Third World liberationism. For by the late 1970s the USSR had acquired a new ideological constituency among Third World radicals that greatly lessened the urgency of preserving at any cost a public image of solidarity with the West European communist parties, even the most influential among them.

91

Until the late 1970s, however, the Kremlin's need for European communist party endorsement of its self-proclaimed vanguard role in the global march toward socialism led to a fair degree of interdependency between the CPSU and its Western communist critics. Thus, despite condemnation of the Soviet march into Czechoslovakia by most Western communist parties and a pointed divergence from the CPSU's ideological norms on the part of some, Moscow expended considerable effort on forging a mutually satisfactory relationship with the West European communist movement.

This chapter examines the CPSU's search for such a relationship during the years following the Czechoslovak crisis of 1968. It begins with an assessment of the contradictory tendencies unleashed within both the major West European communist parties and the CPSU by the onset of détente and the overthrow of the Allende regime in Chile. It then explores the impact of the Portuguese Communist Party's abortive bid for power both on the pan-European communist movement in general and on the USSR's international conduct. With regard to the latter, I will argue that Moscow's decisive military intervention in Angola in the autumn of 1975 and concessions to the emergent "Eurocommunist" entente at the June 1976 European communist conference in East Berlin were but two sides of the same coin: an attempt to buttress the ideological credentials of the CPSU. The third section deals with the Soviet campaign against Eurocommunism that was launched in June 1977 with the *New Times* attack on Spanish communist leader Santiago Carrillo but gained momentum only during 1978. The CPSU's uncommon restraint toward the Italian communists during this period resulted from the threat of polemical retaliation which the PCI then held over Moscow, specifically with regard to foreign policy issues and relations with Peking. All the same, by the end of the decade the gist of Soviet policy toward the Western communist parties was aptly captured by Stalinist cliché, "He who is not with us is against us." The concluding section focuses on the causes of the recent Soviet-PCI rift. PCI opposition to the military crackdown in Poland was the catalyst for the polemical escalation between the two parties during the winter of 1982. But far more worrisome to Moscow was the PCI's call for a united socialist Europe that would play an autonomous role in world politics, indepent of either superpower. Far from welcoming such an eventuality as a harbinger of "Finlandization," the CPSU appeared to view it as tantamount to collusion with imperialism.

Détente, the "Lessons of Chile," and Pan-European Communist Cleavages

The seemingly unrelated phenomena of East-West détente and the military suppression of the Allende regime in Chile gave rise to reverberations and crosscurrents within the pan-European communist movement that were to be felt throughout the 1970s. With regard to the *mode* of revolutionary change in the West after the Chilean debacle, the CPSU's approach remained notably orthodox, whereas that of the Italian, Spanish, and even French communist parties became more innovative. On the other hand, with regard to the *pace* of social transformation, Moscow in effect urged restraint so as not to disrupt détente, whereas the major Western communist parties, particularly the French and Portuguese, exhibited considerable militancy.

The Warsaw Pact invasion of Czechoslovakia tarnished Soviet-style socialism in the eyes of many Western communists. But the fate of the Unidad Popular coalition in Chile had the more practical effect of highlighting the dangers of political polarization and underscoring the need to build a broad popular consensus in favor of socialist transformations. PCI chief Enrico Berlinguer's postulation of the *compromesso storico* on the heels of Allende's overthrow in the fall of 1973 was the clearest evidence of this new outlook.[1] But a similar tendency was also perceptible in the positions of the French communist leaders—for instance, their assertions during the mid-1970s that a "51 percent" majority was insufficient for the introduction of sweeping socioeconomic changes.[2] Simultaneously, however, the onset of détente between Washington and Moscow fostered French and Italian communist hopes of harnessing the rebelliousness of students and workers that had erupted with such unexpected force in the late 1960s. Despite the conservative backlash that led to Gaullist electoral majorities in 1968–69 and the ascendancy of the center-right in the Italian parliamentary elections of 1972, pockets of discontent over socioeconomic inequities and political immobility were growing in both France and Italy. Meanwhile, the blurring of bipolarity at the international level gave the French and Italian communist parties an unaccustomed air of domestic respectability, hence the opportunity to channel that discontent into electoral support.

In Moscow, on the other hand, détente and the dénouement in Chile elicited currents of official opinion within the CPSU that were reconciled only with difficulty. In addition, what happened in Moscow diverged almost completely from the trends developing in most major Western communist parties.

The dominant tendency among Soviet policy makers was a preoccupation with securing improved political and economic relations with the capitalist powers combined with inattention, conscious or otherwise, toward the prospects for political change in Latin Europe. The Kremlin's conspicuous cultivation of the powers that be in the Élysée during the French elections of 1973–74 and the USSR's steps toward normalizing ties with Spain in the early 1970s, the

---

1. For the evolution of the *compromesso storico*, or "historic compromise," stragety, see Stephen Hellman, "The Longest Campaign: Communist Party Strategy and the Elections of 1976," in Howard R. Penniman, ed., *Italy at the Polls: The Parliamentary Elections of 1976* (Washington, D.C.: American Enterprise Institute, 1977), pp. 155–82.

2. For an analysis of French communist strategy during the 1970s, see Ronald Tiersky, "French Communism, Eurocommunism, and Soviet Power," in Rudolf L. Tökés, ed., *Eurocommunism and Détente* (New York: New York University Press, 1978), pp. 138–203.

eve of the post-Franco transition (General Franco was then eighty and ailing), were only the more glaring manifestations of this attitude. Far more serious was the Soviet leadership's consuming interest in seeing the successful completion of the Conference on Security and Cooperation in Europe (Helsinki) even as signs of European radicalization multiplied (growing electoral support for the *union de la gauche*, the massive Italian vote in favor of divorce in May 1974, mounting revolutionary extremism in Portugal).

The impact of the Chilean events was of a different order, at least among some CPSU officials responsible for ideological matters. Here initial interest in the Unidad Popular experiment and its implications for radical change elsewhere in the West, as evidenced by the infusion of administrative support and personnel into the moribund Institute of the International Workers' Movement of the Soviet Academy of Sciences in early 1971,[3] soon gave way to a pronounced campaign in Soviet international affairs journals to equate the parliamentary path to socialism in Chile with the postwar people's democracies in Eastern Europe.[4] Apparently Soviet ideologues feared the attractiveness of the Allende regime's rhetoric on pluralism just as they had feared the contagiousness of the Czechoslovak reform movement of 1968. Indeed, the overseers of Soviet orthodoxy may well have been relieved when the military coup against Unidad Popular enabled them to redirect their attention from the specter of pluralism to the "lessons of Chile." Whatever the case, in a series of well-placed commentaries on the Chilean fiasco they deplored Unidad Popular's failure to dominate the media, infiltrate the military, and destroy the old "bourgeois" state structures of Chile.[5] Written before the collapse of the Portuguese *ancien régime* in late April 1974, their words read like a prescription for the Portuguese Communist Party's abortive attempt to manipulate its way into power during 1975.

In short, there was a real discrepancy between the conservatism of Soviet state relations with the West and the radical rhetoric used by members of the above circles to depict the shape of eventual revolutionary change in the capitalist world. Moreover, both attitudes were bound to clash with the contrary tendencies then evolving within a number of West European communist parties. In retrospect, for instance, it was almost predictable that the Spanish

3. Joan Barth Urban, "Contemporary Soviet Perspectives on Revolution in the West," *Orbis*, 19, no. 4 (Winter 1976): 1359–1402 at p. 1360.

4. Joan Barth Urban, "Socialist Pluralism in Soviet and Italian Communist Perspective: The Chilean Catalyst," *Orbis*, 18, no. 2 (Summer 1974): 482–509 at pp. 495–502.

5. See, for example, A. I. Sobolev, "Revoliutsiia i kontrrevoliutsiia: Opyt Chili i problemy klassovoi bor'by," *Rabochii klass i sovremennyi mir*, no. 2, March-April 1974, pp. 3–22 at pp. 12–22; M. F. Kudachkin, "Opyt bor'by Kompartii Chili za edinstvo levykh sil i revoliutsionnye preobrazovaniia," *Voprosy istorii KPSS*, no. 5, May 1974, pp. 48–60; and Boris Ponomarev, "The World Situation and the Revolutionary Process," *World Marxist Review*, 17, no. 6 (June 1974): 3–15. Ponomarev's article is but a pale reflection of the first two cited above.

and French communist parties, bent on transforming their own societies rather sooner than later, would begin to suspect Moscow of favoring the status quo in Western Europe; and that the Spanish and Italian communist parties, in their search for a pluralist path to socialism, would provoke a polemical reaction from the more orthodox of the CPSU's ideological cadres.[6]

This proliferation of diverse currents throughout the pan-European communist movement requires some kind of classification—however approximate—for the sake of conceptual clarity. The usual distinction between reformers and conservatives is useful for understanding the dynamics of political development within a single party, or party-state. But it lacks what might be called a transnational dimension. A CPSU ideologue concerned with preserving the status quo at home may be equally committed to the revolutionary projection of the Soviet system abroad. The term "conservative" does not lend itself to this kind of nuance. By the same token, a CPSU leader wishing to promote domestic innovation may actually seek to avoid undue Soviet entanglement in foreign "reform" movements for fear of exacerbating East-West tensions.

For analytical purposes I will therefore use the terms "sectarian" and "innovator" to distinguish between those communists who want to maintain or emulate the Soviet model of socialism (a "monolithic" communist party with a monopoly of power over a command economy) and those who envisage a less centralized alternative. More to the point of the topic at hand, I will also speak of "revolutionary sectarians" and "revolutionary innovators" to describe those groups committed to systemic transformation in the West (although this distinction applies primarily to ruling parties, since it may be assumed that the nonruling communist parties are preoccupied with social change at home). Even this fourfold classification does not do justice to reality. For to differentiate between Stalinists and the present Soviet leaders one would have to speak of radical versus cautious sectarianism; one might also do well to subdivide the leaders of a party like the PCI into cautious and radical innovators (with positions on such issues as the degree of accommodation with the Christian Democratic establishment constituting the line of demarcation between the two); and so on. These labels, moreover, are not intended to be mutually exclusive. In his later years Tito, for example, was a cautious sectarian in domestic party affairs but an innovator on questions pertaining to the Yugoslav economy and intercommunist party relations. These caveats notwithstanding, the above categories provide a kind of conceptual shorthand for discussing the transnational linkages and conflicts within the pan-European communist movement.

6. For the most comprehensive treatment of postwar Spanish communism, see Eusebio Mujal-León, *Communism and Political Change in Spain* (Bloomington: Indiana University Press, 1983); for PCI developments in the 1970s, see Joan Barth Urban, "Moscow and the PCI in the 1970s: Kto Kovo?" *Studies in Comparative Communism*, 13, no. 2 & 3 (Summer-Autumn 1980), pp. 99–167.

A clearer picture of the utility of these categories may be had by applying them to the divergences exacerbated, if not triggered, by détente and the military crackdown in Chile. The Italian and Spanish communist parties' defense of democratic pluralism both before and after the coming of socialism marked them as innovators, however cautious the PCI was in terms of the *pace* of social transformation. On the other hand, the French party's popular-front tactics and equivocal position on socialist pluralism (it continued to hail the CPSU's "general law" of communist party hegemony during socialist construction throughout the 1970s) placed it on the fence between sectarianism and innovation. As for the CPSU, the center of political gravity in Moscow was represented by "cautious sectarianism"–that is, by a preoccupation with maintaining CPSU rule at home and projecting Soviet *state* power rather than ideology abroad.[7] Still, the Soviet ideologues' interpretations of the "lessons of Chile" noted above appeared revolutionary sectarian in the extreme.

In 1974–75 the CPSU made an attempt to reconcile these divergent orientations. Alexander Sobolev, head of the Institute of Marxism-Leninism's department of international communist affairs and editor in chief of the new journal of the revitalized Institute of the International Workers' Movement, endorsed the idea of a democratic transitional stage on the path to socialism (Soviet style) in the capitalist West.[8] As I will elaborate below, this formulation is rather similar to both the classic popular-front strategem and the PCF's current line. Designed to bridge the gap between the West European communist party innovators and the Soviet revolutionary sectarians, it might perhaps be awkwardly described as cautious revolutionary sectarianism. However, as we shall see, the attempt to resolve the basic differences between the two groups soon foundered in the face of the intense revolutionary sectarianism of the Portuguese Communist Party.

SQUARING THE CIRCLE: THE CPSU's RESPONSE TO PORTUGAL AND EUROCOMMUNISM

Portuguese developments in the spring and summer of 1975 had the effect of magnifying the contending approaches to revolution in the West within the pan-European communist movement. If Portuguese communist disregard for electoralism and civil liberties spurred the Italian and Spanish communist parties to a clearer articulation of their innovative strategies, the radical momentum in Portugal gave a shot in the arm to the revolutionary sectarians in Moscow. In place of a unified position on these questions, the CPSU was thus obliged to engage in a series of uneasy compromises. On the one hand, in order to maintain a semblance of pan-European communist unity, the Soviets made some

7. This argument is developed in Urban, "Contemporary Soviet Perspectives."

8. A. I. Sobolev, "Voprosy strategii i taktiki klassovoi bor'by na nyneshnem etape obshchego krizisa kapitalizma," *Rabochii klass i sovremennyi mir*, no. 1, January-February 1975, pp. 3–20 at pp. 15–16; cf. Urban, "Contemporary Soviet Perspective," pp. 1374–75.

rather substantial concessions to the Western (and Yugoslav) innovators on such issues as parity in international communist decision making and the legitimacy of interparty disagreements. As a matter of fact, steps in this direction had already begun in October 1974 with the start of preparations for the European communist conference eventually held in East Berlin in June 1976. On the other hand, as the Portuguese crisis heated up, the more extreme revolutionary sectarians within the CPSU enjoyed renewed prominence. A case in point was Konstantin Zarodov's controversial *Pravda* commentary of August 6, 1975, in which he derided majority rule and insisted on communist party dominance even during the transitional period between capitalism and socialism—on the very eve of high-level CPSU-PCI consultations in Moscow.[9] Moreover, although the fortunes of the revolutionary sectarians in Lisbon were on the wane by the end of August 1975, a highly publicized meeting between Brezhnev and Zarodov in mid–September signaled that their like-minded Soviet comrades remained in good standing. Indeed, there is reason to believe that the USSR's decision of late summer 1975 to escalate dramatically its military support of the Movement for the Liberation of Angola (MPLA) reflected pressure from the revolutionary sectarians within the CPSU as well as a general resolve to recoup the international loss of face wrought by the defeat of the unabashedly pro-Soviet Portuguese communists.

Revolution in Portugal and the Rise of Eurocommunism. The "revolution of the red carnations" in Lisbon in April 1974 led to the collapse of almost four decades of right-wing authoritarianism in a virtually bloodless military coup. The victory of the reform-minded Armed Forces Movement (MFA) elicited not only popular acclaim but also a public consensus favorable to socioeconomic reforms and tolerant of left-wing radicalism. Even the politicians at the conservative end of the legal political spectrum chose to label their party the Social Democratic Center.

This public sentiment formed the backdrop for the abortive attempt by the Portuguese Communist Party (PCP) to dominate the revolutionary process according to the guidelines of the CPSU's revolutionary sectarians. Whether the PCP leaders did so because of direct instigation or merely because of a shared political mentality we do not know. That Portuguese communists participated in Soviet-sponsored discussions of the "lessons" of Chile for revolution in Portugal is, however, a fact.[10] Whatever the case, from mid–1974 onward the PCP sought to

9. "Leninskaia strategiia i taktika revoliutsionnoi bor'by," *Pravda*, August 6, 1975. Zarodov, taking the Russian Revolution of 1905 as his frame of reference, called for communist dominance during *democratic* revolutions as the prerequisite for the ultimate victory of socialist revolutions. Applied to the Portuguese context, his argument was viewed by many Western communists as an endorsement of what amounted to a Portuguese communist bid for uninterrupted revolution and total power.

10. Urban, "Contemporary Soviet Perspectives," p. 1366. In addition, PCP leader Alvaro Cunhal visited Moscow as part of an official Portuguese government delegation from October 29 through November 3, 1974.

make its views prevail within the MFA and its Revolutionary Council, which in March 1975 arrogated to itself the right to oversee the civilian authorities and to ban three political groups, including the conservative Christian Democratic Party. And as the months wore on, the PCP's seeming success in infiltrating the revolutionary power structures became ever more pronounced. In May–June 1975, for example, the PCP/MFA-influenced government closed down the widely respected Portuguese socialist newspaper *República* and the Catholic radio station Renascença. Thereafter proposals for a system of dual power (a network of local councils parallel to the constituent assembly democratically elected in April 1975) developed apace with the PCP's preeminence in Portugal's fifth postcoup provisional cabinet named August 8, 1975.[11]

It was soon to become clear, of course, that the PCP, in its urge to emulate Bolshevik tactics, grossly miscalculated the temper of the Portuguese people. Far from being alienated by the exigencies of an ongoing war or bereft of plausible noncommunist leadership, as was the case in 1917 Russia, the Portuguese people were gripped by a Promethean sense of control over their own destiny. The communist bid for power was thus thwarted, on the one hand, by massive grassroots resistance supported by the Catholic Church and the Socialist International and, on the other, by opposition from MFA factions to the left and right of the PCP. All the same, for the pan-European communist movement the end result of Lisbon's hot summer of 1975 was to deepen preexisting cleavages.

The sectarianism of the Portuguese communists certainly galvanized the development of the Eurocommunist phenomenon that attracted so much political concern in both Moscow and Washington during the second half of the 1970s. Ties between the PCI and the still clandestine Spanish Communist Party (PCE) had already been cemented by their common stand against the Warsaw Pact invasion of Czechoslovakia and by the PCI's backing of the PCE leadership in the face of CPSU attempts to undermine it for defying Moscow. The two Latin European communist parties also shared a programmatic commitment to democratic procedures and socialist pluralism.[12] Their credibility on this score, however, was becoming an increasingly topical question among Western establishment circles as Spain approached the post-Franco transition and the PCI's electoral support jumped six percentage points, to about 33 percent of the popular vote in the regional elections of June 1975.

Guilt by association with the intransigently orthodox PCP could only damage PCI-PCE efforts to gain domestic legitimacy. Both parties thus bent

11. For developments in Portugal during 1974–75, see Eusebio Mujal-León, "Communism and Revolution in Portugal," in Tőkés, ed., *Eurocommunism and Détente*, pp. 271–313; and Kenneth Maxwell, "Portuguese Communism," in George Schwab, ed., *Eurocommunism: The Ideological and Political-Theoretical Foundations* (Westport, Conn.: Greenwood Press, 1981), pp. 269–302.

12. See note 6 above.

over backward to distance themselves from their sectarian comrades in Lisbon. They publicly deplored the PCP/MFA-instigated violations of democracy and civil liberties. They jointly proclaimed their own support for pluralist principles, now and in the socialist future, at a much publicized summit meeting between Berlinguer and Carrillo in mid-July 1975.[13] And on August 7–8, 1975, the PCI's international affairs spokesman, Gian Carlo Pajetta, conducted talks in Moscow with Brezhnev's deputy, Andrei Kirilenko, on the Portuguese situation. *Pravda* greeted Pajetta's arrival with the publication of Zarodov's highly provocative call of August 6 for communist party hegemony throughout the revolutionary process. The talks nevertheless ended in a compromise of sorts. Both sides endorsed the need for unity of action between the Portuguese communists *and socialists*[14] at a time when it still seemed that the PCP might succeed in its bid for exclusive power. The following November, for reasons not as directly related to developments in Portugal, the French Communist Party (PCF) added its voice to the emerging Eurocommunist entente.

CPSU Caution in Europe, Ambivalence in Portugal, and Radicalism in Africa. During the mid-1970s the Soviet leadership's response to the ideological challenge posed by the Western communist party innovators was one of caution and compromise, both before and after the Portuguese crisis. The emphasis placed by CPSU ideologues in early 1975 on a democratic transitional stage on the path to socialism has already been noted. Although such flexibility contrasted sharply with the rigidly sectarian approach to events in Chile just a short while earlier, it was not entirely new to Soviet doctrine. One need only recall the popular-front tactics of the 1930s and Khrushchev's endorsement of a parliamentary path to socialism at the Twentieth Congress. What was quite novel (and wholly unacceptable to people like Zarodov), however, was the suggestion that democratic principles should be observed during the actual transitional period between capitalism and socialism. The intent of the more cautious CPSU ideologues in this regard was clear. By calling for an open-ended democratic transitional stage, they supported a revolutionary perspective that would seemingly be compatible with East-West détente as well as acceptable to the communist innovators in Western Europe. Such a strategy would provide an outlet for revolutionary zeal at home and abroad without constituting a direct challenge to the West European systems of government. At a time of Soviet preoccupation with securing international recognition of the postwar division of Europe through Helsinki talks (which drew to a successful close only on August 1, 1975), this was hardly an unimportant consideration.

The CPSU leadership also made compromises of an organizational nature: it agreed in October 1974 to a pan-European communist party conference and a

13. For the text of their joint communiqué, see *l'Unità*, July 12, 1975.
14. "Vstrecha v TsK KPSS," *Pravda*, August 9, 1975.

rapprochement with the Spanish Communist Party. I have argued elsewhere that the idea of an all-European communist summit was directly linked to the Helsinki talks insofar as it enabled Moscow to claim that its pursuance of the Helsinki Accords did not imply acquiescence in the status quo in Western Europe.[15] Charges to this effect had already been made by the PCE and were soon to be echoed by the PCF. Even more galling to the Kremlin oligarchs, Spanish party spokesmen were calling for a socialist Western Europe independent of both the United States and the Soviet Union.[16] Indeed, this was probably the reason why, during the CPSU's bout of post-Chilean ultrasectarianism in early 1974, the Soviet party's agitprop biweekly, Partiinaia zhizn', singled out the PCE for direct castigation while confining its anti-PCI polemics to veiled innuendoes. To be specific, an unsigned editorial in February 1974 lambasted PCE leader Manuel Azcárate for supporting the above-mentioned foreign policy line.[17] Yet in the very next issue Alexander Sobolev merely denounced unnamed "contemporary revisionists" (read the PCE and PCI) for advocating "socialist pluralism."[18]

In any event, CPSU support of a pan-European communist party conference was a way of buttressing its ideological stature as the fountainhead of revolution in spite of Helsinki while simultaneously blunting the Spanish Communist Party's challenge to Soviet foreign policy. Indirect support for this interpretation is to be found in the apologetic tone of Boris Ponomarev's address at the consultative meeting in Warsaw in October 1974 that laid the procedural ground rules for the European communist party summit finally held in East Berlin in June 1976. In a word, Ponomarev conceded that during the 1960s Moscow may have slighted the interests of class struggle in the West because of the overriding necessity (as he put it) of ending the cold war.[19] Reading between the lines, one could conclude that the CPSU was now prepared to rectify that imbalance. Evidently the PCE thought so, for it agreed to the reconciliation with the Soviet party.

For reasons related both to the widening breaches within the pan-European communist movement and to the procedural rule of consensus agreed upon at the Warsaw consultative meeting, the twenty-month preparations for the Berlin conference turned out to be a political can of worms for Moscow. The

15. Joan Barth Urban, "The Ties that Bind: West European Communism and the Communist States of East Europe," in William E. Griffith, ed., The European Left: Italy, France, and Spain (Lexington, Mass.: Lexington Books, 1979), pp. 203–37 at pp. 211–14.

16. Mujal-León, Communism and Political Change in Spain, pp. 103–31.

17. "Po povodu stat'i rukovodiashchego deiatelia Kompartii Ispanii M. Askarate," Partiinaia zhizn', no. 4, February 1974, pp. 54–63.

18. "Aktual'nye problemy bor'by protiv pravogo revizionizma," Partiinaia zhizn', no. 5, March 1974, pp. 75–79 at p. 77.

19. Text in Pravda, October 18, 1974.

joint conference document finally agreed upon by the twenty-eight participants was plainly unsatisfactory in terms of conforming to the requirements of the CPSU sectarians.[20] It omitted any reference to the Suslovian "general laws of socialist construction" formulated by the late guardian of Marxist-Leninist orthodoxy after the Hungarian Revolution in 1956 and retained in force until his death. It substituted the Socialist International's slogan, "internationalist solidarity," for "proletarian internationalism," the CPSU's codeword for foreign communist party alignment with Moscow. And it denied that criticism of a given party's conduct was tantamount to anticommunism. What this meant in plain English was that Western communist criticism of Soviet domestic repression was not tantamount to "anti-Sovietism," as Moscow so insistently maintained. At the same time, the proceedings of the Berlin conference, represented by the delegates' formal speeches, testified to the actual pluralism that characterized the pan-European communist movement by mid–1976. The innovators were given equal time with the spokesmen for varying shades of sectarianism. And all were published verbatim in the GDR's party daily, *Neues Deutschland* (only to be censored in *Pravda*).

What, then, did the Soviet decision makers expect to gain from this spectacle of galloping "polycentrism"? First of all, *failure* to hold the Berlin meeting after so much publicity and preparation would have reflected poorly on the CPSU's pretentions to global ideological authority while deepening the fissures between Moscow and the more autonomist communist parties. Second, through the Soviet media's tested methods of censorship, distortion, and outright falsification, the extent not just of European communist party diversity but of non-ruling party criticism of the USSR's model of socialism was concealed from the Soviet people. Instead, an image of pan-European communist unity was projected in the Soviet central press which may have helped reinforce the domestic legitimacy of the CPSU.[21] Viewed more cynically, the Kremlin may have calculated that an accommodating demeanor toward its innovative European comrades would heighten the suspicions of official Western circles regarding the Eurocommunists' independence from Moscow and thereby undercut their domestic political clout. This, in turn, might ultimately weaken the influence of the innovators in the West European communist movement.

All the same, the CPSU concessions that made the Berlin meeting possible were slow in coming and grudging to the end. Soviet ambivalence toward developments in Portugal certainly complicated the process of forging a compromise with the Western communist party innovators. No sooner did the CPSU spokesmen involved in West European communist affairs start expounding upon the virtues of a democratic transitional stage than the radicalization of the Portuguese scene gave a hollow ring to their words. Indeed, the ostensibly

20. The English text appeared in *New Times* (Moscow), no. 28, July 1976, pp. 17–32.
21. Urban, "The Ties that Bind," p. 221.

102   JOAN BARTH URBAN

monolithic Soviet media began to speak with at least two voices. Throughout the spring and summer of 1975 commentaries in the specialized journals and even sometimes in *Pravda* reiterated Sobolev's winter 1975 initiative on the question of a democratic transitional stage,[22] specifying its relevance to the Portuguese situation on occasion.[23] The emphasis on cautious gradualism and broad alliances often went hand in hand with protests at the very idea of "the export of revolution."[24] Even in the issue of *Kommunist* sent to press on July 21, the height of the summer crisis in Portugal, Ponomarev stressed the importance of "*intermediate stages and transitional forms* on the paths to socialism" in the capitalist world.[25] By the same token, from March through June 1975 *Pravda* often portrayed Portuguese society as passing through a "transitional period defined . . . as the path to socialism in a multiparty framework."[26]

On the other hand, during this same period *Pravda*'s dispatches from Lisbon reported with open praise or barely concealed partiality (i.e., by citing PCP approval) the controversial sectarian maneuvers of the PCP/MFA radicals. Moreover, during the highly critical period from mid-July through mid-August, after the withdrawal of the moderate center-left parties from Portugal's fourth postcoup provisional cabinet in protest against the radicals' violations of democratic procedures, *Pravda*'s on-the-scene reports became even more slanted. News stories emanating from both TASS and the local *Pravda* correspondent began to accuse the Portuguese *Socialist* Party and the MFA moderates of colluding, first "objectively" and then "subjectively," with "counterrevolution and reaction."[27] Zarodov's *Pravda* article of August 6, 1975, represented a high-level imprimatur for this kind of reportorial militancy. At no point in his article did Zarodov actually mention Portugal. However, his attack on communist "moderates," "conciliators," and proponents of broad-alliance and electoral tactics was not just a rebuke of the West European innovators but also a defense of the PCP's exclusionary policies.

It may be recalled that CPSU talks with Italian communist leaders, which began the day after the publication of Zarodov's article, ended with a communiqué urging unity between the PCP and the purportedly "counterrevolutionary" Portuguese socialists! What this underscored was that the Soviet public

22. See, for example, T. Timofeev, "Znamia revoliutsionnoi bor'by proletariata," *Kommunist*, no. 6, April 1975, pp. 98–108; and "Kommunisty v bor'be protiv fashizm i voinu, za mir, demokratiiu i sotsializm: Doklad tovarishcha B. N. Ponomareva," *Kommunist*, no. 11, July 1975, pp. 11–28.
23. Timofeev, "Znamia revoliutsionnoi bor'by proletariata," p. 105.
24. Ibid.; cf. N. Lebedev, "O klassovoi prirode mirnogo sosushchestvovaniia," *Kommunist*, no. 4, March 1975, pp. 52–62 at p. 55.
25. "Kommunisty v bor'be protiv fashizm i voinu," p. 28; emphasis added.
26. *Pravda*, June 22, 1975; cf. Urban, "Contemporary Soviet Perspectives," pp. 1385–86.
27. Ibid., 1389–90.

attitude toward the revolution in Portugal was fraught with ambiguity. The reasons are not difficult to fathom. Considerations of Soviet foreign policy required caution, to say the least. The coincidence in timing between the radicalization of Portugal and the final preparations for the Helsinki summit, the capstone of Brezhnev's diplomatic efforts over four years, explains the CPSU's initial efforts to place Portuguese developments within the framework of the recently articulated strategy of the democratic transitional stage. At the same time, given the ideological matrix of Soviet power at home, the regime could hardly afford to turn its back on a proletarian revolution in progress. The Soviet masses may well have been more concerned with peace and prosperity than doctrinal vindication; indeed, I would argue that Brezhnev's tenacious insistence on the Helsinki summit was partly aimed at buttressing the Soviet regime's *domestic* image as the most active great-power proponent of peace and prosperity. But among CPSU cadres steeped in dogma since political adolescence, there must have been considerable residual commitment to the revolutionary precepts of Marxism-Leninism. This would explain the sectarians' preoccupation with the "lessons of Chile." More to the point, it would suggest broad support among party stalwarts for a forward strategy in Portugal.

The CPSU leadership coped with these contradictory requirements by combining reportorial militancy with editorial restraint in *Pravda, Kommunist,* and other party media. At no point did Moscow authoritatively endorse the PCP's bid for power. It was prepared to accept a *fait accompli,* as evidenced by the tenor of *Pravda*'s local coverage. It was not prepared to endanger détente by inciting a communist takeover. Nor was it ready to risk an open break with the Western communist moderates, as indicated by the compromise reached with the PCI during the talks of early August 1975.

CPSU caution and ambiguity toward Portugal were counterbalanced by Moscow's decision sometime in late August or early September 1975 to give decisive backing to the pro-Soviet MPLA in Angola, in terms of both military equipment and logistical support for the Cuban troops soon to arrive en masse.[28] Much has been written on the possible explanations for this shift in the USSR's policy toward Africa. Angola offered an ersatz "port of entry" for closer Soviet involvement with the hitherto pro-Chinese Frelimo guerrillas in Mozambique, the military revolutionaries in Ethopia, the radical liberationists of Zimbabwe and Namibia, and so forth. The eventual strategic advantage that could accrue to the Soviet Union from a political foothold in these areas was indisputable, especially in the wake of Moscow's setback in Egypt. The "Vietnam syndrome"

---

28. For careful documentation of this specific period, see Jiri Valenta, "Soviet Decision-Making on the Intervention in Angola," in David E. Albright, ed., *Communism in Africa* (Bloomington: Indiana University Press, 1980), pp. 93–117 at p. 102.

in the United States, of which Soviet analysts were well aware,[29] made massive American resistance to the contemplated Soviet action unlikely.

However, the coincidence in timing between the PCP's exclusion from power in Lisbon and the Soviet decision to intervene decisively in Luanda (late summer 1975) suggests that the need to compensate for yet another revolutionary failure after Chile was also an important, and perhaps paramount, motive for the move into Angola. The other considerations—strategic gains, U.S. passivity, pro-Soviet support from radical African liberation movements—remained potential and, in the case of Washington's reaction, uncertain. The need for the CPSU leaders to snatch victory from the jaws of defeat in Portugal was immediate, for all the ideological reasons noted above as well as because of the growing Western communist party charges (Vietnam notwithstanding) that the USSR had become a status quo superpower. The argument that the Soviet Union would have backed the MPLA to the hilt regardless of developments in Portugal is not entirely persuasive. A communist victory on the mainland might well have induced Soviet caution elsewhere. For the magnitude of the USSR's political-strategic gains from a PCP takeover in Portugal would have so stiffened Western resolve as to make any other Soviet course of action unduly provocative.

On September 17, 1975, Brezhnev granted a personal audience to Konstantin Zarodov, an event that was headlined on the front page of *Pravda*.[30] The ostensible occasion for this unusal honor was to congratulate Zarodov for his accomplishments as editor in chief of *Problems of Peace and Socialism* (*World Marxist Review* in its English edition). But the meeting, coming as it did on the heels of the political defeat in Lisbon yet before public knowledge of the CPSU's decision on Angola, was obviously meant to bolster the revolutionary sectarians. It was probably also intended as a rebuff to the French and Italian communist parties for their heated objections to Zardov's piece in *Pravda* on August 6. In any event, divergences among CPSU analysts of Western revolutionary trends once again surfaced in the specialized journals. While articles endorsing variations on the theme of a democratic transitional stage carried the by-lines of such prominent establishment ideologues as Vadim Zagladin, Ponomarev's deputy, more intransigent views also appeared.

A case in point was a commentary by Stepan Salychev in the late November 1975 issue of *Kommunist*. By way of background, in the early 1970s Salychev had conveyed the image of a revolutionary sectarian by arguing, in *Kommunist* and other journals, that mass pressure for the radical economic and political democratization of Western society was unleashing an open-ended revolutionary

29. For persuasive evidence on this point, see Morton Schwartz, *Soviet Perceptions of the United States* (Berkeley: University of California Press, 1978).
30. "Beseda u tovarishcha L. I. Brezhneva," *Pravda*, September 18, 1975.

process that would lead inexorably to the creation of socialism.[31] On the other hand, a review in April 1974 of Salychev's interwar history of the French Socialist Party, in what appeared to be a pointed rebuke, charged that he treated the question of "transitional forms of power" inadequately, especially with reference to its contemporary significance. It also implied that Salychev, by minimizing the Comintern's sectarian resistance in the early 1930s to "intermediate" democratic tasks, was in some sense guilty of the same errors.[32] Thereafter, Salychev faded from public view until late 1975 when in an article he wrote again of revolution in the West, with particular reference to mode rather than pace. Above all, he lambasted "parliamentary prejudices" and insisted that the elimination of bourgeois-democratic institutions, including the separation of powers, and their replacement by a "democracy of a new type" (read people's democracy?), was the precondition for revolutionary victory.[33] He said not a word on the question of a democratic transitional stage but stressed instead the primacy of extraparliamentary mass mobilization over parliamentary activity. In other words, his essay was an implicit defense of the PCP's conduct and a refutation of the PCI-PCF communiqué of mid-November 1975 (about which more will be said below) upholding bourgeois-democratic liberties, democratic alternation, and the separation of powers even under socialism.

CPSU spokesman flatly denied the existence of substantive differences among Soviet analysts on these questions.[34] By way of contrast, an article entitled "Debate in the USSR on Democracy and Revolution" appeared in the PCI daily *l'Unità* on December 9, 1975. The unsigned commentary not only contrasted the simplistic orthodoxy of the Salychev piece with a more nuanced article by Vadim Zagladin that welcomed "the search for new paths, forms, and methods of struggle," but it also rebuked Zagladin for his allusions to "ambiguous maneuvers" and "compromises that can lead to the loss of revolutionary identity" on the part of some Western comrades. For the Italian communists it was a matter of principle, retorted *l'Unità*, that there could be no advance toward socialism without the "consistent development of democracy which is expressed politically in the plurality of protagonists and in the real acquisition of consensus" by the working class and its political vanguard.[35] Implicit in this brief PCI

31. S. Salychev, "Ob osobennostiakh sovremennoi klassovoi bor'by v stranakh kapitala," *Kommunist*, no. 6, April 1973, pp. 71–85 at pp. 76–80.

32. Iu. Krasin, "Sotsialisty Frantsii: Uroki istorii," *Mirovaia ekonomika i mezhdunarodnye otnosheniia*, no. 4, April 1974, pp. 143–46.

33. S. Salychev, "Revoliutsiia i demokratiia," *Kommunist*, no. 17, November 1975, pp. 114–24. Thereafter Salychev's articles appeared with some regularity. See, for example, his favorable review of a book published in 1980 by Konstantin Zarodov in *Pravda*, September 18, 1980.

34. Boris Vesnin, "Anti-Communist Stratagems and Realities of the Communist Movement," *New Times*, no. 50, December 1975, pp. 18–19.

35. "Dibattito in URSS su democrazia e rivoluzione," *l'Unità*, December 9, 1975.

commentary were the three basic approaches to revolutionary strategy that were to form the crux of the pan-European communist debate on this subject for the rest of the decade: the orthodox sectarians' support for manipulation of the majority by a minority of communist activists; the cautious sectarians' acquiescence in a democratic transition to a communist-dominated society; and the innovators' call for electoral competition even during the stage of socialist transformation.

The French Puzzle. If the CPSU's revolutionary sectarians were mollified by Moscow's radical shift in Africa and their own public resurgence, the Kremlin still faced the problem of reaching an accommodation with the Western communist party innovators, as suggested by the *l'Unità* commentary. And here, much to the puzzlement of Western observers and perhaps even the Soviet leaders, a major source of difficulty turned out to be not Moscow's long-time critics, the PCI and PCE, but the traditionally archloyalist PCF. The chief bone of contention between the Soviet and French comrades, moreover, was not revolutionary strategy but Soviet foreign policy. The PCF followed not the PCI's pattern of questioning only the CPSU's ideological credentials but the PCE's pattern of challenging Moscow's foreign policy conduct as well. In a word, the French party strenuously objected to the USSR's cultivation of normal relations with the government of President Giscard d'Estaing. During the early 1970s, as already indicated, the CPSU confined its reaction to the PCI to indirect polemics over ideological nuances, while it subjected PCE spokesmen to explicit attacks in *Partiinaia zhizn'*. Its treatment of the PCF during 1974–76 was equally harsh, albeit of a somewhat different order.

If anything, Soviet overtures toward the French government during this period demonstrated in the most blatant manner possible that the perpetual tension between the raison d'être of the international communist movement and the raison d'état of the USSR had once again been resolved in favor of the latter. The highlights of Moscow's eagerness to pander to the powers that be in the Élysée need only be summarized here: the Soviet ambassador's visit to then presidential candidate Giscard d'Estaing between the first and second rounds of the closely contested presidential race of May 1974;[36] the Soviet media's enthusiastic commemoration of the fiftieth anniversary of Soviet-French diplomatic relations precisely at the time of the PCF's Twenty-first Congress in October 1974,[37] along with *Pravda*'s compression of Georges Marchais's critique at that congress of Giscard's pro-NATO policy into one terse sentence;[38] *Pravda*'s extensive and

36. For details, see Annette Eisenberg Stiefbold, *The French Communist Party in Transition* (New York: Praeger, 1977), pp. 135–37.

37. See, for example, A. Manfred, "SSSR-Frantsiia: Istoriia i sovremennost'," *Pravda*, October 27, 1974.

38. "Doklad general'nogo sekretaria FKP tovarishcha Zhorzha Marshe," *Pravda*, October 26, 1974; the same issue of *Pravda* carried a rather detailed report on President Giscard's press conference description of France's *independent* foreign policy.

glowing coverage of Brezhnev's state visit to Paris the following December; the Soviet leadership's warm reception in March 1975 of Premier Jacques Chirac, followed the next month by a visit to Moscow by Marchais's archrival, François Mitterrand. (Marchais could surely not have been gratified by Suslov's praise on that occasion for what the French socialists had done "in behalf of détente and coexistence."[39]) Then in mid-October 1975 President Giscard made a formal return visit to the USSR.

These Soviet overtures to the French center-right at a time of mounting left-wing electoral appeal in France were apparently taken by the PCF as a slap in the face. Indeed, the Giscard trip to the USSR in the aftermath of the Portuguese crisis suggested Moscow's interest in uninterrupted détente at the expense of revolution of any kind in Europe. As such it was the last straw for the French communist leadership. Again, we need only briefly recall the essentials of the PCF's reaction. On October 13, 1975, the day of Giscard's arrival in Moscow, *l'Humanité* published a Politburo resolution and an interview with international affairs spokesman Jean Kanapa, both of which sounded a categorical "*non*" to the Giscard government and a clarion call for domestic sociopolitical change.[40] The PCF had thrown down the gauntlet to the CPSU's policy of détente cum the status quo in France. This move was soon followed by the French communists' "discovery" of political repression in the USSR, a subject to which *l'Humanité* devoted increasing attention during the fall and winter of 1975–76.[41] Then came the electrifying PCF-PCI declaration in mid-November of common political principles that heralded the French party's shift to the emerging Euro-communist entente. Herein lies, of course, the French puzzle. For within four years the PCF would return full circle to the Soviet fold. Whether its two-pronged initiative of the mid–1970s (its move to distance itself from the CPSU and embrace the strategy of the Eurocommunist innovators) represented a vote-getting ruse or a genuine search for a more effective political profile remains an open question. Of greater concern for our purposes is the impact of the PCF's volte-face on Moscow's conduct toward the West European communist parties.

In a nutshell, the French Communist Party's behavior provoked what we might call a sectarian backlash on the part of the CPSU. The article by the Soviet revolutionary sectarian, Stepan Salychev, in the late November 1975 issue of *Kommunist* was Moscow's immediate riposte to the joint PCF-PCI communiqué. More significant, however, was the CPSU's intransigence at the November 17–19 meeting of the Editorial Commission for the Berlin conference.

39. See Claude Estier's notes on the talks between Mitterrand and the Soviet leaders in "9 Heures d'Entretien: La rencontre de Moscou," *l'Unité*, no. 156 (May 2–8, 1975), pp. 3–7.
40. For further details, see Urban, "The Ties that Bind," p. 218.
41. Ronald Tiersky, "French Communism in 1976," *Problems of Communism*, 25, no. 1 (January-February 1976): 20–47.

In contrast to a preceding meeting in early October when a compromise agreement on the final conference document seemed to be in the offing, the Soviet delegates reverted to their initial 1974 preference for an ideological pronunciamento—that is, a statement of a pan-European communist "general line" compatible with the Suslovian "general laws."[42]

There are several indications that this more rigid CPSU stance was both a reaction to the PCF's foreign policy challenge of mid-October and a bargaining ploy intended to persuade the French comrades to back down. Since the bilateral PCF-PCI statement was not published until November 18,[43] when the Editorial Commission was in midsession, it is unlikely that its pluralist connotations were the cause of the CPSU's obstinacy. The Soviet policy makers had probably assumed beforehand that a tougher stance on "principles" at the November editorial meeting would be to the liking of the traditionally orthodox French communist leaders. It was in fact Kanapa himself who had reacted to the October session's compromises by complaining that "the political content of the document has been reduced, impoverished."[44] At the same time, the composition of the CPSU delegation to the November meeting was "détentiste," or *cautious* sectarian, to the extreme. Not only was the delegation headed by Konstantin Katushev, the CPSU Politburo member in charge of ties with the *East* European communist parties, hence responsive to their interest in the economic advantages of détente; but the delegation also included G. K. Shakhnazarov, a Soviet international relations theorist prominently linked to the advocacy of improved East-West relations.[45] For instance, in an early 1974 *Kommunist* piece Shakhnazarov had argued that détente was essential not merely because of the threat of nuclear extinction but also because it would promote what the PCF so pointedly called for—a further shift in the global correlation of political forces in favor of world socialism.[46] In other words, it is arguable that at the November 1975 meeting the Soviets hoped for the French Communist Party's support for Franco-Soviet détente in exchange for a more sectarian line on the Berlin conference document.

If so, this Soviet maneuver failed because of the PCF's unexpected turn toward programmatic innovation. Consequently, while the French communists remained adamant in their public opposition to the Kremlin's efforts to curry favor with the Giscard regime, the CPSU returned to the policy of accommodation on the

---

42. Kevin Devlin, "The Challenge of Eurocommunism," *Problems of Communism*, 26, no. 1 (January-February 1977): 1–20 at pp. 6–9.

43. Text in *L'Humanité* and *l'Unità*, November 18, 1975.

44. Quoted in Devlin, "The Challenge of Eurocommunism," p. 6.

45. Zagladin was the third member of the delegation; *Pravda*, November 18, 1975.

46. G. Shakhnazarov, "K probleme sootnosheniia sil v mire," *Kommunist*, no. 3, February 1974, pp. 77–89.

Berlin conference noted earlier. PCF-CPSU tensions proceeded thereafter to in-
tensify. At the Twenty-fifth Congress of the CPSU in late February 1976,
Brezhnev, in what can only be considered a jab at the French Communist Party,
declared that Franco-Soviet *state* relations and views on a number of foreign
policy questions had grown closer. He claimed, moreover, that this had met
with "widespread support from the French people and *the majority of political
parties* in France."⁴⁷ Marchais, who had made a point of not attending the
CPSU congress, quickly informed the world that the PCF was not one of those
parties.⁴⁸ The CPSU then proceeded to deal the PCF leaders a behind-the-
scenes blow. According to the ex-Communist *apparatchik* François Hincker,
Moscow sent a scathing letter (apparently in April 1976) to the French party's
Central Committee calling for a reversal of the party's policy and, in effect, the
ouster of the Marchais-Kanapa leadership.⁴⁹ The letter, which Kanapa himself
read to the Central Committee at the beginning of May, elicited instead indignation against Moscow and resounding support for the PCF leaders. Nevertheless, this episode underscored the CPSU's sensitivity to any nonruling communist party challenge to the USSR's foreign policy. As would become abun-
dantly clear during the next few years, in the eyes of the Soviet leaders
ideological divergences among fraternal parties were negotiable; foreign policy
differences were not.

   Still, as of mid-1976 the CPSU appeared to have restored a precarious equilibrium within the pan-European communist movement by making concessions to both the revolutionary sectarians and the Eurocommunist innovators,
through militancy in Angola and compromise in Berlin. Only gradually would
it become evident that Moscow had in fact backed itself into a corner. For soon
the USSR's involvement in Angola would lead to a militarization of Soviet
policy in the Third World that would precipitate outspoken disagreement between the Western communist party innovators and Moscow precisely in the
area of Soviet foreign policy.

He Who Is Not with Us Is against Us

   On the threshold of the 1980s the CPSU's approach to the West European
communist parties underwent an ultrasectarian shift. Moscow's previous forbearance toward interparty divergences receded as foreign policy issues assumed
greater salience in the pan-European communist dialogue. Indeed, in mid-1977

47. *Pravda*, February 25, 1976; emphasis added.
48. On February 26, 1976, the day after Brezhnev's report appeared in *Pravda*, *l'Humanité*
retorted with verbatim excerpts from the PCF leader's biting attack on Giscard's foreign
policy at the French Party's Twenty-second Congress earlier that same month.
49. François Hincker, *Le parti communiste au carrefour: Essai sur quinze ans de son historie,
1965–1981* (Paris: Éditions Albin Michel, 1981), p. 167.

the Soviet party launched attacks against the leaderships of the Spanish, French, and Italian parties who had met as a group for the first—and only—time in Madrid in early March 1977.

"Anti-Sovietism" formed the catchall rubric on the basis of which each group of Western communist innovators was successively denounced. To be "anti-Soviet" was now tantamount not simply to anticommunism but to active collusion with imperialism. The politics of the international communist movement had once again become a zero sum game: he who was not with the CPSU was against it. Nevertheless, the cutting edge of the substantive Soviet attacks had to do more with foreign policy issues than with revolutionary strategy. As a matter of fact, divergences on this latter score between Moscow's own cautious sectarians and ultrasectarians had only intensified in the Soviet media, thereby precluding a concerted CPSU critique of nonruling parties on this account.

Furthermore, the targets of verbal abuse were apparently selected according to the criterion of which deviationist communist party was the most vulnerable at any given moment. Thus, Spanish communist leader Carrillo was first personally castigated in the Soviet foreign affairs weekly, *New Times*, only after the Spanish elections of spring 1977 revealed that support for the PCE amounted to less than 10 percent of the total popular vote. By the same token, *Kommunist* did not openly criticize the PCF until December 1978, after the seemingly definitive collapse of the *union de la gauche* following its defeat in the National Assembly elections of March 1978 and the recriminations that ensued between French communists and socialists as well as within the PCF itself. Soviet relations with the strongest of the Eurocommunist triad, the Italian Communist Party, form a special case in this context. For reasons that will be explored below, the PCI managed to challenge Moscow on discrete points of foreign policy with some impunity until the explosive turning points of Afghanistan and Poland.

The PCE and PCF: Targets of CPSU Pressure. As just indicated, the setbacks to the electoral prospects of the Spanish and French communist parties in 1977–78 made them particularly vulnerable to Soviet pressures—public and otherwise. No longer would overt CPSU criticism aid the Spanish and French party leaders' efforts to distance themselves from the USSR in the hope of enhancing their chance of entering government coalitions. Rather, Moscow could now expect its polemical assaults to encourage pro-Sovietism and orthodoxy at the base of the PCE and PCF. At the same time, attacks on the two parties for foreign policy divergences and "anti-Sovietism" were grounds upon which all CPSU sectarians, cautious and revolutionary, could agree. As for the specific targets, the PCE served as a scapegoat (and surrogate) for the Soviet leadership's apprehension over the more serious challenge to its authority posed by the larger French and Italian parties. By the same token, Soviet anger at the deviationist conduct of the PCF seemed all the more profound because of the French party's role dating back to the 1920s as second to none in pro-Soviet fidelity. Finally, the impact of the CPSU's campaign against the two parties was, in a somewhat paradoxical fashion, successful in both cases. For although Carrillo's reaction was wholly at odds with that of Marchais, whose ultimate capitulation was underscored by his defense over Soviet television of the USSR's invasion of Afghanistan,[50] each party was decisively weakened. The PCE became so factionalized that Carrillo's Eurocommunist stance posed little substantive threat to the CPSU's ideological credentials.[51] On the other hand, the PCF became so isolated on the domestic political scene—largely of course because of its leaders' deliberate undermining of the *union de la gauche* in 1977–78—that there appeared to be little other short-run alternative than to return to the party's traditional role as spokesman for Soviet interests.[52]

The nature of the Soviet polemics against the PCE, beginning with the widely publicized *New Times* attack on Carrillo's book *"Eurocommunism" and the State*, in June 1977,[53] illustrates some of the general observations made above. First of all, the PCE leader's call for coordinated Western communist party efforts in behalf of a socialist Western Europe "independent of the USSR and USA" bore the brunt of the CPSU reproaches, bringing to mind the *Partiinaia zhizn'* rebuke of Azcárate in February 1974. Rather illogically, given the PCE's opposition to Spain's entry into NATO, the anonymous Soviet polemicist also accused Carrillo of favoring a strengthened NATO. But upon reflection this charge simply revealed the CPSU leaders' fears that an independent Europe of any kind, Western or Eastern, socialist or not, would be in fact anti-Soviet if not pro-Atlanticist in international orientation.

The PCE's broad-gauged ideological critique of Soviet-style socialism was, in contrast to the foreign policy differences, played down in the CPSU polemics. For instance, the anti-Carrillo philippic of June 1977 maintained that there were two forms of Eurocommunism, the Spanish one and another supported by "the Left, including the Communist parties," which embraced "the present strategy of the Communist parties of the developed capitalist countries." While the first,

---

50. For Marchais's television interview in Moscow, see *l'Humanité*, January 12, 1980.

51. Eusebio Mujal-León deals with the fragmentation of the PCE into three groupings—Eurocommunist, traditional *ouvrièriste*, and pro-Soviet—in two articles: "Cataluña, Carrillo, and Eurocommunism," *Problems of Communism*, 30, no. 2 (March-April 1981): 25–47; and his contribution to the symposium, "Soviet Policies and Negotiating Behavior Toward Nonruling Communist Parties," *Studies in Comparative Communism*, 15, no. 3 (Autumn 1982): 236–65.

52. For a penetrating analysis of the French communist leadership's political mentality in the post-Stalin era, see the contribution of William J. Friend to the symposium cited in note 51.

53. "Contrary to the Interests of Peace and Socialism in Europe: Concerning the Book 'Eurocommunism and the State' by Santiago Carrillo, General Secretary of the Communist Party of Spain," *New Times*, no. 26, June 1977, pp. 9–13.

the PCE version, was downright anti-Soviet, the second was merely "erroneous" (given the fact that there was only "one" scientific communism). As a follow-up piece in *New Times* bluntly put it, the original commentary contained "not a single word . . . against the strategy" of any communist party. Rather, it dealt with "the *foreign policy* concepts and views set forth in Santiago Carrillo's book."[54]

Azcárate was, to be sure, roundly trounced in a pair of *New Times* articles in early 1978 for his denial of the "socialist" nature of the Soviet state, his rejection of Marxism-Leninism, and his defense of "ideological pluralism" under socialism.[55] Still, even after the PCE formally redefined itself at its Ninth Congress in April 1978 as "Marxist, democratic, and revolutionary"—rather than Leninist!—the Soviet *domestic* press generally limited itself to veiled slurs at unnamed "revisionists" or "leading circles" among Western communist parties who sought to water down Leninist principles.[56] Presumably, the Soviet policy makers were reluctant to reveal to their own people the degree to which some Western communist parties were diverging from the Soviet model of socialism.

This brings us to the final characteristic of the CPSU's anti-PCE diatribes—their publication for the most part in *New Times*, a propaganda weekly destined for foreign rather than domestic distribution. For the purpose of the attacks was to bring about a change in Spanish Communist Party policy or, at the very least, to threaten the PCF and PCI with similar polemical retaliation if they perserved in their mounting challenges to Moscow. The critiques were not intended to discredit the PCE in the eyes of the Soviet public. Far from it. As a matter of fact, the CPSU bent over backward to persuade Carrillo to attend the sixtieth anniversary celebrations of the October Revolution in November 1977. Not only was he assured of an opportunity to present his views during that gala event, but a feature article in *Pravda* in late October 1977 also lauded the achievements of the Spanish party and alluded sympathetically to Carrillo himself.[57] Even when the PCE chief was actually prevented from speaking in the Great Hall of the Kremlin on November 2, 1977 (for reasons not yet clarified), every effort was made to paper over the incident. The Soviet leadership pleaded innocence, claiming that Carrillo had arrived too late for his speech to be translated into the seventeen languages required for the occasion.[58] At the same time, as we

---

54. "Putting the Record Straight," *New Times*, no. 28, July 1977, pp. 16–17 at p. 16; emphasis added.

55. B. Andreev, "Playing up to Imperialist Anti-Soviet Propaganda," *New Times*, no. 3, January 1978, pp. 12–14; and "Why This Distortion of the Truth?" *New Times*, no. 6, February 1978, pp. 10–11.

56. For example, T. Timofeev, "Magistral'nye tendentsii revoliutsionnogo protsessa," *Kommunist*, no. 10, July 1978, pp. 75–83 at p. 79; and B. Leibzon, "Revoliutsionnyi avangard rabochego klassa," *Kommunist*, no. 5, March 1979, pp. 87–95.

57. V. Afanas'ev, "Ispaniia, oktiabr' 1977-go," *Pravda*, October 30, 1977.

58. Urban, "Moscow and the PCI," pp. 149–50.

shall see, they showered attention on Berlinguer as a token of their tolerance toward their Western communist party critics.

For some months the CPSU policy makers treated the PCF's defiant attitude more gingerly, at least on the public level. A curious exception to this general practice was a pair of ultrasectarian commentaries in the issue of *Kommunist* sent to press on March 3, 1978, and thus due to be published on the eve of the first round of the French parliamentary elections scheduled for March 12. In a nutshell, the lead editorial and a companion piece on revolutionary strategy in the capitalist world evoked the extreme sectarianism of the period before and after the overthrow of the Allende regime. The editorial baldly asserted that electoral activity should take second place to infiltration of the state bureaucracy, mass media, and forces of public order. The threat of force, if not its actual use, should remain a key weapon in the proletarian arsenal. Above all, under no circumstances should revolutionaries guarantee the survival of bourgeois political institutions, which must be overturned and replaced.[59] The accompanying article bluntly set forth as "general laws" of the *transitional stage* between capitalism and socialism injunctions that were identical to the Suslovian "general laws"—the leading role of the communist party, wholesale nationalization, the obligatory inculcation of Marxism-Leninism, and so forth.[60] Thus all that had been said since the mid-1970s regarding the possibility, even the advisability, of a democratic transitional stage seemed to have been reversed. This relapse into intransigency was, it turned out, only temporary. A more flexible position on all these questions reappeared in *Kommunist* the following summer under the by-line of Zagladin.[61] But this only begs the question *why* the ultrasectarian position was highlighted at such a delicate moment the previous spring.

One could argue that the radical rhetoric of March 1978 was a defensive ploy aimed primarily at the USSR's own party faithful. According to this interpretation, the criteria for a genuine revolutionary advance were made so stringent that they could not conceivably be met in the foreseeable future in Western Europe. Under these circumstances, it really didn't matter whether the *union de la gauche* won or lost. In light of past Soviet maneuvers during critical French elections, however, one could just as well view *Kommunist*'s orthodox outburst as a backhanded move to discredit the PCF through guilt by association with the CPSU. For Moscow most probably did favor the continuation of the status quo in France. Why upset the applecart of Franco-Soviet détente in exchange for the provocative victory of a leftist alliance whose political profile and inner balance were at best uncertain from the Soviet point of view?

59. "Revoliutsiia i demokratiia," *Kommunist*, no. 4, March 1978, pp. 3–15.

60. Iu. Poliakov, "Nekotorye problemy istorii perekhodnogo perioda ot kapitalizma k sotsializmu," ibid., pp. 53–64.

61. V. Zagladin, "Istoricheskaia missiia rabochego klassa i sovremennoe rabochee dvizhenie," *Kommunist*, no. 11, July 1978, pp. 67–80.

In any event, the CPSU's doubts concerning the PCF were publicly voiced in the late December 1978 issue of *Kommunist*. On the surface a critique of *l'URSS et nous*, an unflattering portrayal of the Soviet system coauthored by five PCF Sovietologists several months earlier, the piece amounted to an indictment of the French party leadership (which had given its seal of approval to the volume)[62] for caving in for reasons of electoral opportunism to "the sharply intensified anti-Soviet campaign and . . . the stepped-up pressure exerted by bourgeois and reformist propaganda on the French Communist Party itself."[63] The bulk of the *Kommunist* article was actually taken up with a detailed rebuttal of such "propaganda," and this explains its simultaneous dissemination beyond the Soviet borders in *New Times*. But above all the Soviet polemicists accused the authors—and their Politburo supporters—of trying to make the PCF's historic links to the USSR the scapegoat for the party's recent domestic setbacks.[64]

This oblique attack on the French communist leadership coincided with the convening of an international ideological conference in Sofia under the joint auspices of the Bulgarian Communist Party and none other than Konstantin Zarodov, in his capacity as editor in chief of *Problems of Peace and Socialism*. While the conference program called for a discussion of the theoretical problems related to building socialism, it turned into a polemical broadside against communist critics of actual, or "existing," socialism. As the Paraguayan Communist Party leader put it, "anti-Sovietism" had now become the "main danger" to the world communist movement.[65] On this score the Peking regime was as usual lambasted. More notable, however, was the chorus of reproaches leveled against Eurocommunism. Explicit attacks by the Czechoslovak leader Vasil Bilak and a half dozen nonruling party representatives (those from Norway, Luxemburg, Israel, Canada, Jordan, and Turkey) were accompanied by veiled innuendoes by many other party spokesmen.[66] The French and Spanish delegates blinked, as it were, and confined themselves to bland expositions of their domestic programs. In contrast, the PCI's Michele Rossi not only pointedly reiterated the entire range of political-ideological issues on which his party differed from the CPSU, he also threatened that the PCI would withdraw from the editorial board of Zarodov's journal should it be involved in organizing such polemical and unproductive conferences in the future.[67] In short, the Italian party was becoming increasingly isolated; but it continued to stand its ground.

62. For the official English version, see E. Ambartsumov, F. Burlatsky, Y. Krasin, and E. Pletnyov, "Against Distortion of the Experience of Real, Existing Socialism," *New Times*, no. 52, December 1978, pp. 18–28.

63. Ibid., p. 19.

64. Ibid., p. 26.

65. *World Marxist Review*, 22, no. 3 (March 1979): 30–33 at p. 33.

66. For abridged texts of the conference speeches, see *World Marxist Review*, 22, no. 2–4 (February–April 1979), pp. 3–27, 3–107, and 3–73.

67. *World Marxist Review*, 22, no. 3, pp. 47–51 at p. 51.

The PCI: Moscow's Recourse to the Carrot and the Stick. In contrast to Moscow's verbal abuse of the PCE and PCF, the CPSU reacted to the PCI's ideological challenge during the late 1970s with veiled and indirect polemics, stopping short of openly accusing the Italian party of anti-Sovietism. This restraint was probably due to the CPSU's fear of detracting from its public image as the vanguard of a worldwide revolutionary movement by attacking the probity of its most numerous nonruling member.

The Soviet leadership's conciliatory approach to the PCI was underscored at the USSR's sixtieth anniversary celebration in November 1977. In contrast to the muzzling of Carrillo on that occasion, Berlinguer was permitted to give an address that stressed the PCI's pluralist program. Moreover, the next day, despite the crush of delegates from over a hundred countries, Brezhnev, Suslov, and Ponomarev found time to meet with Berlinguer for fifty minutes "in an atmosphere of cordiality and friendship."[68] The Soviet leaders' respectful treatment of Berlinguer was plainly intended to prevent the negative publicity surrounding the Carrillo incident from unduly tarnishing the image of international communist unity that they were so determined to project. As for Berlinguer, he graciously went along with the CPSU leaders' attentiveness, not the least because in the eyes of his pro-Soviet constituency (whatever its magnitude) he stood only to gain from the public acclaim accorded him in Moscow.

On the other hand, although the CPSU exhibited considerable forbearance toward the Italian communists' programmatic deviations from Soviet norms, it also threatened to resort to ever more explicit polemical attacks should the PCI embark on a more broad-gauged critique of the CPSU's global ideological authority or international conduct. As in the case of the PCE and PCF, recourse to public polemics would enable Moscow to convey to the Italian party's rank and file the Soviet dissatisfaction with official PCI positions, thereby helping to fan the considerable disagreement that already existed at the PCI's base over such issues as the historic compromise and the party's condemnation of the Soviet invasion of Czechoslovakia.[69]

Yet the CPSU also held out the promise of Soviet-PCI summitry as a carrot to induce Italian communist accommodations to Soviet policies. Berlinguer's meeting with the top Soviet leaders in November 1977 was a case in point. The reasoning behind this Soviet gambit was clear. The Kremlin was well aware that just as the Italian communist leaders feared the impact of direct Soviet attacks on their party's internal cohesion, they also needed evidence of Moscow's approbation as a means of mollifying traditionalist or pro-Soviet elements in their ranks. This was especially true during 1977–78 when the PCI's de facto

68. For details, see Urban, "Moscow and the PCI," p. 150.
69. For survey data on such dissent, see Kevin Devlin, "The PCI and Its 'Afghans,'" *Radio Free Europe Research*, Background Report no. 113, April 23, 1981.

cooperation with the Christian Democratic establishment in Italy exacerbated the disorientation and dissent noted above.

For some time the Soviet leaders' use of diplomatic kid gloves in their dealings with the PCI seemed to work to their advantage: the Italian party's criticism of Soviet foreign policy remained fairly restrained and selective throughout the 1970s. To be sure, the Italian communists took issue with Moscow's handling of its dispute with Peking and condemned out of hand its invasion of Czechoslovakia. But their support for the European Economic Community and accommodation to Italy's membership in NATO were couched in the terms of an adaptation to national conditions, not a dissent from the Soviet position on these questions. Only in 1978 did foreign policy differences begin to impinge on PCI-CPSU divergences over the mode of socialist construction. At that time the Italian party's disagreements with certain aspects of Soviet behavior in black Africa verged on a more general criticism—that is, Moscow's tendency (according to PCI observers) to rely on military force rather than economic and political aid to advance the cause of Third World liberationism.

For example, the PCI reversed its initially favorable view of revolutionary developments in Ethiopia as the new Addis Ababa regime, now armed with Soviet weapons, moved to suppress the Eritrean national liberation movement. Accordingly, in mid-May 1978 l'Unità carried a front-page commentary flatly declaring that the new Ethiopean regime should prove that it was "really new" by recognizing the right of the Eritreans to self-government, a cause to which the "socialist countries" should also commit themselves by virtue of "their presence in Ethiopia."[70] Soon thereafter a second front-page l'Unità piece voiced criticism of overall Soviet military involvement in Africa. While justifying the initial Cuban move into Angola as a response to South African intervention, it expressed alarm over the extension of the "Cuban presence" to a "Soviet military presence of notable proportions," over the reemergence in the African context of "what seems to us a temptation . . . to make the expansion of the liberation process coincide with the stipulation of political-military alliances and the conquest of zones of influence."[71]

Since the new PCI position on Africa paralleled the CPSU ultrasectarian campaign against Eurocommunism qua "anti-Sovietism," there can be little doubt but that Moscow's slurs were also aimed, however obliquely, at the Italian party. The PCI thus sought to defend itself by advertising in multiple ways its readiness for a rapprochement with Peking. During July 1978 l'Unità published an unusual series of favorable commentaries on life in China.[72] In

70. Romano Ledda, "L'Eritrea non è l'Ogaden: La prova di forza etiopica non si giustifica," l'Unità, May 18, 1978.

71. Romano Ledda, "Ma l'Africa non è degli africani?" l'Unità, June 7, 1978, p. 13; emphasis added.

72. Emilio Sarzi Amadè, "Il 'profitto' di Sun Yeh-fang: Cosa cambia in Cina dopo la caduta dei 'quattro'," and "Pechino: I segnali della politica estera," l'Unità, July 19 and 21, 1978.

August the PCI daily carried extensive coverage of Chinese communist leader Hua Guofeng's tour of Romania and Yugoslavia. And in early September Gian Carlo Pajetta discussed at length, in several press interviews, the desirability of normal interparty relations with the Chinese communists.[73]

The CPSU, in turn, held out the offer of a summit meeting with Berlinguer as a means of dissuading him from the rapprochement with Peking, delivering the invitation in mid-September,[74] that is, shortly after Pajetta's public broaching of the normalization idea. Berlinguer probably welcomed the opportunity to re-affirm his party's ideological credentials through a Moscow summit at a time of growing doubt among PCI militants regarding their party's compromising, quasi-governmental status. Indeed, because of the need to dampen innerparty criticism, the PCI leadership was quite prepared to delay the restoration of ties with Peking in exchange for polemical restraint on the part of the CPSU. Still, on October 6, 1978, the very eve of his departure for Moscow, Berlinguer pointedly reiterated the possibility of a rapprochement with the Chinese party as a means of enchancing his bargaining power.[75]

Both the official Soviet-PCI communiqué published on October 10 and sub-sequent developments indicate that a mutual deal had been reached. On the one hand, the communiqué included a joint condemnation of antidétente moves by "certain imperialist, *militarist*, and reactionary circles,"[76] the term militarist denoting the Chinese in the current Soviet lexicon, while Berlinguer conceded in a press conference upon his return to Rome that "for now" the PCI would not normalize relations with the Chinese.[77] On the other hand, the communiqué also reiterated a major Soviet concession made at the 1976 Berlin conference: the legitimacy of disagreements among communist parties. In short, the Italian leader agreed to postpone (not renounce!) a rapprochement with Peking in return for continued Soviet forbearance with regard to the PCI's multiplying divergences from the CPSU line.

The CPSU actually did exhibit considerable restraint toward the PCI for some time thereafter. Although the twin bogies of Eurocommunism and anti-Sovietism continued to be roundly trounced in the Soviet press, it was – as we have seen – the French party rather than the PCI that was singled out for direct attack in *Kommunist* in December 1978. And at the international communist ideological conference of Sofia that same month the PCI was included only by implication in the many attacks on Eurocommunism.

73. See, for example, his interview in *l'Unità*, September 9, 1978.
74. See Frane Barbieri's report in *la Stampa*, October 15, 1978.
75. "Berlinguer a Mosca dopo i colloqui con Marchais," *l'Unità*, October 7, 1978.
76. "Sovmestnoe kommiunike o prebyvanii tovarishcha E. Berlinguera v Sovetskom Soiuze," *Pravda*, October 10, 1978.
77. "L'iniziativa internazionale del PCI: Berlinguer a Roma parla del suo viaggio," *l'Unità*, October 12, 1978.

BEYOND BIPOLARITY: THE MEANING OF THE CPSU-PCI RIFT

The delicate modus vivendi between the CPSU and the PCI collapsed in 1980–81 over Afghanistan and Poland. Public sparring over foreign policy differences had already resumed in 1979, especially regarding the question of theater nuclear forces in Europe. Then the Soviet Army's march into Afghanistan at the end of the year triggered Italian communist accusations that the USSR was engaging in "bloc politics" superpower style. Soviet intimidation of Poland during the fall and winter of 1980–81 further exacerbated tensions. But it was the military crackdown in Poland on December 13, 1981, that caused the Italian communist leadership to spell out in unequivocal terms its vision of the future correlation of forces in Europe. The PCI looked beyond bipolarity to the day when an independent Western Europe would play an autonomous role in the international arena and a reunited European workers' movement would become the "epicenter" of a new phase in the world march toward socialism. The Italian party's views were almost indistinguishable from those articulated by Spanish communist leaders in the early and mid–1970s. And the CPSU's reaction was even more furious and uncompromising toward the PCI than it had been toward the PCE. The Kremlin plainly wanted nothing to do with an independent socialist Western Europe.

The PCI Reaction to Afghanistan: "Bloc Politics" Superpower Style. By way of introduction, the PCI approached the theater nuclear force controversy that erupted in the fall of 1979 by calling from the outset for East-West negotiations to determine the true state of the military-strategic balance in Europe. In other words, it equivocated on whether or not the Soviet replacement of older weapons with the mobile and MIRVed SS–20 intermediate-range missiles had tilted that balance in the USSR's favor. To be sure, the PCI opposed the NATO plan to deploy U.S. cruise and Pershing II medium-range missiles on the Continent and voted against Italy's support for it. But it also refused to accept at face value Brezhnev's October 6, 1979, assertions in East Berlin that the USSR had in no way altered the Eurostrategic balance. Instead the PCI formally proposed, in a *Direzione* resolution of October 16, 1979, that a NATO–Warsaw Pact conference "ascertain the real state of nuclear armaments in Europe," correcting by means of arms reductions any imbalances that might come to light.[78]

Pajetta boasted in a November 1979 report to the PCI Central Committee that the Italian party was free of "any prejudice toward this or that great power" in taking the position it did on the theater nuclear force issue. This remark, however self-serving, was indicative of a growing tendency among the Italian communists to treat the Soviet-American relationship as a great-power confrontation in which ideological considerations had become secondary. All

78. Text in *l'Unità*, October 18, 1979.

the same, the PCI was still not ready for an evenhanded attitude toward Moscow and Washington. For instance, in the same report Pajetta explained the worsening of Soviet-American relations in a manner reminiscent of revisionist interpretations of the origins of the cold war: influential U.S. circles were seeking a confrontation with the Soviet Union as a rationale for imposing American economic and political policies on Western Europe, and this, in turn, was leading Moscow to fortify its own "political-military and economic bloc."[79]

In the wake of the Soviet invasion of Afghanistan, however, PCI analyses became notably less encumbered by ideological arguments. Thus in January 1980 party spokesmen and documents denounced the USSR for its "act of aggression"[80] against Afghanistan and the United States for its provocative hard-line posture toward the USSR (the TNF decision and the shelving of SALT II), inveighing against the "logic of confrontation" between the two superpowers that was threatening the world with nuclear disaster.[81] Similarly, when Berlinguer was asked upon his return from China who most threatened world peace, he replied: "The greatest danger . . . arises from a growing confrontation [*contrapposizione*] between the two supreme powers."[82] This assessment permitted the PCI leaders to take a more evenhanded approach to the transgressions of the two superpowers while upholding their ideological preference for socialism.

The CPSU's initial reaction to this provocative PCI behavior remained relatively restrained. Berlinguer's normalization of party ties with Peking during his April 1980 trip to China met with a direct, albeit mild, reproach in *New Times*.[83] But on the whole, both *New Times* and *Problems of Peace and Socialism* confined themselves to indirect polemics—that is, attacks on unnamed communist party leaders who opposed Soviet conduct in Afghanistan or blamed the deterioration of détente on the logic of superpower confrontation rather than U.S. provocation.[84] At the same time, the sudden convening in April 1980 of a pan-European "peace" conference in Paris was a clear sign of Soviet displeasure over Italian communist policy on Afghanistan and China. Moscow had during the winter of 1980 broached the idea of an all-European communist party meeting to rally opposition to the recent NATO decision to install

---

79. Text in *l'Unità*, November 15, 1979.

80. The phrase is used editorially in a report on Berlinguer's speech to a meeting of PCI provincial secretaries, in *l'Unità*, January 27, 1980.

81. See ibid.; also text of *Direzione* resolution, *l'Unità*, January 6, 1980; and Berlinguer's speech on the fifty-ninth PCI anniversary, *l'Unità*, January 21, 1980.

82. Berlinguer press conference, *l'Unità*, April 28, 1980.

83. I. Ivanov, "On the Visit of the Italian Communist Party Delegation to Peking," *New Times*, no. 20, May 1980, pp. 10–11.

84. See, for example, "World Communist Solidarity with the Afghan Revolution," *New Times*, no. 3, January 1980, pp. 8–10; and Boris Ponomarev, "Pakt mira i pakt agressii," *Problemy mira i sotsializma*, no. 8, August 1980, pp. 3–10.

medium-range nuclear missiles in Europe. But only in the early spring were plans for such a conference abruptly finalized by the CPSU and its once again loyalist PCF supporters—despite the PCI's privately expressed opposition to the very idea of a peace rally limited solely to communists as early as January 1980 in talks with Marchais.[85] The coincidence in timing (mid-March 1980) between the issuance of the invitations to the Paris meeting and the PCI's public announcement of its intention to normalize relations with the Chinese communists the following month hardly seems accidental.[86] Indeed, Moscow's decision to proceed with the Paris conference in the face of PCI opposition may have been partly intended as a rap on the Italian communists' knuckles for their rapprochement with Peking. Notable in this context was the fact that the Spanish, Yugoslav, and Romanian communist parties—all committed to normal relations with the Chinese communists—also boycotted the Paris meeting.

There was a clear line of continuity between the PCI's stand on Afghanistan and China and its reaction to the Polish strike movement that erupted in the summer of 1980. PCI support for the revolutionary changes under way in Poland in 1980–81 was significantly more assertive than its stand in behalf of the Dubček reformers in 1968. Then, the PCI leaders—along with their French and Spanish comrades—had confined themselves to bringing behind-the-scenes pressure to bear upon Moscow in an effort to prevent the military suppression of the Prague Spring.[87] Now, in the case of Poland, the Italian communists not only emphasized the negative aspects of the political system under attack, but they also threatened a rupture with the CPSU should the Soviets resort to military intervention, rejecting the "quiet diplomacy" that had proven so ineffective in deterring the invasion of Czechoslovakia twelve years earlier.

On August 19, 1980, shortly after the outbreak of massive strikes in the Baltic coast shipyards, the editor of the PCI daily blamed the Polish crisis on the "pyramidal and totalitarian" (*totalizzante*) nature of Poland's Soviet-style political structures and called for the development of "democracy and participation" forthwith.[88] Thereafter, the PCI press as well as official party statements steadfastly hailed both the victories of Solidarity and the ascendancy of reformers within the Polish party itself. Meanwhile, as the threat of a Soviet invasion of

85. See Gian Carlo Pajetta's report on the PCI's opposition to the Paris peace rally in *l'Unità*, April 3, 1980.

86. The "mid-March" date was mentioned by Antonio Rubbi in "L'iniziativa internazionale del PCI," *Rinascita*, 37, no. 15 (April 11, 1980): 3–4. The PCI's *public* announcement of Berlinguer's trip to Peking was made at a Central Committee meeting on March 14, 1980; see *l'Unità*, March 16, 1980.

87. Jiri Valenta, *Soviet Intervention in Czechoslovakia, 1968* (Baltimore: Johns Hopkins University Press, 1979), pp. 67–69.

88. Alfredo Reichlin, "Il nostro invito," *l'Unità*, August 19, 1980; cf. unsigned editorial, "La Polonia è già diversa," *l'Unità*, August 31, 1980.

Poland mounted in the fall of 1980, with Warsaw Pact maneuvers on all borders, the Italian party made known its categorical opposition to such a step during top-level PCI-CPSU talks in Rome on December 9 and 10. The precise contents of what was described by both sides as a "long and frank discussion" were not disclosed.[89] The substance of the Italian position can, however, be inferred from a communiqué issued by the PCI *Direzione* on the first day of the talks which warned that "military intervention" in Poland would have the "gravest consequences" and confirmed that this view had been unequivocally communicated to the socialist countries involved.[90] The PCI's message to the CPSU, according to noncommunist sources, threatened a de facto break in relations between the two parties in the event of a Soviet invasion,[91] a report that the PCI neither affirmed nor denied. What the Italians did say publicly in a front-page *l'Unità* editorial on December 10—while the Italian-Soviet talks were still going on—was that even the suggestion of intervention "already represents an unacceptable limitation of sovereignty."

Still, the CPSU refrained from all but the most mild direct criticisms of the PCI during this period. Only in the winter of 1981, after the PCI's blunt warning to the Soviets to keep their hands off Poland during the December 1980 talks between Zagladin and Berlinguer did the CPSU shift to polemics and organizational sanctions aimed explicitly at the Italian party. Even then the Soviets seemed to hold out the possibility of compromise. In the January 1981 issue of *Voprosy istorii KPSS* one Gennadi (Enrico) Smirnov, a close associate of Ponomarev's and former Soviet diplomat in Rome, deplored the PCI's "contradictory search for an 'intermediate' place . . . in a world divided into blocs," and he chided "certain Italian comrades" for avoiding a clear characterization of NATO as "aggressive."[92] Yet he also pointedly dissociated Berlinguer from these reproaches, thereby giving the Italian leader a chance to place himself in Moscow's corner at the forthcoming Twenty-sixth Congress of the CPSU. However, on February 12 the PCI officially let it be known that Berlinguer would boycott the congress,[93] the first time since Stalin's death that an Italian general secretary had done so.

89. *L'Unità*, December 11, 1980; *Pravda*, December 11, 1980. The Soviet delegation was headed by Zagladin. Significantly, the Italian delegation included Antonio Rubbi, who had just returned from three days in Warsaw where, as reported by *l'Unità* on December 7, 1980, he had a "long and *cordial* discussion" with Polish leaders; emphasis added.

90. "Passi ufficiali del PCI presso i PC dell'Est," *l'Unità*, December 10, 1980.

91. *La Repubblica*, December 9, 1980.

92. G. P. Smirnov, "Ital'ianskaia Kommunisticheskaia Partiia," *Voprosy istorii KPSS*, no. 1, January 1981, p. 98; cf. *l'Unità*, February 7, 1981, regarding the identity of the author, known as "Enrico" in Italy.

93. "La delegazione del PCI al Congresso PCUS," *l'Unità*, February 12, 1981; cf. *la Stampa*, February 10, 1981.

At this point the Soviets took the offensive. On February 13 the world learned that a CPSU Central Committee letter to the PCI leadership, evidently written after the abortive Soviet-PCI talks the previous December, had been leaked to the Italian newsweekly *Panorama*.[94] The letter, reportedly drafted by Smirnov and Zagladin and approved by Ponomarev and Brezhnev himself,[95] accused the Italian party of objectively supporting "those forces which have in Poland unleashed a veritable offensive against socialism." Other such letters had apparently been sent to the PCI in the past, but this was the first one to be made public. On the heels of this leak came the Soviet refusal to permit Pajetta, Berlinguer's representative to the February 1981 CPSU congress, to present the PCI's customary greetings from the congress podium unless he deleted some—rather circumspect— criticisms of the Soviet intervention in Afghanistan and intimidation of Poland.[96] This Pajetta declined to do. He was thus prevented from addressing the congress, in a replay of the rebuff Carrillo had received in November 1977. (The only difference was that Pajetta went along with the Soviet concession of letting him deliver his uncensored remarks at a minor gathering some blocks from the Kremlin.) Thereafter, for the remainder of 1981, the CPSU's open attacks on the PCI moved from the pages of such esoteric journals as *Voprosy istorii KPSS* to the more general forum of *New Times*.[97]

The PCI Reaction to Poland: A European Alternative to Socialism Soviet Style. The Polish regime's imposition of martial law on December 13, 1981, brought PCI-Soviet tensions to a head. Italian communists criticized not just the Polish move but also Soviet foreign policy across the board. In addition, the PCI leaders articulated what had hitherto been only implicit in their programmatic statements: the need for a European alternative to socialism Soviet style that would be democratic in the Western sense and serve as an inspiration both to socialist advances in the Third World and to reform of the Soviet-bloc systems themselves. If the PCI's challenge resembled that of the Spanish Communist Party in the mid-1970s, Moscow's reaction can better be compared to its treatment of the Chinese communists two decades earlier. The CPSU denounced the Italian Communist Party leaders by name in its official organs, *Pravda* and

94. "A proposito di un documento pubblicato da 'Panorama'," *l'Unità*, February 14, 1981.
95. Carlo Rossella, "Breznev manda a dire . . . ," *Panorama*, February 23, 1981, pp. 83 and 85.
96. See the reports of this incident in the *Washington Post*, February 27, 1981; *la Repubblica*, March 1–2, 1981; and *l'Unità*, February 28, 1981. The text of Pajetta's speech appears in ibid.
97. Y. Samoilov, "Strange Position: Concerning an Article in the Italian Journal *Rinascita* about the Events in Poland," and E. Fryazin, "The Communists Fight for Peace: Concerning the Speech by Romano Ledda at the Italian Communist Party Plenum," in *New Times*, nos. 26 and 47, June and November 1981, pp. 14–15 in each issue.

Kommunist, and proceeded to mobilize an international communist campaign of collective censure against them. Loyalist communist parties around the world echoed the Soviet polemics. These foreign communist attacks were then reprinted in a series of articles in *New Times* (published in an Italian edition since October 1980) and, beginning in March 1982, in *Pravda* as well. The latest test of pro-Sovietism had thus become a given communist party's readiness to criticize the PCI.

The PCI's immediate response to developments in Warsaw was a number of informal statements by top-ranking party leaders condemning out of hand the crackdown in Poland and linking it directly to the USSR's postwar pattern of rule in Eastern Europe. According to Berlinguer, the Polish military dictatorship demonstrated that the progressive impulses unleashed by the Russian Revolution itself had been exhausted.[98] These ad hoc views received the imprimatur of the PCI *Direzione* in a resolution published in *l'Unità* at the end of December.[99] In a categorical yet nonpolemical manner, the document attributed the suppression of Solidarity in part to the "persisting dogmatism, conservative positions, [and] inertia" within the Polish Communist Party. But it placed equal blame for this turn of events on the Soviet Union's "pressures, undue interference, and battering political and ideological campaign against the effort at renewal in which an important part of the POUP [Polish Communist Party], Solidarity, and the Church were engaged." At the same time, the resolution delivered a ringing indictment of the USSR's postwar imposition of its model of socialism on Eastern Europe and its repeated crushing of all reform initiatives in that area. With the revolutionary credentials of the CPSU thereby discredited, the document enjoined the West European left to take the lead in the worldwide advance toward socialism as well as in the "democratic renewal" of the communist societies in the Soviet orbit. Perhaps most offensive to Soviet Leninist doctrine, it vowed that the PCI would seek to maintain "normal relations" with communist parties just as with all other socialist and progressive groups but "without particular or privileged ties with anyone." The resolution thus rejected once and for all "the idea of a homogeneous communist movement separated from the totality of forces in the international workers' movement."

The position of the PCI *Direzione* on Poland was upheld (with only one negative vote and two abstentions) at a meeting of the party's Central Committee in mid-January 1982. But in his report to that body Berlinguer went even further than the December resolution, explicitly equating the USSR's foreign policy line with that of the United States. The PCI general secretary spelled out what had been implicit in his party's reaction to the Afghan crisis: he accused the Soviet Union, like the United States, of engaging in sheer "bloc politics," of

98. See the articles by Franco Pepitto and Miriam Mafai in *la Repubblica*, December 18, 1981.
99. Text in *l'Unità*, December 30, 1981.

seeking the expansion of its own power not just in Eastern Europe or Afghanistan but on a global scale. As Berlinguer expressed it, "the two great powers [continue to] work for the rigid maintenance of blocs and their logic and, more generally, for the defense and possibly the extension of their mutual areas of influence."[100] It was in this context that he underscored the PCI's vision of moving beyond bipolarity to a situation wherein Western Europe would play an autonomous role in the international arena and a leading role in the global march toward socialism.

The distinction between the challenge to the CPSU's ideological authority represented by the PCI statements on Poland during the second half of December 1981 and Berlinguer's subsequent frontal attack on Soviet foreign policy in mid-January 1982 was apparently crucial. For the Soviet leadership responded to the PCI's opposition to the military crackdown in Poland merely with a confidential letter from the CPSU Central Committee.[101] That letter, to be sure, defended the Polish regime's action (as well as Moscow's innocence in this regard) and deplored the PCI's falsifications and "violent criticisms" directed at both the Polish and Soviet communist parties. Nevertheless, it was Berlinguer's global critique of Soviet conduct that led to a *public* polemical offensive unparalleled in the history of recent CPSU relations with the West European communist parties.

In a biting riposte in *Pravda* on January 24, 1982,[102] the CPSU called the PCI's equation of Soviet and American foreign policies "truly blasphemous," given the "aggressive, militaristic" nature of imperialism and the "NATO bloc." In this sense it was reminiscent of the *New Times* attack of June 1977 on Carrillo for his "monstrous statement" that the Soviet Union was a "'superpower' . . . [that] pursues great-power objectives."[103] But the *Pravda* diatribe recalled the earlier campaign against the Spanish communists in yet another way. It derisively dismissed the Italian party's positive appraisal of the initiatives of some West European "bourgeois" governments (read the Federal Republic of Germany) on such issues as arms control and détente, thereby again betraying Moscow's anxiety over any signs of an independent constellation of West European democratic socialist forces. Only toward the end did the unsigned editorial broach ideological issues, charging that the PCI leaders had over the years engineered "a gradual departure from the Marxist-Leninist platform" under the guise of "cunning theoretical and political 'innovations'" and had "openly come out against world socialism" with their position on Poland. Such

100. Text in *l'Unità*, January 12, 1982; see p. 8.
101. Text in *l'Unità*, March 17, 1982; the letter was received by the PCI Secretariat on January 2, 1982.
102. "Vopreki interesam mira i sotsializma," *Pravda*, January 24, 1982.
103. "Contrary to the Interests of Peace and Socialism in Europe," p. 12.

conduct, the statement concluded, amounted to giving "aid to imperialism, . . . aid to anti-Communism and to all forces hostile to the cause of social progress." *Kommunist* published almost simultaneously an even harsher commentary that lambasted the PCI leaders for "distorting" Soviet foreign policy in general, for supporting counterrevolution in Poland, and for "repeating almost word for word the fabrications of Reagan, Weinberger, Haig, Brzezinski and other imperialist politicians" on the Polish question.[104] Meanwhile, although the Soviet media did not publish the PCI documents in question—just as they had declined to do during the Sino-Soviet polemics of the 1960s—so-called information assemblies were held throughout the USSR for CPSU cadres at which official speakers repeated, often with rhetorical embellishments, *Pravda*'s accusations against the PCI.[105] By late February *New Times* was ready to begin publication of excerpts from the loyalist communist party diatribes against the Italian party.[106] The contents of those polemics varied from party to party. Nevertheless, the PCI's "preposterous" equation of Soviet foreign policy with the superpower politics of NATO and Washington constituted a major focal point. The second installment of the *New Times* series went even further, taking note editorially of the identity of foreign policy views expressed in *l'Unità* and the Chinese communist *People's Daily*, "which openly lines up with imperialist forces against the Soviet Union and détente."[107] In early March the appearance in *Pravda* of an article by the American communist leader, Gus Hall, condemning the "Eurocommunist" views of Berlinguer and Carrillo, marked yet a further step in the escalation of the Soviet-PCI rift.[108]

CONCLUSIONS

A central theme of this chapter has been Moscow's low threshold of tolerance for West European communist party challenges to Soviet foreign policy. Western communist compliance with the CPSU's political-ideological norms may be negotiable, but backing of the USSR in the international arena is not. Indeed, it would appear that for the men in the Kremlin—in recent years as under Stalin—the true measure of a nonruling communist party's ideological probity is its readiness to subordinate its own interests to those of the Soviet state.

104. For the official English version, see "On a Slippery Path: Concerning Recent Statements by the Leadership of the Italian Communist Party," *New Times*, no. 5, February 1982, pp. 18–24.

105. Reported by Adalberto Minucci, "Guardiamo ai fatti e rileggiamo bene Carlo Marx," *l'Unità*, February 14, 1982; p. 16.

106. "Communist and Workers' Parties on the Position of the Leadership of the ICP," *New Times*, no. 8, February 1982, pp. 18–21.

107. "More Comment on the Position of the Leadership of the ICP," *New Times*, no. 10, March 1982, pp. 18–23 at p. 23.

108. "Real'nyi sotsializm i kommunisty mira," *Pravda*, March 10, 1982.

The Soviet leadership's angry reaction to the PCI's searing critique of the USSR's international conduct is therefore hardly surprising. What does require some explanation is the intensity of that anger and the magnitude of Moscow's retaliation, especially when compared with the CPSU's earlier treatment of the Spanish Communist Party. The respective PCI-PCE challenges to Soviet authority were, as we have seen, quite similar. However, whereas Moscow's polemics against the Spanish party were aimed primarily at a foreign audience, via *New Times*, its attacks on the Italian party were widely disseminated inside the Soviet Union. As in the case of the Sino-Soviet confrontation, this suggested that in the CPSU's view relations with the current PCI leadership had reached a point of no return.

Moscow's relative restraint toward the Spanish communists during the 1970s was due in part to their domestic ineffectiveness. Their criticisms of the USSR's foreign policy and socialist system were more insulting than threatening. Stated the other way around, the CPSU's castigation of the PCE stemmed more from hubris than fear. But an even more important reason for the CPSU's caution in regard to the PCE may have been its desire to placate the PCI. There are persuasive indications that the Soviet leaders toned down their original June 1977 attack on Carrillo because of the Italian party's intervention in his behalf during high-level Soviet-PCI talks in Moscow on July 1, 1977.[109] The source of the PCI's leverage over the CPSU at that time, moreover, lay precisely in the area of Soviet raison d'état. Unlike France, the land of the Caesars had precious few Gaullists. Since Moscow had little to anticipate from the pro-American political establishment in Rome, anything that could be gained from the PCI by way of advancing the USSR's national interests was to be encouraged. In fact, the Italian communists remained largely supportive of Soviet foreign policy until 1978.

Another point of contrast with the Soviet-PCE clash was that the PCI's defiance of Moscow in the realm of foreign policy occurred under international conditions markedly different from the mid-1970s. Soviet-American détente was in shambles, creating the psychological climate for a return to cold war tensions. But for that very reason the likelihood of a West European shift "beyond bipolarity" had increased, given European-American disagreements over East-West issues. From the perspective of mid-1982, moreover, Mitterrand's unexpected victory in France and Bonn's unprecedented assertiveness toward Washington—as well as the cautious receptivity of both the French Socialist Party (PS) and the German Social Democrats to overtures from the PCI—suggested that Moscow may have had some cause to fear the Italian party's vision of an autonomous left-oriented Europe maneuvering between Washington and Moscow. No one knew better than the Soviet leaders how attractive such a vision might be to the USSR's restive East European clients.

109. For details, see Urban, "Moscow and the PCI," pp. 145–48.

There are several further explanations for the intensity of the Soviet Union's offensive against the PCI. By the Kremlin's standards, it had for years displayed a rather remarkable degree of forbearance toward the Italian comrades' wide-ranging political-ideological challenge to the CPSU. The onset of the open Soviet-PCI rift thus must have released a wellspring of pent-up fury and frustration on Moscow's side, with the Soviet polemics rapidly spreading beyond the immediate disagreements over Poland and foreign policy to the long-simmering grudges between the CPSU sectarians and the PCI innovators. One may surmise, moreover, that both the revolutionary ideologues and the cautious sectarians in the CPSU were eager to join the fray on this account. In addition, far more to the taste of the cautious sectarians (preoccupied as they were with Soviet state relations with Western Europe) were those European leaders who viewed Warsaw's military overlords as "patriots" and their imposition of martial law as an "internal Polish affair" than the Italian communists who saw the Soviet leaders and their East European paladins as emperors without clothes.

Finally, the cautious and revolutionary sectarians were doubtless equally proud of the USSR's expanding influence in the Third World and resentful of any aspersions in this regard. Both that pride and resentment found veiled expression in the initial Soviet attacks on the PCI. For example, the *Pravda* piece of January 24, 1982, rebutted the Italians' charge that Soviet Marxism-Leninism had outlived its appeal by arguing that ever more "revolutionary-democratic parties emerging from the national liberation movement" were reaching out toward "scientific socialism" while many had actually "proclaimed Marxism-Leninism the theoretical basis of their activity." The *Kommunist* diatribe approached this same question from a somewhat different angle, sardonically accusing the PCI of reverting the "the old social-democratic idea of 'Eurocentrism,'"[110] that is, the position that only a socialist victory in the capitalist metropoles would lead to revolution in the Third World. Significantly, Soviet warnings against "Eurocentrism" had also been voiced during the initial preparatory talks for the East Berlin communist party summit of 1976.[111] Then, however, they were intended to parry Spanish and French communist insinuations that the CPSU was sacrificing the prospects for revolutionary change in Western Europe on the altar of East-West détente.

In light of the foregoing discussion, the puzzling nature of Soviet relations with the French communists during the 1970s also warrants some comment. In a very real sense, Moscow's attitude toward the PCF differed sharply from its treatment of the PCI. Despite the French party's traditional loyalism and conformity to CPSU norms, the Brezhnev regime disregarded its interests and slighted its leaders. On the other hand, despite the PCI's multiple challenges to

110. "On a Slippery Path," p. 21.
111. See, for example, Ponomarev's speech to the Budapest preparatory meeting, *Pravda*, December 21, 1974.

CPSU doctrine, the Soviet oligarchs at times came close to pandering to Berlinguer, for instance during the sixtieth anniversary celebrations of the Bolshevik Revolution. As has been amply discussed in the preceding pages, Soviet foreign policy considerations provide the clue to this paradox. Indeed, there is perhaps no better illustration of the primacy of raison d'état in Soviet decision making than the CPSU's contrasting behavior toward the French and Italian communist parties.

In the end, of course, Moscow's conduct was instrumental in provoking the PCF's mid-1970s flirtation with Eurocommunism. And the French party's initial retreat from that posture was due not to any change of Soviet heart but rather to the identity crisis felt by the French communists themselves at the prospect of playing second fiddle to the revitalized French Socialist Party. It was, finally, only the 1981 electoral landslide of Mitterrand and the PS that really restored the PCF's stature in Moscow's eyes. For with the ascendancy of traditional socialist anti-Sovietism in the Élysée, the communists became once again, as in the pre-Gaullist years, the Kremlin's sole bulwark in France.

But how is one to explain the seeming contradiction between this persistence of foreign policy motives in shaping relations with Western communist parties and the continuing devotion of some CPSU ideologues to the cause of Soviet-style revolution? On one level this dilemma is easily resolved. From the earliest years of the Soviet state, the Bolsheviks perceived an identity of interests between the defense of the USSR and support for world revolution. Success in the first would ultimately lead to victory in the second. This same perspective continued into the 1970s when CPSU leaders regularly claimed that the pursuit of détente would lead to a shift in the East-West power equation in favor of socialism. When such establishment ideologues as Ponomarev, Zagladin, and Sobolev touted the possibility of a democratic transitional stage on the path to Soviet-style socialism, they were—as discussed earlier—suggesting a revolutionary strategy compatible with détente. Yet on another level this begs the question. For was the transitional-stage approach simply a means, conscious or otherwise, of postponing genuine revolutionary change into the indefinite future so as not to rock the ship of state? Publicists such as Zarodov evidently thought so, judging by the impatient orthodoxy and polemical tone of their writings on revolution in the West. And their assessment paralleled that of certain non-Soviet communist parties, such as the Portuguese and even in some respects the PCF.

Here, then, we come back to the original question, stated in somewhat different terms. How, within the Leninist structures of the CPSU, could the revolutionary sectarian viewpoint remain officially acceptable in the face of the political dominance of the cautious sectarians? The answer probably lies in the Soviet regime's continued dependence on Marxist-Leninist ideology as the rationale for its total power. The actions of the men at the top of the CPSU hierarchy may bespeak pragmatism, or cynicism, more than ideological commitment.

Still, the voice of committed orthodoxy is difficult to silence in any system, let alone the Soviet one where its legitimizing role is so central. Thus, when the views of the militant ideologues do not jeopardize Soviet national interest, they are not only heard but they may even be heeded, especially when they enhance the CPSU leadership's influence beyond the borders of the USSR. Such a situation seemed to exist in late 1975 when Moscow sharply escalated its military support for radical liberationism in black Africa. A by-product of that decisive shift in Soviet foreign policy, moreover, was the emergence of an expanded ideological constituency among Third World liberation movements that apparently reduced the CPSU oligarchs' perception of their need for pan-European communist solidarity except with those communist parties that docilely served the interests of the Soviet state. According to that criterion, the Italian and Spanish communist parties had become dispensable—forces to be weakened or even split.

The CPSU had encouraged and abetted the fragmentation of the Spanish communist movement ever since 1969.[112] The emergence in the early 1970s of Moscow-oriented splinter parties led by dissident PCE leaders was followed a decade later by the factionalization of the Spanish party itself. By 1981 Carrillo confronted *internal* party opposition from at least three distinct groups: orthodox working-class militants, pro-Soviet loyalists, and younger intellectuals even more innovative and anti-Soviet than the Carrillo leadership. There is considerable evidence of Soviet and East European organizational and financial aid to the first two—sectarian—factions. Indeed, given their growing strength among PCE cadres, Carrillo was finally pressured into the expulsion of his outspoken ally, Azcárate, from the party Central Committee in late 1981. At the same time, the internal disarray—nay, identity crisis—of the PCE was unquestionably related not just to Soviet meddling but also to the party's own political weakness, its failure to garner more than 10 percent of the national vote in the post-Franco era.

What remained to be seen as of mid-1982 was whether the Italian Communist Party—with its time-tested organizational structures, traditional tolerance of internal party diversity, and electoral support from 30-odd percent of Italian voters—would be able to withstand the even more massive campaign that Moscow had launched to discredit its leadership and divide its cadres. In short, would it suffer the same fate as the Spanish party, ceasing to be a credible political force at home, hence a threat to Soviet authority within the European communist movement?

112. For details see the articles by Mujal-León cited in note 51 above.

Chapter 5

The Soviets and the Noncommunist Left

Trond Gilberg

All political parties face major questions of political orientation, of strategy and tactics, as they grapple with their programs, platforms, and policy directions. First of all, parties must decide if they are to be system supportive or extrasystem oriented; that is, they must decide whether to operate within the confines of the existing political order or to attempt to alter that order in some fundamental way. Second, parties must decide on major and minor adversaries, and primary and secondary allies. Who is the main "enemy," who are the lesser "enemies" of the political system, and who could be permanent or temporary "allies"? Third, the party leadership must decide the circumstances under which allies and enemies may change positions. Is it possible that today's enemy may become tomorrow's ally, and vice versa? Fourth, what are the conditions under which alliances may or may not be made with other players in the political system? When should such alliances be maintained, and when should they be abandoned? A fifth problem is the question of methods of aggregation and articulation: is extensive aggregation the favored method, wherby large numbers of individuals are brought together on a platform of limited common issues; or should the choice be intensive aggregation, with fewer individuals gathered under the party "roof," but these in agreement on more issues, and perhaps more intensely in agreement as well? Should the party articulate its program in such a manner that its ideological precepts are blurred, thus enhancing the chances for coalition building and extensive aggregation, or should the messages transmitted reflect a commitment to principle, to ideology, regardless of the impact this stance may have on coalition building and aggregation? Finally, the party leadership must find a mix between

130

strategic commitment to a program and tactical flexibility in implementing that program.[1]

Communist parties are faced with the same difficult choices about programs, platforms, and policy. During the approximately seventy years of organized existence of communist parties in Europe, the following *specific* problems have been constant companions and headaches for communist party leaders prior to capturing power and even after successful ascendance to control over the political system.

The communist parties that emerged from the splits in the Second International were immediately faced with the fact that they remained part of the larger political left, and therefore must establish relations with the parties and organizations of that side of the ideological spectrum. This problem became aggravated by the fact that the Third International, established by Lenin and soon converted into an instrument of Soviet foreign policy, forced all of the European left to take a stance on the political manifestations of the Russian Revolution and the state that emerged from it—a state that behaved less and less like the headquarters of international revolution.

The new political constellations on the left of the European political spectrum were complex. There were, on the extreme left, the communists; and after the expulsion of Leon Trotsky from the Soviet Communist Party and eventually from the Soviet Union itself, there emerged Trotskyist groups even to the left of the communists, and these entities eventually established the Fourth International. Immediately to the right of the communists were the still radical socialists, who in some cases established their own parties (such as the Independent Socialists, or USPD, in Germany). To the right of the socialists could be found the social democrats, who, in most cases, were divided into leftist, centrist, and right-wing factions, divided on one or more of the basic questions discussed above.[2]

For the communists, these developments raised a number of fundamental questions. They had split with the old socialist parties because the latter were too concerned with reform, thus neglecting revolution; the 1920 postulation of the so-called Cominform theses had pinpointed a number of areas in which the revolutionaries were distinguished from the reformists.[3] Now that the split was organizationally consummated, how should one relate to the socialists? The latter were clearly remiss for refusing to accept revolution and opting for a form of

1. Lenin discussed the nature of communist parties; see R. N. Carew Hunt, *The Theory and Practice of Communism* (London: Penguin Books, 1968).

2. Milorad M. Drachkovitch and Branko Lazitch, "The Third International," in Drachkovitch and Lazitch, eds., *The Revolutionary Internationals, 1864-1943* (Stanford, Calif.: Hoover Institution Press, 1966), pp. 159-202.

3. Henry M. Christman, ed., *Communism in Action: A Documentary History* (New York: Bantam Books, 1969), pp. 62-71.

"peaceful coexistence" between the classes. Ideological parties are not known for tolerating those who betray revolutionary dicta, and it could have been expected that the communists would classify their erstwhile colleagues of the left as renegades, and thus the main, immediate enemy to be combated before proceeding to deal with other enemies. This was indeed a real option, and it was pursued during relatively extended periods of time in the period between the two world wars.

But there were other options. The socialists may have betrayed the ideas of revolution, but they were still on the left ideologically, and in some cases they were dedicated to the eventual destruction of the capitalist order. Their differences with the communists were therefore primarily a matter of timing. With such leftists, coalitions might be possible.

The social democrats, on the other hand, seemed to have removed themselves from the revolutionary path, thus anchoring themselves firmly in the revisionist and reformist camp. With these elements, genuine cooperation would be less likely; tactical collaboration, a marriage of convenience on a temporary basis, was the most that could be expected.[4]

After 1922, it was the Kremlin leadership that determined the main policy question for communist parties everywhere, but especially in Europe: the path to take to political power. There were several options: direct, frontal assault on the capitalist order; various forms of coalition behavior, which might include temporary coalitions with the leadership of the other parties of the left ("united front from above"); or attempts to establish "action unity" with the socialist and social democratic party masses ("united front from below"); loose organizational cooperation with other parties of the left, in which each party remained autonomous and free to criticize its temporary coalition partners ("the Labour Party concept"); or finally, a broad, temporary coalition across the dividing lines between the political left and center in opposition to various "reactionary" political manifestations ("popular fronts"). All of these approaches were tried during the period between the two world wars, but one element remained constant: the communist determination to obtain power eventually. Thus the Kremlin and its loyal shield bearers in the communist parties of Europe exhibited extreme tactical flexibility on the road to power, but strategically nothing changed. Relations between communists and others, including the noncommunist left, depended on this approach to power.[5]

4. *Protokoll des III Kongresses der Kommunistischen Internationale* (Hamburg: Verlag der Kommunistischen Internationale, Carl Hoym Nachf., 1921), pp. 48–90.

5. It appears that nothing much has changed in this respect: Soviet spokesman still express their conviction that communism will prevail. See, for example, Gerhard Wettig, "Das sowjetische Koexistenz-Konzept: Grundlage eines friedlichen Verhältnisses zwischen Ost und West?" *Osteuropa*, 24, no. 3 (March 1974): 180–87.

The tactical flexibility of the loyal European communist parties led to startling shifts and reverses of policy; thus the "main enemy" changed drastically from time to time. There were periods when the main enemy was social democracy, also known as "social fascism" in communist parlance. At other times, the main enemy was capitalism, from its most liberal to its most reactionary manifestations. During certain periods, the principal problem was German and Italian fascism. Depending on the definition of the main enemy, relations with the noncommunist left might be cordial or characterized by intense struggle; the "class brothers" of yesterday became the "class enemy" of today. Throughout all these twists and policy contortions, the shadow of Moscow's influence covered the policies of the European communists, especially in the question of relations with the noncommunist left.[6]

The conflicting policy goals and the various opportunities that presented themselves to the European communist parties up to the end of the Stalin era produced a number of policies. These policies were: united fronts from below and above (1921–27/28), battle against the social democrats in trade unions and other mass organizations of the working class (1927/28–33/34), and the popular front (1933/34–August 1939), in which the communists participated in broadly based coalitions (extending beyond the social democrats to the bourgeoisie) to combat fascism and Nazism. This popular front was reestablished after the Nazi attack on the Soviet Union, and extended past the termination of hostilities in Europe. Thereafter, up to the end of the Stalin era, relations between the European communist parties and the rest of the European left can best be characterized as united front relationships.

POST-STALINISM TO THE CZECHOSLOVAK INVASION: WHO'S WHO ON THE LEFT?

The death of Stalin ushered in a period of uncertainty in international communism, and it took years to reestablish real guidelines for political activity in the movement. By the time such guidelines had been posited, it was clearly too late for the CPSU and the Kremlin to reassert their traditional control over nonruling communist parties, and this had serious consequences for relations with the noncommunist left as well. The main ramifications of Stalin's death were the following:

1. The Soviets lost their unquestioned ideological and political control in Eastern Europe and were forced to engage in military operations to regain their previous position. The events of Hungary and Poland in 1956 were triggered by Khrushchev's anti-Stalin speech at the Twentieth Congress of the CPSU, but they reflected the wider political and socioeconomic malaise of states that had been subjected to the experience of Stalinism imposed from abroad. The political chaos that developed in the region after the speech has been well

6. Drachkovitch and Lazitch, "The Third International," pp. 159–202.

documented elsewhere; suffice it to say that the military intervention in Hungary alienated a substantial part of the West European left and resulted in massive defections from the local communist parties as well. Relations with the socialists and social democrats of the area therefore deteriorated to levels reminiscent of the cold war, despite the improvements that had been registered in this relationship after the death of Stalin, during the era of relative good will characterized as the "spirit of Geneva." Relations were further complicated by the fact that many of the West European social democratic parties had achieved governmental power in their respective systems, and these ruling parties took a staunch anti-Soviet position after the invasion.[7]

2. The death of Stalin led to ideological diversification in the international movement and ushered in the era of polycentrism. The problem of international communism had always been its inability to establish a core of ideological unity while at the same time allowing *real* tactical political flexibility. The main reason for the seemingly monolithic ability of the European communist party leaderships to follow similar policies toward the noncommunist left was the authority of Stalin and the system he represented. After the dictator's death, the focus of ideological unity and communist political activity had disappeared. There resulted a considerable ideological diversification in the movement, as exemplified by Togliatti's conceptualization of polycentrism. Furthermore, in many of the West European communist parties there were elements that reacted sharply to the revelation of Stalinist excesses, as discussed with such graphic detail by Khrushchev in the secret speech. The factionalism resulting from these developments weakened the local communist parties of Western Europe and established the dangerous principle that the CPSU was not above criticism but rather the main focus of it.

3. The weakening of the Soviet ideological position coincided with the rise of Maoism. As if to underline the weakened ideological position of the CPSU and the Soviet Union, the unsettling developments in Eastern Europe and the emergence of polycentrism in the nonruling communist parties were followed, in short order, by the emergence of Maoism as a full-fledged ideological alternative to the Soviet model and also a real alternative to state power as exemplified by the Soviet Union. The resulting splits in the West European communist parties and the emergence of numerous, competing, Maoist groups further complicated the question of Soviet policy toward the noncommunist left. Furthermore, the socialist and social democratic parties of the area were undergoing a series of changes that split some of these parties into two or more structures, in which the more radical elements of social democracy established their own political parties, located ideologically between the communists and the mother

7. See, for example, J. M. Mackintosh, *Strategy and Tactics of Soviet Foreign Policy* (London: Oxford University Press, 1963), esp. chap. 17.

party. The resulting pluralization of the West European left produced numerous problems for Soviet decision makers. Many of these problems persist to this day.[8]

The multifaceted problems faced by the Kremlin in its relations with the West European noncommunist left were balanced by the emergence of a number of opportunities for greater maneuverability on that left. First of all, there was the gradual subsiding of the cold war and the emergence of détente as a major foreign policy fact. This process continued despite occasional setbacks engendered by crises such as the Hungarian Revolution and even the Cuban missile crisis. In the complicated relationships that constituted East-West relations in this period, the persistence of détente, despite a number of other policy developments and events that would normally have changed the trend, produced a major policy advantage for the Soviet Union in its relations with the noncommunist left, because Moscow was now increasingly accepted as a responsible power with which one could do "business" at the state level. This attitude certainly became fairly prevalent among many of the ruling social democrats of Western Europe as the events of the fall of 1956 faded into the background. But the very tendencies that made the Soviet Union acceptable at the state level generated many problems at the level of the international movement, where, increasingly, voices were heard castigating Moscow for its "state socialism" and its preference for the status quo, at the expense of the revolution.

Second, the United States became entangled in a number of controversies that seriously damaged Washington's image abroad, Western Europe included. The most important of these was the American involvement in Vietnam during the 1960s. As that conflict heated up and necessitated greater and greater use of U.S. combat troops, anti-American sentiment increased dramatically all over Western Europe, and this sentiment was by no means limited to the left, but crossed over old ideological dividing lines into the "bourgeois" camp. The Soviet Union therefore gained considerable advantages with the noncommunist left in Western Europe under the guise of peace making and as the representative of the responsible forces among the world powers, while the traditional leader of the West was increasingly perceived as irrational, irresponsible, and imperialist.[9]

Third, the move toward greater economic and political unity in Western Europe benefited the Soviets in at least two ways. The drive to expand the Common

8. An excellent discussion of these problems in Western Europe is found in David E. Albright, "An Introductory Overview," Albright, ed., *Communism and Political Systems in Western Europe* (Boulder, Colo.: Westview Press, 1979), pp. 1–42.

9. I have discussed this campaign in "Sweden, Norway, Denmark, and Iceland: The Struggle between Nationalism and Internationalism," in Albright, ed., *Communism and Political Systems*, pp. 269–318.

Market produced a good deal of opposition, especially among elements of the European left who feared that foreign cartels and multinational corporations would become the dominant forces of the new Europe. Perhaps even more important, may of those same forces that led the drive to greater West European integration were in fact partly anti-American in the sense that they wanted greater European power and autonomy in relating to both of the global powers. Since the Soviets were constantly warning all Europeans about the nefarious effects of Americanization, these developments helped increase the Kremlin's maneuverability in some measure.

Finally, the very growth in Soviet state power, especially military power, helped increase the influence of the Kremlin in Europe, first among ruling social democrats, but also in some measure among other, nonruling elements of the left. The kind of power repesented by the Soviet state simply must be reckoned with, as the eastern giant forged ahead to conventional superiority and eventual strategic equality with the United States.[10]

There emerged out of this welter of opportunities and liabilities a rather sophisticated set of Soviet policies toward the West European noncommunist left. The outlines of these policies in the 1950s and 1960s are sketched below.

1. The Kremlin increasingly disregarded the local communists in relations with the West European noncommunist left, and pursued instead such relations directly, if need be; the local communists would of course be included if they were considered reliable, but they were frequently bypassed if this loyalty was adjudged questionable. This was more than the old problem of relating to *ruling* social democrats because of the needs of Soviet state interests; it was a function of the growing realization in Moscow that many communist parties, under the influence of polycentrism and Maoism, could no longer be trusted to implement Soviet-sponsored policies.[11]

2. The Soviet leaders (and, by and large, the local communist leaders) sponsored action unity with the socialists and the social democrats, regardless of the status of these two parties in the local political systems; thus such action unity was requested with the mass organizations and party structures even of ruling social democratic parties whose leaders were loyal members of NATO and other Western organizations. Several major political issues during this period also lent themselves admirably to such policies, especially the anti-Vietnam War movement and the drive to forestall the expansion of the Common Market. Such issues allowed the Soviet leadership and many local communists

10. An overview of Soviet strategic power can be found in Vernon V. Aspaturian, "Soviet Global Power and the Correlation of Forces," *Problems of Communism*, 29, no. 3 (May–June 1980): 1–18.

11. For an analysis of Soviet views on the so-called Eurocommunists, see Jiri Valenta, "Eurocommunism and the USSR," in Vernon V. Aspaturian et al., *Eurocommunism between East and West* (Bloomington: Indiana University Press, 1980), pp. 103–23.

the luxury of appealing to nationalism, perhaps even national chauvinism, anti-Americanism, and—in some countries—continued, if hidden, hostility to Germany (this could be used by arguing that the Federal Republic would be the dominant force in the Common Market, hence in Western Europe in general).[12]

3. The Soviet Union and the pro-Moscow local communists fought the Maoists, the Trotskyists, and assorted other left-wing associations with great determination and verbal ferocity. There were several reasons for such policies: the extreme leftists represented a threat both to the Soviet claim of preeminence in the international communist movement and to the aggregative capabilities of the local communist parties; the Maoists argued a brand of revolutionism that seemed infinitely more credible to some than the policies of the established communists, who were seen primarily as the errand boys of Moscow; the Sino-Soviet dispute inserted itself into this controversy and soon became the main issue on which the various factions of West European communism split.[13]

4. The Kremlin produced only a vacillating policy toward the radical socialist parties that had been established in some West European countries in the mid to late 1950s. On the one hand, these parties were much closer to the communists and to major elements of Moscow's ideology than the social democrats; on the other hand, the radical socialists refused to accept Soviet ideological control and international discipline, and in many cases were highly critical of Moscow's policies, both domestically and abroad. This kind of radicalism competed seriously with the communists on the left. The pro-Moscow communists, therefore, felt themselves squeezed between the noncommunist ultraleft and the radical socialists immediately to the right on the ideological spectrum.[14]

5. The Soviet leadership, through a variety of vehicles, attempted to deal directly with those elements of the "bourgeois" political forces of Western Europe that could be classified as anti-American, antidefense, or primarily nationalist. Such elements could be found in the pacifist organizations that developed during the period: of considerable significance here were the many church organizations that became involved in the anti-Vietnam movement, but there were also elements that would ordinarily find themselves on the anti-Soviet side of the political fence but now, for various reasons, found common ground

12. An analysis of these and other aspects of Soviet policy can be found in Robert Legvold, "The Problem of European Security," *Problems of Communism*, 23, no. 1 (January-February 1974): 13–33.

13. An excellent analysis of Trotskyism and Soviet attitudes to it is Günter Bartsch, "Der Trotzkismus als internationale Sonderbewegung: Die IV. Internationale und ihre Abzweigungen," *Osteuropa*, 26, no. 5 (May 1976): 369–81.

14. Some of the most successful radical socialist parties could be found in Scandinavia; see my "Communism in the Nordic Countries: Denmark, Norway, Sweden and Iceland," in David Childs, ed., *The Changing Face of Western Communism* (London: Croom Helm, 1980), esp. pp. 239–44.

with the local communists or the Soviet leadership (or both) on limited issues. An example of this is the common stance taken by Norwegian agrarian interests and the local communists on the question of Norwegian membership in the Common Market—a stance that was repeatedly and volubly hailed by the Soviet press.[15]

These policies, like any set of policies, produced some successes, some failures, and a great deal of ambiguity. There can be little doubt that the widespread campaign against the American involvement in Vietnam helped serve Soviet foreign policy goals, insofar as it reduced U.S. prestige and influence in Western Europe and may have had some impact on the eventual decision to "Vietnamize" the conflict through withdrawal of U.S. personnel from that troubled country. Internally, the congruence of communist goals and the goals of substantial numbers of noncommunists helped reintegrate the local communists in their respective political systems. These parties, which had often found themselves outside the pale of rather substantial policy consensus in Western Europe, now could act as nationalists, peace makers, and full-fledged members of their communities at the same time. Since so many West Europeans tended to look upon the local communists as mere creatures of Moscow, these developments helped legitimize the Soviet Union as well. And finally, the constant communist campaigns against the "lunatic fringe" of Maoists, Trotskyists, and assorted other extreme leftist groups helped establish the communists as respectable, system-supportive elements, thus lending further respectability to their perceived masters, the Soviets. And even those communist parties that openly and vociferously criticized Soviet policies helped the Kremlin's interests indirectly, because they established the perception that the Soviet Union no longer attempted to dictate policy elsewhere.[16]

These important gains were considerably offset by other developments. Communist action unity with the socialists and social democrats against American policy in Vietnam did not greatly increase general support for the communists; the West European electorate, by and large, realized that the communist parties of the region could not produce *general* policies that would be in the interests of large sectors of the public. Furthermore, the communists often found themselves outmuscled by the socialists and social democrats in the action committees and other bodies focusing on Vietnam, disarmament, and other promising issues. In fact, may of the other participants in these action unity groups turned out to be more radical than the communists themselves, thus preempting a major element of communist attractiveness.[17]

15. An example of this is the Soviet commentary on the parliamentary elections of 1973, in which the left gained a victory—probably because of the anti-EEC movement. See M. Zubko, *Izvestiia*, September 12, 1973.
16. Valenta, "Eurocommunism and the USSR," pp. 103–23.
17. Communist electoral strength in Western Europe is summarized by David Childs in "Appendix," *The Changing Face*, p. 276.

One of the main reasons for the inadequate success of the Soviets and the local communists in "action unity" policies was the emerging attitude among the West European public that there was a need for a European position apart from both Washington and Moscow. Thus, important elements of the European peace movments castigated both the Soviet Union and the United States for imperialist policies and warmongering; little advantage was gained from such attitudes. It is true that Washington was criticized more heavily and more vociferously, because the United States was the most active "imperialist" power at the moment; but these groups were volatile, and could turn against Soviet interests in a most disturbing way. The reliability that the old, disciplined communist parties of Western Europe had displayed could not be reproduced in this fashion.

The relative success of Soviet policy toward the ruling social democrats on the question of Vietnam did not translate into more lasting achievements, such as the dismemberment of NATO, the promotion of real neutralism, or a substantial reduction of U.S. influence in these systems. The European social democrats might disagree with American policy in Asia, but they clearly perceived the need for continued U.S. support in Europe, and this perception of overriding security interests superseded the policy differences over Vietnam. Thus, NATO remained intact, the Common Market expanded, at least to some degree, and the socialists and social democrats continued to fit the real and perceived needs of substantial numbers of the West European electorate, while the communists did not. Time and time again, the Kremlin learned that the common origin of leftism did not in any way produce policy congruence in the 1960s.

The attempt to deal harshly with the extreme left of the political spectrum in Western Europe may have made the local communists more respectable to certain elements, and it probably helped the general image of the Soviet Union. But it also established as fact the Maoist and Trotskyist assertions that the Soviet Union and the CPSU had left the fold of revolution and now simply wished to use the movement and assorted slogans for their own purposes. Thus, the local communists became targets of the volatile and articulate European left, and the Soviet Union was ridiculed as the most despicable of all systems, a "state capitalist" order masquerading as a genuine member of the revolutionary movement.

The net result of these policies, then, was not overly favorable, but, at the same time, certain tactical goals were achieved. Above all, the stage was set for further developments during the 1970s.

The "New Left" in Europe and the Soviet Quandary

During the 1960s there emerged in the United States and in Western Europe a movement that has been categorized as the "new left" by prominent analysts.[18]

18. For an excellent analysis, see Klaus Mehnert, "Moskau und die neue Linke," *Osteuropa*, 23, no. 9 (September 1973, entire issue).

It was a motley movement of various kinds of antiestablishment groups, ranging from Maoists and Trotskyists to elements that were ideologically close to traditional Marxism-Leninism; anarchists of various persuasions were also numerous. Most of the members, however, were not easily categorized by means of ideological labels; they merely shared a common aversion to the existing political and socioeconomic order, to political—indeed societal—authority, and, perhaps most importantly, to the "ruling generation" (which was sometimes classified as anyone over thirty). This kind of unfocused, rebellious movement needed *issues* to produce any kind of organized action, and there were several forthcoming during the 1960s, most prominently the Vietnam War (which served as a rallying point both in Western Europe and in the United States) and the "events" in France in May 1968 (the effects of the latter issue were more important in Europe than in the United States).

The new left demonstrated an extraordinary vitality throughout the period of the 1960s, temporarily culminating in 1968. Through demonstrations, clashes with the police, sit-ins, and other forms of mass action the new left demonstrated its capability to confront the existing order head on; the May events of 1968 in France showed the capacity of the movement to challenge the existing order in a most fundamental way, even if it proved to be only a temporary challenge.

The extraordinary action capacity of this movement stood in sharp contrast to the placid position undertaken by the social democrats and socialists of Western Europe (many of whom were ruling parties in any case) and the stale sloganeering of the local communists, who were preoccupied with the Sino-Soviet conflict and the persistent problems of Stalinism and de-Stalinization. The elemental revolutionary force that seemed to emanate from the new left rekindled the hopes of fundamental social, economic, and political change. For elements of the European left this was the possible recapturing of the old revolutionary ardor that had characterized the heady days after the October Revolution, only to be smothered by Stalinist bureaucratism, democratic centralism, and alien autocracy, Russian style.

The Soviet leadership reacted with extraordinary caution to this movement. In retrospect, it seems clear that this was the most likely Soviet reaction. Lenin had never accepted revolutionary spontaneity; in fact, he had denied that such spontaneity could exist, even in the working class (let alone among intellectuals). For Lenin and his successors (and Stalin in this respect was a true heir to the mantle of Lenin, just as Khrushchev and Brezhnev followed the lead of Stalin on this issue) spontaneity must be replaced by organization, and revolutionary élan must be tempered by discipline and control. A movement such as the new left in Western Europe and the United States had the wrong characteristics; it was intellectual, not proletarian; spontaneous, not controlled; and, perhaps most important of all, it rebelled against *all* power and authority. In other words, this movement smacked of anarchism, and it carried with it many more dangers than advantages.[19]

This Soviet assessment of the characteristics of the new left was correct, and it produced a major policy problem for the Kremlin; this was not a new problem, but it was now posed in a very clear form, not seen since the early 1920s. Furthermore, it was to stay with the Soviet leadership (and the leaders of the local West European communist parties) for many years to come.

The Soviets produced two sets of policies toward the new left. In the beginning, the response was a nonresponse. The Soviet press discussed the events in France, for example, from the vantage point of traditional class analysis, which included the recommendation that the disparate revolutionary forces of the movement must separate themselves from the anarchistic and crypto-capitalist elements by means of submission to revolutionary and class discipline represented by the French Communist Party (PCF). Similar responses were made to the statements, slogans, and programs emanating from the new left in the United States; here, too, the proper focus must be submission to the class discipline represented by the local communist party.

After a while it became clear that the new left was not amenable to such suggestions, and the Soviet leaders devised another approach, which resembled the action unity programs used by West European communists in the past. Such action unity groups, it was presumed, would allow themselves to be controlled by more disciplined elements, such as the communist parties. If this were the case, the movement could be utilized for Soviet foreign policy goals; after all, the new left did attack the established political and socioeconomic order in the United States and Western Europe, and it did demonstrate against American foreign policy in an area of considerable interest to the Kremlin. Here, then, was another possibility for the expansion of Soviet influence in the heart of capitalism, and one of the vehicles was an element of the noncommunist left. Despite these clearcut advantages, the CPSU leadership retained its serious doubts about a movement that seemed impervious to manipulation and bent upon criticizing the Soviet Union as vociferously as it castigated the United States.

THE INVASION OF CZECHOSLOVAKIA AND ITS AFTERMATH

When Warsaw Pact troops poured into Czechoslovakia in late August 1968, the Soviet leaders were undertaking a policy that would have broad and potentially damaging repercussions in relations with the European noncommunist left. This drastic move might have destroyed the general climate of détente that

19. "Die Arbeiterklasse: Die Führende Kraft im Kampf um Sozialismus und Kommunismus," *Osteuropa Archiv*, September 1973, p. A625 (translated from *Kommunist*, no. 8, 1968, pp. 3–12).

had developed during the 1960s, despite the Vietnam War and the apparent
bellicosity of the United States in areas such as Southeast Asia and the Caribbean
(as witnessed by the Cuban missile crisis). It certainly would jeopardize the newly
improved relations with the Federal Republic, which had been ushered in by
the new Ostpolitik of the Grand Coalition after 1966. The West European communist parties, already severely factionalized because of de-Stalinization,
Maoism, and the problems associated with the new left, were bound to experience a serious crisis of conscience over this policy. The ruling social
democrats and socialists were bound to look upon this move as a signal to draw
closer to the United States. Those elements of the "bourgeoisie" who had
castigated the United States for its involvement in Vietnam might now turn
their attention to Soviet aggression. The new left was likely to turn "anti-
imperialist" and include the Soviet Union in the list of oppressor states, thus
producing a serious fallout on this side of the political spectrum. And the
Maoists and Trotskyists would simply interpret the intervention as proof that
their analysis of the Soviet system had been correct all along.

These were serious risks indeed, but the Soviet leadership was willing to accept them, because the majority of its members clearly valued the maintenance
of Soviet power in Eastern Europe more than they valued their relations with
the West European communists and the rest of the left in that part of the
world. There may also have been an element of historical learning involved in
this decision, based on the experiences of the Hungarian invasion, to wit: the
West European left, despite its howls of outrage at the invasion, did not termi-
nate relations with Moscow; the ruling social democrats of the area did not
break off diplomatic relations; and, after a "suitable" interval, the process of
normalizing relations in Europe under the auspices of détente continued. There
may have been a calculation made in the Kremlin, in the case of Czechoslovakia,
that temporary dislocations in relations with the noncommunist left in Western
Europe would be substantially healed over time. In this calculation the Kremlin
leadership appears to have been right. After an initial deterioration of East-West
relations in general, the period of détente continued, and the process was, in fact,
accelerated. The decade of the 1970s up to 1978–79 was the decade of détente.[20]

As the decade of the 1960s drew to a close, the Soviet leadership could look
back on some major challenges to its position in the international communist
movement, in Eastern Europe, in the global relationship with the United
States, and also in its relations with the noncommunist left in Western Europe.
In the international movement, the "Chinese challenge" represented by Maoism
and the Sino-Soviet conflict had taxed the Kremlin's ability to maintain control, but, by and large, the damage of this challenge had been contained. In
Eastern Europe, the dangers of "socialism with a human face" had been confined
through the successful invasion of Czechoslovakia; the dangers of spreading

20. Aspaturian, "Soviet Global Power," esp. pp. 1–12.

revisionism had been contained. The relationship between Washington and Moscow had stabilized to such an extent that the two leaderships were willing to contemplate further discussions and a formalization of détente, despite the strains produced by the Czechoslovak "affair." The noncommunist left of Western Europe had expressed its concern over the invasion, but there had been no serious disruption of political relations with the Soviet Union as a state; the ruling social democrats deplored the invasion as much and as strenuously as anyone else, but, given the global and regional power relationships, the Soviet Union must be reckoned with, and the CPSU, as the dominant political force in the Soviet state, could not be politically ostracized for long. This was a lesson that even the so-called Eurocommunists learned as the decade drew to a close.[21]

Given this relative consolidation of Soviet power after the unsettling decade of the 1960s, Soviet decision makers could proceed to implement their major goals in Western Europe within the parameters of the global relationship with the United States and the emerging factor of increased Soviet activities in the developing world. The following were the main goals of the Soviet *state* in Western Europe during the decade of the 1970s.

1. The first goal was to weaken U.S. influence in Western Europe, especially on the Continent. This was, of course, a traditional goal for Soviet foreign policy makers; it had been a major element of the Kremlin's European policy since World War II. The Soviet leadership still considered Europe to be the main "battleground" between East and West, and it was therefore logical for the political struggle with the United States to be joined here.

2. The objective described in item 1 could best be achieved through a weakening of the multilateral agencies that helped cement that American influence, such as NATO and any economic organizations, primarily the U.S.-led multinational corporations.

3. Weakening U.S. influence required the division of Western Europe into several "target categories" for Soviet approaches, which would separate the core of pro-American states from those that had doubts about the closeness of the Atlantic Alliance and existing bilateral ties and those where nationalism and anti-Americanism played a major role.[22]

4. The objectives of items 1–3 above would set the stage for an expansion of Soviet political and economic influence in the area. Economically, the Soviets began to depend more heavily on technology transfer and credits from the West to sustain growth rates at home and also to subsidize the faltering economies of

---

21. This aspect of the relationship is discussed in Pierre Hassner, "Moscow and the Western Alliance," *Problems of Communism*, 30, no. 3 (May-June 1981): 37–54.

22. For years the main targets of such Soviet approaches were France and West Germany as well as the Nordic countries. See my "Soviet Policies in West Europe," *Current History*, 61, no. 362 (October 1971): 198–205.

Eastern Europe. The continuation or expansion of this relationship was possible only if the Soviet Union could produce goods and services needed by the West Europeans. Because of the relatively low level of technological sophistication in the Soviet economy and the sorry state of collectivized and state agriculture, the only feasible commodity was energy. A "correct" energy policy would presumably help meet the needs for foreign exchange so badly felt by Moscow and at the same time tie the economies of the Soviet Union and Western Europe more closely to each other.[23]

Closer economic ties could lead to greater political influence for the Soviet Union in the West. This might come about because large numbers of firms, banks, and workers would depend on the "Eastern connection" (it is interesting to note that this was a Soviet version of a similar linkage theory much touted both in Western Europe and the United States at the time). But, despite the possible political benefits from increased economic ties, the Kremlin expected the most important improvement in its position in Western Europe to stem from the altered strategic balance between Moscow and Washington and the substantial increase in all forms of military power. The resulting change in the power balance would set the stage for greater willingness by West European ruling circles to become more accommodating. Thus, limited "Finlandization" was a possibility.[24]

These policy goals were to be implemented by several mechanisms, of which elements of the noncommunist left were a part. The socialists and social democrats indeed constituted an important part of the strategy, because their mass organizations and party structures could be utilized for a variety of action unity projects, while at the same time the party leaderships of the two groups held important positions in ruling coalitions or at times ruled alone in some of the West European states. The socialists and social democrats could therefore be used for both defensive and offensive purposes: they could help limit the influence of the the United States in Western Europe, and the ruling elements of the two parties would be faced with the need to deal with the realities of Soviet military power as well as the economic benefits that might accrue to their respective states through expanded trade and joint economic projects.

While the socialists and social democrats occupied important positions in the Soviet approaches to Western Europe in the 1970s, the extreme left wing of the European political spectrum was treated with a mixture of contempt, outrage, and, occasionally, awkward attempts at partial reconciliation. The Maoists and Troyskyists were recipients of withering criticism, as before; the

23. Chancellor Schmidt defended his government's decision to import natural gas from the Soviet Union at a meeting of top SPD leaders in Bad Godesberg in late February 1982; see *Frankfurter Allgemeine Zeitung*, March 1, 1982.

24. The concept of "Finlandization" is discussed in Ulrich H. E. Wagner, "Finnland und die UdSSR: Das sogenannte Finnlandisierungsproblem," *Osteuropa*, 25, no. 7 (July 1975): 463–76.

various left-wing movements, arranged around specific issues, were treated as possible allies in limited action unity policies; and the new left was gingerly approached and occasionally appreciated for its revolutionary enthusiasm. These elements of the left, bereft of any real chance of obtaining state power in Western Europe, could be dealt with in a more summary and manipulative fashion than the much more powerful socialists and social democrats. But regardless of status in the domestic political system, the Soviet leadership saw the various elements of the noncommunist left in Western Europe as potential supporters (witting or unwitting) of broader goals and objectives of Soviet foreign policy in the region.[25]

In this complicated set of relationships, the increasing complexity of West European communism appeared at times to offer an added element of maneuverability, but occasionally also an obstacle to Soviet foreign policy flexibility. The emergence of several communist parties whose leaderships were severely critical of Soviet policy at the state and movement level produced a major handicap for the Kremlin and forced the CPSU onto the defensive in the politics of the West European left on numerous occasions. The Italian, Spanish, British, Swedish, and Icelandic communist parties had their own ideas about the relationships they might want to undertake and the policies they would like to endorse and condemn, and this clearly produced complications for the Soviets. On the other hand, it was now possible for Moscow to approach other elements of the West European left with relative equanimity and perhaps even greater sincerity, since the local communists no longer required major consideration as a real partner for the Soviet Union, whether at the state or movement level.[26]

The various Soviet policy goals, using a variety of mechanisms (including the noncommunist left), were to be implemented through a set of policies, some of which were innovative while others were variations on approaches in use as early as the 1920s. The most important of these are the five listed below.

1. Sponsorship of the general policy of détente through expanded relations with the moderate elements of the West European left, notably the socialists and social democrats. Since the Soviet leadership had determined the need for détente (which in turn permitted the expansion of technology transfer and economic aid and credits from the West), this state of East-West relations was to be promoted and maintained, and one of the most effective methods was to promote friendly ties with the noncommunist left. This generalization is not

25. The importance of the social democrats in this approach has been discussed in an excellent article by Heinz Timmermann, "Moskau und die Linke in Westeuropa: Aspekte und Perspektiven des Verhältnisses zu den Eurokommunisten und zu den demokratischen Sozialisten (I)," *Osteuropa*, 30, no. 5 (May 1980): 389–400.

26. Ibid. See also Wolfgang Leonhard, "Positionen und Tendenzen der westeuropäischen Kommunisten," *Osteuropa*, 30, no. 1 (January 1980): 3–21.

valid for all the West European states at all times: there were periods in which the relations with one or more of these forces on the European left deteriorated, especially in the immediate aftermath of the Czechoslovak invasion; but on the whole, the Soviet leadership promoted moderate relations with the socialists and social democrats of the area, and the loyal communist parties followed suit (the Eurocommunists promoted such relatively friendly relations for reasons of their own).[27]

2. "Action unity" on issues of mutual concern. The first half of the 1970s provided a ready-made issue for action unity of most leftist elements in Western Europe–the continued and escalating American involvement in Vietnam. As Washington took an increasingly aggressive stance in this conflict, the European peace movement also gathered momentum and provided a forum for expanded communist influence. This escalation on both sides reached its zenith during the systematic bombing of North Vietnam in the early years of the decade, and then tapered off somewhat as the American involvement slowly abated; it lasted, however, until the final collapse of South Vietnam in 1975.[28]

3. The need for "progressive forces" to cooperate in the face of multifaceted American aggression. The Soviet leadership also attempted to further the action unity of the left in Europe by playing to the increasingly nationalistic attitudes found in many countries on the issues of security relations with the United States and U.S. economic expansionism, as exemplified by the spread of American multinational corporations in the West European economic systems and markets. The anti-Americanism demonstrated during the Vietnam War could be nurtured by appeals to European regionalism and the nationalism of each state in the area, and the Soviets used both vehicles to advance their foreign policy goals in the region. This task was made easier by the Watergate scandal in the United States–an event that facilitated the Soviet propaganda claim that the U.S. political system was indeed rotten to the core.[29]

4. The use in some of the West European states of a variety of indigenous movements whose programs lent themselves to such manipulation. An example of this was the ecology movement, which gathered momentum in some states (notably the Federal Republic) during the decade. The Soviets could claim that widespread air and water pollution was directly ascribable to the evils of advanced capitalism, and that the very system that produced such excesses needed serious

---

27. This policy was especially prominent in relations with ruling socialist and social democratic parties; see, for example, the joint declaration of the Soviet and West German governments after Brezhnev's visit to the Federal Republic in May 1978 (*Pravda*, May 7, 1978).

28. The Soviet position here was made clear in a speech by Kosygin at a reception for the visiting prime minister of Italy, Giulio Andreotti, in *Pravda*, October 25, 1972.

29. Interestingly, the Soviet press tended to blame Congress and the U.S. political system, rather than Richard Nixon, for Watergate and the subsequent resignation of the president; see *Izvestiia*, September 3, 1974.

modifications. Since such movements at times became formidable political factors, first at the local and regional and then at the national level, they could also be seen as mechanisms that would eventually reduce the power of "big capitalism," and this added to their attractiveness in Soviet eyes. The Kremlin therefore sponsored and supported such movements throughout the decade, and since elements of the noncommunist left were relatively prominent in the ecology movment, this forum became yet another arena in which to promote relations with the West European left.[30]

5. Endorsement of expanded activity, especially by the ruling social democrats, in selected areas of the world, to maximize the differences between the United States and its allies, coupled with the argument that Europeans must find solutions to European problems without interference by outside forces (not indigenous to the region). This approach was used with a great deal of consistency by the Moscow leadership during the 1970s. Although it was not limited to the noncommunist left, Kremlin strategists clearly assumed that such arguments would have more weight in moderate leftist circles of the region, for whom the lessons of U.S. involvement in Vietnam would, presumably, remain more vivid. (This did not preclude deviations from the rule in certain cases, as exemplified by Soviet wooing of the French conservatives during this period.) Examples include Soviet arguments during the MBFR negotiations, in the discussions leading up to the Helsinki Accords, and in the Soviet commentary on European (especially social democratic) initiatives in the Middle East after the momentum of the Camp David agreement had slowed down. The Kremlin especially hailed attempts by West European social democrats to establish and maintain relations of various kinds with the Palestine Liberation Organization. Differences between some of the Europeans and the Americans in policies toward liberation movements in Africa and elsewhere were also emphasized by the Soviets; such approaches were especially prominent in the question of relations with the Pretoria government and the status of Namibia. Once again, social democrats such as Willy Brandt were recipients of favorable commentary in the Soviet press.[31]

CENTRAL AMERICA, AFGHANISTAN, POLAND, AND PERSHING MISSILES:
OPPORTUNITIES AND LIABILITIES

The various policies promoted by the Soviets in Western Europe in the period of détente had resulted in greatly improved relations with the noncommunist

30. This is not to imply that the ecology movement was communist controlled. The Soviets have been careful to discuss the excesses of "industrialism" primarily with reference to the CDU/CSU and "capitalist" policies generally; criticism of the SPD would jeopardize state relations with the Federal Republic. For a full report on Brezhnev's important visit to West Germany in November 1981, see *Pravda* and *Izvestiia*, November 24, 1981.

31. In 1981 Brandt was hailed for his constructive attitudes on foreign policy, especially during his visit to Moscow during the summer (see, for example, *Pravda*, July 1, 1981).

left in most West European states. The foreign policy requirements of the
Soviet Union when it acts as a global power and as a self-proclaimed leader of
the international communist movement occasionally come into conflict with
the regional goals and objectives of Moscow in a certain area of the world; indeed, perceived policy needs in one region may clash with needs in another.
The last three or four years have seen the clash of such various goals and objectives in Soviet foreign policy, resulting in a relative deterioration of Soviet relations with the noncommunist left in Western Europe. At the same time, certain
developments in other parts of the world have redounded to the advantage of
the Soviet Union, both directly and indirectly. Finally, developments in
Western Europe itself have provided Moscow with a rare opportunity to expand its influence greatly while simultaneously reducing the prestige and power
of the United States in this crucial area. In most of these situations, the noncommunist left in Western Europe has played an important part.

Several policy decisions made by the Kremlin in its capacity as a global power
have produced serious liabilities for the Soviets in the West European noncommunist left. The invasion of Afghanistan scandalized the West in general and
particularly those elements of the European political order that had been the
staunchest advocates of détente; in this category were many socialists and
social democrats, some of whom were ruling elites in their countries. The ensuing debate over policies to be undertaken as a countermeasure to the invasion
augured ill for the Kremlin, because it presaged the reemergence of a kind of
united front of anticommunism and anti-Sovietism from the extreme right to
the socialists and social democrats and indeed beyond. There were cries of outrage against the Soviet action and demands for some form of retaliation, be it
economic, political, or symbolic. In some cases, such retaliation was demanded
by ruling social democrats. In other cases, the party organizations of the
socialists, social democrats, and the so-called Eurocommunists issued remarkably similar denunciations of the Soviet action.[32]

The Soviet response to these charges was predictable. The Kremlin charged
the critical elements of the noncommunist left with submitting to U.S. imperialism and betraying the needs of the "progressive forces" in Europe and elsewhere. Witting or unwitting complicity in American schemes was a common
charge leveled against these leftist elements, and the stridency of the Soviet
argument occasionally harked back to the days of "social fascism"
(1927/28–33/34). Coupled with such attacks were repeated assurances that the
West Europeans had nothing to fear from the Soviet Union, which remained
thoroughly dedicated to the principles of peaceful coexistence. (A careful

32. The Italian communists reacted sharply, for example, in *l'Unità*, January 6, 1980;
the West European social democrats helped push for increased armaments, for which individuals such as Helmut Schmidt were roundly criticized; see *Pravda*, May 28, 1981, commenting on the chancellor's visit to Washington.

reading of the Soviet interpretation of that concept would suggest, however, that the West has plenty to fear from such an approach.)[33] And added into the Soviet hopper were reminders of the necessity of détente, which had improved the relations between East and West in Europe so dramatically earlier in the decade. Was remote Afghanistan really worth the sacrifice of such a favorable development? In any case, the Soviet Union was only safeguarding its legitimate security interests and the needs of the progressive elements in Afghanistan.[34]

The Western reaction to the invasion demonstrated the difference in perceptions between the ruling elites in London, Bonn, Paris, Washington, and other capitals, on the one hand, and important elements of public opinion, on the other. This difference existed even between the leaderships of ruling social democratic parties and substantial elements of their own rank and file. Because of this difference, the Soviets could in fact turn the potential disaster of the invasion partly to their advantage. This became clear as the ruling elites of the Western alliance began to produce policies designed to enhance the military capability of NATO, while significant elements of the populations of Western Europe, including many noncommunists on the left, demanded a continuation of détente and expanded disarmament talks as well as an immediate reduction in the nuclear arsenal on both sides. As the NATO alliance moved to a decision on deploying a new generation of U.S. missiles to conteract the actual deployment of the dreaded SS-20 and other missiles in the Soviet Union, the focus of this movement became the United States and the local West European governments that had accepted the deployment of the Pershing missile.[35]

The debate over missile deployment was not new in Western Europe. President Carter's trial balloon concerning the manufacture of the neutron bomb had touched off major demonstrations in Western Europe, and the Soviet leadership added much verbal ammunition to the arsenal of the protesters.[36] The debate over the Pershing rockets and the possible deployment of the cruise missile exacerbated the controversy and showed the extent to which West European public opinion feared a serious escalation in the arms race, which, from the European perspective, meant a devastating number of missiles and warheads targeted on a relatively small, highly urbanized, and thus exceedingly vulnerable area. The broadly based movement against nuclear deployment in Western Europe includes important elements on the noncommunist left; especially prominent here are large segments of the Social Democratic Party

33. Klaus Mehnert, "Friedliche Koexistenz: Eine deutsche Meinung," *Osteuropa*, 24, no. 4 (April 1974): 270–74.
34. Leonid Brezhnev in response to questions from Soviet journalists, in *Pravda*, January 13, 1980.
35. Brezhnev was clearly making such a bid for dividing the Western alliance in his interview with West German journalists, printed in *Pravda* (and also *Izvestiia*), November 3, 1981.
36. *Pravda*, August 14, 1981 (on the U.S. decision to produce the bomb).

(SPD) rank and file in the Federal Republic of Germany (and also a number of local party organizations and the youth organization of the party), but similar constellations can be found in other West European countries as well. And the movement does not merely include elements of the left: it crosses ideological lines and generational divisions; it bridges regional gaps; and it promises to become one of the largest mass movements of Europe in a long time.[37]

It is clear that this movement promotes policies that indirectly benefit the Soviet Union. This is not to allege that leaders or rank and file of the movement are pro-Soviet or procommunist; in most cases leaders and followers alike are probably motivated by a genuine aversion to nuclear armaments and the escalating arms race. Included in the movement are pacifists and individuals morally committed to ending the frightening escalation of Soviet-American rhetoric, which is becoming increasingly bellicose on both sides. There are also many clergy and others of religious persuasions, and undoubtedly quite a few who are anti-U.S. or at least anti-Reagan; some of these may be veterans of the Vietnam War movement of a decade earlier. Some (probably a relatively small minority) are procommunist or pro-Soviet. The exact mix is of no real concern here. The main point is that this is the kind of issue that lends itself to action unity, not only of the entire left (with the exception of the diehard Maoists and Trotskyists) but of other segments of the population as well. And since the goals of the movement focus on preventing the deployment of U.S. missiles, while the Soviets already have substantial numbers of such missiles deployed and targeted on Western Europe, the net result is a distinct advantage for some important Soviet foreign policy goals.

The peace movement has become well organized and well entrenched in West European politics. The "nuclear malaise" represented by the movement is further enhanced by the persistent economic crisis currently besetting much of Western Europe. This crisis, too, is largely blamed on the United States and its policies. Together, the fears of nuclear holocaust and economic ruin produce the kind of political environment the Kremlin finds congenial to implementing its policy goals in Western Europe.

During the last year or so, the Soviets have been able to capitalize on the existence of such a broadly based peace and disarmament movement in Western Europe. This has been done through repeated Soviet calls for arms reduction. In March 1982, Leonid Brezhnev stated that the Soviet Union would unilaterally establish a freeze on missile deployment; this statement openly and clearly appealed to the fears and hopes of the peace movement. He later responded to an appeal from the International Physicians for the Prevention of Nuclear War by calling for "radical" arms agreements and cutbacks. In May, there was a flurry of statements reacting to President Reagan's proposals for

---

37. This view is reflected in "Neutronenwaffe: 'Schlicht unheimlich'" (cover title: "Reagans Neutronen-Schock: Schlachtfeld Deutschland?"), *Der Spiegel*, August 17, 1981, pp. 17–29.

drastic cutbacks in armaments, hinting broadly that the U.S. president was merely grandstanding to the peace movement, but unable to fool the honest people in it. Later in May, Brezhnev stated (in a speech to a Komsomol meeting) that the Soviet Union was ready for "serious" arms talks. Thus the Soviets have been able to utilize the existence of the European peace movement to force the United States into a temporary defense in the nuclear debate.[38]

Another area of direct or indirect East-West confrontation is producing serious friction between the United States and its West European allies, and elements of the noncommunist left in Europe have become outspokenly opposed to Washington's policies in this field. The area in question is Central America, and the policy issue is the approach to the national liberation fronts that have emerged there, first in Nicaragua and now in El Salvador; other groups are active in many of the other states of the region. Here again, the West European left (as well as most of the ruling elites of Western Europe, whether of the left or the right) take a stand drastically different from that promoted by the Reagan administration. The West Europeans would like to establish a dialogue with the guerrillas, thereby drawing them into political discourse and eventually produce a moderation of their revolutionary views and policies. The United States, on the other hand, has taken the position that many of the rebel leaders and forces are under the direct control of the Nicaraguans and thus, by extension, of the Cubans and their masters, the Soviets. The continued U.S. support of regimes that are widely held to be dictatorial, bloodthirsty, and lacking in concern for human dignity by wide sectors of the European public has hurt American prestige in Western Europe considerably and has resulted in a relative congruence of Soviet and West European views on this issue. Thus, two purposes of Soviet foreign policy have been served: U.S. power has been weakened in crucial areas, and there has developed a considerable split between Washington and its main allies in Europe. In this process of alienation, the noncommunist left in Western Europe has been a major factor.[39]

There remains the issue of Poland. The imposition of martial law in that country brought to an abrupt halt an experiment that went beyond the political pluralism that existed in Czechoslovakia during the Dubček era. It was clearly too much, both for the local communist elite and for the leaders in the Kremlin. Once again, coercion was used, without regard for the reactions that were bound to emanate from the West. But these reactions were far from uniform, and that fact allowed the Soviets some room for maneuver. Consequently there

38. The March proposal by Brezhnev can be found in *Pravda* and *Izvestiia*, March 17, 1982; his response to the physicians' organization is in *Pravda* and *Izvestiia*, May 3, 1982; the commentator Nikolai Prozhogin dealt with Reagan's disarmament proposals in *Pravda*, May 9, 1982; the Brezhnev speech to the Komsomol organization can be found in both *Pravda* and *Izvestiia*, May 1, 1982.
39. See, for example, the lead article in *Der Spiegel*, February 1, 1982.

emerged a policy aimed at separating the states of Western Europe from the United States on this issue. This policy argued that détente must continue, and economic agreements must be made and executed; life goes on. The "saber rattling cowboy" in the White House, who has very little knowledge of politics in Europe, should not be allowed to destroy the "businesslike" relations that have developed on the Continent during the last ten to fifteen years.[40]

This approach from the Kremlin is aimed, in considerable measure, at the noncommunist left in Western Europe, both the ruling socialists and social democrats and those leftist parties that are currently in opposition. It was further aimed at the growing peace movement in the region, which demands rapid and substantial progress at the arms limitation talks under way in Geneva. The beguiling qualities of the Soviet approach stem from a simple set of propositions: most West Europeans are not willing to make massive political and economic sacrifices for a state that has been in the Soviet orbit for an entire generation; there is a substantial (and growing) body of opinion in Western Europe that demands disarmament and continued peace on the Continent and sees the Reagan administration as the main stumbling block to fulfilling this goal; many West European states have extensive economic ties with the Soviet Union and Eastern Europe and fear a cutoff of such relations if the Polish issue becomes a major East-West confrontation.[41]

These attitudes are understandable, given the geographic facts of life in Europe and the current power constellations in the area. Many of the opinions now being expressed by West European statesmen, party leaders, and movement leaders have long been held by many on the left, including the noncommunist left. Prevailing attitudes in the Reagan administration and in important segments of the body politic in the United States question this view, partly because of the different geographical perspective held in Washington, and partly because the United States, a global power, is more likely to adopt a stance of confrontation with the other global actor than are the regional powers of Western Europe, whose leaders are acutely aware of the discrepancies in military capability in Europe at this time and in the foreseeable future. These are serious divergences, and they have created a situation the Kremlin can use to get out of a potentially devastating loss of prestige in the West. The Soviet tactic stands and falls with the ability of the Polish military regime to control the situation in its own country. If Soviet forces were to be used in Poland, it would have the most dramatic effect on public opinion elsewhere, including the

40. See, for example, Academician G. Arbatov in *Pravda*, January 1, 1982. The Soviets also gleefully reported that a spokesman of the West German government disagreed with U.S. sanctions against Poland because of the imposition of martial law (TASS, January 4, 1982, as quoted in *Current Digest of the Soviet Press*, 34, no. 1, February 3, 1982).

41. A good analysis of these Soviet policies can be found in Hassner, "Moscow and the Western Alliance" (see note 21 above).

noncommunist left in Western Europe. So far, the Soviets have been lucky. The Polish issue is therefore yet another element in the growing crisis of the Western alliance and the growing alienation between the United States and important political elements in Western Europe, notably the moderate left.

Compared to the many favorable prospects that seem to emerge in Soviet relations with the moderate elements of the noncommunist left, the extreme left still represents a considerable challenge to the strategists and tacticians in the Kremlin. The Sino-Soviet dispute has continued, and this has meant that the Maoists of Western Europe still consider the CPSU and the Soviet Union renegades and traitors to the revolutionary cause. There is no possibility of reconciliation with the Trotskyists. And the assorted leftists who are emerging within the growing peace movement of Western Europe (as perhaps also in the United States) are of the "new left" type—spontaneous, idealistic and enthusiastic, not easily amenable to control, and, in many cases, anti-Soviet as well as anti-American (this fact is not widely known in the United States, and the misperceptions about the peace movement held by important parts of the U.S. public and apparently elements of the political elite contribute greatly to the deteriorating relations between the United States and Western Europe). In short, these leftists have all the wrong qualities from Moscow's vantage point. Little *direct* advantage can be expected from them in the near future.

IMPROVED RELATIONS WITH THE SOCIALIST INTERNATIONAL

One of the most interesting aspects of the current Soviet attempt to utilize West European fears of a nuclear confrontation to reestablish a broad, "progressive" front against Washington on this issue has been the Kremlin's willingness to expand its relations with the Socialist International. This body, which has often been highly critical of Soviet policies in Eastern Europe and even domestically (especially in the field of human rights violations), has been wooed by the Brezhnev leadership on the issue of nuclear weapons and the need to prevent further emplacement of them in Western Europe. Thus Brezhnev met with Olof Palme, head of the Swedish Social Democratic Party and chairman of the International Commission on Disarmament and Security Issues; Palme is also a prominent leader of the Socialist International.[42] *Pravda* on July 17, 1981, reported favorably on the meeting of the Bureau of the International in Bonn (where the Bureau went on record as strongly supporting nuclear disarmament). The commentator Vitali Korionov argued for a broad front of communists and socialists (as well as social democrats) against nuclear weapons (*Pravda*, October 4, 1981). In February 1982, Brezhnev met with representatives of the Socialist International's Consultative Council on Disarmament, and

---

42. This meeting was reported in *Pravda*, June 13, 1981.

repeated his call for nuclear arms cuts and the need for cooperation among "progressive" forces to achieve this goal.[43]

The Soviet stance on the Socialist International is interesting as an example of Realpolitik. The International is seen as a vehicle for possible coalitions in limited terms (such as "action unity") and for the purpose of weakening the position of the United States in important elements of the West European public. The Soviets cannot possibly harbor any illusions about real *ideological* unity with the Socialist International; the latter organization has lately conducted talks with some of the Eurocommunist parties, notably the Italian Communist Party, and this has enhanced the standing of the PCI in its ideological debate with the CPSU. For tactical purposes, however, the Kremlin leadership finds enough common ground on the issue of nuclear arms to improve its relations with the socialists and social democrats and their international organization to an extent not seen in quite a while.

THE FEDERAL REPUBLIC OF GERMANY AS THE KEY

Throughout the 1970s it became clear that the main focus of the Kremlin's West European policy was the Federal Republic of Germany. This is nothing new in Soviet foreign policy. Ever since the October Revolution Soviet foreign policy makers have considered Germany a key to the success or failure of the Kremlin's goals in external relations. Thus, Lenin and Trotsky expected the European revolution to break out in Germany; the focus of the popular front was collective security against Nazi Germany; and the entire question of European security and East-West relations is intimately tied in with the division of this Central European state, where the two major power blocs of the world meet in direct confrontation across the barbed wire and the no-man's-land. Given this historical concern with Germany, it made sense that the Soviet Union would focus on the Federal Republic during the 1970s.

History was only part of the reason for this Soviet focus. The Federal Republic has all the right ingredients for a target of policy and, presumably, opportunity. It is the strongest state in Western Europe economically; the Bundeswehr is perceived as the mainstay of the European contribution to NATO; the SPD has a radical youth organization whose views on major aspects of European and world security are at odds with U.S. goals and objectives; many regional party organizations are openly challenging the foreign policy of the party leadership; there is a growing ecology movement, which is highly critical of the perceived excesses of advanced industrial capitalism; there is a burgeoning peace movement which may become the largest mass movement in Europe in decades; and important elements at the top of the SPD challenge the policies of the government and appear sympathetic to some of the goals of the peace movement.

43. *Pravda*, February 4, 1982 (also in *Izvestiia*).

Objectively, the goals of that movement will weaken the security position of the United States in Europe, thus producing an indirect bonus for the Soviet Union. These are the kinds of ingredients that may be used to maximum advantage by the Soviet Union in its West European policy. And because the moderate left is so important in the Federal Republic, relations with that left have become a key aspect of the Kremlin's goal setting and implementation in a region still seen as the decisive region in the East-West equation.

The Federal Republic is also a key in several other respects. The West German economy, despite some recent problems, is still the strongest in Western Europe. The enormous problems of the Soviet economy can be alleviated, at least in part, by technology transfer and commercial credits from the powerful West German economy. The Germans also need economic relations with the Soviets. The recently concluded agreement on purchase of Soviet natural gas is an example of the kind of trade agreement an energy-poor but highly industrialized state may find advantageous. A closer economic relationship between these two states in the limited areas of mutual advantage would serve the interests of both parties.[44]

Finally, the Federal Republic has undergone a political maturation process that has taken it from virtually total dependence on the United States to a situation in which significant elements of the population (including much of the noncommunist left) demand a more independent foreign policy for West Germany. This trend is not necessarily anti–United States, and should not be so interpreted here; but from the vantage point of the Kremlin it offers additional opportunities for appeals to nationalism and occasionally neutralism in a population increasingly faced with the difficult choices of major, mature regional powers. It is a scenario that offers the Soviet decision makers added incentives in their West European policy. Thus, in this decade, the Federal Republic will represent the key to the success or failure of the Kremlin's policy in this most important region.

CONCLUSION:
A SCORE CARD FOR SOVIET POLICY TOWARD THE NONCOMMUNIST
LEFT IN WESTERN EUROPE

A serious discussion of Soviet policies toward the noncommunist left in Western Europe will inevitably produce a mixed balance sheet of successes and failures. This assessment will be further influenced by the analysis of the goals of the Soviet foreign policy makers. If the goals change over time, achievements must also be measured differently. How have Soviet goals changed since 1917?

---

44. The extent of these economic ties was discussed in *Pravda*, November 20, 1981, in connection with Brezhnev's visit to the Federal Republic.

First of all, the Kremlin leadership has given up the idea of making Western Europe communist, at least in the short or intermediate term. This goal, which was a prominent feature of the early revolutionary policies emanating from Petrograd and Moscow, soon became illusory; as early as the mid-1920s it was clear that capitalism had reestablished itself in the area, and only major dislocations of a socioeconomic or political nature could change this fact. By the time the Depression had produced this kind of economic dislocation, the Kremlin was worried about collective security and the threat from Nazism; in any case, other, more capable, elements of the European left had taken charge of practical policies designed to alleviate the plight of the masses. When similar opportunities seemed to arise again in the political and socioeconomic chaos of postwar Europe, the American presence precluded any such move on the part of the Kremlin. The goals of the Soviet leaders therefore changed. The focus now switched to political influence rather than political control; the Soviet leadership, acting in the interests of the Soviet *state*, attempted to produce policies that would influence the leaders of the existing order in Western Europe in some way that was perceived as beneficial to the political, economic, or security interests of Moscow.

Once the perceptual change had taken place in the Soviet Union, the nature of the Kremlin's policies in the area also changed. Instead of forcing changes in Western Europe, the Soviet leaders focused on responding to the opportunities that developed as a result of domestic and external changes in the region itself. In the exploitation of these opportunities, the attitudes and policies of the West European noncommunist left became major elements.

Opportunity exploitation did not preclude rather aggressive policies in tactical matters, as discussed above, but this focus did portend a reactive policy from the Kremlin rather than an approach designed to change matters in some fundamental way. In the meantime, the foreign policy capabilities of the Soviet Union increased considerably, especially in military power. At this point, the military preponderance of the Soviet Union on the European continent is rather frightening. Does this presage the return to the early Bolshevik quest for fundamental changes in the West European and socioeconomic systems? And will the Kremlin this time rely on the leverage of superior military capability rather than the ephemeral slogans of revolution that issued from the Soviet capital in 1917–21? The likely answer to this question can only be produced after a careful assessment of the *liabilities* the Kremlin faces in its West European policy and its relation with the noncommunist left in the area.

These liabilities are severe and therefore likely to preclude a massive growth in *direct* Soviet influence in the area in the years to come (even though the *indirect* influence of the Kremlin may increase). First of all, Marxism-Leninism, Soviet style, has very little appeal anywhere in Western Europe, including the ranks of the noncommunist left. Even many of the communist parties of the region strenuously criticize some basic facts of political life in the Soviet Union, especially the continued emphasis on tight political control and the policies resulting from that emphasis (such as the harsh treatment of dissidents, the stultifying effects of party control over the arts, literature, and academia, and the continued denial of basic human rights as they are understood in the West). For large segments of the populations of Western Europe, the Soviet Union represents the worst kind of despotism, which is further aggravated by the cultural and political traditions of autocracy that have always been present in Russia, regardless of regime. This kind of system, emphasizing authority, discipline, control, and collectivism, is abhorrent to a West that increasingly focuses on individual rights and privileges, and personal freedom. This abhorrence is as widespread on the left as it is elsewhere in the ideological spectrum in Western Europe: the socialists and social democrats have always stood for individual rights and political choice; and it should not be forgotten that in the past it was precisely these elements of the noncommunist left in Europe that fought the communists most strenuously and successfully. Out of this kind of "action knowledge" comes caution. The West European socialists and social democrats are not likely to fall victim to the political blandishments emanating from Moscow. As for the ultraleft forces of Western Europe, their alienation from the policies of Moscow is ideological, hence fundamental; no reconciliation can be expected here.

The economic performance of the Soviet Union is a further handicap to any real projection of Moscow's influence in Western Europe. The bankruptcy of the economic policies of the regime is clearly evident in poor agricultural production, shoddy and expensive consumer goods, machinery that is already obsolete, and a stagnation of labor productivity and thus of economic growth. The centralized, planned, and controlled economy of the Soviet Union cannot produce the goods and services required by the population. The resulting standard of living is way behind Western Europe, and the gap appears to be widening. There is no economic appeal in such a model. The socialists and social democrats of Western Europe, basing themselves and their appeal on instrumental legitimacy, find very little that is worthwhile in the Soviet economic model.

The malfunctions of the Soviet political order, the lagging performance of the economy (which now requires massive infusions of technology and credits from the West), and the oppressive and stultifying nature of the social and cultural systems of that vast country combine to produce a sense of alienness exuding from the giant to the east. This image is not likely to appeal to the modernized, secularized, skeptical, and performance oriented elites and populations of Western Europe—least of all, perhaps, to the noncommunist left, which tends to see the political and socioeconomic orders of the Soviet Union as monstrous aberrations of a great idea, socialism.

This impression of Soviet stagnation at home is reinforced by the aggressiveness of Soviet policy in many areas of the world, which has resulted in serious political, economic, and military overextension. Eastern Europe, Afghanistan, Cuba, and assorted liberation movements in Africa—all represent a massive drain on Soviet capabilities that will shortly result in a serious reduction in the capabilities of the Kremlin to conduct any kind of policy short of military threats or the actual use of coercion. Such a system is not likely to produce a great deal of support. The political and economic appeal of the Soviet Union in Western Europe, therefore, is minimal.

What remains is the element of fear. The performance of the Soviet Union in almost all areas of activity is poor, but in the realm of military power it is awesome. This fact, coupled with the simple realities of geography, ensures for the Soviet Union a considerable amount of influence in Western Europe. This fear is clearly present in the goals and demands of the peace movement, and it is an element in the decision making of the ruling political elites of Western Europe, whether they belong to the noncommunist left or not. The malaise and uncertainty of Western Europe at the moment are fueled by the current economic crisis, on the one hand, and the relative decline of American power, on the other. The phenomenally successful economies of Western Europe are now in a rather serious economic crisis; and the populations of the area, accustomed to annual increases in the standard of living and their personal prosperity, have begun to feel helpless. The crisis, at least in part brought on by outside forces such as energy prices and the American recession, appears to be beyond the grasp of remedial action, out of hand. This is a fearful experience for populations used to seeing results for hard work, who have considered it a basic right to control their own economic destinies. And then there is the fact that the "American umbrella" of strategic power is no longer superior to that of the Soviet Union, but rather barely equal to it (if that), and this changes the power equations. It is felt that the fate of Western Europe is in the hands of others, the global powers. This situation, then, establishes the need to reassess relations with both global powers. And this process is currently under way in Western Europe, both among the elites and the general populations.

A reassessment of this kind may take several forms and have several results. It may result in closer relations in the Western alliance—a "closing of the ranks," so to speak. Conversely, it may result in accommodation to the other side, if that side is perceived as more powerful and aggressive. Given the complex nature of this problem, no uniform or clearcut result of this assessment is likely to emerge; instead, the resulting policies will depend on national peculiarities, unforeseen events, and even personalities. Given the unpopularity of communism (especially Soviet-style communism) in Western Europe, the best the Kremlin can hope for in the area is a form of "accommodationism" or "Finlandization." If this were accomplished on a broad scale or in some of the most important West European states, it would be a major accomplishment. Soviet success or failure will, in considerable measure, depend on two factors—the political position of the noncommunist left of the region and U.S. foreign policy toward those political forces. The United States has many real and potential assets in Western Europe, despite some setbacks. What is required now is an imaginative policy for that important part of the world.

Chapter 6

Soviet Economic Policies in Western Europe

John P. Hardt and Kate S. Tomlinson

Two often conflicting tendencies have dominated Soviet policy toward Western Europe: the desire to wield political and ideological influence over a divided capitalist world and a need to draw upon the technological resources of the economically advanced Western countries. The interplay of these tendencies has formed Soviet policy toward Western Europe since the earliest days of the Soviet state. Divisions within the capitalist world present Soviet leaders with the opportunity to exert political and ideological influence over Western Europe. Thus they have eagerly seized upon evidence of division within the West— either among the European countries or, particularly during the post–World War II period, between Western Europe and the United States. Efforts to enlarge or foster such division have been a prominent feature of Soviet foreign policy. Yet the Soviet Union has frequently sought expanded commercial relations within the West, particularly Western Europe, in order to advance its economic goals of modernization and growth. Soviet economic relations with Western Europe have not progressed steadily, but have been marked by interruption and occasional equivocation. Discussions among the Soviet leadership on the risks and opportunities of expanded commercial relations with the West have tended to coincide with periods of division within the West. Judging from the events of the late 1970s and early 1980s, the 1980s are likely to be such a period. The continuation of détente and economic Ostpolitik in Soviet–West European relations during the 1980s sharply contrasts with the return to confrontation, tension, and trade restrictions in Soviet–United States relations. Concurrently,

The views are those of the authors, not necessarily those of the Congressional Research Service or the U.S. Congress.

the Soviet leadership's enthusiasm for technology transfer as a means of attaining growth and modernization may be cooling.

Political factors dominate Soviet policy in the 1980s as in the past. During the Brezhnev era, however, issues of political economy such as commercial relations with Western Europe and alliance relations in Eastern Europe have also been high on the policy agenda. To be sure, when the Soviet leadership perceives threats to political or military security, national sovereignty, or systemic continuity, issues of political economy do not take precedence. During the 1970s, major threats to these values were not perceived and the Soviet leaders felt able to concentrate on the needs of the economy and the agenda of political economy generally. The turn to the West for technology, grain, and credit was central to Moscow's policy of economic modernization.

In alliance relations, the Soviets sought to retain their hold over Eastern Europe by economic as well as military levers. In an era of détente, the Soviets gave the East European countries leeway to build their own economic bridges to Western Europe and the United States. The Soviets hoped that the East Europeans could thereby foster economic modernization, consumer welfare, and political stability. An equally important reason for this leeway granted the East Europeans was to reduce the drain on scarce Soviet energy and other raw materials.

With the revival of fundamental division in the West on relations with the Soviet Union, the Soviet leaders might be tempted to exploit political divisions and move closer to an autarkic system. Reducing the level of interdependence with the West and increasing CMEA (Council for Mutual Economic Assistance, or Comecon) integration would have an appeal for the Soviet leadership. They could thereby reduce CMEA's exposure to economic leverage by the West. But it is economically costly to reverse the trend toward interdependence, and the Soviets may be presented with the even more attractive option of pursuing a divided political and economic policy toward the West—continued détente and economic intercourse with Europe, and a return to conflict and autarky in relations with the United States.

CHANGING CURRENTS IN THE USSR's WEST EUROPEAN ECONOMIC POLICY

In the early days of the Soviet state, the leadership saw the West as subject to escalating economic division and economic crises verging on collapse. In this apocalyptic vision it seemed that wartime division, fatigue, and economic weakness in the capitalist world had opened the path to the spread of the Bolshevik revolution to Western Europe—especially Germany. Again, in the 1980s economic competition, economic crises, and differences in Western policies toward the East have driven wedges into Western unity, especially between Western Europe and the United States.[1]

1. For an analysis of the current situation in the West by an authoritative Soviet commentator, see N. Inozemstev, "XXVI s"ezd KPSS i nashi zadachi," *Mirovaia ekonomika i mezhdunarodnye otnosheniia*, no. 3, 1981, esp. pp. 18–23.

The themes of long-term Soviet policy have been to divide and weaken the West politically and draw on the technological advances of the West: in 1917, conflicts dividing the West were seen as the way to the world socialist revolution; in 1920, the goal of overcoming economic backwardness bound Moscow to the West; and in the 1980s, opportunities to divide the NATO Alliance with the Brezhnev Peace Program and selective economic Westpolitik and to encourage a much-needed scientific-technological revolution with Western technology and credit were equally attractive to the Soviet Union.

These centrifugal political and centripetal economic forces have played across the history of the Soviet Union in Europe for more than the six decades. The policies of the developed Western economies have alternately fostered and impeded the success of these Soviet tendencies. Occasionally Western policies have been unified, but more often they have been divided.

Europe has been a primary focus of Soviet foreign policy since the October Revolution. The United States has also played a critical role because of its technological prowess and acquisition of a leadership role in the Atlantic Alliance after World War II. From the Soviet point of view, the United States frequently acts as a European power through its role in NATO, CoCom, and other international organizations. Since the 1970s, however, the European countries have been playing more independent roles in East-West relations.

The Stalinist System. In the pre-Five-Year Plan period, Western Europe, especially Germany, was to be the solution to both Soviet economic backwardness and political isolation – by revolution if the communist "machine shop" of Germany could be added to the Soviet granary, or by trade as the two outcast nations joined in informal industrial and military cooperation. The aim of the modified autarky of the first Five-Year Plan (1928–32) was to obtain critical technological imports to further industrialization. Trade missions preceded formal recognition as the Depression in the West made Soviet industrial import orders more desirable. With diplomatic recognition came further normalization of trade – tariff and credit privileges. Stalin, however, was chary about accepting normal Western commercial relations, for he feared that interdependence in economic relations would lead to political dependence and vulnerability. His fears proved to have some basis as the German Reich used economic penetration to pave the way for later political and military control in Eastern Europe.

On the eve of World War II in 1938, Soviet bilateral ties with the Western countries were sharply reduced, although the special ties with Nazi Germany were temporarily deepened during the Nazi-Soviet Pact period. With the wartime alliance, Western, especially American military and industrial aid, became critical to Soviet survival. The wartime volume of lend-lease was high but short-lived. Before the war's end the Soviet Union and the Western countries initiated a two-track policy leading to the creation of global institutional relations. The political track continued to San Francisco and the establishment of the United Nations in 1945. The economic track, undertaken in a cooperative mode at

Bretton Woods, was later derailed as the USSR chose not to join the International Monetary Fund (IMF) or World Bank or accept Marshall Plan aid.

Why Stalin renounced an active role in the postwar international economic system is not clear. Perhaps, as some Western analysts suggest, the war had left the Soviet economy so devastated that the Soviet Union could not hope to participate on an equal footing. Or perhaps, as others suggest, Stalin did not see any advantage in participating in organizations likely to be dominated by and oriented to the capitalist countries.[2]

Whatever the reason, Stalin rapidly returned the Soviet Union to the economic autarky of the 1930s. In the "two camps" speech of 1952 he justified the change of policy by describing the world as divided into two opposing systems—capitalist and socialist—between which only a minimum of economic relations were to be desired.[3] Concurrently, Stalin revived the totalitarian system of the 1930s, which had been relaxed during the war years, and sought to isolate Soviet citizens from all foreign influences. Many individuals who had come into contact with foreigners during the war were purged.

In the early 1950s less than 20 percent of Soviet trade was with noncommunist countries. Imports were limited to commodities needed to relieve short-term supply bottlenecks and were carefully balanced with exports to avoid indebtedness. Throughout the decade the East European and Chinese economies were tied to the Soviet economy through interlocking plans.

For its part, Western Europe adopted a policy of economic isolation from the Soviet Union in the wake of the U.S.-Soviet confrontation in Berlin in 1948. Its policy on trade with the East paralleled that of the United States: a virtually complete embargo and economic warfare. Through CoCom (Coordinating Committee for Multilateral Export Controls), the informal export control system that began in 1950, the United States and the West European countries restricted all exports that could contribute to the East's military or economic performance. Slightly looser controls were applied to Yugoslavia, Romania, and Poland to encourage political independence from the Soviet Union. Tariffs on imports from the East were set high; and trade and credit facilities for bloc countries were restricted.

By the mid-1950s, the policy of peaceful coexistence with the capitalist countries began to take a more global, less isolationist, form under the post-Stalinist leadership. In addition, owing to a sharp slowing down of growth rates in the CMEA countries, problems in developing new technology, and the desire for higher quality Western machinery and equipment, Soviet interest in expanding East-West trade greatly increased. But the renewed Soviet interest in Western

2. Thomas G. Paterson, *Soviet-American Confrontation* (Baltimore: Johns Hopkins University Press, 1973), pp. 154–56.

3. In Leo Gruliow, ed., *Current Soviet Policies*, vol. 1 (New York: Columbia University Press, 1953).

imports was not matched by an increased ability to finance these imports. During the 1960s, therefore, trade was restricted by the small size of Soviet export earnings, the limited availability of Western government and private credits, and the small number of industrial cooperation agreements that could be concluded.

Toward Ostpolitik/Westpolitik. When Khrushchev was ousted in October 1964, a collective leadership led by Brezhnev and Kosygin took power. Although the general objectives of Khrushchev's foreign policies in most cases continued under the new leadership—maintain Soviet political, ideological, and economic domination in Eastern Europe; avoid direct military conflict with the West; contain the Chinese threat; maintain Soviet influence over the world communist movement; increase Soviet influence in the Third World; restrain Western military power; and improve access to Western products and technology, the manner in which these objectives were pursued did undergo significant change. Whereas Khrushchev's foreign policy actively utilized military power for political gains (as in Cuba), the Brezhnev-Kosygin leadership, although it aimed at strengthening Soviet power in relation to the West, did not pursue a militarily aggressive foreign policy.

The more narrow Soviet objectives regarding Western Europe also remained essentially unaltered (prevent the development of a powerful West European military bloc; gain de jure recognition of the geographic status quo; gain access to West European technology; retain control of West European communist parties; and maintain a policy of relaxation of tensions with the West European nations). To achieve these ends the Brezhnev-Kosygin leadership encouraged the development of orderly negotiations and the establishment of significant multilateral agreements in arms control, trade, science, and technology.

Concurrent with renewed Soviet interest in East-West trade was a Western movement toward lowering economic and ideological barriers to trade during the 1960s. The Western industrial countries diverged from U.S. policy and began to develop more independent Eastern policies. Chancellor Adenauer's embargo of pipe shipments from the Federal Republic of Germany to the Soviet Union in 1962, which was seconded by U.S. insistence and a NATO embargo order, was probably the end of an era of American dominance in East-West commercial policy. For the Germans it was the end of an era of isolating the USSR and of insisting on political concessions on such issues as the permanence of German borders and reunification as prior conditions for normal trade. Thus the Soviets in 1962 were penalized by denial of critically needed oil pipes until or unless they took favorable political action on borders. The Soviets eventually manufactured their own pipelines, but it took a year or two longer than it probably would have if German piping had been available.

By 1966, the Soviet leadership had begun to develop closer ties with Italy and France, signing a variety of agreements on mutual consultation and scientific/economic cooperation, including an agreement to produce the Soviet version of

the Italian Fiat in the Volga Valley. The Soviet leadership by 1966 was also ex-
changing a growing number of visits with their other European neighbors (with
the notable exception of the FRG)—including two trips to Moscow by British
Prime Minister Harold Wilson, a visit to the Vatican and the Italian government
by Gromyko, and visits to Finland and Austria by Kosygin and Podgorny—in
some cases signing trade agreements and joint cooperation agreements. Soviet
policy toward Europe not only emphasized closer political, economic, and technical ties between the West and the Soviet Union, but also encouraged the idea
of new collective security arrangements as an alternative to NATO, in order to
loosen European ties with the United States.

Soviet initiatives in Europe from 1966 to 1968 were moving in a positive direction until August 1968, when the Soviets invaded Czechoslovakia. The invasion created new problems for Soviet–West European relations and set back a
number of previously attained Soviet policy objectives. By 1969 Soviet efforts
once again centered on creating an atmosphere of détente in Europe. Soviet officials proposed a European security conference to be held in Helsinki in 1970,
began bilateral talks with the FRG for normalization of relations, and agreed to
reopen four-power talks on Berlin. The 1972 and 1973 Brezhnev-Nixon summits
in Moscow and Washington put the U.S. stamp of approval on détente. By
1973, when the Conference on Security and Cooperation in Europe (CSCE)
and negotiations on mutual force reductions (MFR) opened in Europe, economic and technological ties between East and West were beginning to grow
closer, and trade turnover increased dramatically.

Although there was no basic shift in the Soviet European policy after the invasion of Czechoslovakia, there was clearly a shift in emphasis. Gone was the insistence that NATO and the Warsaw Pact be replaced by an all-European security system and that the United States initiate a withdrawal from Europe. The new emphases were (1) a desire to raise the level of consumption without cutting defense expenditures and (2) a stronger desire to acquire Western capital and technology.

SOVIET AND EAST EUROPEAN PERSPECTIVES ON EAST-WEST INTERDEPENDENCE AND DÉTENTE

Break with Stalinist Autarky. The decision, after the removal of Khrushchev, to
contract with Fiat to build a passenger car plant in Togliatti was a critical one
in the setting of the Brezhnev-Kosygin strategy on technology imports from the
West.[4] The Fiat contract, signed in 1966, followed by one year the conclusion

4. John P. Hardt and George D. Holliday, *Technology Transfer and Scientific Cooperation between the United States and the Soviet Union: A Review*, U.S Congress, House Committee on International Relations (Washington, D.C.: U.S. Government Printing Office, May 1977), part 2, chap. 2. Sources of general interest include E. S. Shershnev, *USSR-USA Economic Relations* (Moscow: "Science" Publishers, 1976), and *Economic Ties East-West: Problems and Possibilities* (Moscow: "Thought" Publishers, 1976).

of an agreement for scientific and technical cooperation between Italian firms and the Soviet government. The impact of the Fiat contract and related agreements on Soviet foreign trade was felt later as Soviet imports of Western machinery increased sharply. Donald Green and Herbert Levine quite reasonably see 1968 as the beginning of a new strategy on technology in imports from the West.[5] One aspect of the new Soviet strategy was the conclusion of science and technology exchange agreements with Western governments. The agreements signed with France and Italy in 1966 were followed by agreements with the United Kingdom in 1968, Sweden in 1970, Canada in 1971, the United States in 1972, and Japan and West Germany in 1973. A common goal of the intergovernmental agreements was to complement and encourage commercial contracts on the model of the Fiat transaction.[6]

The decision to import automotive technology was broadened, during the Ninth Five-Year Plan, to include truck technology. As the Fiat arrangement had been the centerpiece of the Eighth Five-Year Plan, the Kama River truck plant became the major focus of Western machinery importation in the Ninth Five-Year Plan. The areas selected for special attention were widened from automotive technology to include technology and equipment for (1) natural gas, oil, timber, metal extraction, processing, and distribution, (2) metallurgical facilities, (3) chemical processes ranging from fertilizers to petrochemicals, (4) computer-assisted systems, (5) agrobusiness, (6) regional development in the Baikal-Amur region of Siberia, and (7) tourist facilities.

Many Western technologies sought by the Soviets represented only "evolutionary" advances, or small incremental improvements in technology, such as automobile designs and tourist facilities. Some technologies, evolutionary only in terms of the level of technology in the West, may bring about a significantly greater improvement in Soviet technological capabilities and result in substantial benefits to the Soviet economy.[7]

In seeking to expand the importation of foreign technology, whether "revolutionary" (involving major technological advances) or "evolutionary," Soviet decision makers appeared to be moving belatedly toward a foreign economic

5. Donald W. Green and Herbert S. Levine, "Implications of Technology for the USSR," paper presented to NATO Directorate of Economic Affairs Colloquium on East-West Technological Cooperation, Brussels, March 17–19, 1976.

6. Lawrence H. Theriot, "U.S. Governmental and Private Industry Cooperation with the Soviet Union in the Fields of Science and Technology," Soviet Economy in a New Perspective, U.S. Congress, Joint Economic Committee (Washington, D.C.: U.S. Government Printing Office, 1976).

7. U.S. Department of Defense, Office of the Director of Defense Research and Engineering, "An Analysis of Export Control of U.S. Technology: A DOD Perspective," a report of the Defense Science Board Task Force on Export of U.S. Technology (Washington, D.C., 1976), pp. 9–14.

policy that conformed with the postwar policies of other industrialized countries. Soviet leaders appeared to have approved the growing technological interdependence of the world economy and therefore apparently decided to end the
autarkic tendencies of Stalinist economic policy, thus terminating a policy of
denying themselves access to the world market. This interpretation does not
conflict with the reality that the Soviet leaders selected particular Western
streams of technological change for top priority.[8] The pattern of cooperative
agreements emphasizing computer applications and chemical and metallurgical
processes followed the same strategy.

Soviet leadership statements and actions during the Ninth and Tenth Five-
Year Plans increasingly advanced the official view that significant growth was
likely to be achieved from selective Western technology transfer. West European exports of machinery and transport equipment to the USSR increased
from $294 million in 1965 to almost $3 billion in 1976.[9] A significant Western
confirmation of the Soviet official view was the econometric assessment of
Green and Levine, which attributed up to 15 percent of Soviet industrial
growth in the period 1968–73 to importation of Western machinery.[10] Sector
analysis by Philip Hanson in the chemical fertilizer industry reached similar
conclusions.[11] These views on the importance of Western imports to the Soviet
economy suggest a certain degree of political influence or leverage in the West.
Just as the Soviet Union may use its energy exports for political reasons, the
West European countries may counter with their technology exports.

Recomputations of the Soviet trade statistics by Vladimir Treml, Jan
Vanous, and others, while using different methodologies, all agree that the imports from the West and CMEA have been undervalued in Soviet computa-
tions and represent increasingly critical inputs for individual sectors of the

8. John P. Hardt and George D. Holliday, "Technology Transfer and Change in the
Soviet Economic System," in Frederic J. Fleron, Jr., ed., *Technology and Communist Culture: The Socio-Cultural Impact of Technology under Socialism* (New York: Praeger
Publishers, 1977), pp. 189–92.
9. U.S. Department of Commerce, Bureau of East-West Trade. This includes Austria,
Belgium-Luxembourg, Denmark, France, the Federal Republic of Germany, Italy, the
Netherlands, Norway, Sweden, Switzerland, and the United Kingdom. Machinery and
transport equipment are classified as SITC 7.
10. Green and Levine, "Implications of Technology for the USSR," p. 56.
11. John P. Hardt, "The Role of Western Technology in Soviet Economic Plans," *East-
West Technology Transfer* (London: Pergamon Press, 1977), pp. 174–80; see also Robert
Campbell, "Technological Levels in the Soviet Energy Sector," paper presented to NATO
Directorate of Economic Affairs Colloquium on East-West Technological Cooperation,
Brussels, March 17–19, 1976; Philip Hanson, "Soviet Mineral Fertilizer Industry," in Paul
Marer and John M. Montias, eds., *East European Integration and East-West Trade* (Bloom-
ington: Indiana University Press, 1980), pp. 252–80; and Stanislaw Gomulka, *Inventive Ac-
tivity, Diffusion and the Stages of Economic Growth* (Denmark: Aarhus, 1976).

Soviet economy.[12] Whether the attendant interdependence and higher foreign trade participation ratios represent dependency or vulnerability is subject to some dispute among Western analysts.

Potential Western political leverage from exports of machinery and technological processes may not be the only Soviet problem. If the Soviets are to obtain the benefits in economic performance suggested in the Green-Levine approach, imports may place heavy demands on their limited domestic supply of high-quality equipment and skilled manpower.[13] Imports, to be sure, may have dual consequences: releasing domestic resources for military use as well as consuming more resources to complete sophisticated civilian projects, diverting resources from military programs.

Several factors support the general conclusion that Soviet technology imports have a net resource-demanding or diverting effect in the domestic economy: (1) The technology transfer process itself consumes domestic as well as foreign resources. The adaptation and absorption of technology that has been developed for another country requires considerable inputs from the Soviet economy. For example, Soviet engineers are needed to adapt foreign production techniques and product designs to local conditions. The Zhiguli passenger car, produced with the assistance of Fiat and modeled after the Fiat-124, required modifications of 65 percent of its parts in order to perform adequately under Soviet conditions.[14] (2) Frequently the highest-quality domestic labor and material resources are needed to ensure that imports of advanced technology are effectively exploited. One example is the apparent diversion of experienced construction crews from high-priority Moscow projects to work on construction of the Western-assisted Volga and Kama river automotive plants. Likewise, skilled production workers have been recruited from other regions for the Soviet automotive industry.[15] (3) Often, Western-assisted projects cannot function effectively without massive domestic investment in complementary industries and facilities. Foreign technology imports may

12. See Vladimir G. Treml, "Foreign Trade and the Soviet Economy: Changing Parameters and Interrelations," in Egon Neuberger and Laura D'Andrea Tyson, eds., *The Impact of International Economic Disturbances on the Soviet Union and Eastern Europe* (New York: Pergamon Press, 1980), pp. 184–211. For a critique of Treml's analysis by Jan Vanous, see Wharton Econometric Forecasting Associates, Centrally Planned Economies, *Current Analysis*, July 14, 1982. Treml's response is in the August 6 issue.

13. On this subject, see also George Holliday, "Western Technology Transfer in the Soviet Union: Problems of Assimilation and Impact on Soviet Imports," in U.S. Congress, Joint Economic Committee, *Soviet Economy in the 1980s: Problems and Prospects* (Washington, D.C.: U.S. Government Printing Office, 1983).

14. Hardt and Holliday, "Technology Transfer and Change," p.204.

15. George D. Holliday, *Technology Transfer to the USSR, 1928-1937 and 1966-1975: The Role of Western Technology in Soviet Economic Development* (Boulder, Colo.: Westview Press, 1979), p. 180.

be likened to the down payment on economic change; subsequent payments must be made by a selective revision in domestic resource-allocation priorities.

The long-term effect of Western technology transfers to the Soviet Union will probably be to strengthen the Soviet economy. But the net effect may be to direct Soviet resource allocations to those sectors of the economy that are the main recipients of Western technology. Furthermore, the sophisticated nature of domestic investment requirements for projects using Western technology competes with the defense industries and other high-priority sectors.

If the resource-demanding function of Soviet imports of Western technology exceeds the resource-releasing function, the traditional Soviet high-priority investment sectors may be affected. For example, resources needed to complement technology imports may have to be diverted from military programs. If so, the traditional advocates of a high priority for military spending would undoubtedly exercise their considerable political power to impede change. They might readily accept the long-run utility of a more modern energy base, but not at the expense of short-run cuts in key military programs. They might, however, be partly appeased by the gains in administrative power over high-technology civilian projects offsetting their loss in resource priority. This would be more attractive if leadership policy seemed to give them no better alternative.[16] For these reasons, the domestic demands on Soviet resources are likely to be for high-quality products severalfold the value of imported products. Moreover, as much high-quality domestic machinery would be used as possible to minimize import requirements. In building a new project in the Urals, the Soviets rapidly constructed an entire urban industrial complex, using a combination of Western imports and high-quality intermediate products. The expenditures were several times the value, in ruble equivalents, of the imported equipment. Several Soviet economists in informal discussions have suggested that imports were held down in 1976–77 not just because of the hard-currency debt but also because imported machinery would place demands on Gosplan for additional scale resources. A resource-demanding ratio substantially above 2:1 seems reasonable. A careful and detailed analysis of several large projects and their effects on supply plans is necessary to determine the ratio more precisely; but it is not possible with the available information.

If high-quality intermediate goods and facilities are required, will there be a choice between military and civilian economic growth?[17] It seems likely that

16. See John P. Hardt, "Soviet Commercial Relations and Political Change," in R. Bauer, ed., *The Interaction of Economics and Foreign Policy* (Charlottesville: University of Virginia Press, 1975), pp. 48–83.

17. For other answers to this question, see in *Soviet Economy in the 1980s*: Daniel L. Bond and Herbert Levine, "The Soviet Machinery Balance and Military Durables in SOVMOD"; Myron Rush, "The Soviet Policy Favoring Arms over Investments since 1975"; and Gregory Hildebrandt, "Trade-offs between Growth and Defense."

any major high-priority project in the civilian sector must draw on the pool of Western type industrial products usually reserved for the military. Accelerating a major Siberian complex would seem to involve decisions that would change civilian-military priorities. This is likely simply because any large-scale, high-quality rapid building in the Soviet Union appears to be done by the military builders, and the only adequate supply of high-quality industrial goods appears to be found within the Ministry of Defense Industries. This hypothesis might, in turn, be supported by a detailed piecing together of available evidence in the defense economics field. However, since such information is largely covered by the Soviet Secrecy Acts, this conjecture will have to be left as an assumption.

Industrial Cooperation: Toward Joint Ventures. A narrowly constrained transfer of technology, such as a one-time purchase of equipment or even turnkey plants (suppliers of a complete product or service by contract) followed by a reduction of Western ties, has not proved particularly successful for purposes other than relieving domestic demand at a given time. The Soviets have often established modern industrial plants based on Western technology imports only to fall behind the rapid pace of technological progress in the West within a few years. Their inability to keep abreast technologically is a result of shortcomings in both their foreign commercial and their domestic economic institutions.

The Soviet leaders' awareness of these and other problems has led them to consider more flexible arrangements for importing Western technology. The traditional Soviet approach has been giving way to a modified systems approach characterized by (1) a long-term or continuous connection, (2) complex or project-oriented management and distribution, (3) systems-related construction, production, management, and distribution, and (4) Western involvement both in the USSR and at home in the training and decision-making process.[18]

Financing Western Technology Transfers. A major constraint on Soviet technology imports from the West is the USSR's ability to finance such imports. During the 1970s it had serious and chronic balance-of-payments deficits in trade with the West and a rising level of hard-currency indebtedness due to short-, medium-, and long-term borrowing from private and official Western banks. This situation temporarily improved in 1974, when the jump in oil prices enabled the Soviets to expand their hard-currency earnings. But in 1975 and 1976, Soviet trade deficits again worsened. Concurrently, net Soviet debt to the West (gross debt minus deposits in Western banks) declined in 1972 to $555 million from a level of $582 million in 1971. Thereafter, net debt rose each year, almost reaching the $10 billion mark by the end of 1976. Unwilling to allow continued increases in trade deficits and debt, the Soviets began to cut imports,

18. Hardt and Holliday, "Technology Transfer," pp. 184–89.

170 JOHN P. HARDT AND KATE S. TOMLINSON

especially of machinery and equipment, from the West. In addition, the Soviets increasingly sought product-payback arrangements with Western firms to avoid having to expend hard currency. According to estimates by the CIA, the Soviets managed to reduce the annual trade deficit from an average of $6 billion in 1975–76 to an average of $2.9 billion in 1977–80. Net debt rose to $11.1 billion in 1977, but then began to decline, sinking to $9.55 billion in 1980.[19]

In 1981, however, Soviet efforts to reduce trade deficits and debt came undone, owing to the need to import large amounts of grain from the West and to give Poland a substantial amount of hard-currency aid, and also owing to soft oil prices on the world market. The hard-currency deficit increased from $2.5 billion in 1980 to $4 billion in 1981. Net debt ballooned from $9.5 billion in 1980 to $12.5 billion in 1981. These unfavorable developments occurred despite a reduction in nonagricultural imports to their 1978 level, large sales of gold in a soft market, increased borrowing, and a temporary downturn in deposits in Western banks.[20]

Equivocation in Brezhnev's Modernization Policy. In the Tenth Five-Year Plan (1976–80), the first plan in the fifteen-year-plan, there appears to have been a major equivocation in the application of the new Brezhnev modernization strategy, especially as it involved Western technology transfer.[21] Serious delays in the plans for modernization in areas such as the following were costly to future Soviet economic performance: (1) projected production of Western automobile and truck models; (2) development of the power-consuming industries and resource-development industries in East Siberia and the region around the Baikal-Amur railroad; (3) development of the agrobusiness complexes required for modernizing the feed grain livestock industry; (4) development of long-distance alternating and direct current (AC and DC) transmission facilities for bringing cheap hydro- and coal-generated power from Siberia to European Russian markets, and of importing transmission, exploration, extraction, and other facilities for petroleum and natural gas complexes to meet the projected plan of output increases both onshore and offshore; (5) development of the Kursk metallurgical project for pelletizing and direct metal reduction; and (6) introduction of an effective, computer-assisted national economic reporting system.

The delays suggest that there was debate within the Soviet leadership on the priority of modernization, especially as it involved increased imports from the primary trading area, Western Europe. These differences of views may represent equivocation on the part of Brezhnev.

19. Joan Zoeter, "U.S.S.R.: Hard Currency Trade and Payments," in *Soviet Economy in the 1980s*, pp. 479–88.

20. Ibid., pp. 482–88.

21. John P. Hardt, "Soviet Economic Capabilities and Defense Resources," in *The Soviet Threat: Myth or Reality?* (New York: Academy of Political Science, 1978), pp. 122–24.

Noting that the Soviet leadership decided to reduce the rate of growth of investment during the Tenth and Eleventh Five-Year Plans, Myron Rush concludes that the Brezhnev leadership was set on a course of sacrificing investment in favor of a continuing defense buildup.[22] Given the secular decline in the Soviet rate of growth in the 1970s and its probable continuation in the 1980s, the decline in both the growth rate of investment and in its share of national income is liable to impose serious constraints on Soviet efforts to modernize key sectors of the economy. Efforts to increase the effectiveness of capital utilization, and thus to foster the goal of modernization without significantly increasingly investment, are unlikely to succeed.

Others, especially Hanson, argue that the earlier enthusiasm of Soviet leaders for imports of Western technology as a means of achieving a scientific and technological revolution in their economy has cooled.[23] The limited effectiveness of some major projects in automotives and computers may fuel this skepticism. The expanded political use of restrictions on key Western exports to the USSR by the Carter and Reagan administrations raises the political cost of using Western technology. Thus far, the natural gas pipelines and the BAM (Baikal-Amur Mainline railroad) are the only major high-priority projects tied to Western trade in the 1980s.

On the other hand, there are those in Gosplan, the Ministry of Foreign Trade, the State Committee on Science and Technology, the academic institutes, and a number of ministries who still argue for an expansion of modernization based on Western technology. Their arguments are deflected for the time being by a shortage of hard currency, a low level of domestic investment, and a deferment of domestic reform.

Energy: The Solution or the Problem? The Soviet Union has been a net exporter of oil since 1955 and of natural gas since 1970. In recent years, exports of oil and oil products have become the largest single earner of hard currency, bringing in over $4.5 billion in 1976. By 1980, natural gas exports had become a major source of hard currency as well.

Because of the enormous demand and significant price increases for energy in 1973 and 1974, the USSR was able to finance a large share of high-priority imports with oil income. Even without further energy price increases, the Soviet Union will likely continue to be a net energy exporter to the West throughout the 1980s in order to earn hard currency and finance imports. Out of a total of 135 million metric tons of oil available for export in 1980, the Soviets exported

22. Rush, "The Soviet Policy Favoring Arms."

23. Philip Hanson, "The Role of Trade and Technology Transfer in the Soviet Economy," paper prepared for the Conference on Economic Interchange with the USSR in the 1980s, April 15–17, 1982, Belmont Conference Center, Elkridge, Maryland, esp. pp. 11–20. (To be published.)

75 million metric tons to Eastern Europe and 35 million metric tons to hard-currency countries; and out of the 59 billion cubic meters of gas available for export in 1980, 33 billion cubic meters were exported to Eastern Europe and 26 billion cubic meters to Western Europe.[24] In 1981, the volume of oil exports to Western countries decreased, while that of natural gas increased.

In order to maintain energy exports as a major hard-currency earner, the Soviets had to produce or import significantly more drilling equipment, pipelines, submersible pumps, and other geophysical equipment. Without this equipment and technology, exploration and extraction would have been unlikely to keep up with energy demand. Therefore, the energy sector laid claim to a priority share of the hard-currency income.

Attainment of the 1985 and 1990 oil production goals depends primarily on the rapid development of West Siberian deposits, on major improvement in the technology and equipment for oil exploration, development, and transport, and on the continued stability of present levels of output in the existing oil fields in West Siberia.

The volume of oil exports to the West is to some extent a function of production goals in the 1980s.[25] Should, for example, the goals for the 1980s be significantly underfulfilled, the Soviets could cut back on oil exports in order to maintain domestic supply and supplies to Eastern Europe. The more important variable that determines the size of oil exports, however, is the ability of these exports to finance large quantities of Western equipment, technology, and grain. As long as oil maintains its potential to earn large amounts of hard currency, it is likely oil exports will be kept high—even at the cost of cutting back on domestic usage—as long as physically possible.

During the 1980s, a high level of oil exports may become difficult if not impossible to maintain in the following cases: (1) if no new large field like Samotlor is discovered and proven out, (2) is adequate geophysical equipment and skilled labor to manage the equipment are not readily available, (3) if investment resources are not sufficient to support necessary roads and facilities, exploration, and extraction plans, and (4) if Western credits are not available to finance crucial imports. Oil exports may represent the critical margin for Soviet hard-currency income in the 1980s. According to one estimate, in 1985 they may range from $11.3 to $19.3 billion in current prices.[26]

24. ECE, Economic Bulletin for Europe, June 1981, p. 233.

25. For a more detailed analysis, see U.S. Congress, Joint Economic Committee, Energy in Soviet Policy (Washington, D.C.: U.S. Government Printing Office, 1981), esp. chaps. 2 and 4, and Hedija H. Kravalis, "U.S.S.R.: An Assessment of U.S. and Western Trade Potential with the Soviet Union through 1985," in U.S. Congress, Joint Economic Committee, East-West Trade: The Prospects to 1985 (Washington, D.C.: U.S. Government Printing Office, 1982), passim.

26. Kravalis, "U.S.S.R.," p. 296.

Exports of natural gas are expected to rise sharply in the 1980s, as the output of gas increases and the pipeline network expands. Attainment of the natural gas production goal of 435 billion cubic meters for 1985 depends largely on substantial production increases from West Siberia, particularly in the Urengoi area. Although this production goal does seem realistic, fulfillment turns on the ability of the Soviets to make major improvements in pipeline construction, technology, and high-performance pipeline equipment. More and better pipelines could result from expanded Western supply and financing arrangements.

The ability of the Soviets to import the large quantity of Western technology necessary for the rapid development of energy resources has been and will continue to be dependent on their ability to earn hard currency, borrow at acceptable and affordable interest rates, arrange compensation agreements, participate in long-term cooperation agreements with the West, and maintain a high level of debt with Western nations.

To encourage long-term energy cooperation between East and West, among other goals, the Soviet Union, along with thirty-four other nations in 1975, signed the Helsinki Final Act, which supported the following long-term projects: (1) exchanges of electrical energy within Europe with a view to utilizing the capacity of the electric power stations as rationally as possible; (2) cooperation in research for new sources of energy, especially nuclear energy; and (3) cooperation in perfecting equipment for multimodal transport operations and for handling containers.[27]

Compensation agreements with the West are perhaps one of the best ways for the Soviets to import Western technology and develop resources, since they often do not involve complex financing arrangements but rely on barter with repayment through exports of the product resulting from the project. Yakutia, Sakhalin, and Orenburg are successful examples of these compensation agreements. In all three cases the Soviets were able to commit future energy production for current purchases of energy services, equipment, and technology. For future East-West trade, the Soviets have indicated a strong preference for this type of agreement.

The Soviets also emphasize exports using substantial energy inputs. Those products that use energy in their production processes are said to "embody energy." The Soviets, therefore, have options when developing their energy export industries, to export the raw materials—oil, gas, and coal—or to export products that "embody energy," such as mineral fertilizers, copper, and aluminum. Because the products can use cheap and available energy resources, such as thermal power, hydropower, and natural gas, they serve three useful purposes to the Soviets: (1) They contribute to the modernization process, for they encourage further development of the energy centers of East Siberia, where

27. See Conference on Security and Cooperation in Europe, *Final Act* (Helsinki, 1975), Bulletin Reprint, U.S. Department of State, Washington, D.C.

much of the natural gas and cheap hydropower is found. (2) Using a relatively small labor force, the production process for these products does not need the high-cost development facilities required for the export of raw materials. (3) By developing an exportable product, the Soviets are able both to reduce their dependence on oil and gas exports and to help finance their growing debt to the Western nations.

The demand for energy-embodied products does exist in some Western countries, because with large energy deficits these countries are looking for ways to cut back on domestic energy consumption yet satisfy their needs for energy-embodied products. It remains to be seen whether the Soviets will choose to use their energy resources to develop energy-embodied products for export or to allocate their resources to other areas. The Soviets have been economically supportive of Eastern Europe at a high cost to their own economic welfare. The Soviet Union in 1975 exported a total of 63.6 million metric tons of oil, 11.3 billion cubic meters of gas, and 14.8 million metric tons of coal to Eastern Europe. In 1980 the Soviets exported 75 million metric tons of oil and 33 billion cubic meters of gas to Eastern Europe.[28]

When the Soviets export energy to the Eastern countries, they forgo the hard currency that might have been earned had they exported the energy to Western Europe. In 1975 alone the Soviets might have earned approximately $5.25 billion by selling to hard-currency countries instead of to Eastern Europe.[29] The Soviets maintain a high level of energy exports to Eastern Europe presumably because of concern over East European performance and because it gives them a strong say in political and economic decisions made there. The decision to reduce oil deliveries to Czechoslovakia, Hungary, and the GDR by as much as 10 percent per annum, which was announced in late 1981, is thus a measure of Soviet concern about hard-currency earnings and debt levels. The CIA estimates that the Soviets could earn as much as $1 billion annually by switching the destination of this oil to the West.[30]

Although the Soviets—from a desire to increase energy exports to hard-currency countries—have encouraged the East European countries to make arrangements with the Middle Eastern countries to exchange energy for goods and services, no major deals have been made. The Middle Eastern nations generally prefer to exchange their oil for hard currency rather than make barter arrangements, but the East European countries have very little hard currency available for purchasing oil. Therefore, it does not appear that the Middle East will contribute significantly to Eastern Europe's supply of energy.

28. *Economic Bulletin for Europe*, June 1981, p. 170.
29. The Soviets sold 38.6 million metric tons of oil to hard-currency countries, earning $3.2 billion. They sold 63.3 million metric tons of oil to Eastern Europe. If they had sold the 63.3 million metric tons to hard-currency countries, they could have earned $5.25 billion.
30. Zoeter, "U.S.S.R.," p. 495.

The Soviet leadership, in a continued effort to earn more from energy exports, has raised the price the Eastern nations must pay for oil and gas. Although prices have not yet been raised to the world level, starting in 1975 the East European nations were placed on a multiyear moving average related to world market prices, which will draw them closer to Organization of Petroleum Exporting Countries (OPEC) pricing levels. Still, since soft or nonmarketable goods by Western standards are accepted in payment, the returns to the USSR are less than the price equivalents would suggest. Oil and gas prices will continue to rise, but because of the Soviet policy of maintaining economic order and control over Eastern Europe, they will not rise enough to cause permanent economic damage and will probably end up less than world market prices.

Raw Materials and Agricultural Prospects. Traditionally, raw materials have been a large export item for the Soviet Union. Metals—nickel, palladium, platinum, and chromium—in particular have been exported in large quantities to the developed West, as have wood, wood products, diamonds, and foodstuffs. Future prospects for increased export earnings will depend on (1) raw material price trends in the West, (2) ability to increase the volume of raw material exports, and (3) ability to increase the volume of manufactured exports. Because of problems such as quality, marketing, servicing, and strong Western competition, it is unlikely that exports of manufactured goods will contribute significantly to future export earnings.[31]

During the 1960s, the value of Soviet exports to the developed West rose because of an increase in the volume of exports rather than an increase in the price received. Oil, coal, wood, and wood products were the fastest growing exports. During the 1970s, by contrast, the value of exports to the developed West grew because of an increase in the prices received for major Soviet exports—oil, wood, cotton, metals—rather than an increase in the volume exported.

The volume of Soviet export did not increase during the 1970s primarily because of bottlenecks in raw material supply. An increase in both domestic and CMEA demand for raw materials, combined with rising investment costs for exploitation, was the main reason. To help solve the problem, the Soviets have encouraged increased CMEA and Western investment in raw materials projects.

The volume of Soviet exports during the 1970s was also limited by the Western recession. As early as 1974, economic activity in the West began to contract and inventories increased because of the recession. Hence the demand for Soviet exports fell. This situation, combined with rising prices for industrial equipment—resulting from Western inflation—and poor harvests, caused balance-of-payment problems for the Soviet Union. Imports of Western grain

31. See N. Smeliakov, "Zapiski zamestitelia ministra vneshnei torgovli," *Novyi mir*, no. 12, December 1973, pp. 203–39, for a discussion on Soviet problems in exporting manufactured goods to the West, and Kravalis, "U.S.S.R.," pp. 291–94.

and technology, while helping somewhat to relieve short-term shortages and bottlenecks, were particularly expensive for the Soviets because they coincided with reduced demand for Soviet exports.

Future increases in exports of raw materials will depend on the ability to commit more resources to development and exploitation, the availability of Western credits, and the ability to make compensation agreements and other payback arrangements with the West.

Multilateral and Bilateral Agreements. Although both the European Community (EC) and CMEA have submitted drafts for a treaty, the two organizations have not reached an agreement. The Soviet Union would encourage such an agreement, because it would bring a stronger commitment by the East European countries to CMEA, but many of the East European and Western countries prefer bilateral arrangements. The East European countries generally prefer bilateral contacts, because they can minimize Soviet economic dominance and in some cases obtain more concessions with the West. Similar considerations seem to motivate West European countries to prefer bilateral arrangements. Yet, it is conceivable that an agreement could be reached because the EC and CMEA draft treaties mention some areas of agreement—such as economic prognoses, statistics, environmental protection, and standardization.[32]

Most commercial agreements between East and West have been bilateral rather than multilateral. Dating as far back as the 1960s, starting with the Federal Republic of Germany, and then expanding to other West European countries, the number of bilateral agreements in scientific, technical, and economic areas grew rapidly. Over time, these agreements evolved from simple licensing arrangements to highly complex joint-production and coproduction ventures and turnkey projects involving product compensation arrangements.

For Soviet purposes, turnkey projects have been most useful, for they are the most efficient method of importing needed Western technology equipment, management skills, and marketing capabilities. These projects are used primarily in oil and gas development, exploration, and exploitation; major technological improvements in the production of computers, cars, trucks, and steel; developing, processing, and storing agricultural products; and livestock raising.

There is some question whether Western equipment and technology transfers in the form of turnkey projects or Western credits will have a major impact on the export capabilities of the Soviet Union. It seems more likely that such imports will have a marginal impact on Soviet productivity and will relieve critical short-term bottlenecks.

---

32. For a detailed analysis, see Max Baumer and Hanns-Dieter Jacobsen, "CMEA's 'Westpolitik' between Global Limitations and All-European Potentials," in U.S. Congress, Joint Economic Committee, *East European Economic Assessment*, part 2: Regional Assessments (Washington, D.C.: U.S. Government Printing Office, 1981), pp. 872–86.

Nontrade Income. Tourism has been a modest earner of hard currency for the Soviet Union. According to the CIA, net receipts from tourism were between $300 and $400 million in recent years.[33] In the past, the uneven quality of Intourist, Aeroflot, and other Soviet facilities restricted the growth of tourism, but the construction of new facilities for the Moscow Olympic Games in 1980 significantly expanded and improved existing facilities.

Soviet merchant shipping has expanded at an impressive rate in the 1970s, allowing it to earn substantial hard currency. Its earning capacity will undoubtedly continue to grow again after the recession in the West ends and if East-West agreements on merchant marine activities are renewed.

CMEA's Impact on Soviet Policy.[34] Détente between the superpowers and increasing East-West trade moved together. Political understandings between Moscow and Washington provided more maneuvering room for Eastern Europe to deal bilaterally with both the United States and Western Europe—its traditional trading partner. A renewal of tensions between the Soviet Union and the United States, reinforced by economic recession in East and West, led Moscow and Washington to press for political conformity and control—more integration in Warsaw Pact and CMEA in the East and U.S. efforts to persuade or, through extraterritoriality, force Western Europe to restrict strategic exports to the Soviet Union and Poland. The East European countries have always resisted unilateral Soviet control of CMEA, insisting on the principle of unanimity and other provisions in CMEA to retain their sovereign influence. Western Europe has been unified in its resistance to unilateral extensions of Washington's control to its Western political and economic relations with the East, especially embargoes and sanctions.

Like the Soviet Union, the countries of Eastern Europe have been concerned with their technology lag and inadequate consumer incentives. However, they have neither the Soviet degree of constraint against reducing security programs nor the Soviet ability to meet the needs of economic modernization from their own resources. The East European countries' attitude toward CSCE is indicative of their avowed desire to reduce the defense burden on their economies. By increasing economic interdependence with Western Europe, Brezhnev's policy may encourage CMEA diversion of resources from the Soviet economy and increased diversity in political and economic policies.[35]

---

33. Zoeter, "U.S.S.R.," p. 486.

34. For a European perspective on CMEA, see Heinrich Machowski, "Rat für gegenseitige Wirtschaftshilfe [Council for Mutual Economic Assistance]," in *Handbuch der Finanzwissenschaft* (Tubingen: J. C. B. Mohr (Paul Siebeck), 1982), pp. 365–92.

35. For analysis of the forces encouraging and impeding CMEA integration, see Paul Marer, "Prospects for CMEA Integration," *International Organization*, 30, no. 4 (Autumn 1976): 631–48.

The different geopolitical positions of Brezhnev, on the one hand, and the East European party secretaries, such as Wojciech Jaruzelski of Poland and János Kádár of Hungary, on the other, help to determine their different outlooks on economic priorities. The massive, resource-rich Soviet economy has different development options than the lesser-endowed, smaller East European economies. Moreover, the Soviet Union may be able to translate expanded military capability into meaningful political power, whereas Poland and Hungary have greater difficulty achieving a marginal benefit to their national security from an increment in defense spending.

In addition to their national defense role, the Warsaw Pact forces have played the role of maintaining internal security—that is, they have served to keep the East European nations in line with Soviet policy and the populace in step with the indigenous party line. Expanding military capability to support the Brezhnev Doctrine, however, as the Warsaw Pact forces did in Prague in 1968, is surely of limited current popularity in Eastern Europe, even within East European party leaderships. Perceptible economic benefits and political relaxation may be perceived as more effective measures for keeping the party in power than increased security forces. In this vein, one might argue that the choice in favor of civilian improvements over military programs is less difficult to make in Eastern Europe than in the Soviet Union. East European leaders, left to their own preferences, seem less likely than their superpower Soviet neighbor to perceive technology transfers from the West as an opportunity to avoid allocation of resources away from military programs, if indeed that is a viable option.

The needs of small-scale East European economies for Western trade in high technology products are probably greater than those of the larger Soviet economy. The East European need combines the domestic requirements for modernization and consumer welfare with the commercial requirements of raising their potential exports to an acceptable quality for sale on the world market. The Soviet Union has provided little technological aid to assist in the modernization of the East European economies. The Soviet modernization policy of CMEA integration has been largely one of sharing problems, what Radislav Selucky calls the "mutual exchange of inefficiency." Indeed, many of the joint ventures pressed on the East European nations by the CMEA Comprehensive Program initiated in 1971 have furthered the long-term Soviet policy of extracting technological transfers from Eastern Europe in return for raw materials. A case in point is the CMEA agreement of 1974 tying the supply of natural gas from the Orenburg field to the East European recipients' willingness to construct the transmission lines and to finance—with hard currency—the importation of compressors and large-diameter pipe. In this instance, as in many others, the West offered the best technological potential for meeting East European requirements for growth and modernization. This pressing need for Western technology is illustrated by East European willingness to entertain comparatively greater institutional flexibility and to institute superior techniques to absorb imported technology and techniques.

Soviet policy in the late 1960s and early 1970s, however, inhibited the ability of the East Europeans to finance needed imports from the West. Emulation of the Yugoslav formula for financing a commerical-technological bridge with the West through tourism, remittances by Yugoslavs working abroad, credits, and industrial cooperation was restricted by the example of Soviet policy and even by direct Soviet intervention. These kinds of economic transgressions were on the bill of particulars accompanying Soviet tanks into Prague in August 1968.

The Soviet détente policy has relaxed constraints in all these areas and thus materially improved East European prospects for exploring new ways of financing increased trade with the West. There were some signs of relaxation before the Moscow and Washington (1972) and Vladivostok (1975) summits, but there is no doubt that the superpower détente encouraged the following two policy changes.

1. The relaxation of the Soviets' policy of controlled tourism, signaled by their own hotel-building program, has stimulated a burgeoning of East European investments in tourist facilities.[36] Not long after the Soviet airline, Aeroflot, negotiated rights to exchange flights with Pan Am on the Moscow–New York run, the Poles arranged for their airline, LOT, to fly from Warsaw to New York. Soviet discussions of Western involvement in hotel construction and servicing have been accompanied by contracts for new tourist facilities in Eastern Europe. West European tourists, who had previously sought inexpensive vacations in Spain, Portugal, and Yugoslavia, were partly diverted to Poland, Hungary, Romania, and Bulgaria.

2. Industrial cooperation between Yugoslavia and Western Europe led to capital and plants emigrating to Yugoslavia (facilitated by more liberal laws on foreign investments) and workers emigrating on a short-term basis—Gastarbeiter—to West Germany.[37] While Soviet policy has permitted new forms of industrial cooperation in Eastern Europe, a large-scale foreign worker phenomenon is not likely to occur in the Soviet Union. What seems more likely is a combination of foreign involvement in the economies of Eastern Europe emphasizing labor-intensive activities. This would be a Western technology and credit bridge, made possible by "domestic Gastarbeiter" (migrants from labor surplus to deficit regions). The Italian Fiat plant in Poland may be such an example.

36. For a study of prospects for the tourist industry in the East European countries, see Paul Marer and John W. Tilley, "Tourism," in U.S. Congress, Joint Economic Committee, *Reorientation and Commercial Relations of the Economies of Eastern Europe* (Washington, D.C.: U.S. Government Printing Office, 1974), pp. 744–71.

37. Paul F. Myers, "Population and Labor Force in Eastern Europe: 1950–1966," and Paul Marer and Egon Neuberger, "Commercial Relations between the U.S. and Eastern Europe: Options and Prospects," both ibid.

The arrangements of Western companies in Romania and Hungary provide other examples. Hungary and Romania have adopted investment laws to facilitate foreign equity ownership in East European enterprises. Their experience may have set the parameters of permissible change for Poland and other East European countries considering the same step.[38]

Against the background of less concern about defense priorities and greater need for high technology Western imports, the East European nations may be more inclined to develop high-priority export industries. Aided by Western credits and cooperation, more significant industrial exports to the West may well become possible. The earlier assessment of the Romanians that most favored nation (MFN) tariff status in the United States was important to them is an indication of the desire to develop just such export industries. In the wake of the oil embargo, however, a new constraint on East European economic relations with the West emerged. The limited quantities of East European industrial and agricultural products of world market quality have gone increasingly to the Soviet Union and to the Middle East to finance necessary oil and gas imports. The Soviet Union is willing, however, to continue to meet the East European needs at low fixed-energy prices; for example, petroleum prices continued to be a fraction of the world market prices.[39] In the current five-year plans for the East European countries, however, some increases in petroleum products may have to come from the Middle East, and the Soviet prices for their current level of deliveries will more closely approximate world market prices. Although this grim picture, especially important for Hungary, Czechoslovakia, the GDR, and Poland, may be modified, East European balance-of-payment problems will be even more difficult in the 1980s than they were in the 1970s.

Current Soviet use of its economic control levers in Eastern Europe centers on efforts to integrate further the economics of CMEA with the USSR, as illustrated by increasing intra-CMEA trade, and the increasing integrative effect of Soviet energy policy. With rising energy prices, the Soviets may make greater demands on East European leaders for conformity in economic policy, and the changing terms of trade may tend to tie the CMEA countries closer to the Soviet economy.

But concurrent with this movement toward increased CMEA integration are efforts by Soviet policy makers to modernize the economy and increase consumer welfare—a policy based on expanding Western economic relations. It is this Soviet need to expand Western economic relations that permits greater East European involvement with Western economic institutions. Prospects for continued involvement were reinforced in 1975 by the Eastern acceptance of

38. Patrick J. Nichols, "Western Investment in East Europe: The Yugoslav Example," in *Reorientation and Commercial Relations*, pp. 740–43.

39. See Michael Marrese and Jan Vanous, "Soviet Policy Options of Soviet Trade Relations with Eastern Europe," in *Soviet Economy in the 1980s*.

Basket II of the Helsinki Final Act on economic, scientific, and technological relations. The principles adopted in the Final Act on "sovereign equality" – "respect of the rights inherent in sovereignty" coupled with the principle adopted by Warsaw Pact and CMEA nations of "mutually advantageous cooperation" – provide a range for independent East European action that could still be defined as within Soviet-approved guidelines. To expect the individual countries to accept a "profoundly Western orientation" of the agreement is beyond the permitted parameters of the Soviet party line, but the area for economic sovereignty or individual-country action appears to have been widened, both in practice and in principle.

In addition, for every change in Soviet policy toward Western Europe and the United States, the East European nations may be willing and able to take steps of substantially greater magnitude: the Soviets agree on a trade center in principle, and a trade center is opened in Warsaw; the Soviets consider industrial cooperation, and the Romanians change their investment laws to permit joint ventures; the Soviets discuss membership in the General Agreement on Tariffs and Trade (GATT) behind the scenes, and Romania, Hungary, and Poland apply for membership; and so forth. Whether a step backward by the Soviet Union would be followed by two steps backward by East European nations cannot be tested at this time, but appears unlikely. However, forward movement in Eastern Europe would probably be arrested, if not set back, by a reversal of the Soviet commercial policy of normalization. The principle of two East European steps in compliance with Western conditions for normalized trade to one Soviet step is applied unevenly. In need of technology and credit at various times, Romania, Poland, and Hungary have broadly acquiesced in the more demanding American requirements. Hungary's tacit acceptance of the Jackson-Vanik amendment (which limits credit to the communist countries unless they allow freer emigration), Poland's promulgation of an investment law, and Romania's adoption of liberal forms of industrial cooperation would not be evidence of opposition to Soviet policy under these circumstances but illustrations of the wider range of acceptable choices possible under the Soviet policy on importation of Western technology and the Eastern interpretation of the Helsinki Final Act provisions. The Soviet Union would have to weigh the political implications of this diversity against the economic advantages of measured increases in East European sovereignty and economic interdependence with the West.

The end of autarky or economic isolation in the commercial trade of the Eastern countries with the West leads in time to a degree of interdependence difficult or costly to reverse. Some Soviet commentators suggest that a failure of détente would mean more than a return to the *status quo ante* – that is, they feel that relations would be worse. In addition, most Western analysts agree that the costs of undoing this measure of interdependence would likely be greater than the costs of establishing it. An assessment of the costs of reversing commercial policy is certainly important to any Western decisions on risks involved in East-West trade.

The inclusion of Western imports in individual CMEA plans for 1981–85 is reversible in part or whole, but the damaging impact on economic performance from the bottlenecks created by substituting Eastern goods for Western deliveries would probably be greater than during the predétente period. Similarly, export production designed for particular Western markets might garner lower returns if sold elsewhere. The Soviet loans to Poland of over one billion rubles after the 1976 price riots, and aid in 1980–81 before and after the declaration of martial law, may illustrate the costs the Soviets will bear to avoid a reversal of East-West economic relations.

The dominance of Soviet policy in Eastern Europe is likely to remain a major constraining factor in CMEA–West European trade. The continued maintenance of overwhelming political, military, and economic leverage in the hands of Moscow's decision makers is likely to circumscribe any independent East European foreign policy actions. The Soviet Union, in turn, is likely to be influenced in permitting this degree of polycentrism and pluralism in East European relations by actions in the other world power centers—the United States, Western Europe, Japan, and the People's Republic of China (PRC). Some argue that the Polish sanctions, which were intended to encourage polycentrism and pluralism, may have the opposite effect of isolating Poland and forcing it back to economic reliance primarily on the Soviet Union.

Likewise, the effects of increasing interdependence between Eastern and Western Europe could lead to outcomes significantly different from those commonly predicted. The industrial nations of Western Europe may become more dependent on Soviet raw materials, including energy, but the Soviet Union and the rest of CMEA may, at the same time, become increasingly reliant on West European technology. Mutual reductions in military forces may leave Warsaw Pact forces stronger than NATO in Europe. At the same time, the increasing threat from China and the U.S. nuclear umbrella may offset these negative developments for European security. In Eastern Europe, Soviet military, political, and economic leverage will doubtless continue to be dominant if the Soviets choose to exercise their power fully and pay the price a dominant policy entails. But the increasing East European reliance on Western sources of high technology products, the lessening of Soviet reliance on East European industrial products, and the diversion of Soviet raw materials from East European markets may permit and perhaps even encourage greater freedom for Eastern Europe in economic relations with the West.

In addition to achieving a greater degree of economic interdependence with Western Europe, the East European countries have extended their economic relations with the developing economies. At the forefront of this policy has been Romania with its triadic policy of trade with CMEA, the West, and the developing countries.[40] The other East European countries have had to move in this direction. However, there is a basic asymmetry between Soviet and Western leverage on Eastern Europe. Soviet energy policy, in particular, requires a reassessment by the East European nations of commercial relations with the oil-exporting nations. Romania, again, with its special relations with the PRC and the Middle Eastern nations, has been a major non-Western supplier of energy processing, refining, and equipment. The limits on expansion of exports to members of AOPEC (the Arab Organization of Petroleum Exporting Countries) and the desire to increase Middle Eastern oil imports have spurred interest in industrial cooperation among CMEA, Western, and developing-country partners. But faced with expanding energy needs, limited domestic supplies, and hard-currency shortages, Soviet energy policy is potentially an effective and powerful lever.

Although the Soviet policy of interdependence has brought many economic gains for the USSR and Eastern Europe, it has also resulted in some disturbing political side effects for the Soviet Union. The Fiat cooperation is an example. Perhaps seeking improved markets for its automobile production equipment and more stable labor conditions for production of automotive parts, Fiat exported jobs that might have been performed by the PCI-controlled Italian unions. By making a deal with Giovanni Agnelli, the head of Fiat, the Soviet Union created an atmosphere of acceptability that allowed the PCI to qualify for more participation in the national government with the Christian Democratic Party dominated by the same northern Italian industrialists. Future political interaction between the PCI and the Christian Democrats could include agreements on domestic wage policy and tax reform. Such a compact would place the PCI in the position of favoring parliamentary participation and letting national policy take precedence over the issues of the international communist movement. This indirect effect of Soviet economic policy encouraging a West European communist party's policy of economic cooperation with bourgeois parties is an aspect of Eurocommunism most disturbing to Soviet ideologists.

These kinds of economic/political policy implications stemming from Eurocommunism in Italy, Spain, France, and Portugal reinforce East European independence from the USSR. They may foster moves by East European parties toward diversity by widening the range of policies on relations with the West and in domestic affairs that are acceptable to the Soviet Union. If indeed the Second International were revived it might have no greater impact than the continuation and acceptance of Eurocommunist trends in Western Europe.

40. John M. Montias, "Romania's Foreign Trade: An Overview," in *East European Economies Post Helsinki*, pp. 871–77.

EUROPEAN PERSPECTIVES

The sanctions imposed by the Carter administration after the Soviet invasion of Afghanistan and the European response to them highlight some of the divergences between the West European countries and the United States on East-West trade.[41] In the view of many Europeans, the Carter administration did not fully consult with them before declaring the sanctions against the Soviet Union on January 4, 1980, but actively sought their support once the response was chosen. On the January 24, 1980, the undersecretary of state for economic affairs, Richard N. Cooper, stated the administration's view of the commonalities in Western perceptions and prescriptions:

> We all share the basic analysis that the Soviet action is a sharp deviation from past Soviet policy and that it constitutes a threat to countries on the periphery of the Soviet Union. There is also allied agreement that we must demonstrate to the Soviets that their conduct will involve heavy costs for them. It is not just United States–Soviet relations or the broader concept of détente which is at stake, but rather the fundamental rules of international behavior which all nations must observe if we are to live in a peaceful and harmonious world.
>
> I would emphasize that allied solidarity is not limited to shared perceptions of the crisis. It extends to a widespread willingness to take measures.[42]

In Cooper's words, the administration envisaged "parallel and mutually supportive actions by individual countries" and recognized that the allies would not all take the same measures. As reasons for the probable divergence in responses, Cooper cited the allies' "different capabilities"; for example, those without large exportable grain surpluses could hardly be expected to emulate the scale of the American restrictions on grain sales. Cooper could have also cited different degrees of vulnerability to Soviet retaliation and different domestic political considerations as reasons for divergent responses.

Few would deny that the United States and the Western allies shared a basic analysis of the invasion. Yet even on this fundamental point there was significant divergence. Many Europeans were know to discount President Carter's characterization of the invasion as the most serious crisis since World War II.

---

41. A version of this section appeared in U.S. Congress, House, Committee on Foreign Affairs, Subcommittee on Europe and the Middle East, *An Assessment of the Afghanistan Sanctions: Implications for Trade and Diplomacy in the 1980s* (Washington: U.S. Government Printing Office, 1981), pp. 98–104. For another view, see Angela Stent, *From Embargo to Ostpolitik: The Political Economy of West German–Soviet Relations, 1955–1980* (New York: Cambridge University Press, 1981), pp. 233–47.

42. U.S. Congress, House, Committee on Foreign Affairs, Subcommittee on Europe and the Middle East, *East-West Relations in the Aftermath of the Soviet Invasion of Afghanistan*, Hearings, 96th Congress, 2d sess., January 24 and 30, 1980 (Washington, D.C.: U.S. Government Printing Office, 1980), p. 2.

Referring to the president's remark, Chancellor Helmut Schmidt expressed this view: "I understand how it could have been said from an American point of view. Given the difference in the geopolitical situation . . . the Berlin crisis comes to mind."[43]

Moreover, the Europeans tended not to believe the notion prevalent in the United States that Soviet acceptance of détente implied a restraining "code of conduct" in the Third World. While U.S. observers, particularly within the Carter administration, understood détente as indivisible and tended to view the Soviet action as an East-West issue, the Europeans generally were willing to accept détente as divisible and did not view the invasion as a threat to détente in Europe.

Between the United States and the Western allies there were also serious divergences on appropriate responses to the invasion. A fundamental divergence between the United States, on the one hand, and France and the Federal Republic of Germany, on the other, centered on the appropriateness and effectiveness of economic sanctions as a diplomatic tool. In contrast to that of the United States, the French policy rejected the use of economic measures for political purposes. Although the Federal Republic's policy did not reject this concept, Schmidt said that a policy of "punishing" the Soviet Union for the invasion would be difficult, given the size of its economy, and "was unproductive and could be dangerous."[44] Thus the German reaction to the Carter sanctions, while approving the political message of deep concern, questioned the rationale of economic punishment, especially if the punishment policy was expected to bring about a Soviet reversal—that is, withdrawal from Afghanistan.

In addition, a number of the West European governments were known to believe that in a period of tension official and unofficial communication with the Soviet Union should be stepped up, not curtailed. Whereas the Carter administration postponed most exchanges from the highest to the technical working levels, the Schmidt and Giscard governments continued—if not expanded—use of channels at all levels.

Many European leaders were loath to return to the cold war era and feared that full adoption of economic sanctions would jeopardize the gains achieved during the late 1960s and early 1970s: a reduction in tensions in Europe and increased trade with the East. At the same time they felt compelled to demonstrate their solidarity with the United States and to avoid giving the Soviet Union an opportunity to exploit the divergences within the Atlantic Alliance.

For Schmidt, the tensions between the goals of maintaining détente with the East and demonstrating solidarity with the United States were particularly acute. In October the chancellor had to defend the Social Democrats' decade-old

43. Quoted by John Vinocur in "Schmidt Calls for More Coherence in Western Policy on Afghanistan," *New York Times*, March 7, 1980.
44. James Reston, "A Talk with Schmidt," *New York Times*, March 7, 1980.

policy of Ostpolitik against the Christian Democrats, led by Franz Josef Strauss. Strauss's anticommunist and pro-U.S. position probably reinforced Schmidt's expression of solidarity with the United States, which is simultaneously the Federal Republic's nuclear guarantor, a major political ally, and sixth largest trading partner. At the same time, the left wing of the SDP and business exerted conflicting pressures on Schmidt.

One of the by-products of Ostpolitik has been a surge in the Federal Republic's trade with the East. OECD (Organization for Economic Cooperation and Development) trade statistics show that exports to the Soviet Union are important for several industrial sectors of the Federal Republic's economy, but only for the farm sector in the United States. On the import side, the Federal Republic imports 17 to 18 percent of its natural gas from the USSR and significant quantities of oil as well.

Therefore, as Schmidt aptly put it, "sanctions vis-a-vis the Soviet Union are a sword with two edges" from the point of view of the Federal Republic of Germany.[45] Moreover, since much of its trade with the Soviet Union is conducted through long-term agreements, government and business leaders in the FRG were concerned that trade could not be easily resumed if the agreements were broken. In the wake of the Carter sanctions the Soviet Union did allude to the potential weapon provided by the magnitude of its trade with the FRG. While in the Federal Republic, Soviet Deputy Minister of Trade Yuri Krasnov threatened it with irreparable damage to bilateral trade if it imposed economic sanctions—in particular, if it agreed to the $100 million limit on individual transactions reportedly proposed by the United States. Krasnov stated that the USSR "could turn off the natural gas tap" in an extreme case.[46] What role, if any, such threats played in the Federal Republic's decision making is not known. The Germans also noted that energy independence is not even a remote goal for Europeans. The choice of suppliers of oil and gas is between such states as Iran, Iraq, Algeria, Libya, and the USSR.

The policy of Ostpolitik is said to have generated political as well as economic benefits—reduced danger of another Berlin crisis, closer relations with the German Democratic Republic, and repatriation of ethnic Germans from the USSR and Eastern Europe—which the FRG seeks to retain. The leadership is proud that about a quarter of a million Germans have been allowed to resettle in the FRG since 1975. The government ascribes this success to a conciliatory policy that eschews explicit linkage of trade and emigration. Noting that many ethnic Germans still seek resettlement in the Federal Republic of Germany, Schmidt has said:

45. Thomas J. Bray and Karen Eliot House, "An Interview with Helmut Schmidt," *Wall Street Journal*, March 10, 1980.

46. Reuters, *East-West Trade Newsletter*, no. 17 (April 23), 1980, p. 4, and no. 18 (April 30), 1980, p. 3. For a related article, see Marshall I. Goldman, "Interaction of Politics and Trade: Soviet-Western Interaction," in *Soviet Economy in the 1980s*.

All this could come to a standstill. So you will understand that the divided nation of Germans–more than 16 million Germans are still living in the Communist world–is not in a position to act as a spearhead or as a forerunner in a conflict between two superpowers.[47]

French Foreign Minister Jean Francois-Poncet announced that the government was not considering "reprisals," but that France would not take advantage of the restrictions on U.S. sale to increase exports to the Soviet Union. The French government, moreover, was thought to oppose both economic sanctions against the Soviet Union and a response on a European scale, by which it evidently meant sanctions by the West European countries as opposed to a response specific to Southwest Asia, such as aid to Pakistan. From a 1978 case in which a French company stepped in to sell TASS a computer that President Carter had prevented an American company from selling, many concluded that the French government might define its pledge narrowly.

The West European governments pledged not to take commercial advantage of U.S. restrictions on exports of high technology items. Most of the major CoCom members, including the Federal Republic of Germany, Japan, and Great Britain, declared their willingness to reconsider tighter restrictions on high technology sales to the Soviet Union within the CoCom framework. But in most cases such willingness was predicated on like responses by the other CoCom countries. As Cooper explained, the other CoCom members did not agree "to restrict high technology per se."

As in the case of industrial exports, the European Community's response was to pledge not to increase exports above the traditional levels–in other words, not to replace the grain embargoed by the United States.[48] For 1980 the EC had an estimated exportable surplus of 7.3 to 8.3 million metric tons of grain, or about half of the Soviet Union's potential import gap, but had not made major grain sales to that country since 1974. With respect to its other agricultural exports the EC also pledged not to exceed "traditional" levels or to make up the Soviet shortfall in other agricultural commodities embargoed by the United States.

Among observers in the United States, there was a widespread perception that most of the Western allies conducted business as usual–or almost as usual–with the Soviets, especially after their initial reaction to the invasion. While the West European countries did not pledge to restrict transfers of technology per se, a number of cases in which an American or Japanese firm appeared

---

47. Bray and House, "An Interview with Helmut Schmidt."

48. Two useful studies of the grain embargo are John C. Roney, "Grain Embargo As Diplomatic Lever: A Case Study of the U.S.-Soviet Embargo of 1980–81," in *Soviet Economy in the 1980s*, and Hanns-Dieter Jacobsen, "Economic Asymmetries and Economic Sanctions: The Partial Grain Embargo of the US against the USSR, 1980/1981," contribution to the Twelfth World Congress of the International Political Science Association, Rio de Janeiro, August 9–14, 1982.

to lose a contract to a West European company were particularly galling to observers in the United States and Japan.

Nonetheless, the West European countries did agree not to seek exceptions to the CoCom controls for exports to the Soviet Union. Since most of the exceptions granted by CoCom involve exports to the Soviet Union, this measure represented a significant change in CoCom's operations. Yet the dollar value of the exports thus forgone—one measure of the impact on Western firms and on the Soviet Union—was probably fairly modest. It was estimated as approximately $50 million by the Carter administration.[49] Moreover, several West European countries, notably Great Britain and Italy, introduced temporary restrictions on credits to the Soviet Union. Support for the Olympic boycott was not particularly widespread in Western Europe, but it should be noted that the European governments could not order their national Olympic committees to join the boycott.

AMERICAN PERSPECTIVES

During the postwar years, U.S. policy on East-West trade and attitudes toward Western Europe's economic relations with the Soviet Union have undergone several fundamental shifts. The United States, from the Soviet point of view, is a European power exercising a major policy role in Western Europe. This fact is symbolized by the United States' central role in the Helsinki Accords. The U.S. commercial position in Europe and its military leadership in NATO are the instruments of its policy role.

In the 1950s, the United States enlisted Western Europe in its policy of economic warfare against the Soviet bloc. During the 1960s, the United States relaxed its policies on trade and economic cooperation with the Soviet Union. Since then, U.S. enthusiasm for East-West trade has cooled, and under the Reagan administration the United States has led a campaign against European participation in the construction of a natural gas pipeline and for tighter controls on exports to the Soviet Union. Underlying these significant shifts in U.S. policies are several fundamental attitudes: (1) Industrial trade with the East is an option rather than a necessity for the United States. (2) Trade with the East can be used as a weapon or a lever to advance U.S. national security interests. (3) The Western countries should strive to maintain a unified policy on East-West trade.

Industrial trade with the East was viewed as an option not as a necessity even at the height of U.S. enthusiasm for trade with the Soviet Union during the early 1970s. Since then, however, the U.S. farm sector and members of Congress from farm states have increasingly come to view the Soviet and, to a lesser

---

49. Paul Lewis, "Allies Discuss More Curbs on Sales to the Soviet Bloc," *New York Times*, January 20, 1982.

degree, the East European market as crucial for U.S. grain exports, even critical for maintaining farm incomes and profits.

The U.S. belief that the leverage of trade can be used to advance its foreign policy goals is reflected in legislation that authorizes the president to impose controls on exports for foreign policy purposes. The economic warfare policy of the 1950s was based on the idea that trade could be used as a weapon. The use of the leverage of trade throughout the 1950s and 1960s may be characterized as a penalty-reward approach, as restrictions on trade were the norm.[50] Exceptions to the restrictions in the form of MFN tariff status and less severe export controls were made for Poland, Yugoslavia, and Romania as rewards for varying degrees of independence from the Soviet Union or for more liberal domestic policies.

While the Nixon and Ford administrations continued to use the leverage of trade to advance U.S. goals, the approach changed. The goal of the new policy associated with Henry Kissinger was to draw the Soviet Union into a "web of relationships" with the United States and the other Western countries, which would lead the former to modify its foreign and domestic policies. As the emphasis shifted from penalties to rewards, the policy of the Nixon and Ford administrations might be termed a reward-penalty approach.

In its first three years the Carter administration continued this approach, but applied it in an ambiguous manner. On the one hand, the Export Administration Amendments Act, which was passed by Congress and signed by the president in 1977, seemed to imply that trade with the Soviet Union was to be placed on a more normalized basis. The amendments included the presumption of the right for U.S. citizens to export to all countries, including the Soviet Union; changed the basis of licensing decisions to a country's current policy and relations with the United States, not its system of government; and mandated quicker processing of licenses with clearer criteria for license decisions and more certainty in the licensing process. Yet, on the other hand, the Carter administration placed greater emphasis on foreign policy controls, which are less predictable for U.S. exporters and the Soviet Union. In two publicized cases the Control Data Corporation and Sperry Univac were denied licenses to export computers, on foreign policy grounds. In the latter case the Carter administration almost explicitly connected the denial of a computer for the Soviet news agency TASS with the Shcharansky trial. Moreover, the administration placed equipment for the oil and gas industry under foreign policy controls in 1978. These controls were described as "a

50. This formulation was originally developed in John P. Hardt, "United States–Soviet Trade Policy," in U.S. Congress, Joint Economic Committee, *Issues in East-West Commercial Relations* (Washington, D.C.: U.S. Government Printing Office, 1979), pp. 277–85.

flexible foreign policy tool to be used when necessary and appropriate, to sensitize the Soviets regarding actions that are damaging to U.S. foreign policy interest."[51]

Following the Soviet invasion of Afghanistan in December 1979, the ambiguity in the Carter administration's approach was resolved in favor of a penalty-reward approach to trade with the Soviet Union. In 1980 the president imposed a partial embargo on grain sales and a full embargo on phosphate exports to the Soviet Union; he imposed additional foreign policy controls and other restrictions on high technology exports; he led a boycott of the Moscow Olympics and banned U.S. exports connected with the games; and he restricted Soviet landing and fishing rights and official bilateral exchanges. The intent of the sanctions was to punish the Soviet Union by inflicting economic costs and to signal U.S. disapproval of the Soviet action. In recognition of the fact that the East European countries did not participate in the invasion and in some cases quietly told the administration that they did not endorse it, a reward-penalty approach was taken in trade policies toward Eastern Europe.

Although the Reagan administration lifted the grain embargo, it retained the other sanctions against the Soviet Union. After reviewing previous U.S. policies on trade with the East, it concluded that Western exports of strategic goods to the Soviet Union should be controlled more strictly, but that the United States could promote exports of nonstrategic goods. Like previous administrations, the Reagan administration emphasized the need for a common Western policy on trade with the East, particularly because the United States no longer has a monopoly on the production of high technology goods. The administration's efforts to forge a common Western policy have focused on, but not been limited to, the CoCom forum.

Since the mid-1970s some U.S. observers have come to believe that East-West trade is a trap for the United States and especially for the West Europeans. They argue that far from moderating Soviet policies as previous administrations had predicted, the trade lever works against its users as the West becomes dependent on Eastern markets. In their view, the West should avoid any interdependence with the East. This attitude is reflected in the administration's view of the proposed Soviet–West European pipeline. Members of the administration have argued that the FRG, France, Italy, and the other participating European countries will become dependent on the Soviet Union for too high a share of their natural gas imports, and will thus become economic hostages to Soviet policy.

ISSUES IN SOVIET RELATIONS WITH EUROPE

Energy Policy and Interdependence. Conservative Europeans and some Americans fear that the construction of the pipeline from the Soviet Union to

---

51. U.S. Department of Commerce, International Trade Administration, Office of Export Administration, *Export Administration Annual Report FY 1980* (Washington, D.C., February 1981), p. 151.

the border of Western Europe during the 1980s may make an economically unified Gaullist-type Europe "from Brest to Brest" a reality, but with Moscow playing the dominant role rather than Paris or another West European capital. In their view, the Soviet Union might at some point use its economic leverage to encourage the removal of all Western export controls and to influence the extension of Western preferential credits and other trade concessions. Coupled with the perceived shift in the military balance to the Warsaw Pact, this trend, they warn, might lead to Soviet dominance of Europe.

On the other hand, there is another more widely held view that stresses the leverage that the pipeline will confer on the West European countries, the increasing independence of the East European countries, and the tendency among the West European communist parties to diverge from the Soviet position on important political issues.[52]

In the 1980s, Soviet plans call for increased development of all energy sources—oil, coal, hydro, nuclear, and gas.[53] Since proven Soviet gas reserves are equivalent to Saudi Arabia's oil reserves and since the Soviets are encountering difficulty in continuing to increase oil output, natural gas is projected to account for the predominant share of incremental energy production and hard-currency earnings for the Soviet Union.

The key to the Soviet's ambitious plans for natural gas and for the maintenance of hard-currency earnings is the construction of the export pipeline and domestic pipelines to bring the gas from Siberian fields to the center. This network of pipelines would exceed the rate of pipeline construction in any other country by several times. According to Soviet estimates, the pipeline construction program will cost over 25 billion rubles. There may have been some opposition in the Politburo to the militarylike priority for natural gas production, but when Brezhnev announced in November 1981 that the pipelines would have to be completed "without fail" by the end of the current Five-Year-Plan (by 1985), the issue was settled. The export line is to be completed and European deliveries are to begin by late 1984 as contracted.

The gas supply agreements signed by the Soviet Union and the West European countries have long-term implications. Gas deliveries through the new export pipeline will continue for twenty-five years. The FRG, the largest purchaser, will import 10.5 billion cubic meters annually; France, the next largest,

52. On the last point, see Joan Barth Urban, "The West European Communist Challenge to Soviet Foreign Policy," in Roger E. Kanet, ed., *Soviet Foreign Policy in the 1980s* (New York: Praeger, 1982), pp. 171–93.

53. For background on Soviet energy policy, see in *Soviet Economy in the 1980s*: Edward A. Hewitt, "Near-Term Prospects for Soviet Natural Gas Industry and the Implications for East-West Trade"; Jonathan P. Stern, "CMEA Oil Acquisition Policy in the Middle East and the Gulf: The Search for Economic and Political Strategies"; and Thane Gustafson, "Soviet Energy Policy."

will purchase 8 billion annually. Other European countries have either agreed to or are likely to import smaller quantities. While deliveries via the new pipeline are to begin in 1984, they need not reach maximum contracted levels until 1987. These commitments are over and above the amount of Soviet gas that has been flowing into the West European gas network through the Orenburg and Northern Lights pipelines since the 1970s. With the deliveries of gas from the new pipeline, the share of Soviet gas in French, German, and Italian imports of gas from all sources will rise to about one-third. Soviet gas will account for 5 to 6 percent of all primary energy in these countries.

West European interest in the pipeline stems primarily from the policy of reducing dependence on OPEC oil and of diversifying sources of natural gas. These policies are also designed to hold down the cost of energy. Unlike some on the other side of the Atlantic who believe that energy independence is an option for the United States, West Europeans do not perceive it as a viable option for Europe. In the European view, the way to achieve energy security and hold down prices is to diversify sources of supply. Thus, West European governments viewed the Soviet proposal as a means of offsetting the risks entailed in importing oil from OPEC and natural gas from other suppliers, such as Algeria. The Italian energy agency used the Soviet price concessions to hold down the Algerian price for gas from a new pipeline via Sicily. Moreover, they viewed the large Soviet equipment orders placed with firms in importing countries as providing substantial job and production prospects for many years. The orders would benefit the metallurgical and equipment sectors, which are highly competitive and have been stagnant in the past few years. A third motivation was the West European view that economic interdependence with the East may stabilize political relations and provide a useful tool for Western diplomacy.

The Reagan administration disagreed with the European assessment and attempted to dissuade the West European countries, especially the FRG, the key participant, from accepting the Soviet offer. The administration's chief argument was that the additional gas deliveries would make major NATO allies dependent on Soviet gas, hence vulnerable to Soviet threats to cut off the gas during a political crisis. The administration also argued that the pipeline would provide the Soviets with large amounts of hard currency—perhaps as much as $11.1 billion annually by the mid-1980s, according to the Defense Intelligence Agency—which could be used to pay for major purchases of high technology from the West. The administration proposed U.S. coal and revival of plans for development of nuclear electric power as substitutes for Soviet gas. As a minimum precaution, the United States urged the West Europeans to arrange stand-by facilities (e.g., Dutch or Norwegian gas).

For much the same reasons some members of Congress—notably Senator E. J. Garn and Representatives John LeBoutillier and James Nelligan—actively opposed the pipeline and urged the president to take a stronger position against West European involvement and to oppose any U.S. participation. Other members, such as Senators Charles Percy and Charles Mathias, and Representatives Gillis Long and Henry Reuss, called for reexamination and clarification of U.S. policy with appropriate concern for differing European perspectives.

The Federal Republic claims to have a virtually complete "safety net"—alternative supplies of non-Soviet gas and other fuels—through Dutch "surge capacity" contracts, new gas from Norway, domestic gas, and stand-by energy sources. An Algerian-Italian gas line would provide additional gas to Western Europe in the 1980s. Liquefied Nigerian gas and more Norwegian gas may be available in the 1990s as well as increased U.S. coal supplies. Public opposition to nuclear plants may limit expansion of nuclear electric power in all major West European countries except France. Premier Mitterrand seems to have sufficiently qualified his preelection opposition to enable resumption of the ambitious French nuclear program.

In response to the presumed Soviet role in the Polish declaration of martial law on December 13, 1981, President Reagan banned U.S. sales to the Soviet Union of equipment and technical data for the refinement and transmission of gas and oil. This measure, which went into effect December 30, 1981, effectively precluded U.S. companies from completing sales related to the pipeline. In particular, it blocked the General Electric Company (GE) from exporting patented rotors for the compressors the West European companies were to supply. After the declaration of marital law in Poland, France and West Germany reaffirmed their commitment to a policy of equipment supply to the pipeline, although that policy was more controversial in Italy.

Much to the consternation of the West European countries, President Reagan decided to expand the ban on U.S. sales of oil and gas equipment to include overseas subsidiaries of U.S. firms and foreign companies that produce oil and gas equipment under U.S. licenses. The decision, which was announced on June 18, 1982, was aimed at preventing U.S. subsidiaries in Europe and European-owned firms from shipping turbines with patented GE rotors to the Soviet Union for the pipeline, but oil and gas equipment for other uses was also affected.[54] Statements by the administration stressed the lack of improvement in the Polish situation as the main reason for the president's decision, but there remained some uncertainty in both Europe and the United States about the reasons for, hence the necessity of, the broadened control.[55]

The European response was angry and unified. The British, French, Italian, and German governments and the European Community protested that the extraterritorial application of U.S. law was counter to international law and was an affront to European sovereignty. They also objected to the retroactive application of the controls to preexisting contracts, and to the U.S. decision to

54. 47 FR 27250.
55. See, for example, Dan Quayle, "A Worthy Objective—But You Wouldn't Know It," *Washington Post*, August 29, 1982.

extend its grain agreement with the Soviet Union for another year. They did not accept the Reagan administration's argument that grain sales and pipeline equipment exports should be viewed differently because the former reduced the Soviet Union's hard-currency supply while the latter would increase it. Given the recession and high rates of unemployment, European governments were also concerned about the potential loss of employment connected with the contracts. For these reasons, the governments of Britain, France, Italy, and the Federal Republic ordered or, lacking legal authority to do so, encouraged their companies to defy the ban. Since enough components for part of the Soviet order were already on European soil or could be manufactured by a French company, Alstom-Atlantique, the European response could partly frustrate the U.S. goal. The Reagan administration responded by blacklisting European firms as the banned equipment was shipped.

Without a compromise, the pipeline controversy, which coincided with a serious dispute over steel imports, will remain an irritant in U.S.–West European relations. The European Community's protest note, which may be taken as an authoritative statement of its members' view, predicted that the expanded controls would not "delay materially" the pipeline.[56] Most evidence indicates that President Reagan believes otherwise.

Strategic Trade and CoCom. Throughout the postwar period dual-use exports to the East (products and technologies with military as well as civilian applications) have been a contentious issue within the Atlantic Alliance. Since the establishment of CoCom in 1950 as a mechanism for coordinating the export policies of the Western countries, both the criteria for deciding which exports to restrict and the lists of embargoed goods have undergone substantial changes. At the U.S. lead, in the 1950s and through most of the 1960s, CoCom sought to deny the Eastern countries all exports that would contribute to their economic as well as military capabilities. The late 1960s saw the adoption in U.S. legislation and, concurrently, in the CoCom guidelines of criteria for controlling only those goods that would contribute to the military capabilities of the East. Along with the demise of the policy of economic warfare against the East and the change in the criteria for deciding which goods could be exported came a reduction in the length and scope of the lists of controlled goods.

Over the years there have been broad areas of agreement and disagreement between the West European countries and the United States.[57] All agree that "strategic" goods and technologies should be controlled in order to preserve Western security. There is general agreement, even in countries such as France

56. Bradley Graham, "European Community Protests U.S. Sanctions against Pipeline," *Washington Post*, August 13, 1982.
57. See, for example, Stephen Woolcock, "Western Policies on East-West Trade," *Chatham House Papers*, no. 15 (1981).

and Italy, which are officially discreet about their participation in CoCom, that a mechanism for coordinating Western export policies is necessary. Beyond that, however, there are disagreements about what constitutes "strategic" goods and which ones with which capacities should be restricted. From the beginning the United States has tended toward a broader definition of strategic and has generally sought to control a broader array of goods than most of the West European countries. In addition, the process of compiling the lists of restricted goods and authorizing exceptions almost inevitably leads to charges that some members are seeking commercial advantages for their firms.

Another important divergence between the West European countries and the United States concerns the linkage of political and commercial relations with the communist countries: the West European countries tend to view them as separate, the United States to link them. Some of the West European countries do occasionally link commercial policy to political relations, but they tend to use "positive" linkages (benefit-penalty) as opposed to the "negative" (penalty-benefit) linkage generally used by the United States. The United States alone uses export controls for foreign policy purposes as well as national security. Thus West European members have not accepted the American use of foreign policy controls in the CoCom forum.

Another factor underlying the differences between Europe and the United States is that in Europe the consensus on the nature of East-West trade and the respective roles of Western countries in CoCom has shifted, whereas in the United States this shift is more ambiguous. The current U.S. legislation, the Export Administration Act of 1979, reflects changes in perceptions of the nature of the Soviet threat, in views on the appropriate balance between preserving U.S. and Western security and maximizing economic benefits from trade, and in approaches to the use of trade in diplomacy. While the legislation is basically in tune with European views, the philosophy of American leadership and the implementation of policy in the Carter and Reagan administrations hark back to the Export Control Act of 1949, the Battle Act of the 1950s, and even to the Trading with the Enemy Act of World War I. The new consensus in Europe, Canada, and Japan is in sharp contrast to the return to older perceptions in Washington. The contrast was brought into focus by the divergent European and American responses to the Soviet action in Afghanistan and martial law in Poland.

A similar phenomenon may be said to exist in the East. The CMEA Six and Yugoslavia have accepted as desirable and preferable their broader Western connections, with greater maneuvering room in terms of system flexibility and external relations. Changes in Hungary and Poland represent the range of Soviet toleration in practice. Paralleling the change in U.S. policy, the Soviet Union in the 1980s has shown a marked inclination to return to great-power dominance, adversarial relations, and Eastern system integration and independence from the West.

The Carter and Reagan administrations made two proposals for significant changes in Cocom's operations: (1) the incorporation of the "critical technologies" approach in Cocom's licensing guidelines, and (2) a tightening of controls on exports to the Soviet Union.

The critical technologies approach evolved from a study by the Defense Science Board, which was completed in 1976. Its chief conclusion was that the direct mechanisms of technology transfer that may accompany East-West commercial relations, such as technical documentation and training of Eastern personnel, are a more important means of technology transfer than exports of specific products.[58] Instead of focusing on the product being considered for export—the traditional approach to export licensing—the Board recommended focusing on the technology being transferred through a given transaction. Or, as it is often described, a "case" approach should be substituted for the "list" approach. As a follow-up to the study, the Export Administration Act of 1979 mandated the compilation of a list of militarily critical technologies, which was completed in the fall of 1980.

West European officials are thought to doubt that this approach is workable. Nonetheless, the other CoCom members seem willing to adopt at least some elements of the approach. For example, during the 1978–79 review of the CoCom lists they agreed to the U.S. proposal to add specific references to technologies as well as products to the CoCom strategic criteria and to include controls on technology in the CoCom lists themselves instead of in an "administrative principle" appended to the lists.[59] At the High Level CoCom Meeting in January 1982, the other CoCom members reportedly agreed to "redefine" CoCom's guidelines and procedures and to include modern technologies on the lists.[60]

Under President Reagan the United States has continued and intensified the Carter administration's efforts to tighten CoCom's controls on exports to the Soviet Union. The Reagan administration has claimed some success in obtaining West European agreement to stricter controls on exports to the Soviet Union and Poland and to more rigorous enforcement of CoCom's controls. Since CoCom's deliberations are generally treated as confidential, it is somewhat difficult to assess the administration's statements. A reading of the official statements released after the Ottawa Economic Summit in July 1981, the High Level CoCom Meeting in January 1982, and the Versailles Economic Summit in June 1982 suggests that some movement in the direction of the American

58. "An Analysis of Export Control of U.S. Technology" (see note 7 above).

59. John P. Hardt and Kate S. Tomlinson, "Economic Interchange with the U.S.S.R. in the 1980s: Potential Role of Western Policy toward Eastern Europe in East-West Trade," paper prepared for Conference of California Seminar on International Security and Foreign Policy, April 1982, p. A-9.

60. "U.S. Allies Agree to Redefine Rules on Sales to Soviets," Wall Street Journal, January 21, 1982.

position has occurred, but that the agreement remains general and has yet to be developed into a workable form.

At the Ottawa Economic Summit the leaders of the United States, the United Kingdom, the Federal Republic of Germany, Japan, France, Canada, and Italy signed a declaration stating, in part, that their economic relations with the Eastern countries would continue to be compatible with their political and security objectives. At the time they did not reveal how they intended to maintain the desired compatibility. The generality of the wording, in fact, concealed divergent views on how trade and diplomacy ought to be related. The heads of state further agreed to hold a high-level meeting to discuss controls on exports to the Soviet Union. In the U.S. view, the High Level CoCom Meeting was to be "the first broad reconsideration of our technology control system in nearly thirty years."[61]

In addition to its proposals on the "critical technologies" approach discussed above, the United States made a number of proposals for tighter controls on exports to the Soviet Union at the High Level CoCom Meeting, which was held in Paris on January 19 and 20, 1982. Specifically, the United States proposed tighter controls on advanced computers, other electronics, fiber optics, semiconductors, and several metallurgical processes.[62] It probably also sought restrictions on the construction of turnkey plants in militarily relevant industries and Western agreements to train Easterners in militarily relevant technologies. In the same vein, the United States was reported to have proposed that all contracts worth $100 million or more be subject to CoCom's approval to make sure that they did not transfer any critical technologies.

According to at least one account in the press, the United States also sought agreement to stop granting exceptions for exports to the Soviet bloc.[63] While a moratorium on exceptions involving the Soviet Union was instituted after the invasion of Afghanistan, a "no exceptions" policy for the entire Soviet bloc would be a major change in CoCom's operations. This report is probably accurate, since it squares with statements by the administration before the meeting that it intended to propose tighter controls on exports to certain communist countries—the Soviet Union and, after General Jaruzelski's declaration of martial law, Poland as well. In all probability, at the meeting the United States also continued its push for better enforcement of controls.

From comments to the press by administration officials and the statement released after the meeting, it seems that the Reagan administration met with some success: the other members apparently agreed not to make requests for

61. Caspar W. Weinberger, "Technology Transfers to the Soviet Union," Wall Street Journal, January 12, 1982.

62. Lewis, "Allies Discuss More Curbs" (see note 49 above).

63. Ibid.

exceptions until review of the 1982 list was finished.[64] An anonymous U.S. official explained that many differences still remained. This is not surprising, given the radical nature of the U.S. proposals.

Even after the Economic Summit of the Seven held in Versailles on June 5 and 6, 1982, the differences between the West European and American positions did not appear to be fully resolved. In reference to East-West trade the communiqué released at the end of the meeting stated:

> We agree to pursue a prudent and diversified economic approach to the USSR and Eastern Europe, consistent with our political and security interests. This includes actions in three key areas:
>
> First, following international discussions in January, representatives will work together to improve the international system for controlling exports of strategic goods to these countries and national arrangements for the enforcement of security controls.
>
> Second, we will exchange information in the O.E.C.D. on all aspects of our economic, commercial and financial relations with the Soviet Union and Eastern Europe.[65]

Credit as a Carrot or a Stick. Few in Europe are in favor of precipitating a formal or de jure Polish default on its foreign trade debts. Part of the reason is that West European governments and banks, which have extended more credit to Poland than their U.S. counterparts have, stand to lose more in the event of default. But they also fear that if a formal declaration of default were made, Poland would no longer have any incentive to repay its debts and would have no other option than a closer Soviet orientation in economic and political policy.

U.S. commercial banks and some private citizens have proposed conditionality as a means of avoiding defaults, ensuring repayment, and maximizing benefits to the West. Economic conditionality is familiar from its use by the International Monetary Fund. As applied to Poland and, in the future, possibly to other East European countries on the verge of formal default, economic conditionality might include the following elements: (1) provision of adequate and verifiable information, (2) establishment of a consistent long-range stabilization program by the indigenous government, and (3) progress with the two preceding elements as a condition for rescheduling old loans. U.S. commercial banks have taken the lead in arguing for applying economic conditionality to rescheduling the Polish debt despite the initial lack of enthusiasm on the part of the West European banks.

64. Ibid.; Paul Lewis, "Soviet Pipeline Called Vulnerable," *New York Times*, January 21, 1982; and "U.S. Allies Agree to Redefine Rules" (see note 60 above).

65. Reprinted in *New York Times*, June 7, 1982. The third of the key areas referred to is export credit, which is discussed in the next section of this chapter.

Political conditionality is a more delicate issue with less clear precedent. But it is certainly not unknown for a country in debt to another or dependent on another for needed imports to be responsive on political and economic issues. Political conditionality is the key to new loans to many Eastern countries, and is therefore an issue primarily for Western political leaders, not bankers. The West European governments appear even more reluctant to apply political than economic conditionality. The Reagan administration has not raised the issue per se, but political conditionality would appear to be compatible with its use of economic leverage in diplomacy. The possibility of applying political conditionality may come up in the future; it was not included in the ten Western governments' agreement to reschedule official Polish debts for 1981. The United States did, however, indicate that it intended to apply leverage by refusing to reschedule official Polish debts falling due in 1982 until martial law was lifted. European governments seconded this use of leverage.

Active use of credit and debt in East-West relations is a divisive policy in the West.[66] Some in the United States would foreclose on the Eastern countries in arrears and close the government credit window to all Eastern countries, including the creditworthy USSR. At the other extreme are those in the United States and Europe who would use debt rescheduling, availability of new loans, and credit management as tools to encourage reform and political pluralism. Private banks and commercial interests tend to use a more apolitical, market approach, with the government of the country receiving the loan acting as a passive guarantor of repayment and stability.

PROSPECTS FOR THE 1980S AND 1990S

Constraints on Soviet Economic Interdependence. Through the mid-1970s, the trend of Soviet trade with the West and, by extension, the level of Soviet interdependence with the West was upward. During the late 1970s, and the first two years of the 1980s, however, the trend was reversed. In 1977 the Soviet Union began to reduce nonagricultural exports, especially machinery and equipment, to improve its trade balance and debt position, and probably to reduce demands on high-quality domestic resources. According to calculations by Joan Zoeter, real imports increased by a modest 2 percent per annum during the 1977–81 period, compared with an annual average of 20 percent during the 1971–76 period.[67] Similarly, Philip Hanson notes the post–1977 decline in Soviet imports of technology, which in his view was broken temporarily by an increase in equipment imports for the pipeline in 1981. He concludes that "in

66. For German views on credit, see Axel Lebann, "Financing German Trade with the East," *Aussen Politik* (English ed.), 33, no. 2 (1982): 123–37, and Joachim Jahnke, "Westliche Kreditpolitik gegenüber osteuropäischen Staaten: Die Problematik angesichts wachsender politischer Spannungen," *Europa-Archiv*, no. 15 (August 10), 1982, pp. 459–66.

67. Zoeter, "U.S.S.R."

some respects the Soviet Union could even be said to have reduced its economic involvement with the Western world."[68]

The outlook for Soviet-Western interdependence during the 1980s and 1990s will depend on financial and political factors such as the Soviets' ability to pay, Western willingness to engage in trade with the Soviet Union and to extend credit, Soviet attitudes on interdependence and Soviet perceptions of the ability of the West to exert leverage through trade, and the course taken by Brezhnev's successor.

The Soviet liquidity crisis of 1981–82, during which the USSR requested deferral of payments to suppliers, complete as opposed to 85 percent financing of equipment imports for the pipeline, and gold sold on declining markets, has raised new questions about the Soviet Union's ability to pay. The consensus of Western analysis is that the Soviet hard-currency position will probably be more difficult for the remainder of the 1980s than it was during the early 1970s, but that it will not be a serious constraint on the Soviets' ability to continue critical imports of machinery and equipment.[69]

Likewise, Western willingness to export to the Soviet Union is unlikely to be a serious constraint. The West Europeans have shown no indication of plans to change their policies of promoting exports to the Soviet Union. Under the Carter and Reagan administrations, the United States has restricted technology exports. But, even if U.S. policy remains more restrictive in the 1980s and 1990s, the Soviet Union will probably be able to turn to West European suppliers for most of its import orders. The Soviet Union is considered to be the most creditworthy borrower in Eastern Europe. Even so, current repayment problems in Poland and Romania may have an effect on the Soviet Union's ability to borrow on international markets at least in the short run. Wharton Econometric Associates predicts that the Soviet debt will increase by 40 percent in real terms from 1980 to 1985.[70]

As Hanson suggests, political considerations may be more important constraints on Soviet trade and interdependence with the West than financial exigencies. Soviet decisions about the amount of interdependence they are willing to accept will be made during the transition to a new generation of leadership. In all probability this period will also be a period of slow growth.

68. Hanson, "The Role of Trade and Technology Transfer," p. 1. For a discussion of Soviet export performance in the 1970s, see Philip Hanson, "The End of Import-Led Growth? Some Observations on Soviet, Polish, and Hungarian Experience in the 1970s," *Journal of Comparative Economics*, 6, no. 2 (June 1982): 130–47.

69. See Zoeter, "U.S.S.R.," Kravalis, "U.S.S.R.," and Hanson, "The Role of Trade and Technology Transfer."

70. Daniel L. Bond, "CMEA Growth Projections for 1981–85 and the Implications of Restricted Western Credits," paper prepared for the NATO Economic Colloquium, Brussels, March 31–April 2, 1982, pp. 13, 24.

While a policy of muddling through—that is, keeping economic policy as it is—is an option for the Soviet leadership, it is liable to result in a significant slowdown in growth and shortfalls in key sectors. Nor would such a policy be likely to advance Soviet international security goals. The two likely alternatives for change in Soviet economic policy tend to be divergent: (1) policies that foster economic modernization and interdependence with the global economy, and (2) neo-Stalinist policies of extreme centralization, tight control, and isolation from the noncommunist world.[71] The modernization/interdependence and control/security tendencies can be described in terms of the policies they would entail for national economic development: the allocation of resources for "guns," "butter," and "modernization"; reform of planning and management; economic relations with the industrialized West; and relations with the smaller members of CMEA. Of the two tendencies, the modernization/interdependence one is liable to yield the better economic results and is more likely to be chosen if economic improvement is the first priority. If considerations of internal and external security are paramount, the control/security option is more likely to be adopted.

These two tendencies have sharply divergent implications for Soviet policy on Western Europe. A policy of modernization/interdependence is likely to emphasize international cooperation over competition. Under the neo-Stalinist control/security option, competition and confrontation with the capitalist countries are liable to be the focus. A major factor in determining the tendencies in Soviet policies will be the nature of the domestic power struggle for succession. Western policies will have some influence on succession outcomes. The influence is likely to be enhanced if the West has a unified position on relations with the East.

Prospects for Western Unity. Underlying the current disarray in the West's policy on economic relations with the East are fundamental differences in European and American views on the importance of East-West trade and how it should be conducted. Yet evidence of divergence in views—hence in policies on such issues as the pipeline, CoCom controls, and credits—obscures the important areas of agreement between the European countries and the United States, which should not be overlooked in the effort to forge a common Western policy on East-West trade. In practice, the commonalities are at such a general and nonoperational level as to provide little or no basis for specific policies. At

71. An earlier version of these groupings appeared in John P. Hardt and Kate S. Tomlinson, "Economic Factors in Soviet Foreign Policy," in Kanet, ed., *Soviet Foreign Policy in the 1980s*, pp. 37–57. For another view, see Morris Bornstein, "Soviet Economic Growth and Foreign Policy," in Seweryn Bialer, ed., *The Domestic Context of Soviet Foreign Policy* (Boulder, Colo.: Westview Press, 1981), pp. 227–55.

the operational level, the divergences tend to take over. The commonalities and divergences between American and European views on East-West trade are presented below in schematic form.

COMMONALITIES IN GENERAL POLICY POSITIONS:

1. *The agreed upon basis of CoCom export licensing: denial of exports of military significance.* Restrictions on security-related exports to all Eastern countries are appropriate in the view of all CoCom members.

2. *The agreed interest in use of economic influence for foreign policy purposes.* Some interaction of trade and diplomacy is considered appropriate and likely to be effective, in view of the Eastern need for Western technology.

3. *The agreement on a polycentric, individual-country approach to the East.* Commercial relations with the East are best handled on a country-by-country basis—that is, bilateral relations with the Soviet Union, the individual countries of Eastern Europe, the People's Republic of China, and other communist countries.

4. *A common perception of Western economic benefits in expanded commercial relations with the East.* The Eastern countries are perceived as a potentially expanding market.

DIVERGENCES IN SPECIFIC POLICY APPLICATIONS:

1. *On commercial restrictions and benefits.* The divergence in CoCom and Western councils: there is no common definition of security-related exports; there is no common policy on appropriate restrictions, such as tariffs, quotas, market disruption, or dumping proceedings; nor are there common perceptions of appropriate credit policies.

2. *On the interaction of trade and diplomacy.* No OECD or CoCom country accepts current American use of "foreign policy criteria" in linking specific exports such as energy equipment to specific Soviet foreign policies or internal issues such as trials of dissidents.

3. *Individual-country policy.* A high degree of preference is given to individual countries, such as permitting dual-use or nonlethal military exports to the People's Republic of China or Yugoslavia. This is generally a divisive issue. Traditional balance-of-power policies are one thing; explicitly playing the "China card," the "Romanian card," or the "Yugoslav card" is another.

4. *Eastern market prospects.* West European countries view potential markets in the Soviet Union and Eastern Europe as economically as well as politically important, even vital. The dominant U.S. view is that, excepting the grain trade, the prospects of economic benefits for the United States from Eastern markets are modest, important only to specific sectoral and regional interests.

Alternative Scenarios for the Atlantic Alliance. Western economic relations with the East may follow one of the following three courses during the 1980s: (1) A discriminatory policy of restricting Eastern access to Western technology and credits. Such a policy would be an extension of the sanctions imposed by the Carter and Reagan administrations. In classical economic terms, this policy could be called neomercantilist and, in more modern terms, economic warfare. (2) A neutral policy of governmental nonintervention in East-West trade. Since the forces of supply and demand would determine Soviet access to Western goods and credits, this policy may be considered a market policy. It may also be termed a laissez-faire policy. (3) A competitive policy, under which governments would actively promote East-West trade by offering Eastern countries guaranteed access to supplies and favorable terms of credit. This policy may also be called the Helsinki option, after the Final Act signed there at the conclusion of the Conference on Security and Cooperation in Europe in 1975. These three policies would have divergent implications for Western unity and for the Eastern economies.[72]

Under a discriminatory policy, governments would actively intervene in commercial relations to discourage East-West trade. Such a policy would represent a return to the economic warfare of the cold war era. The United States and its CoCom partners would significantly tighten criteria for licensing exports to the East. U.S. licensing policy, in particular, might resemble that of the late-1940s and 1950s, when the Export Control Act of 1949 was applied in such a way as to deny the Eastern countries goods that could enhance their economic as well as military capabilities. Embargoes and foreign policy controls would logically be prominent features of such a policy.[73] Current legislation, the Export Administration Act of 1979, might be modified to provide a legislative basis for such a policy. Official credit would not be available to most of the Eastern countries, and its absence would discourage commercial banks from extending credit. This policy may be called neomercantilist in that the political benefit to the state would be deemed paramount.

This policy is grounded in a zero-sum view of East-West trade, in which a state reaps political benefit only at the expense of others. Since East-West trade—in this view—cannot be mutually beneficial, any gains from trade that accrue to the East must be at the West's expense. Consequently, it is vital to deny the Eastern countries—particularly the Soviet Union—resources. Trade-denial policies would focus on the Soviet Union as the West's chief adversary,

---

72. For an alternative view, see Pierre Hassner, "American Policy towards the Soviet Union in the 1980s: Objectives and Uncertainties," paper prepared for the Twenty-third Annual Conference of the International Institute for Strategic Studies, Williamsburg, Virginia, September 10–13, 1981.

73. For background on recent U.S policies, see in *Soviet Economy in the 1980s*: Thomas A. Wolf, "Choosing a U.S. Trade Strategy towards the Soviet Union"; Jack Brougher, "The United States Uses Trade to Penalize Aggression and Seeks to Reorder Western Policy"; and William H. Cooper, "An Overview of Soviet-Western Trade."

but might be applied selectively to the smaller CMEA members according to their relations with the West and Moscow.

Paradoxically, a discriminatory policy might not be a no-trade option. Absorbing hard currency in order to deny the Soviet Union the ability to import Western technology might well be an element of a discriminatory policy. In this case, grain sales would be encouraged, since they require the Soviet Union to expend its limited supply of hard currency. Equipment exports, however, would be discouraged, because they ultimately provide the Soviet Union with hard currency from export sales.

Some of the objectives of a discriminatory policy would seem to be mutually exclusive: trade reduction with the Soviet Union, and use of trade for leverage; reduction of trade with the CMEA Six on the assumption of a monolithic Eastern bloc, and the use of trade to promote polycentrism in both CMEA and the Warsaw Pact; reduction of imports of energy and other materials from the Soviet Union by the Western industrial nations to limit its hard-currency earning capabilities on the assumption that other sources would provide reliable and economically competitive supplies. (Although reduced West European energy imports from the USSR would mean a reduction in hard-currency income to the communist powers, alternative sources have not been available, let alone reliable and competitive. Were Norway able to provide more gas at competitive prices, that independent, apolitical, and stable source would resolve the dilemma. But the Norwegians maintain that all the gas that can be extracted by 1990 has already been contracted for.)

Adoption of a discriminatory policy by the United States would be extremely divisive for the Atlantic Alliance. The West European countries have shown little inclination to join the United States in a sanctions policy. In contrast to the United States, they do not accept the use of foreign policy controls. Nor are they likely to endorse a marked tightening of export controls.

A discriminatory policy would be intended to have a detrimental impact on economic growth and modernization in the East. The impact would be greater on the economically weaker East European countries than on the Soviet Union. Soviet and East European leaders would have the opportunity to blame their economic failure on the United States. A U.S. policy of economic warfare might strengthen the Soviet Union's inclination to use force, tighten controls, and reinforce integration in Eastern Europe. In the unlikely event that the West Europeans joined the United States in adopting a policy of discrimination or economic warfare against the Eastern countries, there might be a return to the mutual East-West isolationism of the 1950s. Since West European economic sectors now rely on Eastern trade, such an outcome might well make slow economic growth more likely for Eastern and Western Europe and exacerbate East-West tensions.

Outside the communist world, one may expect adjustments that offset apparent costs or losses. Grain not sold to the USSR will find other markets.

Say's law, that supply creates its own demand, is operative in this view. Credit not extended to further Soviet development will be used for Western projects. This static, full-employment assumption tends to justify a policy of embargoes, since no short- or long-term change is borne by Western economies, businesses, or farms.

In a more dynamic world, however, the Argentineans may plant more corn and export to both the USSR and their traditional markets rather than diverting their supplies. In a market with less than full-employment equilibrium, goods and credits denied to the Eastern markets may be underutilized and production forgone.

Under the second or laissez-faire option, governments would reduce their involvement in East-West trade and rely on market forces to determine trade and credit flows. East-West trade, however, would probably not be entirely unrestricted, for national security controls would most likely be retained. This is the preferred option of U.S. bankers and some businessmen. It is also broadly compatible with the Reagan administration's preference for free trade with other regions.

Adoption by the United States of a laissez-faire trade and credit policy toward Eastern Europe would probably be viewed as discriminatory by East and West Europeans. Without the Western governmental umbrella, commercial relations between Eastern Europe and the West probably could not continue as in the past, given current economic woes in Eastern Europe. For their part, U.S. banks and firms might conclude that without the U.S. governmental umbrella, they could not deal profitably with communist countries because of Eastern control of domestic markets and foreign trade monopolies. Moreover, because the Polish debt problems have already dispelled the previously held views of the reliability, stability, and creditworthiness of Eastern countries, governmental assurances are more likely to be needed to support trade and credit in the future.

Since European and Japanese governments are heavily involved in all of their trade—East-West, West-West, and North-South—they are unlikely to adopt a laissez-faire or market approach for East-West trade.[74]

Under the third or competitive option, governments would intervene to promote East-West trade. The basic elements of this approach are outlined in Basket II of the Helsinki Final Act: trade facilitation, reduction of restraints on trade, governmental credits and guarantees, promotion of industrial cooperation, and encouragement of government-to-government, private, and academic exchanges to promote trade.

74. For German views on East-West trade, see Eberhard Schulz, *Die deutsche Nation in Europa* (Bonn: German Council on Foreign Relations, 1982), and Jochen Bethkenhagen and Heinrich Machowski, "Entwicklung und Struktur des deutsch-sowjetischen Handel und Seine Bedeutung für die Volkswirtschaft der Bundesrepublik Deutschland und der Sowjetunion" (Berlin: German Institute for Economic Studies, May 1982; mimeographed).

A preferential Western credit policy to Eastern Europe might not necessarily involve any new loans to any of the CMEA Six at this time or in the 1980s, especially from commerical banks. Even with strict conditionality for payment of interest and rescheduled principal, new resources from Western banks might not be available on commerical grounds for Poland, Romania, or the other CMEA countries. Yet some Western governments might be willing to make credit and credit guarantees available to the economically stronger East European countries and—under certain political conditions, including some forms of economic reform—to the economically weaker nations such as Poland. In that case, Western commercial banks might reevaluate their lending policies based on prospects of improved East European planning and management. Reform might facilitate the application of rules of conditionality in rescheduling and repayment. Specific U.S. bank proposals for joint ventures with Poland currently reflect this approach, which combines private bank economic and governmental political conditionality.

Since the Soviet Union is likely to continue to remain creditworthy and expand its net Western debt—in contrast to the CMEA Six—a more explicit use of the "umbrella" by Moscow might permit more loans to Eastern Europe; for example, the Soviet Union might individually guarantee other East European loans directly or indirectly through CMEA banks. The USSR might also directly or indirectly encourage compliance with the terms of Western economic and political conditionality within the CMEA Six.

Since it has been endorsed by virtually all the European nations, the United States, and Canada, a competitive option could be the basis for a unified Western policy. West European signatories have always been more in tune with the provisions of Basket II than the United States. The economic organization of their commercial institutions as well as those of the Japanese is designed to implement a governmentally competitive trade policy. These non-U.S. economic institutions are geared to implement commercial policies that follow the Helsinki agreement: government intervention to foster commercial exchange, to facilitate freer flow of economic factors without trade restraints, and to provide for government credit on more favorable terms than those offered by commercial facilities.

Western adoption of the Helsinki option might directly and indirectly benefit the economic performance of the CMEA Six. Preferential Western policies would be of more benefit to the East European countries than to the Soviet Union. Western preference would likely serve as a counterweight to Soviet influence. Preferential Western policies might also benefit Eastern Europe indirectly by encouraging preferential Soviet policies on energy supplies. Western analysts generally consider Soviet energy policy toward Eastern Europe preferential, since the Soviets supply oil and gas to East European countries at less than the OPEC or world market price and accept a mixture of hard and soft currencies as payment. They conclude that Soviet terms for energy sales confer an implicit trade subsidy to Eastern Europe. A preferential Western policy would tend to strengthen Eastern Europe's position in relation to the Soviet Union and might thereby encourage a similar preferential Soviet policy toward Eastern Europe: continued preferential energy supplies and forbearance on payment of rising East European debts to the USSR. To the extent that preferential Soviet policy is encouraged toward Eastern Europe by West European preferential policy, this interaction of European and Soviet policy in Eastern Europe may tend to reinforce European inclination toward the Helsinki option.

The Helsinki approach opted for by the Europeans would not necessarily be incompatible with a U.S. choice of the market option. This combination of Western policies might encourage the adoption of the German notion of spheres of commercial interest and division of responsibilities among the Western countries. As applied to East-West trade, such a division might find the United States as the leading exporter of grain, the Federal Republic of Germany as the major supplier of mining and energy equipment, and France and Britain as the major exporters of chemicals.

If the United States is to accomplish the goal set by President Reagan of reestablishing itself as the Soviet Union's major supplier of grain, limited adoption of the Helsinki option might be necessary.[75] In order for the United States to be accepted as a "reliable supplier," the Soviets insist that some steps be taken to ensure that U.S. grain contracts will not be abrogated for foreign policy purposes. Some additional steps may be deemed necessary to stimulate the communist buyers to return the United States to the position of preferred supplier. A precedent for a selective, preferential grain trade was the extension of agricultural credit facilities to China before the conclusion of a trade agreement. The extension of agricultural credit guarantees and loans (CCC) to the USSR without modifying the Trade Act of 1974 would be politically controversial, but would nontheless be a means of serving the purposes outlined in President Reagan's speech to the Iowa corngrowers on August 2, 1982.[76]

A combined policy, however, would involve some political and economic compromises for U.S. policy makers. It might well make direct U.S. participation in the Soviet market less competitive. Indirect participation through foreign-based affiliates of U.S. companies would provide a basis for continued competition by U.S.-owned offshore facilities, but would deny jobs and production to the U.S. domestic economy. Of course, if extraterritorial reach, retroactivity, and other contractual issues raised by the pipeline equipment sanctions have the chilling effect on U.S. foreign competitiveness feared by the National Association of Manufacturers and U.S. Chamber of Commerce, the competitiveness

75. For projections of U.S. grain exports to the Soviet Union, see Angel O. Byrne, Anto Malish, James E. Cole, and Thomas Bickerton, "U.S.-U.S.S.R. Grain Trade," in *Soviet Economy in the 1980s.*

76. Reprinted in *Congressional Record* (daily ed.), pp. 9849–50.

of U.S.-owned firms abroad may also suffer. Some would argue that a sharp restriction of U.S. use of "foreign policy criteria" in licensing would be necessary in order to return the United States to a competitive position equivalent to those of other Western nations. Thus, although the laissez-faire or market approach in nonagricultural trade may be an attractive concept to the leadership in the United States and preferable to the unilateral, denial strategy because of its potential for effectiveness, it would have its limitations in terms of U.S. commercial benefits.

The likely outcome of a combined policy would be that the United States would find itself virtually closed out of Eastern markets for nonagricultural commodities. It would be difficult for the United States to affect East-West commercial policy, because it would not be directly and heavily involved. Therefore, U.S. influence on terms of credit for industrial trade with the East would be severely limited. In addition, a laissez-faire policy would allow the United States to be more economically restrictive in dealing with the Soviet Union, but would also force the administration to seek alternative channels outside the commercial sphere for influencing Eastern trade, even in the grain trade not covered by the laissez-faire policy. Thus political influence would take on a heightened role in U.S.-Eastern trade.

Conversely, while a policy closer to the Helsinki approach might allow the United States to compete more effectively with the other Western industrial nations for a share of Eastern trade, it would be more beneficial to the Soviet Union. The overall American policy toward the Soviet Union would be based on mutual benefit as long as the Soviet military was not directly served by trade: this would be the policy of the Export Administration Act rather than a return to the philosophy of the Export Control Act that limited all trade of economic as well as military benefit to the East.

Chapter 7

Trends in Soviet Military Policy

Benjamin S. Lambeth

The American defense community and the attentive public are once again in the throes of a wide-ranging debate over the nature of the Soviet military challenge. This debate has been partly abetted by a skillful Soviet effort to project a contrast between Soviet "reasonableness" and American obduracy in the superpower relationship. Mainly, however, it has stemmed from a steady erosion of the fragile national consensus regarding Soviet motivations and their implications for Western security that was first formed in the aftermath of the Soviet invasion of Afghanistan in 1979.

The sources of this resurgent disagreement over the Soviet threat (and thus over the appropriate agenda for U.S. defense planning) are both internal and external. On the first count, the massive increases in defense spending sought by the Reagan administration have not been well received by many constituencies, in light of pervasive economic difficulties, mounting pressures for budgetary stringency, and the administration's continued lack of success in articulating a coherent strategy that might justify its program proposals.[1] On top of this, the substantial toughening of the administration's declaratory rhetoric toward the Soviet Union has conjured up widespread popular fears of an increased danger of nuclear war.[2] Not only has this exacerbated the administration's effort to

Any views expressed are solely those of the author and should not be attributed to Rand or any of its governmental or private research sponsors.

1. For elaboration, see Kevin N. Lewis, *The Reagan Defense Budget: Prospects and Pressures* (Santa Monica: Rand P-6721, December 1981).

2. Among the more notable journalistic tracts that have successfully influenced and exploited this mounting undercurrent of popular concern are Jonathan Schell, *The Fate of*

place U.S. defense back on a strong footing, but it has also given rise to increasingly vocal Congressional and public demands for a negotiated nuclear "freeze," which most defense analysts believe would be highly premature given the numerous military imbalances that favor the Soviet Union.[3]

In the external realm, these domestic difficulties have been compounded by a powerful blend of nervous indecision within NATO and a carefully orchestrated Soviet propaganda campaign aimed at discrediting official U.S. depictions of the Soviet strategic threat.[4] This latter effort, coupled with Moscow's "peace offensive" and vigorous advocacy of all varieties of arms control, has fostered a rising groundswell of neopacifism and resistance to nuclear force modernization in Western Europe and thereby deepened further the traditional division of outlook between the United States and NATO. It has also lent encouragement to those individuals within and around the American defense community who have always been disposed to interpret Soviet military programs and behavior in the most benign possible light. The fact that Soviet power and assertiveness have continued to grow uninterrupted in the years since the collapse of détente, with motivations clearly inimical to Western security interests, has failed even to produce a commonly agreed upon Western understanding of the problem, let alone a military response appropriate to its demands.

In an era that has become increasingly dominated by cold war battle fatigue and resistance to high defense budgets when more immediate economic and social needs remain unattended, it is easy to understand how the administration's efforts to dramatize the Soviet challenge should merely serve as a lightning rod for domestic controversy rather than as a credible foundation for a

the Earth (New York: Alfred Knopf, 1982), and Nuclear War: What's In It for You? (New York: Pocket Books, 1982). The latter is largely the product of a former Carter administration National Security Council staff member. Both convey a tone of having just "discovered" certain unpleasant realities of the deterrence dilemma that have long been well-known facts of nuclear life.

3. See Barry Sussman and Robert G. Kaiser, "Survey Finds 3-to-1 Backing for A-Freeze," Washington Post, April 29, 1982. This, it bears noting, is despite the fact that the same respondents also indicated by two to one their belief that the Soviet Union is ahead of the United States in nuclear weapons and by six to one that the USSR would secretly violate any nuclear freeze agreement the two nations might sign.

4. Spearheading this campaign have been two widely cited Soviet English-language pamphlets written expressly for foreign audiences in response to the Reagan administration's various statements on the Soviet military challenge: The Threat to Europe (Moscow: Progress Publishers, 1981) and Whence the Threat to Peace (Moscow: Military Publishing House, USSR Ministry of Defense, 1982). Soviet public repudiation of any doctrinal orientation toward offensive war-fighting, however, goes back to the Carter years. See, for example, Don Oberdorfer, "Soviet Marshal Denies Kremlin Seeks Nuclear Superiority," Washington Post, August 3, 1979.

broadly supported national strategy. Given the striking contrast between Soviet military program momentum and continued U.S. irresolution over what to do about it, one must fear that disagreement over Soviet motivations will remain a permanent feature of the defense policy process—*whatever* the realities of Soviet conduct might be.

Much of the reason for this continued confusion over the nature of Soviet military activity lies in the tendency of American defense debates to fixate on technological marginalia rather than concentrate on the more fundamental premises that have energized Soviet military programs over the past decade and a half. This chapter aims at helping correct that misdirected focus. It is not principally concerned with hardware specifics, such as the numbers and performance of Soviet weapons. Although these specifics cannot be ignored by defense planners, they are less important for informing a purposeful defense policy than awareness of the broader underpinnings of Soviet military conduct—how the Soviets perceive their security predicament, why their programs have assumed the shape they have, and what these programs reveal about underlying Soviet strategic goals.

Concentration on the material elements of Soviet power runs the risk of missing the forest for the trees. It obstructs consideration of the important operational axioms that shape the context in which Soviet defense decisions get made. Yet these broader axioms that make up Soviet strategy and constitute the key link between Soviet budget planning and force capabilities are critical to a correct understanding of the Soviet strategic challenge. It is not any specific weapon (or combination of weapons) in the Soviet inventory that gives rise to the Western security problem. Through proper countervailing R&D and procurement programs, such things can be readily accommodated if only the resources and willingness to commit them are present. What is more important for clearheaded Western defense planning is a solid appreciation of the overarching strategic vision that lends direction and purpose to Soviet military programs. Without this, U.S. and NATO responses to Soviet force improvements will continue to be episodic and shortsighted, reactive solely to the hardware manifestations of Soviet strategy rather than to the strategy itself.

Another cost of narrow concentration on hardware rather than on Soviet concepts and operating styles is its tendency to perpetuate the widespread misconception that the two superpowers are engaged in a purely technological "arms race" divorced from any political or strategic context. Of course, the Soviet Union and the United States both employ comparable systems in their respective arsenals (ICBMs, SLBMs [submarine-launched ballistic missiles], long-range bombers, and so on). But a perspective on these tangibles that ignores their underlying rationales can easily mislead us into believing that both sides are driven by common views of the security problem and are pursuing similar strategies toward similar ends. The truth is that the superpowers are worlds apart in their view of the deterrence dilemma and speak anything but a common strategic language.

To be sure, certitude about the sources of Soviet military conduct is not easy to come by. Although the Churchillian image of the USSR as a "riddle wrapped in mystery inside an enigma" is plainly inappropriate to the transparent facts of Soviet military capability, we obviously have few reliable insights into the inner workings of Soviet defense decision making. After all, the Soviet Union does not publish annual military budget figures, posture statements, its equivalent of our Congressional deliberations, and other sorts of raw data freely available in the West. As a consequence, many of the factors that influence the Soviet force posture necessarily remain obscure.

Moreover, even overt indicators such as formal doctrine are not always self-explanatory. Fritz Ermarth and others who have thoughtfully pondered the dilemmas of threat assessment over the years have usefully distinguished between what might be termed intelligence "secrets" and intelligence "mysteries." The former involve hard knowables that we are simply prevented from un-covering (the nature of Soviet war plans, weapons capabilities, targeting objec-tives, and so on). The latter involve intangibles that may not be entirely clear even to the Soviets. These are matters of interpretation rather than fact and must be derived largely through analysis and informed inference. The relation between doctrine and policy, the interactive influences between technology and strategy, and what the Soviet leadership might do in a given contingency are examples of this class of questions.[5]

It is to this latter category of concerns that this chapter is principally directed. It will review the major doctrinal inputs into Soviet military policy, indicate im-portant distinctions between Soviet and American approaches where ap-propriate, and survey the changing nature of Soviet military capabilities so as to underscore their growing congruence with long-standing Soviet strategy.

THE DOCTRINAL BASIS OF SOVIET DEFENSE POLICY

The central elements of Soviet thinking on the requirements of deterrence are embodied in Soviet military doctrine, a formal body of authoritative precepts on the nature of the threat environment and its imperatives for Soviet weapons acquisition and use. This doctrine is a product of the services, the military academies, and the General Staff. It is continually reviewed at the top echelons of the Defense Ministry and carries the endorsement of the party leadership. Unlike the strategic "doctrines" of the United States, which have

5. Even putative matters of "fact" can entail important elements of ambiguity. An ex-ample can be seen in the issue of the CEP (circular error probable) of the Soviet SS–18 ICBM. The "secret" component of this question—denied to Western observers—is what the Soviets *believe* to be the accuracy of that weapon, based on the evidence provided by their rather limited flight tests. The residual "mystery" concerns what the CEP of the SS–18 force as a whole actually is. This cannot be confidently known, even by the Soviets themselves, in the absence of a full-fledged ICBM exchange.

been repeatedly buffeted over the years by budgetary pressures and shifting fashions in strategy as each successive administration has sought to reshape U.S. defense policy into its own preferred image, Soviet doctrine has remained remarkably constant since it first began to crystallize in the early 1960s. It is described by Soviet writings as a comprehensive body of views on the nature and requirements of modern war which enjoys the status of accepted national policy.

In its conceptual fundamentals, Soviet doctrine combines a Hobbesian world outlook with Clausewitzian teachings on war. Soviet military theory regards the superpower relationship as one dominated by irreconcilable differences and laden with dangers of war sufficient enough to oblige Soviet planners to undertake every necessary measure for its eventuality. Although the Soviets concede that the destructiveness of nuclear weapons has dramatically reduced the probability of such a war, they maintain that global conflict can nonetheless occur through accident, inadvertence, or willful enemy aggression. Given the awesome consequences of nuclear war, deterrence is naturally the top Soviet priority. Yet unlike many in the West, the Soviets reject the complacent notion that deterrence is automatically guaranteed merely by the existence of large inventories of nuclear weapons on both sides. Instead, they recognize that deterrence can fail despite the best efforts of each side to preserve it.

In these circumstances, the Soviets feel obligated to maintain a capacity to take prompt military initiatives aimed at seizing and holding the operational advantage in any crisis in which war, sooner or later, has become inescapable. One of the problems for Soviet-American stability posed by this Hobbesian view of the threat is the inability of Soviet leaders to settle on any natural end point to their efforts at arms accumulation. Instead, they appear determined to seek absolute security regardless of the cost in heightened East-West tension. While this orientation does not bespeak any inherent Soviet tendencies toward gratuitous aggressiveness, it necessarily implies a situation of absolute insecurity for everybody else. This, for good reason, is unacceptable to the United States and goes far toward explaining the persistence of superpower arms competition notwithstanding efforts to ameliorate it through such measures as SALT—and now, under the Reagan administration, START (Strategic Arms Reduction Talks).[6]

This belief that war is a continuing possibility requiring relentless force improvement naturally leads to a corollary in Soviet strategic thinking: victory for the Soviet Union—even in unrestricted nuclear warfare—is theoretically attainable if the proper measures are undertaken. Here, Soviet theory follows a path markedly divergent from that pursued by the United States since the

---

6. For fuller development of this argument, see Benjamin S. Lambeth, "Soviet Strategic Conduct and the Prospects for Stability," in Christoph Bertram, ed., *The Future of Strategic Deterrence*, Adelphi Papers no. 161 (London: International Institute for Strategic Studies, 1980), pp. 27–38.

beginnings of the nuclear age. American views on the nuclear issue have their origins in a body of academic writings running back to the late 1940s, when the revolutionary implications of the Hiroshima experience were first pondered in U.S. intellectual and scientific circles. The consensus that emerged and gradually came to shape authoritative U.S. civilian leadership thinking held that the advent of nuclear weapons marked a fundamental disjuncture in the trend of arms development that had characterized all prenuclear history. Because of their unprecedented damage potential, nuclear weapons had, in this view, invalidated all the preexisting rules of strategy and made war involving their use unacceptable as a tool of policy. Since no one could rationally contemplate meaningful "victory" in such a war, so this argument went, deterrence had become the sole legitimate function of military power and thus the only appropriate goal of strategic planning.[7]

Over the nearly four decades since this initial groundswell of theorizing, these ideas have remained persistent undercurrents in the various permutations of U.S. nuclear policy. Flirtations by Secretary of Defense Robert McNamara (1961–68) with a counterforce doctrine, Secretary James Schlesinger's (1973–75) attempted reforms aimed at imposing a measure of controllability on nuclear crises through development of selective targeting, and the more recent (1980) attempts to refine U.S. options even further via PD-59 (presidential directive) and subsequent amendments to U.S. nuclear planning guidance have all sought to provide the American leadership with alternatives other than suicide or surrender. Yet despite these laudable efforts to acquire more flexible employment options, neither the public rhetoric of any American president (the present incumbent included) nor the U.S. nuclear hardware accumulation has shown a substantial departure from the abiding disbelief in the "winnability" of nuclear war that has always influenced U.S. nuclear policy.[8] Despite notable advances

7. This perspective was first articulated by Bernard Brodie in "The Atomic Bomb and American Security," Memorandum no. 18 (New Haven: Yale Institute of International Studies, 1945) and was amplified in his landmark volume, The Absolute Weapon (New York: Harcourt, Brace, 1946). It was reaffirmed in its essentials over three decades later in Brodie's last article before his death in 1978, "The Development of Nuclear Strategy," International Security, Spring 1978, pp. 65–83.

8. The most recent official expression of this view was Secretary of Defense Caspar Weinberger's assertion that despite the Reagan administration's determination to deny the USSR a credible war option, "we do not believe there could be any 'winner' in a nuclear war" (Letter to the Editor, Los Angeles Times, August 25, 1982). Weinberger notes, however, that "we are certainly planning not to be defeated." When pressed on one occasion as to the implied difference here between "winning" and "prevailing," he replied: "You show me a Secretary of Defense who's not planning to prevail and I'll show you a Secretary of Defense who ought to be impeached" (quoted in Richard Halloran, "Weinberger Angered by Reports on War Strategy," New York Times, August 24, 1982). Despite the greater than usual heat the Reagan administration has invited upon itself as

in the operational capabilities of U.S. forces and comparable increases in the sophistication and coverage of U.S. targeting plans, the American arsenal still lacks any significant means of active defense against nuclear attack and relies heavily on mutual vulnerability for enforcing Soviet restraint and preserving deterrence.

For their part, the Soviets have shown no attraction to this intellectual baggage that has been associated with American and NATO defense planning throughout the postwar years. They reject "mutual assured destruction" as a consummate abandonment of leadership responsibility. Instead, they have sought to prevent war by relying on the classic injunction, *Si vis pacem, para bellum*. In modern terms of strategic discourse, they have long articulated (and increasingly sought forces to support) a strategy of deterrence based on denial rather than punishment. Moreover, not only have they sought to deny the West a credible war option, they have gone the significant further step of striving to develop a plausible war-waging option of their own. They have done this not merely out of doctrinal preference, but from their conviction that the responsibilities of national stewardship allow no other choice.[9]

This distinctive approach to the nuclear problem has led the Soviets to adopt and refine what has come to be called in the West a "war-fighting" survival doctrine.[10] That they have done so does not mean the Soviets are spoiling for war or have confidence that any "victory" worth having would actually be attainable by the Soviet Union, even in the most optimistic scenario. It does mean, however, that Soviet leaders regard "mutual assured destruction" as a suicide pact and would prefer even a Pyrrhic victory to a Pyrrhic defeat. In their view, a force capable of dominating events in war is more likely to ensure deterrence in peacetime and crises than is one—whether for reasons of choice or neglect—that lacks those operational attributes. There is a vast difference between a theory of war that includes a well-defined image of victory and high confidence in its attainability (neither of which the Soviets show any evidence of possessing) and

---

a consequence of some of its less circumspect pronouncements on nuclear policy matters, its strategic guidance does not differ in its conceptual fundamentals from that of the Carter administration or the Nixon/Ford administrations.

9. This point was expressed with elegant simplicity by Khrushchev in his memoirs: "If the enemy starts a war against you, then it is your duty to do everything possible to survive the war and to achieve victory in the end." *Khrushchev Remembers*, trans. Strobe Talbott (Boston: Little, Brown, 1970), p. 518.

10. By "the Soviets," we are talking about those civilian and military officials at the highest levels of the Soviet defense establishment whose views on the threat and the requirements that stem from it largely govern the complexion of Soviet military programs. Undoubtedly widespread—if often unobservable—differences obtain within this community concerning questions of resource priorities and other implementation matters. It is a premise of this chapter, however, that a broad consensus exists throughout the Soviet elite regarding fundamental Soviet military needs.

the idea that a credible war-waging posture for worst-case contingencies is something worth having in principle. It would be a considerable exaggeration to assert that the Soviet leadership is anywhere close to nurturing self-satisfied convictions that it "could fight and win a nuclear war," as one periodically hears from some quarters in the defense debate.[11] Nevertheless, Soviet strategic planning takes place in a conceptual universe fundamentally unlike that of the Western powers and has force posture implications that are anything but good news for U.S. and NATO security.

THE IMPACT OF DOCTRINE ON FORCE POSTURE

A closer approximation of Soviet strategic goals than either the "war-fighting" or "victory" formulas may lie in the notion that military planning should aim at providing the Soviet armed forces a capability to control events at all levels of conflict, ranging from local and theater conventional war to unrestricted intercontinental nuclear warfare. The more one becomes captured by the technical details of Soviet hardware and combat repertoires, the easier it is to forget that the main motivation for Soviet force improvement remains deterrence, not war. In this image of preparedness, elusive absolutes like "superiority" and "victory" are less important than the maintenance of a force structure whose attributes, in an inherently uncertain world, might impose an "asymmetry of anxiety" on the Soviet Union's adversaries and thereby enhance deterrence on terms congenial to Soviet interests.

Put differently, it is plausible that the Soviet buildup over the past fifteen years has not really sought so much a high-confidence capability to achieve victory in war as a capacity to secure and enforce the *fruits* of victory without the need to resort to war in the first place. Richard Pipes argues that Lenin and his various successors effectively turned Clausewitz on his head by "transforming politics into the waging of war by other means."[12] This idea is certainly compatible with the apparent contradiction between the Soviet Union's propensity to engage in global interventionism and its well-developed aversion to risk.[13] It makes particular sense, moreover, in light of the Soviet belief that nuclear weapons have by no means invalidated the legitimacy of intimidation strategies, even as they have rendered them far more dangerous.

11. See, in particular, Richard Pipes, "Why the Soviet Union Thinks It Could Fight and Win a Nuclear War," *Commentary*, 64, no. 1 (July 1977): 21–34. A more balanced and properly qualified treatment of this controversial issue may be found in Stephen Meyer, "Would the Soviets Start a Nuclear War?" *Washington Post*, December 4, 1981.

12. Richard Pipes, "Why the USSR Wants SALT II," Occasional Paper (Washington, D.C.: Committee on the Present Danger, September 1979).

13. For further discussion, see Benjamin S. Lambeth, *Risk and Uncertainty in Soviet Deliberations about War* (Santa Monica: Rand R-2687-AF, October 1981).

One way out of this dilemma for the Soviets is a force-development approach that tries to make the best of all worlds by providing Moscow advantages in military muscle whose actual combat effectiveness might be problematic, yet whose capabilities (as perceived by adversaries) might be sufficient in peacetime to allow Soviet leaders to pursue their ambitions in an environment in which the danger of war would be minimized. Whether or not this logic entirely reflects private Soviet leadership thinking and planning, one can observe enough disturbing tendencies to the Soviet advantage that have emanated from the changed "correlation of forces" over the past decade to appreciate its attractions.

To cite some examples, Moscow's attainment of parity in central systems has all but neutralized the capacity of the U.S. strategic posture to ensure escalation dominance in Europe and has thereby substantially decoupled the latter from its erstwhile role as a linchpin of NATO's defense. At the same time, by successfully exploiting a decade of SALT negotiations to help postpone the development of enhanced U.S. hard-target kill capabilities (ability to destroy land-based missiles with precision), the Soviets have thus far avoided what almost surely would otherwise have been massive pressures to ensure the continued survivability of their own ICBM forces. This, in turn, has freed them to concentrate Strategic Rocket Forces (SRF) resource allocations in recent years on improving their theater nuclear capabilities through extensive deployment of the SS-20 and follow-on systems. Finally, under this expanded umbrella of intercontinental and theater nuclear capabilities, the Soviets have continued to broaden their conventional options through improvements in ground-force versatility and the acquisition of new, deep-penetration tactical fighter assets.

The result of all this has been to alter considerably the former imbalances in the NATO-Warsaw Pact confrontation that favored the Western powers during the days of American strategic superiority. Of course, it would be wrong to attribute solely to this changed strategic balance all the current ills of NATO (renascent pacifism and popular antinuclear sentiment, deepening separatism, unresolved disagreements over theater nuclear force modernization, and flagging appreciation and support for U.S. global concerns that bear heavily on NATO's security, among others). There is little doubt, however, that the growing convergence of Soviet doctrine and capabilities has created problems for the Atlantic Alliance that have yet to be met by an equally coherent U.S. and NATO response.

Formal doctrine is far more influential in governing the direction and character of Soviet force development than it tends to be in pluralistic societies, where doctrine is frequently a less than authoritative statement of highest-level national goals. In the United States and NATO, military "doctrine" is more often than not a reflection of narrow service or other parochial interests. As such, it has to contend with a variety of crosscutting secular interests, institutional pressures, and budgetary demands in the continuing process of force improvement. This is why American declaratory policy, R&D planning, action policies, contingency plans, and force developments have so often been out of phase with each other. The inevitable results have been "strategy/force mismatches," dramatic shifts in the slogans of U.S. national security policy, and periodic domestic crises over funding practices that show no obvious relation to any unifying theme. The Soviet Union is hardly immune in day-to-day governmental activity to its own version of bureaucratic politics, organization processes, and related strains that are part of politics in any modern industrial society. Nevertheless, it remains a distinctive feature of totalitarian systems—not only in the military sphere but in other realms—that while their leaders may be wrong, they are rarely confused about their goals.

This has not always been true in the case of the Soviet Union. It would thus be wrong to infer from the foregoing remarks that there is anything *automatic* about the connection between Soviet doctrine and force structure. Although in recent years there has emerged a very close correlation between the two, the essential catalyst bringing them into harmony has been the Soviet political process. The changed character of party support to military interests, and not doctrine in isolation, has been the real force behind the major gains in size and versatility enjoyed by the Soviet armed forces since the advent of the Brezhnev regime. After all, as noted above, the basic content of Soviet doctrine has remained relatively stable since the early 1960s, when the initial post-Stalin military debates finally produced the broad policy consensus reflected in Marshal Sokolovsky's *Voennaia strategiia*.[14] Such basic themes as surprise, shock, simultaneity, mass, momentum, superiority, and the feasibility of victory have long been familiar refrains of the Soviet military literature. What has changed has not been doctrine but the Soviet force posture itself. That development can only be explained by the disposition of the incumbent leadership to underwrite the edicts of doctrine with appropriate resource allocations.

Throughout the Khrushchev era, one may recall, the party and armed forces were locked in a thoroughgoing adversary relationship. Khrushchev delighted in heaping scorn on what he termed those "thickheaded types you find wearing uniforms."[15] He once remarked during an interview: "I do not trust the advice of generals on questions of strategic importance."[16] His own military policies—including

14. The standard English translation is Marshal V. D. Sokolovsky, *Soviet Military Strategy*, with an introduction and commentary by Herbert S. Dinerstein, Leon Gouré, and Thomas W. Wolfe (Englewood Cliffs, N.J.: Prentice-Hall, 1963).

15. *Khrushchev Remembers: The Last Testament*, trans. Strobe Talbott (Boston: Little, Brown, 1974), p. 13.

16. Quoted at a Kremlin press conference, *New York Times*, November 9, 1959. Khrushchev's disparaging attitude toward military men was almost legendary. A firm disbeliever in the value of surface combatants in the nuclear age, he would often point to children's toy boats in ponds during strolls through Moscow parks with foreign visitors

plans for massive manpower reductions, his dismissal of air and naval forces as being obsolete in the nuclear age, his propensity to rely on a minimum deterrence based solely on strategic missiles, and ultimately his abortive venture in Cuba in 1962—were all informed by notions that lay well outside the mainstream of professional Soviet military thought. Although Khrushchev's failings in the military realm were by no means the only ones that led to his undoing in 1964, he clearly had no use for martial values and was anything but a willing supporter of the military's institutional interests. In the aftermath of Khrushchev's ouster, Chief of the General Staff Zakharov transparently indicated the military's relief when he openly scored the "harebrained schemes" and so-called "strategic far-sightedness" of "persons who lack even a remote knowledge of military strategy."[17]

Obviously things have changed a great deal in the intervening years. Essentially, the Brezhnev regime apparently accepted Soviet military doctrine as its own belief system and agreed—at least in principle—to observe its broad teachings as appropriate guides for Soviet military development. Perhaps the most revealing indication of this transformation, aside from the Soviet buildup itself, has been the virtual disappearance of those party-military animosities that dominated the Khrushchev era, especially the sharp cleavages over resource allocations and institutional roles that formerly divided the civilian and military leadership. The current defense minister is a civilian by background and upbringing, Brezhnev was a self-appointed marshal of the Soviet Union, and military interests are solidly represented in a variety of high-level governmental organs, ranging from the Defense Council and the Military-Industrial Commission to the CPSU Central Committee and the Politburo itself. This reaffirms that whatever doctrine may insist upon, it is conscious leadership choice—in the Soviet Union no less than elsewhere—that most heavily affects the character and direction of military investment programs. What is distinctive about the Soviet case is that harmony between doctrine and programs (given the necessary leadership cooperation) is made all the easier when adjudication of internal conflicts can be carried out with the iron discipline that has long been a hallmark of the Soviet political process.

---

and refer to them jokingly as "our navy," no doubt to the profound irritation of his admirals. Another symbolic illustration was provided in a remark he reportedly made to Pierre Salinger during a visit at one of the Kremlin's country dachas. The two men were practicing at shooting clay pigeons with shotguns. When Salinger proved himself clearly the inferior marksman, Khrushchev commented: "Don't feel badly. I've got generals who can't hit anything either." Pierre Salinger, *With Kennedy* (New York: Avon Books, 1966), p. 285.

17. Marshal M. V. Zakharov, "The Imperative Demand of Our Time," *Krasnaia zvezda*, February 4, 1965.

CHARACTER AND GOALS OF THE SOVIET MILITARY BUILDUP

Throughout the post-Khrushchev era, a major motivation of the leadership has been to add substance to the image of Soviet military power and thereby invest Soviet doctrine with a degree of credibility it plainly lacked during the Khrushchev incumbency. The impetus for this redirection of effort can be traced to a number of embarrassments the Soviet Union sustained as a result of Khrushchev's failure to provide adequate support to the material needs of the Soviet armed forces. These included, most notably, the explosion of the missile-gap myth through U-2 and satellite photography, the failure of Soviet threats to command American respect during the several Berlin crises and other confrontations of the late 1950s, and particularly the humiliating debacle the Soviet Union experienced as a result of superior American power and resolve during the Cuban missile crisis. The effect of these accumulated insults to Soviet pride was to instill in the new leadership a firm determination never again to tolerate such effrontery on the part of its major enemy.[18]

Although details are hard to come by, the military programs of the Brezhnev regime that have yielded such an impressive force posture today most likely did not emanate from a single decision. At the outset, the new leadership was probably not concerned about much more than eliminating the pronounced inferiority that had characterized the Soviet position in the military balance. Most notably by means of the SS-11 (a small, relatively inexpensive, and technically retrograde ICBM by prevailing Soviet standards), the Soviet leadership initially sought only to close the numbers gap with the United States as quickly as possible and probably did not nurture more ambitious strategic goals.

With the deepening American involvement in Vietnam and consequent slackening of effort in the strategic competition, however, the Soviets may have come to sense an attractive opportunity to press ahead toward more expansive force improvements. Such a perception may have been further encouraged by the beginnings of SALT and détente, which reflected a growing American willingness to settle for some vaguely defined nuclear "parity" and to forgo further arms competition in the interests of "stability"—a concept long anathema to Soviet military logic.

18. The Cuban missile crisis has frequently been touted as a casebook example of successful U.S. coercive diplomacy. Viewed with two decades of hindsight, however, it should more properly be seen as a brilliant tactical victory that produced some very discomfiting long-term consequences for the United States. A former U.S. ambassador to Moscow reminded us several years ago that the Soviet negotiator during the deliberations leading to the missile withdrawal, Vassili Kuznetsov, repeatedly told his American counterpart, John J. McCloy, that "the Soviet Union would never again face a 4-to-1 missile inferiority." Jacob D. Beam, "Dangers of Relying on Weapons Superiority," *Washington Star*, July 15, 1979.

In all events, by the end of the 1960s the Soviet Union had entered full swing into a military construction effort aimed at providing the means to fight credibly across the entire range of conflict, both nuclear and conventional. Whatever deliberations and decisions may have gone before it, this buildup represented an impressive confirmation of the leadership's commitment to the "all-arms" rhetoric that, for years, had dominated Soviet military declaratory policy.

One of the more disturbing features of the Soviet defense effort for U.S. and NATO planners is the apparent absence of any sizing criteria for determining its ultimate magnitude. Instead, the Soviet leadership appears determined to acquire as much military hardware as its armed forces can reasonably assimilate, within the limits of technical and fiscal constraints and the willingness of the United States to tolerate it without implementing determined offsetting measures. This prospect is not encouraging for the future of arms control or Soviet-American relations, but it is a natural outgrowth of the pronounced combat orientation of Soviet military doctrine. Given its pervasive war-fighting focus, Soviet doctrine simply recognizes no measures of "sufficiency" or arbitrary stopping points in the acquisition of weapons and materiel. There is, for example, no known Soviet political-bureaucratic or budgetary constraint of the sort that, until recently, required the U.S. Air Force tactical air forces to remain limited to twenty-six active fighter wings. To be sure, the Soviets can probably be counted on to observe the letter of verifiable arms-control agreements to which they are signatories. Beyond that, they are likely to continue pressing for every quantitative and qualitative advantage in relative military power that their military structure can accommodate.

One of the certitudes of Soviet doctrine is that there are no certitudes in war. As a consequence, commanders require as much quantitative strength in combat forces and support assets as they can get to hedge against the tendency of things to devolve in unexpected ways in the confusion of battle. Particularly if resource constraints are not a prime driver of military investment programs (as appears the case in the Soviet Union), one of the surest ways to minimize risk and uncertainty in strategic planning is to overinsure against anticipated needs with large numbers of first-echelon and reserve forces, whether intercontinental nuclear weapons or general-pupose assets. Aside from the leadership's principled support for a robust military posture, there is probably no single factor behind the continuing Soviet force expansion effort more influential than the notion that one can never have enough strength to confront the unknown and cope comfortably in the fog of war.

There is little uniquely "Soviet" about this approach to military requirements. Not only their stress on the importance of numbers, but virtually all their major doctrinal edicts (on the commanding importance of the offensive, on the indispensability of seizing and maintaining the initiative, on the necessity of tailoring ends to means and not attempting the impossible, and so on) can be traced back to the pages of the nineteenth-century European military classics.[19] The profound differences that separate Soviet strategy from that of the United States mainly reflect dissimilarities between Soviet and American strategic cultures and defense processes, not any inherent incapacity of one side or the other to appreciate military logic. As noted earlier, American strategic concepts are largely artifacts of civilian thinkers and decision makers, who have set the drumbeat of U.S. national security policy over the years. Although the services continue to predominate in formulating action policy (the SIOP [Single Integrated Operational Plan], RDF plans [Rapid Development Force], and similar contingency options), they have only tangential influence on resource allocation—which ultimately determines the size and composition of U.S. forces.

In the Soviet case, by contrast, those responsible for formulating doctrine and strategy, setting R&D requirements, selecting weapons for deployment, and so on, wear uniforms and are all but indistinguishable from one another. Put differently, contemporary U.S. strategic policy is less characteristically "American" than merely "civilian." Soviet doctrinal views, for their part, are less uniquely "Soviet" than simply "military." The differences between the two stem principally from asymmetries in the composition of the strategic elites of the two countries, rather than from deeply rooted societal or intellectual differences between the superpowers.[20] Most American military professionals would find themselves readily conversant with their Soviet counterparts, and a visitor from the Prussian *Kriegsakademie* steeped in traditional Clausewitzian philosophy would most likely adjudge the United States, not the Soviet Union, to be the country more egregiously out of step with his understanding of military common sense.

A question of continuing concern to U.S. and NATO planners involves the ultimate ends toward which this Soviet military effort is directed. Obviously, there is no basis in the evidence publicly available to permit anything other

19. Lenin himself insisted that Clausewitz's axiom regarding war as a violent extension of politics constituted the "theoretical foundation for the meaning of every war." Quoted in Edward Meade Earle, "Lenin, Trotsky, Stalin: Soviet Concepts of War," in Earle, ed., *Makers of Modern Strategy* (Princeton: Princeton University Press, 1944), p. 323. For a summary review of how the military classicists (particularly Clausewitz and Jomini) influenced the formation of Soviet military thought during the years prior to World War II, see Raymond L. Garthoff, *Soviet Military Doctrine* (Glencoe, Ill.: The Free Press, 1953), pp. 51–58. See also R. H. Baker, "The Origins of Soviet Military Doctrine," *Journal of the Royal United Services Institute*, March 1976, pp. 38–43.

20. As Stanley Sienkiewicz has aptly put this point, "the explanation for the Soviet solution to the problem of security in the nuclear age derives more from the fact that it is a solution devised by the *military* profession, and not that it was devised by the *Soviet* military profession. . . . The notion of sufficiency or parity, on the other hand, is not merely an *American* invention. It is more importantly a *civilian* invention." "SALT and Soviet Nuclear Doctrine," *International Security*, Spring 1978, p. 92.

than informed speculation on this score. Insofar as the outlook for Soviet military programs is caught up in the uncertain vagaries of domestic politics, even authoritative Soviet planners probably cannot say for sure what the long-term future holds. Probably the best answer we can give here, based on historical precedent and the facts of Soviet organizational life, is that the Soviet leaders are pursuing no "master plan" beyond simply striving to underwrite Soviet military doctrine to the best of their ability. Those inclined to impute more sinister motives or unitary purpose to Soviet force improvements fail to appreciate either the Soviet Union's healthy respect for the consequences of war or the extraordinary capacity of the Soviet bureaucratic byzantium to keep the left hand from knowing what the right one is doing.

It would be foolhardy to deprecate the willingness of Soviet leaders to use force in any circumstances where they felt there was no alternative. Nevertheless, they are anything but prone to cavalier adventurism—whatever their objective military capabilities might be. Perhaps the most balanced explanation of the Soviet buildup was that offered over a decade ago by Herbert Goldhamer, who described it as an exercise in "banking" power against the uncertain requirements of a future crisis whose contours and consequences the Soviets, by definition, could have no way of anticipating.[21]

DEVELOPMENTS IN COMBAT MISSIONS AND FORCES

The Soviet defense effort under Brezhnev has been directed at striving to close gaps between mission requirements and operational capabilities in all categories of force employment addressed by Soviet doctrine and strategy. Throughout the postwar era, Soviet ground forces have remained more than adequate (both numerically and qualitatively) to support Soviet tactical repertoires and theater war objectives, particularly against NATO. Until the present buildup moved into high gear beginning in the late 1960s, however, most other declared Soviet mission needs were left substantially unmet by actual capabilities in the field. In the strategic realm, the peacetime deterrence function could claim a measure of backing by the embryonic ICBM and SLBM inventories of the Strategic Rocket Forces and the Soviet Navy, but it was never clear to Soviet leaders (as Moscow's backdown in the Cuban crisis attested) whether those capabilities would enforce Western restraint when fundamental interests on both sides were at stake. Moreover, the counterforce preemption option that lay at the heart of Moscow's emerging strategy for nuclear war stood completely devoid of any tangible backstopping, owing to the gross numerical and performance deficiencies of early-generation Soviet ballistic missiles.[22]

21. Herbert Goldhamer, *The Soviet Union in a Period of Strategic Parity* (Santa Monica: Rand R-889-PR, November 1971).
22. At the time of Khrushchev's ouster in 1964, the Soviet YANKEE-class SLBM submarine had not yet been deployed, and the SRF possessed only some 200 SS-7 and SS-8

Adding further insult to this inadequacy were a variety of shortcomings in the composition and strength of other Soviet combat arms. With the Soviet Navy essentially a coastal defense force lacking significant strategic reach and Military Transport Aviation configured solely for intratheater and rear-area resupply, Soviet global power projection assets were all but nonexistent. Soviet tactical airpower remained in the shadow of the ground forces, was restricted to providing only local battlefield interdiction and close-air support, and had no independent offensive capabilities. Long-Range Aviation possessed only a token intercontinental attack capability and was grossly outmatched by the U.S. Strategic Air Command (SAC). Its numerous medium bombers oriented toward peripheral strike missions were outmoded and vulnerable to enemy air defenses. Even the widely proliferated home-defense fighters and SAMs (surface-to-air missiles) of PVO Strany (antiaircraft defense), despite their vast numerical strength, afforded scant intercept capabilities against U.S. bombers flying in the low-level ingress mode that had become the standard SAC penetration and survival tactic. Altogether, despite the numerically imposing size of the Soviet armed forces, the Soviet concept of war remained virtually a paper doctrine for all practical purposes.

Even today, the Soviet Union has yet to meet adequately some of the more important of these mission needs—particularly in the realm of homeland defense. Nevertheless, the progressive shakedown of the Soviet mission set and the determined efforts of the Brezhnev regime to match its military requirements with appropriate hardware equities have plainly resulted in a Soviet posture with diverse potential and substantially enhanced credibility for supporting Soviet global ambitions. It remains now to consider briefly where Soviet military capabilities stand today and where they may be headed over the coming decade.

To begin with, the growing consistency between doctrine and forces, the progressively tighter matching of mission needs with deployed assets, and the fact that most capital Soviet weapons likely to be procured by the end of the 1980s are already observable in R&D or prototype testing all suggest that trends in Soviet force improvement in the foreseeable future will be more incremental and less dramatic than those that marked the greater portion of the Brezhnev era. Of course, we can expect the Soviets to continue to press hard for technological breakthroughs (especially in air and missile defense and antisubmarine warfare) that might permit them to alter the strategic balance to their decisive advantage. By and large, however, they will probably continue pursuing their

---

ICBMs, mostly in soft-site launch configurations. By contrast, the United States was well on its way to completing a missile deployment program featuring 1,000 Minuteman ICBMs and 656 Polaris SLBMs.

mission support efforts primarily by relying on their proven approach of gradual product improvement rather than radical innovation.[23]

Moreover, with the mounting buy-in costs of complex and sophisticated weaponry (to which the Soviets are no more immune than anyone else) and the steadily expanding lead times between concept definition and operational deployment of such weapons, Soviet planners will most likely be driven increasingly to reassess their traditional practice of routinely substituting quantity for quality. The result, if this occurs, will be a steady decline in the numerical growth of Soviet forces—even though this may be offset by commensurate improvements in their performance and combat leverage. A by-product of this development could well be a Soviet military management system increasingly plagued by the same sorts of maintainability problems and cost versus quality dilemmas that have recently risen to such public notoriety in the United States.[24]

In the realm of intercontinental attack, the main Soviet emphasis will continue to be on acquiring a comprehensive hard-target capability against U.S. land-based ICBMs that will give the Soviet Union a credible preemption option and also permit retention of substantial reserve forces for follow-on operations. Barring a complete collapse of the arms-control process, the overall numbers of ICBMs and SLBMs (both launchers and warheads) will probably remain capped by tacit Soviet obeisance to prevailing SALT II restrictions.[25] Within these numerical constraints, however, we can expect to see steady Soviet improvements in accuracy and targeting flexibility.

23. Among the most perceptive analytical treatments of this Soviet weapons acquisition style may be found in Arthur J. Alexander, R&D in Soviet Aviation (Santa Monica: Rand R–589–PR, November 1970) and, by the same author, Armor Development in the Soviet Union and the United States (Santa Monica: Rand R–1860–NA, September 1976). See also Richard D. Ward, "Soviet Practice in Designing and Procuring Military Aircraft," Aeronautics and Astronautics, September 1981, pp. 24–38.

24. Much of this notoriety has been occasioned by a recent (and highly controversial) journalistic critique of U.S. weapons acquisition practices by James Fallows, National Defense (New York: Random House, 1981). Fallows makes a major point of contrasting allegedly oversophisticated and technically unreliable U.S. weapons such as the F–15 fighter and the M–1 tank with their cheaper, simpler, and more serviceable Soviet counterparts. In doing so, he fails to recognize and give proper weight to the significant differences in manpower availability and cost that confront the American and Soviet defense establishments, respectively, and largely allow the Soviets to pursue "quantity" solutions to their military requirements. He also fails to note that several of the new fighters about to enter the Soviet Air Force inventory are quite comparable (in terms of sophistication and technical complexity) to those U.S. aircraft he so roundly deprecates.

25. This seems all the more possible given recent indications of serious Soviet interest (whether genuinely motivated or as another delaying tactic) in discussing deep bilateral arms cuts in the START arena. The tantalizing feature of the Soviet proposal is its suggested ceiling of 1,800 strategic nuclear delivery vehicles for each side, which would entail

In the event that MX, with its own appreciable counterforce capability, should ever see the light of day in a survivable basing mode, Soviet planners will also want to hedge against this threat with appropriate countermeasures. A high-confidence U.S. silo-killing capability could be very disruptive to Soviet strategic planning, since the Soviet Union relies on fixed ICBMs to a far greater extent than the United States does. Such countermeasures could come in the form of both increased Soviet silo-hardening efforts and a gradual trend toward land mobility along the lines of the SS–20, perhaps in their fifth-generation ICBMs now in advanced development. Finally, we might see over the coming decade a gradual blurring of the former distinctions between land- and sea-based missile forces, as the USSR continues to perfect SLBMs with enhanced accuracy and intercontinental ranges that would allow them to be launched from protected sanctuaries beyond the reach of Western ASW (antisubmarine warfare).

On the receiving end of the strategic equation, Soviet prospects for aerospace defense look substantially less appealing because of the numerous difficulties that will continue to frustrate Soviet efforts to deal with enemy penetration capabilities that exist now or lie on the immediate horizon. Much has been made of Soviet R&D efforts in lasers and directed-energy weapons; most knowledgeable observers agree, however, that any deployable Soviet capability of this sort will not be available until the latter years of this century at the earliest. As for near-term possibilities, the Soviets are known to be developing AWACS-type (Airborne Warning and Control System) battle-management systems; improved interceptors with look-down/shoot-down capabilities against bombers and cruise missiles; advanced surface-to-air missiles for engaging low- and medium-altitude airbreathing threats; and better exoatmospheric ABMs for engaging enemy ballistic missiles. Constraints imposed by the ABM Treaty (assuming it survives its impending ten-year review relatively intact), however, are likely to inhibit any major Soviet deployment efforts in the last category. The numerous tactical circumstances that appear likely to continue favoring the penetrativity of airbreathing vehicles (especially once low-observability "stealth" systems become operational toward the end of this decade) also promise to render PVO Strany's efforts to deal with these threats a continued uphill battle.[26] Probably the only realistic counsel of optimism for Soviet planners

---

a force reduction of some 10 percent for the United States, yet upward of 25 percent for the Soviet Union. The ground for suspicion is that the proposal appears expressly aimed at the cruise missile and Trident D–5—the two programmed U.S. weapons most feared by the Soviet Union. See Robert C. Toth, "U.S. Weighs Surprising Soviet Offer on A-Arms," *Los Angeles Times*, September 13, 1982.

26. The most detailed official commentary on the prospective capabilities of "stealth" aircraft may be found in "Statement by Secretary of Defense Harold Brown" and "Statement by William J. Perry, Undersecretary of Defense for Research and Engineering," Office of the Assistant Secretary of Defense (Public Affairs), Washington, D.C., August 22, 1980.

for home defense is the hope that a truly effective Soviet counterforce capability might be able to draw down American, British, and French nuclear offensive forces substantially in a preemptive attack, thereby offering PVO Strany the comparative advantage of dealing with a heavily degraded offensive threat from a fully generated alert posture. This prospect can only be regarded by Soviet leaders as cold comfort. The likelihood that even such a degraded enemy capability would still be able to inflict grave retaliatory damage on the USSR promises to remain a major factor inhibiting the Soviets from indulging in much risk taking.

For lesser levels of conflict, the Soviet armed forces are on a much more positive footing. The Soviet ground forces have undergone fewer dramatic changes than other force elements in recent years, as a consequence of their enduring mission charter and their continued numerical impressiveness. Indeed, notwithstanding some overall manpower growth during the past decade, the ground forces have sustained a perceptible adverse shift in their tooth-to-tail ratio as a result of heightened allocations of troop strength to battlefield support and command and control functions. Nevertheless, the gradual tapering off of Soviet ground-force manning promises to be more than handily offset by Soviet efforts to achieve greater flexibility, versatility, and operational leverage by emphasizing interchangeability between armored and motorized rifle divisions. These efforts stand to be supplemented by activities aimed at developing specialized divisions for discrete missions (such as airborne operations and remote power projection) and discrete theaters of operation (China or the Persian Gulf) that lie outside the boundaries of traditional Soviet planning for the European scenario.[27]

As for intratheater "strategic" forces, the expanding SS-20 inventory, along with other Soviet nuclear systems deployed opposite NATO, has eliminated NATO's former advantage in escalation dominance. With Soviet parity in central forces now holding U.S. intercontinental attack assets at bay, and Moscow's strengthened theater nuclear capabilities pressing hard on the credibility of NATO's threat to escalate with its own nuclear forces, the Soviet Union has increasingly moved toward a position where it could dominate a NATO–Warsaw Pact war as a result of its superior conventional capabilities.

Regarding possible applications of this technology to ballistic reentry vehicles, see also Richard L. Garwin, "The Implications of Stealth," *Federation of American Scientists Public Interest Report*, December 1980, p. 3.

27. For further discussion, see John Erickson, *Soviet–Warsaw Pact Force Levels*, USSI Report 76-2 (Washington, D.C.: United States Strategic Institute, 1978); Chris N. Donnelly, "Options in the Enemy Rear: Soviet Doctrine and Tactics," *International Defense Review*, no. 1, January 1980, pp. 35–41; and Donald L. Madill, "The Continuing Evolution of the Soviet Ground Forces," *Military Review*, August 1982, pp. 52–68.

In the tactical air realm, Frontal Aviation has decisively shed its former status as a subordinate adjunct of the ground forces and has acquired both the mission and the necessary hardware to conduct deep offensive strikes against virtually the entire NATO rear area. Because of its continued lack of good hard-structure conventional munitions, Frontal Aviation remains incapable of destroying aircraft shelters and runways with high confidence and would be hard put to disarm NATO's theater nuclear forces in a surprise air offensive. Nevertheless, it has an impressive capability for severely hampering NATO's fighter sortie capability. This, in turn, could contribute substantially to the Pact's ability to achieve theater air superiority under the protective umbrella of a Soviet nuclear preemptive threat.[28] In such circumstances, combined Soviet and Warsaw Pact ground elements might have enough time to carry out a conventional blitzkrieg aimed at seizing and consolidating a large portion of NATO territory. This capacity to hamper effective NATO conventional opposition is even more disconcerting if one considers the possible use of chemical weapons, which currently remain a virtual Soviet monopoly.[29]

None of this is to say that NATO planners are without effective counterthreats and options that might disincline Soviet decision makers to attempt such a campaign in the first place in most conditions of East-West crisis. However, were a conventional war between NATO and the Warsaw Pact to occur for whatever reason, the Soviet side would be able to call on disturbingly effective capabilities for prosecuting it to a favorable conclusion, as long as its opponents remained unable or unwilling to raise the stakes through nuclear escalation.[30]

28. See John Erickson, "Some Developments in Soviet Tactical Aviation (Frontovaia Aviatsiia)," *Journal of the Royal United Services Institute*, September 1975, pp. 70–74; Colin Gray, "Soviet Tactical Airpower," *Air Force Magazine*, March 1977, pp. 62–71; and Colonel Lynn M. Hansen, "The Resurgence of Soviet Frontal Aviation," *Strategic Review*, Fall 1978, pp. 71–81. For a brief treatment of some operational impediments that might hinder a successful Soviet air campaign against NATO, see also Joshua M. Epstein, "On Conventional Deterrence in Europe: Questions of Soviet Confidence," *Orbis*, 26, no. 1 (Spring 1982): 71–86.

29. See Amoretta Hoeber and Joseph D. Douglass, Jr., "The Neglected Threat of Chemical Warfare," *International Security*, Summer 1978, pp. 55–82. U.S. development of chemical weapons was unilaterally halted during the Nixon administration and has remained moribund ever since. During the Carter years, it was commonly suggested by U.S. defense officials that a NATO threat to use tactical nuclear weapons would suffice to deter Soviet chemical weapons use. There were, and continue to be, good grounds for questioning the credibility of such a threat in the absence of a countervailing NATO chemical warfare capability. In 1981 President Reagan sought to reinstitute the production and deployment of U.S. chemical weapons but was turned down by Congress.

30. This would be especially true were the Soviets to withhold attacks against selected countries (for example, France) or indicate a willingness to limit their operations to all or part of West Germany. Although there is no evidence that such options are a part of current

The Soviets have made major strides over the past decade in their capabilities for war at sea and through power projection. On the first count, the Soviet Navy has moved well beyond its traditional role as a "spoiler" of enemy naval activities and has become a truly multimission service with global reach. Its expanded mission now includes strategic nuclear attack, antisubmarine warfare, and selective sea control in open-ocean areas increasingly removed from Soviet shores. Within these broadened mission areas, Soviet naval weapons and forces continue to improve and offer new combat options to Soviet planners. Examples include the nuclear cruiser *Kirov*, the ALFA fast-attack submarine (probably intended for use against U.S. carrier battle groups), and the prospective development of a large-deck carrier intended for launching and recovering high-performance fighter aircraft.[31]

For peacetime and intracrisis power projection, the Soviet Navy has increased its heavy-lift transport capability and is acquiring the rudiments of a credible assault force through such platforms as the *Ivan Rogov* roll-on/roll-off amphibious landing craft. The lift and remote deployment potential of the Soviet Navy is further complemented by the expanded assets of Military Transport Aviation. The latter's new-found operational leverage was first vividly displayed during the Soviet invasion of Czechoslovakia in 1968. It has periodically supported Soviet foreign policy in subsequent years with equally effective and professional service in such areas as Angola, Ethiopia, and—most recently—Afghanistan.

Soviet air and sealift capabilities will undoubtedly continue to grow in the coming decade in consonance with Moscow's determination to seek enhanced global influence and "presence." To support this ambition to the fullest, of course, the Soviet Navy will have to improve considerably its means of resupply and support, either through development of an overseas basing infrastructure (which has hitherto remained elusive) or a substantially reinforced under-way replenishment capability. Nevertheless, the Soviet Navy has become a mature and sophisticated blue-water fleet with unquestioned worldwide mobility. Its evolving missions and capabilities leave little doubt that the Soviet Union has entered the power projection game in a major way.

OVERVIEW AND OUTLOOK

A dominant hallmark of the Soviet defense buildup under Brezhnev has been the remarkable continuity of effort that has sustained it. The Soviet leaders see

---

Soviet contingency planning, they could be plausible given the right circumstances of crisis and Soviet war objectives.

31. The Reagan administration has indicated that the Soviets could deploy a nuclear-powered carrier of some 60,000 tons with catapults and an air wing of sixty fighter aircraft toward the end of this decade. See *Soviet Military Power* (Washington, D.C.: Department of Defense, 1982), p. 41.

themselves in a long-term competition with the West for global influence and ascendancy. In this contest, persistence and patience are among their most enduring attributes. Their advantages include an ideologically rooted sense of purpose, an established institutional memory, and a decision-making environment largely unfettered by the sort of internal pressures that so heavily complicate the policy processes of democratic societies. Barring a fundamental change in the structure of Soviet politics, these comparative advantages (if one can call them that) promise to guarantee the Soviets a continued edge in strategic competitiveness for the indefinite future. By contrast, the United States and its NATO allies will necessarily continue to do their own defense planning largely from budget cycle to budget cycle. Given the fractious nature of their internal debates and the inherent tendencies of recurrent leadership turnover to keep their defense programs in continual turmoil, there is little chance that the Western powers can ever match the Soviet Union in the constancy of its strategic vision.

This chapter has emphasized the stability of Soviet military thought since the early 1960s. None of the foregoing, however, was intended to suggest that Soviet operational concepts are unamenable to change. The comprehensive expansion and modernizaton of Soviet forces since the advent of the Brezhnev regime have brought Soviet combat capabilities into close congruence with long-standing Soviet doctrinal edicts. At the same time, these Soviets postural innovations have increasingly made possible new Soviet force employment options either expressly ruled out or hitherto unaddressed by the Soviet military literature.[32] In the years ahead, we can anticipate a steady maturation of Soviet doctrine, contingency plans, and operating repertoires in a way that accommodates the broadened range of options afforded by these new Soviet capabilities. Whatever changes may occur, however, are unlikely to make life for U.S. and NATO defense planners any easier. While implementation strategies will continue to evolve and diversify in parallel with improvements in Soviet technology and capability, the underlying principles of Soviet doctrine that stress the importance of assuring deterrence through the pursuit of plausible war options show every likelihood of remaining established Soviet articles of faith.

Given this prospect for continued doctrinal stability and continued force refinement aimed at lending enhanced support to Soviet doctrinal principles, any resurgent U.S. effort to draw the Soviets into an arms dialogue based on a common strategic language would most probably be in vain. Far more likely to impress the Soviets would be a measured effort to match U.S. and NATO capabilities with mission needs—without flourish or fanfare—in a way calculated to deprive Soviet operational plans of any realistic possibility of success. Fortunately,

32. Examples include limited strategic warfare, counterforce-only attacks, selective attacks against enemy command and control facilities, war in space, crisis management and escalation control, and the use of land-based missiles against targets at sea.

both American and most European defense officials now recognize and accept the necessity of this approach. Those who continue to lament the "Reagan defense buildup" and a "new arms race" fail to appreciate that current U.S. policy is largely an attempt to make up for numerous years of failure on the part of the United States to hold up its end of the competition due to preoccupation with the Vietnam War, fixation on misguided "mutual assured destruction" thinking, and consequent underfunding of a broad variety of strategic and general-purpose force needs.[33] Today, the United States and NATO face multiple deficiencies in military capability that all constitute "top-priority" problems. Restoring U.S. ICBM survivability, replacing the aging B–52, acquiring a credible remote-area power projection capability with associated naval and airlift components, and attending to the legitimate demands of tactical air and theater nuclear force modernization are only four among many. In light of these, the real question is not whether U.S. programs threaten a new "arms race" or constitute an unprecedented military "buildup," but whether the fiscal resources and popular support available in the immediate future will be sufficient to sustain these planned force improvements long enough to permit the United States to undo the legacy of their neglect.

Despite the magnitude of this challenge, engaging the Soviet Union in the long-term competition need not be an insurmountable task for the West. What the United States and the NATO countries may lack by way of institutional mechanisms for imposing extended discipline on their defense programs is offset by their superior technological prowess and adaptability in the face of changing political-military circumstances. The preceding discussoin has emphasized the more disturbing elements of Soviet doctrine and planning. It has not, however, suggested that the Soviet Union is without significant problems in the military realm. This is not the place for a detailed review of those liabilities, but it bears stressing that the Soviet leadership has ample reasons to look to the future with less than exuberant self-confidence. For one thing, despite the ongoing Afghanistan episode, the Soviet Union has had no significant direct combat

33. The Soviet Union over the past decade has massively outspent the United States in military procurement. Between 1973 and 1979 alone, the Soviets are authoritatively estimated to have exceeded the American effort in this category by some $100 billion. According to a Rand study conducted several years ago, an equivalent sum available to the United States would have completely covered procurement costs (in 1979 dollars) for the following U.S. programs that were planned at that time: the complete B–1 buy; the full MX ICBM force in its "race-track" shelter configuration; all programmed Trident missiles and submarines; all 7,000 M–1 tanks planned for deployment, along with a matching number of infantry fighting vehicles and a full complement of new transport aircraft to give them intratheater mobility; and the total package of F–14, F–15, F–16, F–18, and A–10 aircraft intended for U.S. Air Force and Navy tactical airpower modernization. See Arthur J. Alexander, Abraham S. Becker, and William E. Hoehn, Jr., *The Significance of Divergent U.S.-USSR Military Expenditure* (Santa Monica: Rand N–1000–AF, February 1979).

experience since World War II and doubtless harbors genuine uncertainties about how its forces (both material and human) would fare under the stresses of a full-blown confrontation with the West. And the very rigidities of the Soviet military management system that permit uninterrupted planning and orderly implementation of Soviet defense programs in peacetime may well deny the leadership the flexibility and responsiveness that would be required to cope effectively in a crisis.

Even in peacetime, Soviet leaders face internal and external pressures that almost surely raise valid questions about the limits of achievable military growth. The continued intractability of the Poland situation, for example, offers them a daily reminder of the burdens of empire. The continued presence of a hostile China on the Soviet Union's eastern flank constitutes another planning uncertainty unique to the Soviet leadership and doubtless occasions much circumspection in Soviet contingency planning against the West. The increasingly prominent racial tensions generated by the steady growth in percentage of ethnic minorities in the manpower composition of the Soviet armed forces make up a third ground for legitimate Soviet anxiety by raising questions about how reliable Soviet ground forces would be in any circumstance short of a fundamental threat to Soviet survival.[34] Finally, the Soviet Union—like all modern powers—is saddled with seemingly irreversible growth trends in the development and procurement costs of capital weapons systems. Every year since 1960, Soviet defense expenditures have increased in percentage of total outlays without interruption, encroaching deeper and deeper on needed investment in other sectors of the economy.[35] The Soviet leaders have thus far appeared willing to accept this burden as a necessary price for meeting their baseline force requirements, and show no indication of feeling threatened by the specter of a bilateral military spending contest with the United States. Nevertheless, the increasing strains on the Soviet economy that have been generated by this continuing buildup raise the possibility that they may eventually have to impose more stringent budgetary constraints on their defense effort, with a commensurate tapering off in the rate of Soviet military expansion.

For these and other reasons, the Soviet military challenge should be regarded not merely as a "threat" but also as a lucrative opportunity for purposeful Western counterplanning. To be sure, because of the high stakes and severe penalities for misjudgment, the pressures to hedge against worst cases are understandably compelling. Certainly it would be dangerous in the extreme to underestimate the effectiveness of Soviet military forces in unrestricted war, however valid our assumptions about Soviet caution and risk aversion may be.

34. For further discussion, see S. Enders Wimbush and Alex Alexiev, *The Ethnic Factor in the Soviet Armed Forces* (Santa Monica: Rand R–2787, March 1982).

35. See Abraham S. Becker, *The Burden of Soviet Defense: A Political-Economic Essay* (Santa Monica: Rand R–2752–AF, October 1981).

This does not mean, however, that Western planners are reduced solely to accepting worst-case possibilities as certainties or to engaging Soviet programs head on in a mindless confrontation of coutervailing weapons procurement. As Major General Jasper Welch has observed, "there is a certain unbecoming fatalism about routinely allowing the Soviet military a free ride on their existing vulnerabilities just because we 'might' be wrong or they 'might' fix them."[36]

Conversely, we must resist the temptation that has recently become fashionable in some circles to discount Soviet strengths on the misguided premise that known Soviet weaknesses constitute an adequate basis for Western complacency.[37] The challenge before American and NATO defense analysts lies precisely in the middle ground of soberly recognizing Soviet strengths for what they are—and then systematically considering how known Soviet vulnerabilities might be exploited through clever tactics and planning to compensate for our inability to match the Soviet defense effort weapon for weapon and dollar for ruble.

36. "A Conceptual Approach to Countering Invasion Threats to NATO" (unpublished manuscript, June 1976), p. 6.

37. For a typical example, see Les Aspin, "The Soviet Soldier," New York Times, June 8, 1982.

Chapter 8

Soviet Studies of the Western Alliance

Michael J. Sodaro

The relationship between the United States and its West European allies has inevitably occupied a dominant position in Soviet foreign policy considerations throughout the postwar period. Soviet perceptions of the relative strengths and weaknesses of the Atlantic Alliance, its capacity for cohesion and its susceptibility to disunity, have formed the basis of Soviet policy initiatives from the earliest days of the cold war right up to the present period of renewed East-West tension. Only in comparatively recent years, however, have Soviet analysts of international affairs published comprehensive investigations of the U.S.-West European relationship in all its complicated political, economic, and military dimensions. Although quite a few articles and several books on the foreign policies of various West European countries appeared in the late 1950s and early 1960s, along with occasional works on U.S. relations with individual West European states, Soviet scholars began focusing on the Western alliance as a problem area in itself primarily in the second half of the 1960s. Not surprisingly, this growing interest in the subject coincided with the breach in NATO unity occasioned by France's withdrawal from the military structure of the alliance in 1966, an action that occurred in the context of proliferating frictions between the alliance partners over a variety of political and economic issues. The quantity of books and articles appearing in the USSR on U.S.-West European relations mushroomed over the course of the 1970s, and reached a peak in the second

I would like to thank the other contributors to this volume, my colleagues at the Institute for Sino-Soviet Studies, and David E. Albright for their comments on an earlier draft of this chapter, which I presented at the Kennan Institute for Advanced Russian Studies, Washington, D.C., May 6, 1982.

half of the decade. This outpouring was matched by qualitative improvements in sophistication of analysis, reflecting the Soviets' stated conviction that they can "take advantage" of developments in the West only if they properly understand them.[1]

Western analysts of Soviet foreign policy have thus far paid little systematic attention to this burgeoning Soviet literature on U.S.–West European relations. In spite of this gap in our familiarity with these Soviet writings, however (and perhaps, to some extent, because of it), Western scholars have advanced a wide variety of explanations and assumptions about the way the Soviets perceive the Atlantic Alliance. At one extreme are the proponents of the so-called Finlandization thesis, who contend that the Soviet Union believes it can split the alliance apart and draw its leading West European members (particularly the Federal Republic of Germany, and perhaps others) either into a state of neutralism or into some form of inclusion within the Soviet orbit.[2] Obviously this view rests on the assumption that Moscow regards the ties connecting the United States and certain of its key allies in Europe as so tenuous that Finlandization is a viable policy option. At the other extreme are those who maintain that the Soviets perceive the Western alliance primarily in terms of its cohesiveness. Hannes Adomeit, one of the few Western scholars who have examined at least some of the recent Soviet writings on U.S.–West European relations, concludes that by the mid-1970s Soviet authors were stressing interdependence and integration as the predominant features of the Atlantic relationship. While noting that Soviet scholars generally recognize the existence of both conflict and cooperation among the Western allies, Adomeit contends that "what is beginning to emerge among Soviet experts in international affairs is the tacit acknowledgement that Kautsky may have been right after all, that there is appearing on the horizon some sort of 'Ultraimperialism' in the Atlantic area where conflicts are solved by peaceful means and where cooperation and some forms of integration . . . are inherent features of relations among capitalist states."[3]

1. M. K. Bunkina, *USA versus Western Europe: New Trends*, trans. Jane Sayer (Moscow: Progress, 1979), p. 9.

2. For variations on the view that the Soviet aim is to detach Western Europe from the United States, see Robert Strauss-Hupé, "The European Policies of the Soviet Union," in George Ginsburgs and Alvin Z. Rubenstein, eds., *Soviet Foreign Policy toward Western Europe* (New York: Praeger, 1978), pp. 235–58; Richard Pipes, "Detente: Moscow's View," in Richard Pipes, ed., *Soviet Strategy in Europe* (New York: Crane, Russak, 1976), pp. 23–24, 29; Walter Laqueur, "The West in Retreat," *Commentary*, 60, no. 2 (August 1975): 45, 47; and Hans-Peter Schwarz, "Die Alternative zum Kalten Krieg? Bilanz der bisherigen Entspannung," in Hans-Peter Schwarz and Boris Meissner, eds., *Entspannungspolitik in Ost und West* (Cologne: Carl Heymanns, 1979), p. 303.

3. Hannes Adomeit, *The Soviet Union and Western Europe: Perceptions, Policies, Problems* (Kingston, Ont.: Center for International Relations, Queen's University, National Security Series, no. 3, 1979), pp. 33–34.

Between the extremes of these two viewpoints lie a number of more nuanced analyses of Soviet perceptions of the Atlantic Alliance that reject the Finlandization concept while asserting that the Soviets seek to exploit—and indeed promote—disagreements among the alliance partners. These studies tend to infer Soviet perceptions of U.S.–West European relations primarily from Soviet policy actions and statements by Kremlin leaders.[4]

A detailed examination of a substantial number of books and articles by Soviet specialists on the Western alliance indicates that they share neither the "Finlandization" nor the "ultraimperialist" version of U.S.–West European relations. On the whole, the Soviet writers whose works are analyzed here tend to take a dialectical approach that underscores the growing severity of conflict between the United States and Western Europe while also indicating that there is a web of political, economic, and military interests that holds the capitalist world together. In a sense the views expressed by Soviet scholars on this subject come a bit closer to those advanced by the third group of Western analysts noted above, although, quite predictably, the Marxist-Leninist mode of argumentation employed by Soviet writers differs markedly from the analytical approaches of their Western counterparts.

It is virtually impossible to determine from the writings analyzed here exactly what these specialists believe the long-term fate of the Atlantic Alliance may be. Only rarely, if ever, do they divulge their speculations (or hopes) about the distant future. Their focus is almost exclusively on short-run expectations based on past trends and current realities. Should these realities change dramatically, it is conceivable that the conclusions these Soviet scholars would draw from such developments would change accordingly. Nevertheless, as the analysis that follows makes clear, none of the writers I have investigated predict a radical transformation of the essentially dialectical nature of U.S.–West European relation.

The chief aims of this chapter are to explain how Soviet scholars perceive the Western alliance and to assess the policy relevance of whatever differences of opinion may arise among them. Before proceeding to these tasks, however, I wish to place this study in a broader context by clarifying its methodological assumptions and by outlining its general theoretical relevance to the field of Soviet foreign policy analysis.

To be sure, any attempt to understand the perceptions of the world entertained by Soviet academic specialists or political leaders involves serious methodological complications. How do we know, for example, that what we read in Soviet publications represents the full spectrum of opinion expressed in the discussions that take place behind the closed doors of a closed political system? Lacking access to policy debates that in the West are more open to public scrutiny, analysts of Soviet affairs must content themselves with the information contained in publications officially sanctioned by state censors. (Interviews with Soviet foreign policy specialists can also yield significant insights into domestic policy debates; unfortunately, I did not have the opportunity to conduct interviews with the writers analyzed in this chapter.) Another problem centers on the connection between academic specialists and Soviet decision makers: to what extent do the views propounded by the former represent, or influence, the opinions of the latter?

Since no definitive answers can be given to these questions, all we can do is assume that the analyses and opinions published by Soviet specialists on international affairs reflect a politically acceptable body of thought to which Kremlin leaders may turn when looking for advice on major policy matters. The ideas published by Soviet academicians are, so to speak, "in the air" and may thus be considered both a reflection of the way Soviet policy makers generally conceive of international affairs and a source of influence on actual policy decisions. This relationship must be construed in rather generalized terms, however, as it is very difficult to trace the links between specific academicians and their viewpoints and specific policy makers and their policies. Moreover, at least some Soviet political leaders must hold views completely at variance with those conveyed by Soviet academicians. Nevertheless, the fact that virtually all the leading Soviet specialists on international affairs are members of the Communist Party of the Soviet Union (some are attached to high party organs such as the Central Committee and its departments), together with the fact that most are affiliated with such prominent state-supported institutes as the Institute on the World Economy and International Relations (IMEMO) or the Institute on the USA and Canada (IUSAC), indicates that some linkage of this sort undoubtedly exists. It is therefore reasonable to assume that the perceptions of U.S.–West European relations put forward by the Soviet scholars examined here to some extent reflect, and seek to influence, the perceptions of leading Soviet decision makers.

The principal theoretical consideration underlying this study focuses on the policy implications of the analyses presented by the Soviet writers treated in the following pages. This is a matter that goes to the heart of Western conceptions of how to study Soviet foreign policy. Two questions are particularly relevant in this context. First, what is the relation between the *analyses* of the international situation written by Soviet scholars and the actual *policy prescriptions* to be derived from these analyses? Second, what do these analyses tell us about the diversity of opinion (if any) within the Soviet elite on foreign policy issues?

The first issue concerns the way Western analysts interpret the meaning of Soviet perceptions of world affairs. Inasmuch as Soviet scholars usually refrain from making explicit policy recommendations in their writings, it is left to

Western readers to draw their own inferences about the policy directions advocated by these authors. At times this can be a fairly straightforward task. Soviet policy analyses frequently mirror intramural policy debates, in which contending views are expressed through corresponding contrasts in the description and analysis of the issue in dispute. Thus writers who analyze international politics in ominous terms, painting a sinister portrait of a hostile, aggressive Western camp, quite often skew their analyses in this direction in order to justify higher military expenditures in the Soviet Union or promote a more militant hard line in international affairs. By contrast, analysts whose conception of the internatinal environment is more placid, and who contrast the weaknesses of the West with the strength of the socialist bloc, can be implicitly arguing for a reduction in Soviet military spending or a less militant foreign policy.[5] In most of the examples of this kind of policy interpretation by Western analysts, a particular line of analysis by a Soviet writer can be logically associated with a particular policy orientation. The analysis of Soviet writings on U.S.–West European relations presented here, however, suggests that this one-to-one correspondence between analysis and policy orientation in Soviet writings is not always so clear-cut. On the contrary, the evidence presented below indicates that the relation between analysis and prescription in Soviet foreign policy literature is considerably more complex, permitting multiple—at times contradictory—policy interpretations for each analytical point of view.

The second question concerning the policy implications of Soviet foreign policy writings centers on the degree of divisiveness within the Soviet elite. On this question there is serious disagreement among Western specialists. Some maintain that there is little or no variation in Soviet perceptions of world politics. These analysts tend to view the Soviet foreign policy elite as a relatively unified, if not unanimous, group.[6] Others have concluded that there is within the Soviet elite an identifiable spectrum of opinion extending from left to right on a number of major foreign policy issues. In Marxist-Leninist parlance, a "leftist" would favor a militant foreign policy designed to promote the aims of Soviet expansionism or Soviet-inspired revolutionary movements, while a "rightist" would prefer a more cautious international posture based on an accommodation with the West of indefinite duration.[7] In some Western formulations, the terms

5. A classic example is the dispute between Khrushchev, who supported higher military spending, and Malenkov, who wanted less, in 1954. Proponents of the two views presented diametrically opposite images of the international situation in *Pravda* and *Izvestiia*, respectively. See H. S. Dinerstein, *War and the Soviet Union*, rev. ed. (New York: Praeger, 1962), p. 99.

6. See, for example, Paul Nitze, "A Plea for Action," *New York Times Magazine*, May 7, 1978, and other sources cited in William B. Husband, "Soviet Perceptions of U.S. 'Positions-of-Strength' Diplomacy in the 1970s," *World Politics*, 31, no. 4 (July 1979): 495.

7. For a comparative listing of traits of the traditional left and right, see Alexander Dallin, "Soviet Foreign Policy and Domestic Politics: A Framework for Analysis," in Erik P.

"left" and "right" correspond to "hawks" and "doves," or simply to "hardliners" and "moderates."

Between the polar extremes of left and right there exists a gradation of intermediate positions. As Jerry F. Hough has pointed out, policy discussions in Soviet publications usually revolve around an approved centrist position, with differing points of view emerging to the left and right of this norm.[8] The critical problem confronting analysts of Soviet foreign policy, however, is how far to the left and right these opposing viewpoints actually go. That is, how wide is the spectrum of foreign policy debate in the USSR? How far apart are the opposite ends of the pole? These questions are of crucial importance not only for our understanding of Soviet foreign policy but also for the conduct of Western policy toward the USSR. In the view of many proponents of the homogeneous view of the Soviet leadership, Kremlin decision makers are virtually all "hawks," and their behavior can be favorably influenced only by an equally hard-line Western position. Many of those who view the Soviet foreign policy elite as a more diversified body, however, insist that, along with the "leftists," there is a group of Soviet "rightists" whose views on such matters as the avoidability of conflict and the nonutility of force can and should be encouraged by Western policy makers.[9]

As the analysis that follows demonstrates, however, neither of these views—of a uniquely hawkish Soviet elite or of a heterogeneous elite containing rightists with policy orientations conducive to East-West harmony—applies to Soviet specialists on relations among capitalist states. On the one hand, there is noticeable diversity in their analyses of U.S.–West European relations. On the other, none of the writers I have read express a concept of international cooperation or détente predicated on the desirability of reducing conflict in a manner that might be acceptable to American or West European leaders. In short, the spectrum of discussion within the Soviet foreign policy elite (at least on this sensitive issue) is relatively narrow, with divergent viewpoints hugging close to a central point of consensus.

As to the methodology employed in this study, I have limited my research to publications by Soviet specialists in international political, economic, and military affairs who have written directly on U.S.–West European relations. Most of this literature is contained in books and in articles in such specialized

---

Hoffmann and Frederic J. Fleron, Jr., eds., *The Conduct of Soviet Foreign Policy* (Chicago: Aldine-Atherton, 1971), p. 45. For a discussion of alternating periods of left and right foreign policies in the Stalin era, see Marshall D. Shulman, *Stalin's Foreign Policy Reappraised* (New York: Atheneum, 1965).

8. Jerry F. Hough, "The Evolution in the Soviet World View," *World Politics*, 32, no. 4 (July 1980): 509–10.

9. William Zimmerman and Robert Axelrod, "The 'Lessons' of Vietnam and Soviet Foreign Policy," *World Politics*, 34, no. 1 (October 1981): 1–24.

journals as *Mirovaia ekonomika i mezhdunarodnye otnosheniia* (*The World Economy and International Relations*), *SShA* (*The USA*), *International Affairs*, and *Kommunist vooruzhennykh sil* (*Communist of the Armed Forces*). Thus I deliberately excluded most material in Soviet newspapers and weeklies, on the grounds that they are more likely to convey short-term, impressionistic accounts of day-to-day events than the scholarly journals, which usually examine long-term trends in a more thoughtful and detailed manner. Having located some twenty-five books and a host of articles dealing with intercapitalist relations, I undertook what might be called a contextual analysis of their content. Rather than engage in a strictly quantitative analysis of particular words or phrases, I read these materials with a view to determining the position taken by the authors within the context of the entire book or article. My purpose in this procedure was to determine how each author characterized the Western alliance with respect to its propensities to unity and disunity. In each case I came to a summary judgment as to whether the author tended to stress one tendency more than the other, or tended instead to adopt a more balanced position elucidating both tendencies but placing special stress on neither. I was also attentive to variations among Soviet writers in their arguments and conclusions, and in this connection I particularly looked for (1) evidence indicating the degree of variation among the different authors, (2) variations over time, (3) variations in the analysis of the political, economic, and military spheres, respectively, of U.S.–West European relations, and (4) institutional patterns of variation (i.e., the extent to which there was a shared position advocated by IMEMO authors, IUSAC authors, military economists, etc.). I also looked for explicit policy recommendations, and when none were evident (as was usually the case), I attempted to make reasonable inferences of my own.

General Features of Soviet Characterizations of the Western Alliance

The basic Soviet line on intercapitalist relations derives from Lenin, who laid down the thesis that "two tendencies" exist in relations among capitalist states.[10] The first is a tendency toward "contradictions," or conflict, the second toward cooperation and "common class interests." Although one tendency may at times gain ascendancy over the other, Lenin regarded them as operating simultaneously, with rivalries in some areas (e.g., the "imperialist partition of the world") coexisting with elements of cooperation in others (e.g., opposition to world communism). If Lenin stressed either of these two tendencies, it was the conflictual one. He specifically rejected Kautsky's thesis on ultraimperialism, and declared that in the long run the ferocity of intercapitalist competition would lead to a calamitous war between the leading capitalist powers.

---

10. V. I. Lenin, *Collected Works*, vol. 27 (Moscow: Progress, 1965), p. 369.

Contemporary Soviet authors accept these Leninist propositions except the inevitability of an intercapitalist war. Ever since the Khrushchev era, Soviet doctrine has renounced the concept of the inevitability of war between capitalism and socialism, and has explicitly discounted the possibility of an intercapitalist war, purportedly because the existence of a powerful socialist state system makes war too risky for the capitalists to contemplate.[11] Otherwise, Soviet writers faithfully adhere to Lenin's principal tenets regarding intercapitalist relations. They echo his denunciations of Kautsky's concept of ultraimperialism,[12] and emphatically reassert the dialectical unity of the "two tendencies." As one writer summed it up: "In reality the two contradictory principles are always interconnected and operate as two aspects of one and the same process."[13]

Within this framework, Soviet authors are free to stress one or the other of these tendencies. Accordingly, some writers accentuate conflictual relations between the United States and Western Europe (or among the various West European states), while others highlight the cooperative aspects. However, these contrasting positions are almost always differences in emphasis rather than rigidly defined antipodal positions. In nearly every book examined, for example, the author (or authors) invariably referred to the simultaneous presence of both currents. In several cases it was difficult to determine precisely where the emphasis lay, as the authors adopted a balanced approach that did not convincingly stress either of the two tendencies.[14] Even when the Soviet authors clearly indicated the predominance of either the "centripetal" or the "centrifugal" factors at work in the alliance, they always included specific examples of the opposite tendency and expressly acknowledged their importance. In some of these cases, the writers specified that cooperation prevailed over conflict in U.S.–West European relations during certain periods, while the reverse was the case at other times. But in these writings, too, the authors pointed to numerous examples of both tendencies acting simultaneously at all times. Thus, one author asserts that during the ten years following World War II, the United States was able to suppress conflicts with its allies owing to Western Europe's

11. See M. K. Bunkina, *Razvitie mezhimperialisticheskikh protivorechii v usloviiakh bor'by dvukh sistem* (Moscow: Moscow University Press, 1966), pp. 26, 30.

12. See, for example, I. M. Ivanova, *Kontseptsiia "Atlanticheskogo soobshchestva" vo vneshnei politike SShA* (Moscow: Nauka, 1973), p. 10; M. K. Bunkina, *Tsentry mirovogo imperializma: Itogi razvitiia i rasstanovka sil* (Moscow: Mysl', 1970), p. 57.

13. Bunkina (1979), p. 11. See also Ivanova, *Kontseptsiia "Atlanticheskogo soobshchestva,"* p. 9.

14. Examples include A. E. Efremov, *Evropeiskaia bezopasnost' i krizis NATO* (Moscow: Politizdat, 1975); I. N. Puzin and M. A. Balanchuk, *Mezhgosudarstvennye sviazi stran NATO: Voenno-ekonomicheskii aspekt* (Moscow: Mezhdunarodnye otnosheniia, 1979); G. A. Vorontsov, *SShA i Zapadnaia Evropa: Novyi etap otnoshenii* (Moscow: Mezhdunarodnye otnosheniia, 1979).

economic dependence on the United States, whereas the contradictions inherent in the Atlantic relationship increasingly rose to the fore in the period
after 1955, once Europe's economic recovery took off.[15] Another book argues
that the contradictions in U.S.–West European relations predominated in
1971–73, while efforts to resolve these conflicts gained the upper hand during the
next three years.[16] The contributions to the journal SShA by another prominent writer provide vivid example of how Soviet specialists have perceived
changes in U.S.–West European relations in recent years, with the emphasis on
cooperation within NATO in the mid–1970s gradually giving way to an emphasis on the strains besetting the alliance in the early 1980s.[17] All of these
writings, however, are replete with allusions to disintegrative processes during
periods allegedly dominated by transatlantic cooperation, and to consensual
undertakings during periods of maximum interallied disagreement.

What this dialectical approach signifies is that the differences between Soviet
writers in their estimations of the Western alliance are not great. Only on rare
occasions (to be specified below) do Soviet specialists single out either the conflictual or the cooperative tendency with such overwhelming force that evidence of the opposite tendency is nearly (though never entirely) excluded. In
the vast majority of the books and articles examined, the accent placed on the
dominant tendency in Atlantic relations is at least partly counterbalanced by
references to significant movements in the opposite direction. Thus one may
conclude that the degree of variation in the Soviet analysis of U.S.–West European relations is relatively small.

Table 1 indicates in abbreviated form (and, for want of space, without the appropriate source annotations) the factors Soviet analysts point to when analyz-
ing some of the principal developments in U.S.–West European relations since
the late 1950s. The column marked "contradictions" consists of actions or
policies that characterize the divisive elements in the Western alliance with
respect to the issues listed in the first column, while the column marked "partnership" includes occurrences that over the years have signaled the continuing
cohesion of the alliance in relation to these issues. Once again, although some
Soviet authors, when studying these events, might concentrate mainly on
either the contradictions or the elements of unity, in most cases one can find
references to both sides of each issue in the same work.

15. A. V. Kirsanov, The USA and Western Europe: Economic Relations after World War
II, trans. David Skvirsky (Moscow: Progress, 1975).

16. V. F. Davydov, T. V. Oberemko, and A. I. Utkin, SShA i zapadnoevropeiskie "tsentry sily" (Moscow: Nauka, 1978).

17. Iu. P. Davydov, "SShA–Zapadnaia Evropa: Predely kompromissa," SShA, no. 6,
1975, pp. 30–41; "Razriadka, SShA i Zapadnaia Evropa," SShA, no. 3, 1979, pp. 20–31;
"Kurs Vashingtona na napriazhennost' i Zapadnaia Evropa," SShA, no. 10, 1980, pp.
31–42; and "Antipol'skaia isteriia Vashingtona i Zapadnaia Evropa," SShA, no. 5, 1982,
pp. 53–57.

TABLE 1
U.S. WEST EUROPEAN RELATIONS SINCE THE LATE 1950S

Issue	Contradictions	Partnership
Suez crisis, 1956	U.S. aims to supplant British imperialism in Third World; "the start of the competitive struggle"	U.S. knew of British-French-Israeli plans in advance
Establishment of the EEC	Promotion of U.S.–West European economic rivalry	U.S. favors integration, seeks to promote U.S. hegemony
Kennedy Round	U.S.-EEC conflicts over trade issues	Partial compromises reached
Cuban missile crisis, 1962	U.S. risks dragging allies into nuclear war	De Gaulle and other allies support U.S.
French withdrawal from NATO command, 1966	Major break in NATO military cooperation	France remains in Atlantic Alliance; stimulates new cooperation between U.S. and other allies
Vietnam War	Some European governments and most Europeans oppose U.S.; support from British, FRG governments halfhearted	FRG and other provide material support for U.S.
Flexible response doctrine	Undermines credibility of U.S. defense guarantee; leads to "crisis of confidence"	Europeans want U.S. troop presence; FRG wants rapid "coupling"
Multilateral force	France, others oppose it	Many in FRG favor it
U.S. investments in Western Europe	Promotes anti-U.S. sentiment in Europe	Promotes European economic development; multinational corporations cooperate
Monetary crises	French assault on dollar in 1960s; plans for a European currency in 1970s	Cooperation between U.S. and European banks; Nixon-Pompidou compromise

Issue	Contradictions	Partnership
Harmel Report	No collective decision making agreed upon for East-West relations	Agreement on détente and on need to coordinate policies
FRG's Ostpolitik	U.S. reluctant to accept it, efforts to retard it	Four-power Berlin agreement; impetus to U.S.-Soviet détente
"Year of Europe"; "new Atlantic Charter," 1973	Europeans reject U.S. proposals	Brussels Declaration affirms NATO solidarity
October War, 1973	Europeans disallow U.S. use of bases	Crisis is serious but temporary
Energy policy	France rejects U.S. plans for International Energy Agency; Europeans deal directly with OPEC	Compromise on International Energy Agency
U.S.-European summits of 1970s	No recognition of U.S. leadership; major problems remain	French initiative to coordinate U.S.-West European economic cooperation
Human rights	Europeans object to Carter policy	Some Europeans adopt Carter policy
NATO modernization; 3 percent defense spending increase; decision to install Pershing II and cruise missiles, 1979	U.S. pressures allies into accepting these measures; peace movement rejects them	Some Europeans support these measures
Afghanistan	U.S. seeks to disrupt détente in Europe, while West Europeans want to retain it	Some European governments risk return to tensions
Martial law in Poland	U.S. "internationalizes" the Polish issue to reassert its dominance of NATO, disrupt Western Europe's economic ties with USSR	West European leaders express support for Solidarity, join in limited economic sanctions

Issue	Contradictions	Partnership
Gas pipeline deal	Europeans oppose U.S. efforts to block agreements with USSR	"Leading NATO circles" oppose pipeline deal; those favoring it insist on need for NATO solidarity

CONTRADICTIONS IN THE WESTERN ALLIANCE

As Table 1 demonstrates, Soviet scholars recognize that for nearly every area of conflict in U.S.–West European relations during the past several decades, countervailing factors have set limits to the impact of the fissiparous tendencies and maintained the integrity of the alliance. Nevertheless, there is total unanimity among these specialists that the contradictions in the intercapitalist relationship are growing. Actually there has been little deviation from this standard maxim since Lenin first formulated it. However, one can discern distinct changes in the way it has been applied by Soviet scholars over time.

First of all, the quality of Soviet scholarship on relations among capitalist states has greatly improved over the course of the postwar period. Although much of what is written bears the obvious imprint of Marxist-Leninist categories and selective scholarship, Soviet writings in recent years have become less polemical and tendentious, and have shown a greater awareness of the complexities of political reality. Gone are the days when a Soviet scholar could suggest (as one did in 1955) that the conflicts between the United States and Great Britain far outweighed their common interests.[18] The increasing sensitivity of Soviet scholars to the scope and limits of contradictions in the Western camp is even observable over the brief time that has elapsed since de Gaulle pulled France out of NATO's military structure. During the second half of the 1960s, at least some Soviet specialists were convinced that France's action proved the existence of "irreversible" differences between the United States and its key allies, and that other West European states would soon follow de Gaulle's example, placing the future of the NATO alliance in serious jeopardy. One article, in particular, reflected this sense of euphoria over the possible implications of de Gaulle's démarche. The essay by O. N. Bykov entitled "The Policy of the USA in Relation to Western Europe (1956–1966)" was one of several analyses published in 1968 under the auspices of IMEMO in the first major Soviet book devoted to the question of U.S.–West European relations.[19] The essay is by far the most emphatic analysis stressing the conflictual elements in the Western alliance. Bykov

18. I. M. Lemin, *Anglo-amerikanskie protivorechiia posle Vtoroi Mirovoi voiny* (Moscow: Akademiia nauk SSSR, 1955).
19. D. E. Mel'nikov, ed., *Zapadnaia Evropa i SShA* (Moscow: Mysl', 1968).

argued that the states of Western Europe faced the choice of either continuing their dependence on the United States or of joining, "without the USA," a European security system to be formed in cooperation with the socialist states of Eastern Europe.[20] This stark either/or proposition apparently held considerable weight with Kremlin decision makers, whose policy initiatives during this period sought to entice Western Europe into an all-European security system without American or Canadian participation.

Few Soviet scholars, however, adopted Bykov's arguments. In fact, another essay in the same volume stressed France's continuing adherence to the Western alliance, in spite of deep conflicts with the United States, while others stressed the undiminished allegiance of Great Britain and West Germany to their American ally.[21] As Soviet hopes for a French-inspired dissolution of NATO faded by 1969, Soviet specialists (including Bykov himself)[22] increasingly counterbalanced their evaluations of Western contradictions with an acknowledgment of continuing centripetal trends.

Another sign of growing sophistication in the Soviet analysis of the NATO Alliance is the increasing attention devoted to bilateral relations between various alliance members, particularly within Western Europe. In the 1970s, Soviet scholars developed a more differentiated approach to international relations among Western states, in contrast to their concentration in the 1950s and 1960s on NATO as a bloc or on bilateral relations between a key West European country and the United States. This refined appreciation of the particular interests of individual West European states can to some extent be traced in the works of the economist M. K. Bunkina. Writing in 1966 and 1970, Bunkina contended that there were "three levels of contradictions" among capitalist states, including (1) rivalries between the West European trading blocs—European Economic Community (EEC) and European Free Trade Association (EFTA)—and the United States, (2) rivalries between individual states belonging to these blocs, and (3) "traditional" intercapitalist rivalries, such as those between Germany and Britain, the United States and Japan, and so on.[23] Although he took note of the presence of conflicts among the European members of the alliance, Bunkina maintained that "the main element of imperialist rivalry, the fundamental interimperialist contradiction" in the contemporary world was the one that set the United States against the bloc of nations forming the European Economic Community. It was on this larger U.S. conflict with Western Europe as a whole, and especially on Western Europe's emergence as a "special imperialist

20. Ibid., p. 136.

21. Ibid., chaps. 2, 3, and 4.

22. See, for example, his contribution to a subsequent book published by IMEMO, in D. E. Mel'nikov, ed., *Mezhdunarodnye otnosheniia v Zapadnoi Evrope* (Moscow: Mezhdunarodnye otnosheniia, 1974), pp. 93, 95, 97.

23. Bunkina (1966), p. 68; (1970), p. 250.

power center," that Bunkina's earlier works focused.[24] In 1976, however, Bunkina elaborated the notion that the capitalist world now consisted of two "triangles of power." The "big triangle" was the United States, Western Europe, and Japan, while the "small triangle" consisted of Britain, France, and the Federal Republic of Germany. In addition to conflicts engendered among these states, Bunkina also referred to bilateral contradictions between particular West European states and the United States or Japan. Although the U.S.-West European relationship remained the most significant of these combinations, Bunkina concluded that rivalries among the West European states were so intense that they effectively precluded the possibility that Western Europe might establish itself as a "third force" equal to the United States or the Soviet Union.[25]

Other Soviet writings in the 1970s also displayed a growing interest in the opportunities for foreign policy maneuver available not only to the larger countries of Western Europe but also to the states of the Iberian Peninsula, the Mediterranean area, and Scandinavia.[26] In short, although they generally accept the centrality of the rivalry between the United States and the West European "imperialist power center," Soviet scholars have come to view the NATO Alliance as increasingly subject to the forces of "polycentrism," a term once popular among Western analysts of the world communist movement.[27]

Another change that has occurred in the Soviet perception of the Western alliance is the idea that the contradictions eroding its structure have gained in both scope and intensity during the 1970s. Such is the general conclusion to be drawn, for example, from a recent book containing seventeen chapters on the entire gamut of U.S.-West European relations by writers connected with IUSAC in 1978.[28] Although de Gaulle is lionized for having led the way to a more independent West European outlook, and opposition to U.S. involvement in Vietnam is said to have multiplied U.S.-West European problems in the 1960s, Soviet scholars maintain that the 1970s saw "unique" and "unprecedented" conflicts among the allies, resulting in a "fundamental difference" between the NATO of today and the NATO of earlier periods.[29] Many Soviet specialists regard 1973 as a turning point in Western Europe's assertion of independence from its American partner.[30] Four developments in that year, in the Soviet

24. Bunkina (1966), p. 70; (1970), pp. 4, 252.

25. Bunkina (1979), pp. 33-34, 184.

26. Mel'nikov (1974); Davydov, Oberemko, and Utkin, *SShA i zapadnoevropeiskie "tsentry sily."*

27. Vorontsov, *SShA i Zapadnaia Evropa*, pp. 24, 322.

28. Iu. P. Davydov, ed., *SShA-Zapadnaia Evropa: Partnerstvo i sopernichestva* (Moscow: Nauka, 1978).

29. Bunkina (1979), p. 36; Vorontsov, *SShA i Zapadnaia Evropa*, pp. 21, 308; Davydov, ed., *SShA-Zapadnaia Evropa*, p. 155.

30. E. S. Khesin, Iu. I. Iudanov, and Iu. I. Rubinskii, eds., *Zapadnaia Evropa v sisteme mezhdunarodnykh otnoshenii* (Moscow: Mysl', 1979), p. 73.

view, substantially undermined the foundations of U.S. primacy within the alliance: Britain's entry into the EEC, Western Europe's cool rebuff to Secretary of State Kissinger's proposal for a "new Atlantic Charter," the refusal of key NATO members to assist American efforts to aid Israel during the October War, and the decision of most EEC members to seek political and economic accommodations with Arab energy suppliers. This constellation of events appears to rank even higher in the minds of many Soviet analysts than West Germany's historic accords with the USSR and Poland in 1970 as a determining factor in the evolution of Western Europe's assertion of foreign policy autonomy.

As described by Soviet analysts, the 1970s witnessed a significant extension in the intensity of interallied conflicts, involving not only new patterns of conflict between the United States and Western Europe writ large, but also a host of bilateral disputes between these various countries, as well as new challenges to both the United States and Europe from Japan.[31] In addition, the scope of these conflicts widened from the sphere of economic rivalry to include new areas of contention over political, military, and ideological matters.

Soviet scholars have traditionally regarded the economic arena as the main area of conflict between capitalist states. This was still the case in the 1970s, when economic problems between the United States and the EEC, in particular, assumed larger dimensions. For Soviet Westernologists, the United States has always been ambivalent about European economic integration. Initially, they contend, the United States applauded the idea because it appeared to offer a fertile field for the political domination and economic penetration of the Continent by the United States. However, as the economic strength of the Common Market partners grew, a process abetted by certain protectionist barriers against U.S. goods, American "ruling circles" cooled off to the idea that European integration conformed with U.S. interests.[32] By the 1970s, according to a view commonly held by Soviet specialists, the United States had come to regard the EEC as a "dangerous rival."[33] Although the Nixon administration is seen as having paid official lip service to the desirability of European integration, some Soviet scholars believe that the United States in the 1970s ceased to encourage European economic unity and instead, in a radical departure from

31. On the course of relations between Western Europe and Japan, see R. Aliev, "Iaponiia i Zapadnaia Evropa: Partnerstvo i sopernichestvo," *Mirovaia ekonomika i mezhdunarodnye otnosheniia*, no. 9, 1981, pp. 69–80.

32. For this standard account, see Bunkina (1979) and Kirsanov, *The USA and Western Europe*.

33. Vorontsov, *SShA i Zapadnaia Evropa*, p. 323. Also Davydov, ed., *SShA–Zapadnaia Evropa*, pp. 41, 44, 248. Also cf. Kirsanov, *The USA and Western Europe*, with his earlier version of the same title in Russian (Moscow: Mezhdunarodnye otnosheniia, 1967). The later work places greater emphasis on the economic conflicts between the United States and Western Europe, and offers more illustrative material.

past policy, sought to promote the functional unity of the entire alliance (in such areas as energy and weapons production) precisely for the purpose of blocking further European separatism from the United States. In many instances, the United States is regarded as having sought to circumvent Common Market strictures through bilateral dealings with EEC members. Moreover, U.S. efforts to secure a common Western front against OPEC, allegedly contrived to reestablish Western Europe's energy dependence on the United States, led to "a new stage in interimperialist contradictions."[34] Although some Soviet scholars underscore the cooperative undertakings of the alliance partners sparked by the economic crisis of 1973–74,[35] they and others note that the positive results achieved were at best only partial, with disagreements festering over currency issues and competition for Third World markets, and with protectionism and trade wars looming as a distinct danger.

The Soviet analysis of U.S.-EEC relations in the 1970s appears to be a relatively new development in Soviet evaluations of the Common Market. Although Moscow remains averse to according the EEC formal diplomatic recognition, Soviet scholars since the 1960s have recognized that the EEC constitutes an important independent force in world affairs. With the recent emphasis on the Common Market's determination to pursue its own course independently of the United States on a variety of issues, Soviet scholars in a sense have come around to a more positive judgment of the EEC. The strength of the Common Market is viewed as all the greater as a result of its enlargement to include Britain, Ireland, and Denmark.[36] As long as it is seen to promote "intercapitalist contradictions," the EEC may eventually come to be regarded in more acceptable terms by Soviet decision makers as well.

One of the most novel aspects of U.S.-West European relations in the 1970s, in the view of several Soviet scholars, is the extent to which economic rivalries are spilling over into the political and military domains. Earlier analyses had commented on the relative stability of U.S. political and military influence over its allies, in spite of its declining economic preponderance.[37] More recently, the Middle East crisis of 1973 and its repercussions represent for Soviet writers perhaps the most salient example of how economic, political, and military problems intertwine in new forms. Several observers agree that Europe's reluctance to go along with U.S. pressures for larger defense budgets—a perennial source of conflict in NATO—has also intensified in the 1970s, stimulating new political and military dissensions.

34. Davydov, ed., SShA-Zapadnaia Evropa, pp. 52–55, 311.
35. Davydov, Oberemko, and Utkin, SShA i zapadnoevropeiskie "tsentry sily," p. 4; A. I. Utkin, Doktriny atlantizma i evropeiskaia integratsiia (Moscow: Nauka, 1979), p. 204.
36. Davydov, ed., SShA-Zapadnaia Evropa, p. 15.
37. Bunkina (1970), pp. 103–4. See also Kirsanov, The USA and Western Europe, p. 171.

In addition, changes in the military area in the 1970s are seen as compounding these problems. Soviet specialists contend that the declining importance of force as a rational policy instrument in the era of détente reduces the opportunities available to the United States to use its pledge to defend Western Europe as a "lever" to elicit political and economic concessions from its partners. As a consequence, the importance of interallied economic relations has risen, with the result that Western Europe's relative equality with the United States in the economic sphere enables it to promote its autonomy from the United States with greater vigor.[38] These and related considerations lead some scholars to believe that the interrelationship between conflicts in the economic, political, and military spheres will grow stronger in the future.[39]

Finally, in the ideological sphere, Soviet analysts assert that the 1970s dealt a serious blow to the concept of Atlanticism. Prior to the second half of the decade, the Soviets' treatment of Atlanticist ideas in the West tended to stress their function as the ideological justification of American hegemony over Western Europe, and it took due note of their popularity among prominent West Europeans, even as "Europeanism" was taking root as an alternative concept.[40] Subsequently, the emphasis shifted to the reputed crisis in Atlanticism owing to the "profound transformations of the 1970s," as a growing number of American and West European academics and political leaders challenged its premises. The Soviets argue that the United States has consequently been forced to modify its concept of Atlanticism in order to take account of the surge of Europeanist and nationalist sentiments on the other side of the ocean.[41]

Perhaps the most important change in the Soviet analysis of intercapitalist contradictions over the years centers on its explanation of their causes. Until the 1970s, Soviet scholars generally attributed these conflicts to the inherent laws of capitalism (above all to the "law of uneven development" among capitalist states) and to the existence of the world communist movement, spearheaded by the USSR. Both explanations have a firm foundation in Leninist doctrine, and retain their validity in Soviet scholarship. Over the course of the 1970s, however, Soviet writers increasingly singled out the role of Soviet détente policy in creating or exacerbating disagreements between the United States and Western Europe. Some proclaimed openly that Moscow's détente policy has become

38. Davydov, ed., SShA–Zapadnaia Evropa, pp. 16, 19, 34, 98.

39. Ibid., pp. 20, 159, 268; Vorontsov, SShA i Zapadnaia Evropa, pp. 187, 319–21; A. I. Utkin, Tsentry sopernichestva (SShA i Zapadnaia Evropa) (Moscow: Mezhdunarodnye otnosheniia, 1973), p. 4.

40. See, for example, Ivanova's essay in Mel'nikov, ed., Zapadnaia Evropa i SShA, chap. 5, and her book, Kontseptsiia "Atlanticheskogo soobshchestva," pp. 173, 275.

41. See the chapter by Utkin in Davydov, ed., SShA–Zapadnaia Evropa, pp. 336–58; also Utkin, Doktriny atlantizma, pp. 68, 135–202, 206; Vorontsov, SShA i Zapadnaia Evropa, p. 6.

"the main and decisive factor" in influencing the situation in Europe, while others pointed to its "catalyzing effect" on interallied contradictions.[42] What distinguishes these characterizations of the Soviet impact on U.S.-West European relations from earlier ones is not only their prominence among the factors currently mentioned by Soviet writers as affecting tensions within NATO but also the fact that, since the 1970s, Soviet analysts have had an easier time substantiating them with detailed references to actual events. In the 1950s and 1960s, invocations of "the growing might of the socialist commonwealth" or "the political and economic superiority of the USSR" as major influences on intercapitalist relations tended to have a largely rhetorical quality, to no small extent because of the Soviet Union's well-known economic and military weaknesses at that time. Since the advent of Moscow's more active role in promoting détente, however, combined with the growth of East-West trade in Europe and the USSR's attainment of military parity, Soviet scholars have been able to draw on a large body of accumulated evidence to support their assertions of Moscow's direct influence on relations among the Western allies. They have also been able to point to specific examples of acute tension between the United States and its key allies in Europe in the 1970s over a variety of political, economic, and military issues concerning East-West relations.

Thus when Soviet scholars write that West European cooperation with the USSR "objectively weakens the leading role of the USA in NATO," or that the "relaxation of tensions" (i.e., détente) "objectively" promotes contradictions within the Western alliance, these statements carry greater weight than the ritualistic references to "socialist might" did prior to the 1970s.[43] They are grounded in considerable evidence that Western Europe (particularly France and the FRG) embarked on the path of détente with the USSR before the United States was ready to do so, and that at various times during the 1970s and early 1980s certain West European states evinced a greater interest in the political, economic, and military aspects of détente than the United States did.[44]

The economic aspects of détente are seen as particularly beneficial for the West Europeans, as trade with the USSR helps them overcome their own economic dislocations and energy shortages, and assists them in closing the technology gap with the United States.[45] For their part, the military transformations of the 1970s are described by Soviet authors as having a decisive impact on U.S.-West European ties. As noted above, Soviet writers have referred to the declining effect of military power on the ability of the United States to

42. Efremov, *Evropeiskaia bezopasnost'*, p. 269; Davydov, ed., *SShA-Zapadnaia Evropa*, p. 75.
43. Davydov, ed., *SShA-Zapadnaia Evropa*, pp. 36, 62.
44. Vorontsov, *SShA i Zapadnaia Evropa*, pp. 22, 318-19.
45. Khesin et al., *Zapadnaia Evropa*, p. 87; Davydov, ed., *SShA-Zapadnaia Evropa*, p. 310; Bunkina (1979), pp. 190-92.

extract political and economic advantages from its allies. Scholars who observe this phenomenon see it as intimately bound up with the USSR's acquisition of military parity with the United States in the 1970s. In the words of one prominent specialist: "The fact of the achievement of parity has an impact on inter-imperialist relations, particularly in that, in losing the position of a practically invulnerable country, the USA to a significant degree has lost the means of pressure over its allies which it once had by virtue of the promise given to the ruling classes of the capitalist countries to protect the foreign and domestic status quo with its might."[46]

Soviet specialists on U.S.–West European relations thus clearly regard the nonutility of force in the contemporary world as a factor contributing to U.S.–West European contradictions, and they explicitly credit the Soviet Union's success in attaining military parity with the United States in the 1970s as creating the conditions for this development. Viewed in this light, the Soviets seem to regard the USSR's growing military force as having a great political utility for the Soviet Union, whereas the decreasing ability to translate military force into political influence seems to apply mainly to the United States.

Soviet scholars have thus concluded that Soviet détente policy decidedly expanded Western Europe's "opportunities" and room for political maneuver in international affairs, thereby greatly reducing its dependence on the United States and reinforcing its own particular interests.[47] These interests, in turn, are viewed by Soviet scholars as primarily regional, a consideration which reputedly spurs West European unwillingness to become embroiled in the far-flung adventures of American globalism.[48] Hence it is not surprising that by the end of the 1970s, there was virtual unanimity among these Soviet analysts that one of the chief results (and virtues) of détente was its disruptive effect on U.S.–West European relations. Rather than regarding détente as a policy contributing to the overall diminution of international tension as such, they emphasized its role in promoting conflict within the Western camp. At least some of these scholars drew the conclusion that a "policy of confrontation" in Europe could only reinforce Western Europe's dependence on the United States and encourage the unity of the Western allies, whereas "if that threat relaxes the contradictions rending them may be aggravated."[49]

46. Utkin, *Doktriny atlantizma*, p. 135.

47. Utkin, *Tsentry sopernichestva*, p. 76; Khesin et al., *Zapadnaia Evropa*, p. 81; Vorontsov, *SShA i Zapadnaia Evropa*, p. 327.

48. Mel'nikov, ed., *Mezhdunarodnye otnosheniia v Zapadnoi Evrope*, pp. 85, 110–11; Vorontzov, *SShA i Zapadnaia Evropa*, p. 327. In this connection, Bykov wrote in 1968: "The war in Vietnam proved that, in similar situations in the future, the USA cannot rely on its basic allies." Mel'nikov, ed., *Zapadnaia Evropa i SShA*, p. 132.

49. Khesin et al., *Zapadnaia Evropa*, p. 81; Kirsanov, *The USA and Western Europe*, p. 162.

PARTNERSHIP IN THE WESTERN ALLIANCE

In sum, there appears to be ample support among Soviet analysts of the NATO alliance for the dictum that "the contradictions between the imperialists are absolute, while the unity between them is relative."[50] Nevertheless, practically all of these scholars (including the one just quoted) do not hesitate to draw attention to the elements of partnership that tend to impose limits on the contradictions and prevent the Western alliance from splitting apart. Moreover, the Soviets note that these integrative tendencies persisted (and in some cases increased) throughout the 1970s, existing alongside the heightened disagreements in the political, economic, and military spheres of alliance activity.

On the political level, Soviet writers continued to refer to the fundamentally anti-Soviet orientation of NATO, an attitude around which all the "ruling circles" of the member countries were said to rally, in spite of the supposed dissolution of the "myth of the Soviet threat" in Western Europe. Western leaders were also portrayed as maintaining an interest in the domestic political and social status quo in their respective countries, a situation challenged in the 1970s by the rise to prominence of communist parties in several West European states. Soviet scholars varied somewhat in their assessments of this leftist challenge. Some held that it stimulated dissension between the United States and Western Europe (since West European governments resented American interference against communism in their countries), while others emphasized the concerted efforts among the Western partners to stem the leftist tide. Still others adopted a middle position, affirming that the rise of the left promoted alliance conflict in some countries and cooperation in others.[51] Whatever the case, all Soviet scholars either affirmed or assumed that Western leaders were still united by strong "class interests" in the maintenance of the capitalist system and bourgeois democracy.

On the economic level, Soviet analysts testify to the bonds of interdependence that join the Western economies. Even such contentious issues as the role of U.S. investment and multinational corporations in Western Europe are said to have their positive aspects for the Europeans as well as the Americans. Soviet economists point out, for example, that Western Europe has profited from the advanced technology used by multinational corporations, and that American firms often cooperate with European corporations in a variety of ways besides competing with them. Some Soviet scholars have even dismissed European

50. Kirsanov, The USA and Western Europe, p. 14.

51. For accounts stressing the contradictions, see V. S. Shein, SShA i Iuzhnaia Evropa: Krizis atlanticheskogo partnerstva (Moscow: Nauka, 1979), p. 185; and Vorontsov, SShA i Zapadnaia Evropa, pp. 159–73. References to the unifying effects are in Davydov, Oberemko, and Utkin, SShA i zapadnoevropeiskie "tsentry sily," p. 142. The middle position is in Davydov, ed., SShA–Zapadnaia Evropa, pp. 99–124, and A. F. Gorelova and Iu. P. Davydov, "SShA i levye sily v Zapadnoi Evrope," SShA, no. 2, 1978, pp. 3–14.

fears of a *défi américain* in the 1960s, while noting that the flow of capital from Western Europe to the United States has increased appreciably in the 1970s. Thus Bunkina likened predictions that U.S. multinationals would one day take over Western Europe to "Ray Bradbury's social science fiction." Other Soviet writers have suggested that capitalists on both sides of the Atlantic are fully cognizant of the mutually damaging effects of protectionism and trade wars, and are anxious to avoid these perils.[52]

The most enduring military link between the United States and Western Europe is the presence of U.S. troops on European soil. Soviet scholars who address the question of military relations within NATO admit that all the governments of Western Europe strongly favor the continuation of the American presence. This applies even to the Soviet Union's most valued interlocutors in Western Europe, Charles de Gaulle and Willy Brandt.[53] Although the Europeans may have their doubts about the flexible response strategy urged on them by the United States (doubts which, in the Soviet view, are reinforced by Soviet military power), these lapses of confidence in the U.S. military guarantee do not lead them to request a withdrawal of American forces. If anything, they have stimulated West European efforts to coordinate their own military activities in the framework of NATO's Eurogroup.

Soviet pronouncements on the Eurogroup display the equivocal judgments typical of the dialectical approach. While some authors state that it has furthered West European "military separatism" from the United States, others describe its effects on NATO as a mixture of contradictions and unity.[54] Still others stress the unifying impact the Eurogroup has had by recalling that its operations take place within the structure of NATO, and that the organization itself meets with the approval of the United States.[55]

Indeed, few issues reflect the ambivalence of the Soviet position concerning NATO more vividly than the progress of military cooperation among the European members of the alliance. On the one hand, Soviet scholars seem heartened by the contradictions it provokes in the alliance, since it reinforces Western

52. Bunkina (1979), p. 147; Kirsanov, *The USA and Western Europe*, pp. 198, 227, 263; also Davydov, ed., *SShA–Zapadnaia Evropa*, pp. 43–44, 264, 269–90. For an example of a study stressing economic contradictions in the West, see E. S. Shershnev, *SShA: Tamozhennyi protektsionizm* (Moscow: Nauka, 1970). For a study emphasizing economic cooperation, see R. A. Novikov and Iu. V. Shishkov, *Mezhdunarodnaia kooperatsiia kapitalisticheskikh firm* (Moscow: Mysl', 1972).

53. See, for example, Kirsanov, *The USA and Western Europe*, p. 162; Davydov, ed., *SShA–Zapadnaia Evropa*, pp. 161, 190, 193, 196–97.

54. Davydov, ed., *SShA–Zapadnaia Evropa*, pp. 42, 163, 166; Efremov, *Evropeiskaia bezopasnost'*, pp. 155 ff.

55. Khesin et al., *Zapadnaia Evropa*, p. 197; Puzin and Balanchuk, *Mezhgosudarstvennye sviazi stran NATO*, pp. 115–16.

Europe's autonomous tendencies. On the other, the Soviets do not seem particularly enthusiastic about the possibility of a separate European nuclear force. Although several scholars offer reassurances that the various schemes for nuclear sharing advanced by the French and the British have specifically excluded the FRG, there are occasional expressions of concern about alleged West German hopes for access to nuclear weapons. One author made no attempt to conceal his opposition to a European nuclear force (with or without the Germans), warning that it would jeopardize prospects for U.S.–Soviet arms control agreements and would be "logically regarded by the Soviet Union as an attempt on the part of the countries of the West to obtain unilateral strategic superiority."[56] It is quite likely that Soviet writers who describe the present prospects for European nuclear cooperation as minimal do so with a sigh of relief.[57]

Other military issues also evoke ambivalent reactions on the part of Soviet scholars, who discern both positive and negative features in them. The problems of NATO weapons standardization and U.S. efforts to enlist West European military support in the Third World (at times successful, at times not) are among the more prominent ones. More recently, the NATO modernization program, including the decision of the alliance in December 1979 to install 572 Pershing II and cruise missiles in Western Europe, has aroused considerable attention, with Soviet scholars pointing to both American "pressure" on its allies to fall into line behind these plans and the receptive attitude manifested by a number of West European governments, including the FRG.[58]

On the whole, however, it is in the area of military affairs that Soviet analysts most often stress the cooperative apsects of U.S.–West European relations.[59] From an institutional standpoint, Soviet analysts who specialize in military affairs (some of whom are active or retired military professionals) are the group

56. Davydov, ed., *SShA–Zapadnaia Evropa*, p. 233.

57. On U.S. attitudes for and against a European nuclear force, see ibid., pp. 237–44; on the likelihood of such a force, see ibid., pp. 160, 162. See also Mel'nikov, *Mezhdunarodnye otnosheniia*, pp. 126 ff., 143; Efremov, *Evropeiskaia bezopasnost'*, p. 252; Bunkina (1979), pp. 21–22.

58. Bunkina (1979), p. 15; Vorontsov, *SShA i Zapadnaia Evropa*, pp. 178, 181; G. Trofimenko, "Politika bez perspektivy," *Mirovaia ekonomika i mezhdunarodnye otnosheniia*, no. 3, 1980, pp. 17–27; B. D. Piadyshev, "Voennaia razriadka v Evrope: Dva podkhoda," *SShA*, no. 11, 1980, pp. 3–14.

59. See, for example, the essay by D. M. Proektor in Khesin et al., *Zapadnaia Evropa*, chap. 7. See also V. Lutskevich, "Mirovaia kapitalisticheskaia sistema: Imperializm–vrag narodov i obshchestvennogo progressa, istochnik voennoi opasnosti," *Kommunist vooruzhennykh sil*, no. 4, 1978, pp. 76–84, and no. 5, 1978, pp. 75–92; Iu. P. Sedov, "Sredizemnomore v ekspansionistikh planakh imperialisticheskoi reaktsii," *Kommunist vooruzhennykh sil*, no. 7, 1981, pp. 80–85; and V. Mikhnovich, "Zapadnaia Evropa–'zalozhnik' iadernoi strategi Vashingtona," *Kommunist vooruzhennykh sil*, pp. 77–82.

most inclined to emphasize the elements of partnership in the NATO alliance. Whereas economists and analysts of political relations (whether connected with IMEMO or IUSAC) usually take either a more balanced view of the alliance or tilt slightly in the direction of NATO's contradictions, the military analysts generally accent the integrative factors. This should not be surprising, since Soviet military specialists have traditionally drawn a picture of a strong, unified adversary for the purpose of justifying higher defense expenditures in the Soviet Union.

One book in particular captures the essence of the military's vision of the Western alliance. *The USA and NATO: Sources of the Military Threat*, written by four senior military officials and published in 1979 by the Soviet military press,[60] consistently projects the most extreme view of NATO unity on a variety of issues, in stark contrast to other Soviet writers whose depiction of these events is either more evenhanded or somewhat more sensitive to their implications for Western disharmony. Although the authors tersely acknowledge the existence of détente and intercapitalist contradictions, their main message is that NATO preserves its "aggressive essence." The current NATO modernization program, agreements on weapons standardization, and the coordination of Eurogroup activities with the United States, and other developments are all presented as the products of interallied cooperation, with little or no reference to the controversies they provoked within the alliance. Whereas most other writers attest to the difficulties for the alliance created in the 1970s by Greece, Spain, and Portugal, the military authors concentrate on the abiding ties of these countries to U.S. military interests. Whereas other authors are unanimous in characterizing the Kissinger proposal for a "new Atlantic Charter" in 1973 as a failure, and generally regard the Atlantic Declaration adopted in Brussels the following year as a *pis aller* that papered over interallied disagreements, Petrov and his coauthors devote several pages to portraying the Brussels document as a testament to NATO solidarity and bellicosity. And whereas most nonmilitary Soviet writers look upon the refusal of the West European states to join the United States in assisting Israel in 1973 as an unprecedented crisis within NATO, the authors of this book pass over these events in silence and focus on U.S. support for Israeli "aggression." Other aspects of U.S.–West European relations are treated in a similar vein. Quite predictably, the authors conclude by warning that the USSR and its allies "cannot but be concerned about strengthening the defense capability of the socialist commonwealth."[61] This is about as close as any of the writers come to making an explicit policy recommendation.

This exaggerated perception of NATO unity is strikingly different from the accounts presented by Soviet scholars from the more academic disciplines. One

60. N. Petrov, N. Sokolov, I. Vladimirov, and P. Katin, *SShA i NATO: Istochniki voennoi ugrozy* (Moscow: Voennoe izdatel'stvo, 1979).

61. Ibid., p. 155.

final example of the more balanced approach generally followed by the non-military writers concerns the Soviet analysis of bilateral relations between the United States and its principal European partners, Britain, France, and the FRG. Studies by "international affairs generalists" on these relationships, published in 1968, 1978, and 1979,[62] invariably counterbalance their portrayal of the contradictions in these ties with copious examples of centripetal factors. In the more recent of these analyses, Britain is perceived as being increasingly torn between its special attachments to the United States and its new European connections; France since de Gaulle is seen to maintain its independent posture while reestablishing cooperative military links with NATO; and the FRG is viewed as having acquired a vital stake in good relations with the Soviet bloc, while striving to supplant Britain as the "special partner" of the United States and assume the leadership of the EEC.[63]

THE SOVIET EVALUATION OF ATLANTIC RELATIONS

Given these contrasting centrifugal and centripetal elements in the Western alliance, what conclusions do Soviet scholars draw from them? On this point the majority of the authors investigated are quite forthcoming. In contrast to the notions of "Finlandization" and "ultraimperialism," the current state of the alliance is described in terms of an increasing equality between its two main pillars, the United States and Western Europe. In essence, the contradictions that have transformed relations within the alliance over the years have not led to a breakup but to a change in the power relationship between the two sides in favor of Western Europe. In Leninist jargon, what has transpired is a change in the "correlation of forces" between the two alliance partners. In this conception, the West Europeans' pursuit of greater independence from the United States is not aimed at producing a rupture of the alliance, but rather at enhancing Europe's role. Western Europe is therefore not opposed to the United States as such, but only to the exercise of American hegemony over its allies.[64]

62. Mel'nikov, ed., *Zapadnaia Evropa i SShA*, chaps. 2, 3, and 4; Davydov, Oberemko, and Utkin, *SShA i zapadnoevropeiskie "tsentry sily"*; and Vorontsov, *SShA i Zapadnaia Evropa*, chap. 5.

63. See, for example, S. Madzoevskii and E. Khesin, "Velikobritaniia v sovremennom mire," *Mirovaia ekonomika i mezhdunarodnye otnosheniia*, no. 8, 1980, pp. 50–63. On the FRG, see A. A. Trynkov, "Atlanticheskii soiuznik SShA nomer odin?" *SShA*, no. 1, 1976, pp. 61–64; V. Fedorov, "Aktual'nye voprosy ekonomicheskikh sviazei SSSR-FRG," *Mirovaia ekonomika i mezhdunarodnye otnosheniia*, no. 9, 1980, pp. 95–105, and the same author's essay, "Nekotorye aspekty militarizatsii v FRG," *Mirovaia ekonomika i mezhdunarodnye otnosheniia*, no. 5, 1982, pp. 119–27. On France, see Michael J. Sodaro, "Moscow and Mitterrand," *Problems of Communism*, 31, no. 4 (July–August 1982): 20–36.

64. Efremov, *Evropeiskaia bezopasnost'*, p. 68; Davydov, ed., *SShA–Zapadnaia Evropa*, pp. 20, 159; Utkin, *Doktriny atlantizma*, p. 103; Bunkina (1979), p. 24; Vorontsov, *SShA i Zapadnaia Evropa*, pp. 38, 85.

In the Soviet view, the West European members of the alliance, led by France, the Federal Republic, and (at times) Britain, have made great strides toward equality with the United States in the 1970s. Although the United States continues to possess the most powerful and diversified economy within the alliance, the EEC as a whole has pulled even with the United States, or surpassed it, in a number of important economic indicators. Furthermore, although the United States continues to carry the main weight in the political and military affairs of the alliance, it can no longer dictate to its European partners as in the past. On the contrary, Soviet writers observe that in recent years, the United States has been compelled to reach compromises with its allies on a number of issues. Because both Western Europe and the United States carry a mixed bag of strengths and weaknesses, Soviet specialists believe that this tendency toward compromise will continue to assert itself as the dominant characteristic of the alliance in the foreseeable future.[65] This means that, even though the United States may on occasion seek to reassert its hegemony, the Europeans will resist these attempts without seeking a radical change in the alliance itself.[66]

From the vantage point of Soviet foreign policy, all of this adds up to a situation in which Western Europe is increasingly able to assert its own interests, and to influence U.S. policy accordingly. Soviet analysts refer to a number of instances in which West European states led a reluctant United States along the road to détente with the USSR. In the Soviet view, the West's acceptance of Europe's territorial status quo, of expanded trade with the USSR and Eastern Europe, of the Conference on Security and Cooperation in Europe, as well as of other milestones of détente, all involved an initial positive response to Soviet initiatives by key West European governments, who then induced the United States to go along. One writer suggested that, whereas in the past the United States exploited U.S.-Soviet tensions for the purpose of controlling Western Europe, in the period of détente Western Europe uses U.S.-Soviet tensions to influence U.S.-Soviet relations.[67] Another author put it this way: "Proceeding from détente, they [the West Europeans—MJS] have endeavored to use Atlantic relations as a counterinfluence on the USA's position."[68]

Meanwhile, Soviet writers also note that the improvement in U.S.-Soviet relations in the early 1970s exerted a positive influence on the West Europeans,

65. Davydov, ed., SShA–Zapadnaia Evropa, chap. 1; Utkin, Doktriny atlantizma, p. 168; Ivanova, Kontseptsiia "Atlanticheskogo soobshchestva," p. 63. Unlike other authors, Vorontsov contends that Western Europe and Japan seek long-term predominance over the United States, but he admits that they have a long way to go before achieving this goal (p. 326).

66. Vorontsov, SShA i Zapadnaia Evropa, pp. 26–27; Bunkina (1979), p. 86.

67. Davydov, ed., SShA–Zapadnaia Evropa, p. 70. See also pp. 7, 21–22, 63, 65, 68–69, 169, 176, 179.

68. Vorontsov, SShA i Zapadnaia Evropa, p. 58.

reinforcing their own commitment to détente and making matters difficult for European foes of the détente process.[69]

In short, what emerges from the Soviet analysis of the Western alliance is a perception of U.S.–West European ties as a relationship of reciprocal influence. The Soviets consequently see themselves in a position to encourage the West Europeans to influence the United States in favorable directions, or, when appropriate, to induce the United States to influence Western Europe. Whether Moscow chooses to exert its principal leverage on Western Europe or on the United States may, of course, vary with the issue or with the general international atmosphere; indeed, the Soviets may wish in some cases to try to influence both sides at the same time, in hopes of promoting mutually reinforcing influence patterns between the NATO partners. However, the literature surveyed makes it plain that the Soviets regard the most likely situation to be one in which the West Europeans will be "out in front" of the United States in taking positions favorable to Soviet interests, and thus it is to the key West European countries that the Soviets will in all probability continue to direct important overtures.

Precisely what policies should Soviet leaders pursue in order to take advantage of these circumstances most effectively? Here the Soviet scholars are for the most part either silent or, at best, oblique. As is usually the case in Soviet foreign policy analysis, it is up to Western observers to strike their own interpretations of the policy implications of Soviet analytical writings.

POLICY IMPLICATIONS OF SOVIET ANALYSES

The process of extrapolating policy prescriptions from political perceptions in Soviet literature is a tricky one. One of the chief pitfalls is that the meanings of terms used by Marxist-Leninists frequently differ—at times considerably—from the usages ascribed to them in the West. This is especially true of politically ambiguous or controversial terminology. Thus it is not enough for Western analysts to say that certain Soviet writers are for or against "détente." Western scholars need to be aware that such terms as the "relaxation of tensions" (i.e., détente) and the "nonutility of force" often carry different denotations and connotations in the Marxist-Leninist lexicon than in the vocabulary of Western social scientists or political leaders. It is essential that Western interpretations of politically charged words and phrases conform as closely as possible to the context in which they are used by Soviet writers. One of the hazards of quantitative content analysis is that it tends to divorce selected terms from their full context, a procedure which can lead either to distorted notions of what these terms mean to the Soviets or to no clear notion at all.[70]

69. Efremov, *Evropeiskaia bezopasnost'*, p. 215.

70. For an example of the former tendency, see Zimmerman and Axelrod, "The 'Lessons' of Vietnam and Soviet Foreign Policy" (see note 9 above); for an example of the

Another general difficulty encountered in the interpretation of the policy implications of Soviet perceptions is that it is rarely, if ever, possible to infer
precise policy recommendations from the analyses themselves. One can at most
deduce the general policy direction or orientation of the Soviet source in question. Even here, however, the categories used by Western analysts to characterize these orientations ("hard" or "moderate," "left" or "right", etc.) can at times
misrepresent reality because they suggest a more coherent, clearly demarcated
policy than may be the case. Indeed, there are good reasons for believing that
the terms "left" and "right" as traditionally applied to Soviet foreign policy are
no longer valid.[71] Certainly they no longer carry the full baggage of domestic
and foreign policy preferences outlined by Dallin (leanings toward utopianism,
violence, voluntarism, etc., on the part of the left, and toward pessimism,
pluralism, determinism, etc., on the part of the right).[72] As my own analysis
suggests, Soviet specialists on U.S.-West European relations by no means exhibit the highly polarized and systematically defined positions associated with
contending left and right factions in the Soviet elite in earlier phases of Soviet
history. On the contrary, the writers studied here might all be described as
"centrist dialecticians," whose differences of opinion extend only marginally in
one direction or the other.

Because the left-right spectrum is probably ineradicably ingrained in our conceptions of political life, and also because I can offer no superior substitute, I shall
continue to use the terms "left" and "right" in attempting to define the policy implications of Soviet perceptions of U.S.-West European relations. More precisely,
however, I wish to qualify these terms by stressing their marginality—that is, their
proximity to a center point of general consensus and, consequently, to each other.
Thus the "marginal left" viewpoints in the contemporary Soviet foreign policy elite
are not all that far removed from "marginal right" positions. Rather than embody-
ing the polarized ends of a wide political spectrum, they reflect a prevailing consensus in the basic orientation of Soviet foreign policy specialists (and, by implication, of Soviet decision makers as well). Above all, both outlooks have in
common certain features of the traditional Soviet right, such as a generally pragmatic approach to world politics, a commitment to professional expertise, and a

---

latter, see Elizabeth J. Kirk, "Cognitive Complexity in the Language of Politburo
Members: Reflections of Soviet Attitudes towards Detente with the West," paper prepared
for the Third Annual Scientific Meeting of the International Society of Political
Psychology, Boston, June 5-7, 1980. The Zimmerman-Axelrod study makes an a priori
assumption that the Soviets ascribe more or less literal meanings to such terms as the
"nonutility of force" and the "avoidability of conflict." Kirk reports on "pro-detente" and
"anti-detente" attitudes among the Soviet elite, but does not define "detente."

71. For a similar view, see Seweryn Bialer, ed., The Domestic Context of Soviet Foreign
Policy (Boulder, Colo.: Westview Press, 1981), p. 392.

72. See note 7 above.

desire to avoid war with the West, together with certain features of the traditional left, such as a dialectical view of the world that stresses the inevitability of conflict (short of war) in East-West relations. It bears reiterating that, in this generally accepted world view, the Soviets believe that violence is to be shunned in the USSR's direct dealings with the West, but conflict short of violence cannot, and indeed should not, be avoided in pursuing Soviet state interests in relation to the NATO countries. As noted above, even the most emphatically prodétente writers on U.S.-West European relations emphasize the divisive, conflict-provoking impact the "relaxation of tensions" has on the West. Similarly, those who proclaim the declining utility of force in contemporary world politics apply this concept primarily to the United States, not the Soviet Union. Thus, for the writers examined in this study, concepts such as "détente" and the "nonutility of force" have the notion of conflict built into them. Rather than signaling a Soviet interest in the avoidance of conflict, they are conceived of as heightening conflict within the Western camp, thus providing the Kremlin with the opportunity to manipulate dissensions within the Western alliance to its own advantage. This is hardly an outlook Western leaders would wish to encourage.

Furthermore, it should be emphasized that the terms "marginal left" and "marginal right" as used here refer to *policy orientations*, not to distinct groups of individuals. Although some Soviet scholars or decision makers may consistently identify themselves with one or the other of these orientations, it may be quite possible for a person to combine elements of the two positions, favoring marginal left policies in some areas and marginal right policies in others. That such a mixture of the two orientations is possible further attests to their mutual proximity along the main axis of the Soviet political spectrum.

As to their differences, the marginal left orientation would stress a somewhat "harder" approach than the marginal right tendency in matters relating to the Western alliance. Supporters of the marginal right viewpoint would thus seek to maximize or "push" Moscow's exploitation of U.S.-West European contradictions. Such individuals would also seek a robust military posture for the USSR (designed in part to intimidate the West Europeans) as well as a firm stand in arms control negotiations with the West. For their part, proponents of the marginal right orientation would counsel a more cautious approach in the Soviet exploitation of conflicts between the NATO partners, and would display a greater willingness to seek realistic compromises with the West on arms control and related issues. Ironically, each side would draw on both aspects of the "two tendencies" in intercapitalist relations as analyzed by Soviet specialists. This is possible in part because both the marginal left and the marginal right positions are based on the dialectical approach to U.S.-West European relations to begin with, and in part because neither the emphasis on the West's contradictions nor the emphasis on its unity automatically lends itself to any particular policy orientation. Rather, each of these two analytical perspectives is capable of supporting either marginal left or marginal right policies.

The notion that "contradictions are inevitably growing" in the West can therefore be used to sustain marginal left arguments in favor of more vigorous Soviet efforts to promote conflict between the United States and Western Europe. To this end, those arguing this position might recommend greater Soviet defense efforts, both in Europe and on the strategic level (to further undermine the credibility of the U.S. pledge to defend Europe, and to provoke renewed interallied squabbling over the question of boosting West European military spending). They would also be willing to countenance a more interventionist Soviet engagement in the Third World (to stimulate conflicts between U.S. "global interests" and European "regional interests"). By contrast, the notion of inevitably growing contradictions can just as well be used by advocates of marginal right positions, who would remind Kremlin policy makers that it is the "relaxation of tensions" that promotes intercapitalist contradictions, and that confrontationist policies are only counterproductive, since they serve to drive the capitalists together.

Meanwhile, the emphasis on NATO partnership is also capable of being interpreted to justify either marginal left or marginal right arguments. As the analysis put forward by the military writers examined earlier concluded, NATO's persisting unity and strength require a strong military position on the part of the Warsaw Pact. The proponents of increased Soviet military spending and force deployments, arguing from the marginal left, can thus seize upon evidence of NATO partnership to buttress their viewpoints. Meanwhile, those affirming a marginal right position might take the opposite tack, arguing that manifestations of Western unity are real and disturbing but that excessively militant foreign and defense policies will reinforce these integrative tendencies. They might also note that since a certain degree of partnership is inherent in intercapitalist relations, in any event, it would be fruitless for the Soviet Union to try to push the West too hard, and more productive to play on inevitable U.S.–West European disagreements through policy initiatives on economic cooperation and arms control.

This reconstruction of how Soviet specialists on U.S.–West European relations might go about deriving policy recommendations from their analyses of the NATO Alliance therefore suggests that a particular line of analysis does not necessarily yield one, and only one, policy orientation. As shown here, each of the two contrasting analytical emphases can substantiate both marginal leftist and marginal rightist policies. The relation between policy analysis and policy orientation in Soviet foreign policy writings can therefore be somewhat complicated, with each analytical conclusion capable of supporting contradictory policy prescriptions. While this need not always be the case, Western analysts of Soviet foreign policy should at least be attentive to the possibility that certain Soviet analyses (or perceptions) can have multiple policy implications.

How then do we characterize Soviet policy toward the Western alliance today, and what does it tell us about the Soviet foreign policy decision making process?

Soviet détente policy in the Brezhnev era may be looked upon as involving a mixture of marginal rightist and marginal leftist elements. The Soviets have sought to extract political and economic benefits from the West through agreements based on mutual concessions (the rightist aspect), while at the same time engaging in an unprecedented military buildup culminating, at the very least, in parity with the United States, and pursuing an active involvement on the side of Third World clients (the leftist elements). As far as its effect on the West is concerned, this combination of the two policy orientations is not necessarily internally incompatible, since both can be used to promote disunity between the United States and Western Europe. Incompatibility arises when the Soviets move too far to the left, prompting the Western allies into a concerted response.

Since the mid–1970s, the Soviets seem to have leaned in the direction of the marginal left in their Western policies. The installation of a new generation of intermediate-range nuclear missiles (SS–20s), together with the decision to invade Afghanistan in spite of possible Western objections, has resulted in the most serious East-West tensions since the early 1960s. In addition, the Soviet leadership in the early 1980s has sought to exploit the growing strains between the United States and its allies (particularly the FRG) by using both carrots (natural gas and other economic agreements) and sticks (propaganda support for the West European peace movement, East German pressures on the FRG) to reinforce Europe's interest in cooperation with the USSR.

Like détente, the current phase of tensions is seen by Soviet analysts as evoking a mixture of conflict and compromise between the United States and Western Europe. Once again, Soviet scholars tend to take a dialectical approach, with some writers stressing NATO's contradictions and others the persisting bonds of partnership.[73] Although they are fully cognizant of the "unprecedented" controversies surrounding such issues as the planned installation of Pershing II and cruise missiles in Western Europe, or the desire of West European governments to proceed with the gas pipeline and other economic agreements with the Soviet Union in the face of U.S. efforts to block the implementation of these

---

73. For examples of the emphasis on contradictions, see O. Bykov, "Glavnaia obshchechelovecheskaia problema," *Mirovaia ekonomika i mezhdunarodnye otnosheniia*, no. 3, 1980, pp. 3–16; V. Shamberg, "SShA v sovremennom mire," *Mirovaia ekonomika i mezhdunarodnye otnosheniia*, no. 7, 1980, pp. 43–57; and S. A. Ulin, "Oppozitsiia v Zapadnoi Evrope amerikanskim planam razmeshcheniia novykh raket," *SShA*, no. 1, 1982, pp. 80–83. For an example of the emphasis on cooperation, see A. Nikonov and R. Faramazian," Opasnyi kurs nagnetaniia voennoi napriazhennosti," *Mirovaia ekonomika i mezhdunarodnye otnosheniia*, no. 2, 1981, pp. 47–59. For analyses that combine references to both contradictions and cooperation, see G. Vorontsov, "SShA i Zapadnaia Evropa v usloviiakh obostreniia mezhdunarodnoi obstanovki," *Mirovaia ekonomika i mezhdunarodnye otnosheniia*, no. 11, 1981, pp. 32–42, and V. M. Kudrov, "Tri tsentra imperializma: Tendentsii sootnosheniia sil," *SShA*, no. 9, 1981, pp. 3–13, and no. 10, 1981, pp. 15–25.

agreements (especially after the imposition of martial law in Poland in December 1981), many of these writers continue to perceive elements of partnership that help maintain alliance cohesion. Soviet analysts note that in some cases the West Europeans refuse to give in to strong American pressures to adopt a more anti-Soviet posture (in economic dealings with the USSR and Eastern Europe, for example), while in others they succumb to these pressures (as in the military and ideological spheres). However, these same writers note that West European officials have reaffirmed the need to maintain NATO solidarity in spite of U.S.–West European differences on economic exchanges with the Soviet Union, have imposed limited economic sanctions of their own on the USSR, have joined with the United States in condemning martial law in Poland, and in some instances have assumed a responsibility of their own in NATO's decision to deploy the new intermediate-range Pershing II and cruise missiles.[74]

While it is still too early to determine what the Soviets might do next, it can be stated as a general hypothesis that a return to marginal right policies may be a distinct possibility. If Soviet decision makers conclude that excessive tensions are only fostering intercapitalist unity, they may decide to move to the right (for example, by offering major concessions at the current Geneva talks on intermediate-range nuclear forces). The point here, however, is not to predict what Moscow will do, but to suggest that Soviet leaders are able to shift between marginal left and marginal right policies without effecting a radical reorientation of policy attitudes. In either case, the Soviets will seek an optimal mix of policies allowing them to pursue their aim of exploiting intercapitalist contradictions without promoting excessive anti-Soviet cooperation.

In the end, the Soviets' ability to shift back and forth in this manner offers further evidence that the contemporary Soviet foreign policy elite is not divided into extreme dichotomies of right and left, but is joined around a general centrist consensus. Not only is this spectrum of Soviet policy options a narrow one, but it might also be thought of as a sliding scale, permitting marginal movements to the right or left as circumstances warrant.

For the West, this implies that there do exist opportunities for influencing Soviet foreign policy behavior, but the degree of change resulting from these influences must be seen as occurring within a fairly limited perspective. Perhaps the most effective action the West can take to influence Soviet policies is to maintain as much unity as possible in dealing with Moscow. In any event, the West should be aware that however preferable it might be to encourage marginal right policies from the Soviet leadership as opposed to marginal left ones, in general both positions share many of the same fundamental assumptions about East-West relations.

74. See V. Lukov and A. Zagorskii, "Belyi dom protiv 'proekta veka,'" *Mirovaia ekonomika i mezhdunarodnye otnosheniia*, no. 3, 1982, pp. 104–7; Davydov, "Antipol'skaia isteriia" (see note 17 above); and Trofimenko, "Politika bez perspektivy" (note 58 above).

All this is not to say that there are no individuals in the Soviet foreign policy establishment who are genuinely interested in a substantial, worldwide, permanent reduction in East-West tensions as a matter of principle rather than for tactical considerations. Perhaps there are. If so, however, they have not manifested themselves in Soviet scholarship on the Western alliance.

Chapter 9

Implications for U.S.-European Relations

Pierre Hassner

In a discussion of contemporary Soviet relations with Western Europe, Polish events seem to have a central place comparable to that of Czechoslovakia for the decade of the 1970s. And one of the obvious questions to ask, but one that at this point I do not feel prepared to answer, is: What did "Poland" change? Along with that: What does it tell us about Soviet policy? What effect has it had on the Atlantic Alliance?[1]

But the rush of events is such that the same questions can be posed about other developments that—in 1982 and at the beginning of 1983—seem to have been rapidly replacing the Polish situation in the headlines: the dispute between the United States and the West European allies over the gas deal and economic relations with the East, the increasing rift between French and German attitudes on security questions, the German elections and the new dimensions of the struggle over the deployment of intermediate-range missiles in Europe, the passivity of the Soviet Union during the Falklands and Lebanon wars, the development of the Sino-Soviet dialogue, the rise of Andropov and the question

1. This essay is in a sense an interim discussion. It relies on a number of published or unpublished contributions by the author, but most of them were written before the Polish coup of December 13, 1981. In particular: "West European Perceptions of the USSR," *Daedalus*, 108, no. 1 (Winter 1979): 113–50; "Moscow and the Western Alliance," *Problems of Communism*, 30, no. 3 (May–June 1981): 37–54; "Soviet Policy in Western Europe: The East European Factor," to appear in a book edited by Sarah M. Terry on *Soviet Policy in Eastern Europe* for the Council on Foreign Relations; and "Recurrent Stresses, Resilient Structures," in Robert W. Tucker and Linda Wrigley, eds., *The Atlantic Alliance and Its Critics* (New York: The Lehrman Institute, 1983), pp. 61–99.

marks raised by the apparent increase in the activities of the KGB–in the Soviet Union and abroad–in controlling Soviet society and in encouraging terrorism, before and after Brezhnev's death.

All these events can be seen as mere episodes or as straws in the wind indicating fundamental changes. The same goes for the evolution in Poland itself, where the Soviet success in maintaining control with a minimum of cost in the short run is matched (as well as for the rest of Eastern Europe, where pacifism, economic discontent, or national unrest has spread in various forms) by the certainty that no long-range problem has been solved and other dramatic crises or political dilemmas are already emerging. In all these cases the Western evaluation of recent Soviet policy toward Western Europe and of possible responses to it seems subordinated either to immediate events whose real meaning is not yet clear or to a broader and perhaps insoluble problem–the coexistence, interplay, and respective priorities of three basic dimensions: the East-West confrontation, based on the incompatibility of communism and liberalism; the common danger of nuclear war and of economic collapse, and the mutual interest in preventing them; and the emergence or reassertion of separate national or regional identities or interests. Do planetary or parochial factors (from–to take the most burning issue–anxiety over nuclear weapons to a renewed Central European consciousness) challenge the primacy of the East-West conflict, or are they manipulated by the Soviet Union in a way that is more an outcome of this conflict than ever, and do they call for a common Western response along the same lines? Do the new concerns for national and regional diversity and for universal, transideological values and dangers render Western unity obsolete, or, on the contrary, do they lead us back to it as a necessary precondition? This is the fundamental question that neither this chapter nor this book can answer any more than the more immediate ones inspired by current events. But at least we can and should be aware of it.

Perhaps the best way to explore some of these issues is to look first at three basic questions about Soviet policy and the Western alliance. First, to what extent is there such a thing as a Soviet policy toward Western Europe? Or to what extent are Soviet actions toward Western Europe the result of narrower (e.g., bilateral) or broader (e.g., global) or of other regional policies (e.g., directed at Eastern Europe)?

The second question is the same one, seen from the Western side. To what extent are various, and often diverging, attitudes and policies within the Western alliance reacting to Soviet policies toward Western Europe, or to what extent are they prompted by Soviet policies elsewhere, for instance in the Third World, or even by what the Soviet Union *is* as much as by what it *does*–by the Soviet Union's military power, or economic weakness, or totalitarian regimes, rather than by its foreign policy?

The third question is addressed directly to the divergences within the Western alliance. Are they based on differences of perception and of strategy, of situation and of interests, or at least of attitudes?

WESTERN EUROPE AND SOVIET POLICY

The first question belongs more to the province of the other chapters. But much of the debate between Americans, between Europeans, and – above all – between Europeans and Americans that does concern this question has to do with whether the Soviet Union really has a strategy specifically aimed at Western Europe (in order to keep it divided or to separate it from the United States, or to dominate it, or to "Finlandize" it, or to neutralize it, or to denuclearize it, and so on) or whether its West European policy is rather the result of two basic priorities – concerning Eastern Europe, which it wants to keep, and the United States, with which it is engaged in a global confrontation.

My provisional answer is threefold. Moscow has always tacitly or explicitly struggled with three dilemmas: between controlling Eastern Europe and influencing Western Europe, between basing its West European policy on the isolation of West Germany or on a privileged dialogue with it, and between trying to eliminate the United States, so as to dominate the whole European continent, or trying to maintain a basically bipolar status quo guaranteeing the control and the division of Germany. Second, the Soviet Union has never really had to choose between these alternatives; it has always tried to have its cake and eat it too, and to keep all its options open. While the control of Eastern Europe, the combination of dialogue and intimidation toward West Germany, and the combination of competition and negotiation with the United States have probably always been its main priorities, this has never prevented it from trying to influence Western Europe even at some cost or risk in Eastern Europe, and to play off other West European states against Germany, and Western Europe as a whole against the United States. Third, in the 1970s the successes of détente in the first half of the decade have made it even easier for the Soviet Union to escape or mitigate these dilemmas; the crisis of détente in the second half of the decade has sharpened them and at the same time has brought Western Europe more to the forefront and has made it cut a more distinctive figure in the global picture of Soviet foreign policy; but the events of 1982 from the Polish coup to the dialogue with Peking seem, again, to provide the Soviet Union with new opportunities for escaping its traditional dilemmas and for exploiting favorable situations on the global as well as the European scene.

In the era of détente and negotiation the Soviet Union has pursued the same policy as Willy Brandt: recognize the status quo in order to change it. Having consolidated its dominance of Eastern Europe through its intervention in Czechoslovakia, Moscow achieved some success in obtaining (from the West) the recognition of the GDR, of existing borders, of, to some extent, existing regimes, and of its own primacy; hence it considered it could afford to play the game of mutual influence and interdependence and to allow a certain opening of its bloc for the sake of economic benefit and of influence in Western Europe. This bid for influence, in turn, was no longer based on asking for radical solutions – such as the separation of Berlin from West Germany, the neutralization of the latter, the dismantling of the European Community and of NATO, the expulsion of the United States from Europe—but rather on trying, within existing structures, to encourage as much division and dilution as possible. The European security process was meant at the same time, by encouraging a pan-European perspective, to marginalize the United States and water down the Common Market. After having intermittently encouraged Germany's hopes of reunification until 1955, and having tried to isolate it and use it as a scapegoat between 1955 and 1969, the Soviet Union has apparently embarked on a policy of rapprochement based on the status quo, using the relationship between the two Germanies both to bring the Federal Republic into a special position compared with its Western allies and to make it exercise its influence with them in the direction of East-West trade, negotiation, and détente.

In the first half of the 1970s this went together with cultivating a bilateral détente with the United States on the strategic and—Moscow hoped—economic levels. Clearly the United States and the Federal Republic were the two pillars of Soviet Westpolitik, with other bilateral relationships, such as the one with France, and the European collective framework serving as instruments or as background.

As the 1970s ended, so did hopes in the U.S.-Soviet détente, particularly in SALT, and in a massive input of American technology in the Soviet empire. On the other hand, the USSR was increasingly hit by economic crisis. For a while, the Third World appeared as a theater of Soviet successes, both indirectly or negatively (through the succession of anti-Western coups and revolutions) and through the direct projection of Soviet power. On the other hand, a certain "revitalization of containment," to use Robert Osgood's expression, was taking place on the American side, and, added to Moscow's own difficulties in Afghanistan, was making further Soviet advances in the Third World more risky or more painful.

In Europe itself, the NATO decision of December 1979 on Euromissiles was signaling a Western counteroffensive against the Soviet military buildup. The only bright spot for the USSR, then, was the growth of the pacifist movement in reaction to this NATO decision, adding to the growth of American-European, particularly American-West German, friction over the issue of détente, and over the reaction to East-West crises, especially the Afghanistan one.

In a world that appeared more and more black and dangerous—certainly when it was looking to the United States and to Eastern Europe, and to some extent when it was looking to the Third World—Moscow increasingly saw trends in Western Europe as the only bright ones and, in particular, the Federal Republic's apparently unconditional attachment to détente as the main hope for leverage, including in the economic and arms control fields. Since France, under Giscard d'Estaing, was more or less adopting the same attitudes, it looked as if the Soviet Union was for the first time putting a positive policy toward Western Europe at the top of its priorities, encouraging even Franco-German

270   PIERRE HASSNER

collaboration as long as it did not lead to military unity and autonomy, and, on the other hand, trying to link this policy toward Western Europe with other regional ones, such as relations with the Persian Gulf, in order to hint at a triangular relationship in which West European money and skills would be married to East European needs and Persian Gulf resources through the mediation of Soviet power.

On the other hand, these perspectives remained fairly vague and the only solid elements, the increasing rift within the Atlantic Alliance and the trend toward peace at any price in Europe, particularly in West Germany, looked increasingly in danger because of developments in Poland, where the old choice of control over Eastern Europe or influence over Western Europe was revived in harsher terms than ever before.

In 1982, however, the horizon began to brighten for the Soviet Union. In the Third World, the death of Sadat and the favorable developments in Iran and in the Iran-Iraq war, as well as the difficulties experienced by the United States in Central America, seem to have opened new avenues for the USSR. Of course, the Falklands war and, even more, the Israeli intervention in Lebanon have shown the limits of its ability to project power on distant shores and must have diminished its standing with its Third World potential or actual allies. But it has stepped up at least its verbal support for the Salvadorian rebellion (in contrast with its discretion at the time of the Twenty-sixth Party Congress, when it was still trying to placate the newly elected Reagan administration), and, after a time of mutual recrimination, it has resumed its arms deliveries to Syria and increased their level of sophistication.

But even more important are three other factors. First, the more conciliatory Chinese attitude, already apparent during Brezhnev's last year, seems confirmed under Andropov; and the latter seems (if his conversations at Brezhnev's funeral are any guide) to exploit it in the direction of a more dynamic Asian policy, using both sticks and carrots, and including certainly Pakistan and probably Japan. While in Afghanistan itself the Soviet Union is more unable than ever to defeat the resistance, the occupation is less and less an obstacle in the way of its relations with Afghanistan's neighbors, such as Pakistan and China. On a more global level, while in the late 1960s and early 1970s Soviet policy was aiming at isolating China with the help of the United States, and while in the middle and late 1970s it could fear being encircled itself by a de facto alliance including China, Japan, the United States, and Western Europe, now it seems on the offensive again, with the aim of isolating the United States by exploiting American difficulties with Peking and Bonn and cultivating a series of separate Asian and European "détentes." The change in the mood of Congress because of the size of the budget deficit and the relative success of the freeze campaign seem to challenge the Reagan program of "rearmament first" and to push the United States back on the road of negotiations and perhaps concessions on arms control and even on conflict resolution around the world. This immediately reduces the specific importance of Western Europe. Third, and most important, the December 13, 1981, coup in Poland seems, at least for the short run, to provide the Soviet Union almost miraculously with a way out of its dilemma: it can stop or control the process in Poland without having to sacrifice détente with Western Europe (least of all with the FRG) or even, to some extent, with the United States.

When, as in France, the reaction of public opinion and, to some extent, of the government is harder, this too can be turned by the Soviet Union to its own advantage. Increasingly, on the issue of "peace versus human rights" or "missiles versus Poland" and, more generally, on attitudes both toward the Soviet Union and toward nuclear weapons, a gap, and perhaps a rift, is developing between the French and the German left, including the two socialist parties. This enables Moscow to return to its traditional tactics of encouraging Franco-German divisions as well as European-American ones. The new emphasis given by Andropov to the inclusion of the French and British nuclear deterrents in the INF negotiations clearly carries this political implication.

Of course, some difficulties arise in relations with the Eurocommunist parties and the peace movement. But on the whole, while nothing is solved in its internal crisis or in that of its empire, the Soviet Union seems again able to play with various options in its relations with Western Europe as well as with the rest of the world, including even communist China. Again it may be hampered in the playing out of these options both by autonomous developments in the East (succession in the Soviet Union, a dramatic turn of East European events in Poland or elsewhere) or in the West (where the combination of crises makes for exceptional volatility and ambiguity of public opinion—witness the rapid disappointment with Reagan and Mitterrand, or the gap between the evolution of the SPD, the Labour Party, and active minorities on the one hand and silent majorities on the other) and by the effects of its own successes (as in the case of the fallout of pacifist movements, which it encourages in the West but fears in Eastern Europe, particularly in the GDR).

The constant element is, has been, and is likely to remain the preference for détente, or negotiation, or arms control, in conditions of superiority. Détente without superiority may produce undesirable effects in the Soviet empire; superiority without détente may produce an unwelcome Western or West European hardening. But this particularly successful combination can itself run into trouble.

For instance, the remarkable feat of appearing as an ally of the peace movement in spite of the SS-20s and the invasion of Afghanistan may reach its limits when (as in the spring of 1982) the independent fractions of the movement (such as the German Greens and the British END) discover they are being manipulated by their communist companions or, more important, when East Germany clamps down on the religious pacifists it has been encouraging for propaganda purposes and bans the use of the same slogans and the passage of the same marches it encourages in the West.

Similarly the combination of practicing détente with Western governments yet helping to destabilize their societies by encouraging terrorism can easily backfire once it becomes too obvious. In 1981 enough evidence of Soviet involvement (which obviously does not mean control) in Turkey, Italy, Spain, and, even more strikingly, of diplomatic exploitation through very thinly veiled threats (reminding the Spanish government that entry into NATO, or the French socialists that the expulsion of the communists, would have bad effects on the terrorist problem), has surfaced for the issue to affect the peaceful image of the Soviet Union. The question is whether this may actually serve Moscow (in virtue of the "Oderint dum metuant" principle) or whether it may backfire by depriving even appeasers of the kind of alibi that fig leaves like the military rule in Poland or Andropov's and the Warsaw Pact's "peace" proposals have been providing. The most spectacular and mysterious example is the Bulgarian connection in the case of the attempted assassination of the Pope. Sometimes, in virtue of that other principle, "On ne prête qu'aux riches," the Soviet Union may suffer the blame for actions it may have been distantly involved with but by no means initiated or controlled.

The West and the Soviet Union

This brings us to the second question. It is by no means obvious that changes in Western attitudes or even policies toward the Soviet Union have been primarily prompted by changes in Soviet policies, particularly toward Western Europe. Soviet interventions in the Third World and in Eastern Europe, and Soviet domestic repression and military power, may have been much more important. Of course, the modernization of the Warsaw Pact and the building of the SS–20s are a part of this buildup specifically aimed at Western Europe, and a case can be made that the goal of holding the latter hostage is a powerful factor explaining some apparent oddities in Soviet programs (such as the priority of MRBMs over ICBMs under Khrushchev) and has slowly sunk into European as well as American consciousness. Still the fact remains that the attitudes of the West toward the Soviet Union have suffered much more spectacular changes than have Soviet foreign policies toward the West.

In the American case, the disaffection with the Soviet Union and détente has been prompted, first, by the Yom Kippur War and by various Western failures in the Third World, attributed, rightly or wrongly, to Moscow's "breaking the code of détente" in the case of Angola, Shaba, or Ogaden. Second, the post-SALT II strategic buildup, particularly in heavy missiles, encouraged a sense of betrayal of the hopes put in arms control, and of suspicion that the Soviet Union was aiming at superiority or at victory. Third, of course, the invasion of Afghanistan and the coup in Poland tipped the balance in the direction toward which it was already leaning.

But underlying and amplifying all these reactions was the more general one to Vietnam, to Watergate, to Iran—all contributing in various ways to a feeling of American humiliation and impotence. In this respect, Europe plays a role less through the direct effects of Soviet policy than through the lack of solidarity attributed to West European allies. The cry "Where are our allies?" was strongly heard at the time of the hostage crisis and sanctions against Iran, and against the Soviet Union after Afghanistan. It was heard again in 1982, as a reaction against the reluctance of the Europeans and Japanese to follow the American lead on sanctions against Poland and the Soviet Union or, for that matter, against Libya or Nicaragua. It is a cry that, while partly inspired by anti-Soviet feelings, must be music to Soviet ears, since (especially when accompanied by threats of American withdrawal) it corresponds exactly to the long-standing goals of Moscow's European policies.

In France, the hardening toward the Soviet Union, such as it is, was perhaps more directly inspired by Soviet policies, although not necessarily toward Western Europe. As far as left-wing intellectuals are concerned, the decisive occasions were the various interventions of the Soviet Army in Hungary, Czechoslovakia, and Afghanistan and the indirect intervention in Poland (the same could be said for the Eurocommunist parties, especially the Italian one). Just as important, however, were what has been called "l'effet Soljénytsine" (the impact of the Soviet dissidents and the sinking into public consciousness of the reality of Soviet concentration camps, or psychiatric wards) and the autonomous evolution of French intellectuals from Sartre to the "nouveaux philosophes," who, after the usual passage through Maoism, have adopted Soviet totalitarianism as the incarnation of evil and its victims as their heroes or models.

At the same time, during the Fifth Republic, French governments from de Gaulle to Giscard d'Estaing have moved in the direction of seeing the Soviet Union as a partner in a diplomatic game (to balance the United States or West Germany) or in economic cooperation based either on commercial interests or on a gamble in favor of the liberalizing and pacifying effects of interdependence and affluence. The former was more the rationale of de Gaulle, the latter of Giscard d'Estaing. Domestic reasons concerning the French Communist Party certainly played a role too, but so did an evaluation of Soviet power, which could be seen in the 1960s as weaker than American power—hence a useful card to play against American domination—or in the 1970s as getting too strong to be ignored or defied.

With the new socialist government some of this has begun to change: partly through the impact of public opinion, which, particularly on the left, had criticized Giscard's softness and was especially moved by the Polish events; partly through Mitterrand's judgment that the balance in Europe was tilting dangerously in favor of the Soviet Union and needed to be redressed by American missiles as well as by France's independent efforts; partly, too, because an anti-Soviet stance in Europe was calculated to buy American good will or tolerance on economic or Central American matters; and, last but not least, because of the fear of an unstable, unpredictable Germany sliding toward the East.

All these elements—which, again, are only partly based on Soviet policies—are still there, but the old imperatives based on economic and domestic considerations are making themselves felt again in the signing of the gas deal. The pro-American stance on security matters is, in turn, compensated by an anti-American one on cultural matters which puts France in the same camp as radical Third World countries in denouncing American influence. The fear of an exclusive West German–Soviet dialogue leads France at the same time to want to maintain America's presence in Europe but also to maintain a dialogue of its own with Moscow.

Finally, the West German case is the most difficult one both by its complexity and by its ambiguity. Neither the wanderings of French intellectuals from Marxism to antitotalitarianism nor the American identification of all the hot spots in the world with the Soviet Union has a German equivalent. On the other hand, Soviet policies, while remaining essentially constant, are being reinterpreted by a more and more vocal fragment of public opinion in a more and more favorable fashion. The general public, as seen by the polls, after one or two years of optimistic neutralism in the heyday of Ostpolitik, in 1970–71, has switched back to an ever more distrustful attitude toward the Soviet Union. The West German government is well aware of the growing Soviet power and of the need to balance it with a strong commitment to détente, arms control, and dialogue with the Soviet Union—not least because of the latter's influence, actual or potential, on intra-German relations. But the most unexpected and interesting phenomenon concerns the active minorities who dominate the media—the pacifist movements or, in general, the educated among the eighteen-to-thirty-five year olds. There one finds a predominance of anti-Americanism (the United States being identified with technology and the danger of nuclear war), which leads if not to pro-Sovietism at least to an "anti-anti-Soviet feeling," in which both guilt and condescendence toward a past and potential victim coincide, in contrast to the feelings toward the powerful but irresponsible American ally. On the other hand, a minority of German elites reaches the same conclusions from opposite premises: the Soviet Union having reached superiority militarily, any effort to reestablish the balance would be dangerous; one should rather try to tie its hands through arms control and economic concessions. Independent intellectual authorities such as C. F. von Weiszäcker (who describes his position as starting from a hawk's premises on the Soviet Union's power and ambitions but reaching a dove's conclusions on the policies to adopt in response) and important journalists such as Peter Bender and politicians such as Egon Bahr (who profess a more reassuring view of Soviet intentions but also favor competing with Moscow in fields other than the military one, where it should be left to enjoy the only advantage it has) are interesting examples of a position that is rarely stated in this way but may be less isolated than it looks.

THE ROOTS OF WESTERN DIFFERENCES

We are right at the heart of our third question, about the inner and deeper roots of Western differences on East-West relations and, in particular, on policies toward the Soviet Union. Some see in them above all differences in *perception*—for example, about the reasons for the Soviet invasion of Afghanistan, or about the roots of the civil war in El Salvador, or about the dangers of nuclear war, or, in general, about the relative importance of the Soviet danger versus local factors, and so on.

At the other extreme, one can see the root of transatlantic divergences less in differences of perception than in differences of *interests*. It is indeed true that instead of the global structure of peace based on converging interests, as envisaged by Henry Kissinger, what has emerged is a duality between, on the one hand, a global theater of conflict (as the East-West struggle extends more directly and more actively to regions, such as Africa, where it had been more marginal), in which America's interests, as a global superpower, are more immediately and inevitably involved, again following Kissinger, than those of the regional European ones, and, on the other hand, a European structure of peace, based on economic interdependence and human contacts, in which the interests of Europeans, particularly Germans, are much more directly and heavily involved than those of the United States. Similarly, the differences over deterrence have often been seen by Americans as stemming from differences in doctrine or from an inadequate European perception of strategic realities, whereas many Europeans have stressed the objective difference of interests between the United States and Europe concerning, for instance, the use of nuclear weapons in a limited war.

This brings us to the third interpretation, which stresses above all differences in *strategy*. According to this view, Europeans do not perceive the character of the Soviet threat any differently from the way the United States does, nor do they have less of an interest in stopping it—just as the continuation of détente and arms control are also in the American interest. They only disagree on the way to achieve these aims. The Europeans favor a more differentiated approach, which, instead of punishing the Soviets across the board, would combine, for instance, local resistance, and the restoration of regional equilibrium in areas where it is threatened, with a continuation of détente and arms control where they are in the mutual interest.

Of course this is exactly the professed position of the Soviet Union, which never tires of pointing out that it was holding the Moscow summit and signing the SALT agreements at the time that Hanoi was being bombed. Similarly, Brandt has declared that Ostpolitik and détente ought to survive Afghanistan just as they have survived Vietnam. One can very well argue, as Robert Legvold has done, that just because a view is held in common by Moscow and Bonn does not mean that it is not in the interest of Washington, and the West as a whole.

Indeed, he would argue that it provides a more effective basis for the containment of the Soviet Union.

While there undoubtedly is some truth in this view, I would personally combine it with an interpretation less charitable to at least some Europeans. To a great extent, the evidence, particularly as it appears in public opinion polls, shows that the image of the Soviet Union and the perception of its actions are no more favorable or reassuring in Europe than in the United States; but the reactions to them and the willingness to take risks, especially that of violent confrontation, in resisting them, vary dramatically. This is less a matter of rational strategy, however, than of moral and psychological attitudes, or of perception of one's own situation more than of Soviet intentions. Very often an apparent optimism about the latter hides a deeper pessimism about oneself. Publicly or consciously, one is committed to the more reassuring interpretation of Soviet policies precisely because deep down one feels one cannot afford to act on the implications of the more worrying one. Von Weizäcker would only be saying aloud, more lucidly and more honestly, what many Europeans feel without admitting it, even to themselves.

Beyond the rational dimension of perceptions, interests, and strategies, one finds, then, the more intangible or elusive but—I feel—even more crucial one of *attitudes* based on different or differently perceived *situations*. On the rational level, interests are more common than conflicting between the two sides of the Atlantic, and some kind of consensus on the nature of the common threat and on the best strategy against it should not be impossible to reach. But these very perceptions and strategies cannot help being interpreted differently on the basis of deep-seated differences in attitudes, which are themselves based on differing historical experiences and on different shades in each partner's feelings of security or vulnerability, as well as of solidarity and responsibility. And this is what is coming out, not only between America and Europe, but within Europe itself, between small and middle powers, between nuclear and nonnuclear, between Protestant and Catholic ones, and, above all, between Germany and her neighbors or allies.

This would help explain why, while in the past détente tended to encourage independent policies and East-West crises tended to reunify the Western alliance, in 1980 the crises of Iran and Afghanistan tended to split it, and in 1981 the continuous friction about European reluctance to get involved in American-led efforts outside Europe (such as those in the Gulf), the revival of the peace movement in Europe and of bellicose rhetoric in Washington, and the divergences (again, at least at the level of rhetoric) in reaction to the Polish coup indicate—despite the efforts of governments to compromise and cooperate—a continuing and deepening crisis over relations with the Soviet Union.

How structurally based and hence how inevitable is this crisis? In 1980, at the time of the crisis between the Carter administration and the Europeans over Afghanistan, I proposed—while emphasizing that this had to be taken with a grain of Salt—to interpret these crises in the light of an instant philosophy of history by distinguishing their effects on three types of cycles: the short-term cycle on confrontation and détente in East-West relations, the middle-term cycle of retreat and activism in American foreign policy, and the long-range cycle of warlike experience and civilian attitudes in European and Japanese societies. I still present it here, but more as a warning against the danger of extrapolation, for, in the light of American reactions to the dangers of involvement in El Salvador and to the defense budget, and of the spectacular revival of American antinuclear feelings, the grain of salt should be multiplied, even if, as I believe, it should not entirely bury a residual grain of truth.

It is tempting indeed to interpret the present crises in the light of an instant philosophy of history, by distinguishing their effects on three types of cycles. A well-known short-term cycle in East-West relations is that of confrontation and détente. Usually a Soviet move is followed by a period of outrage and tension, itself followed by a resumption of détente a few months later after a peace offensive. This is what happened, for instance, after the invasion of Czechoslovakia. But from now on the pattern may be modified by its overlapping with two different kinds of cycles.

One is the middle-range cycle of American foreign policy. After fifteen years of retreat, if one follows Samuel Huntington's calculations, it may, since 1979, have entered a new phase of activism. The events in Iran and Afghanistan may have given the decisive push to a switch that was already in the making (at least as far as the mood of the public was concerned) for four or five years, thereby contributing to Ronald Reagan's election and to decisions on arms policies and on military reinvolvement in the Third World that may have their full effect only at the end of the decade but meanwhile make confrontations more likely and a return to the old style of détente more difficult.

Conversely, in the case of Europe and Japan, there may be a secular trend—at work since 1945—toward becoming "civilian powers without power" and against running any risk of war through active confrontation. In one case, the reaction to the crises may be harder than usual and exclude the usual return to détente; in the other, the attachment to détente may have become unconditional and exclude even the usual show of firmness and unity—however superficial and short-lived—during a crisis.

The immediate effect may well be that even if the Soviet Union were to withdraw from Afghanistan, dismantle all the SS-20s, and encourage a return to the pre-December 13 situation in Poland, the American turn toward a harder, more nationalist, and more assertive policy would continue; and even if the Soviet Union were to launch a full and open invasion of Poland, there would be many important European voices (particularly West German) that would claim that this is all the more reason to stick to still more détente and trade and not fall into the trap of a return to the cold war.

The trouble is that both attitudes may be incompatible not only with each other but also with the requirements of the situation. The prevalently American dream of returning to the cold war of the 1950s and the prevalently European (in particular West German and Nordic) dream of sticking to the détente of the 1970s may be equally unrealistic. Yet on both sides of the Atlantic there exist "moral majorities" (which are, of course, but vocal and more or less influential minorities) who see politics in absolute terms: in America they identify morality with the supremacy of the United States and the destruction of communism; in Protestant Europe they identify morality with peace at any cost and immorality with nuclear weapons—even in a deterrent function—as long as they are on the Western side.

This neat opposition (which I presented, albeit with the qualifications called for by Mormons, Quakers, and others, in various papers published in 1981) is weakened by the emergence of another "moral majority" in the United States, more like the European one, and by the apparent decline of the "new right." Of course, it is much too early to tell: the antinuclear feeling in the United States is both less extreme (after all, to call attention to the horrors of nuclear war or to favor a nuclear freeze or a "no first use" agreement may, as I believe, have a negative effect but is not tantamount to calling for unilateral disarmament) and less massive than the German one, although it should be substantial enough to make the latter more understandable to American critics. The resistance to military intervention to Central America is not tantamount to resistance to an active foreign policy or even to the use of force per se; on the contrary, polls seem to indicate a very discriminating attitude in the general public, with an actual increase in the willingness to intervene in some areas (e.g., Europe) together with a decrease in others (e.g., the Middle East) and an overwhelming refusal in third ones (e.g., Central America).[2] Even if the convergence between the attitudes of American and European elites were confirmed, it would remain to be seen whether the ethos of Western democracies (and indeed of developed secularized societies as such, if one is to compare Czechs and Poles to Afghans and Iranians), including the United States, is to be interpreted in the light of the long-range cycle we have mentioned in relation to Western Europe, or whether the whole exercise is to be dropped and we should be prepared for belligerent allies (for instance, under F. J. Strauss—or rather under a future German or Japanese generation) as well as for pacifist Americans.

Even before this change at the level of vocal minorities, the contrast was much less stark at the level of governments and of less "moral" but more real majorities, as indicated by opinion polls or elections. After all, the Schmidt government, widely (and partly rightly) suspected of having succumbed to the three-headed monster of pacifism, neutralism, and anti-Americanism, staked its existence on

2. *Le Point*, March 15, 1982.

accepting the deployment of missiles that could reach the Soviet Union, which that archetype of German pro-Western trustworthiness, Konrad Adenauer, had refused in the 1950s as too dangerous. Conversely, the fierce, reckless, and unilateralist Ronald Reagan is accepting negotiations on Euromissiles and proposing a zero option meant—against his better judgment on the substance—to placate the European mood and help the West German government. Against Castro and Qaddafi, as well as against the Soviet Union itself, his verbal denunciations have been more consistent than his effective action. The socialist French government has been on the American side with a vengeance on nuclear issues in Europe, and while it stands at the other extreme from the United States on Central America, it has been most pragmatic and concerned with blocking Soviet expansion in Africa and the Middle East. On the Polish crisis, the initial reaction of all Western governments was one of caution and noninterference. The apparent hardening of the French and American positions, in subsequent weeks, was both limited and, in part at least, short-lived. It had more to do with placating public opinion than with actual policy.

The public opinions themselves, on both sides of the ocean, are less far apart than their respective vocal elites. A great majority of the West German people distrusts the Soviet Union and is in favor of the Atlantic Alliance and American presence; a small majority used to favor the NATO decision on long-range theater nuclear forces (TNF),[3] although by now it opposes their deployment when the question is asked in this form. Conversely, in the United States, increasing numbers fear nuclear war and a majority suspects that the deployment of long-range missiles in Europe may increase the danger of war and favors arms control no less than the Europeans.[4] Between France and West Germany, too, the general publics are less different than it would appear from the atmosphere in the politically active elites: the French are more neutralist and more ready to capitulate in case of war; the Germans are more Atlanticist than their current reputation.[5]

Between the two countries, the yet unexplained paradox is that while the two governments and the two silent majorities are largely converging, the attitudes

3. See the results of two major polls, one by the Allensbach Institute, in *Capital*, no. 8, 1982, and the other in three issues of *Der Spiegel*: no. 48, November 23, 1981, pp. 56–70; no. 49, November 30, 1981, pp. 94–106; and no. 50, December 7, 1981, pp. 85–101. A more recent Gallup survey finds 41 percent for and 27 percent against TNF. See *Le Point*, March 15, 1982.

4. See the poll in *Time*, December 29, 1981. However, according to the Gallup survey quoted by *Le Point*, 50 percent of Americans think the deployment increases the protection of Western Europe and only 14 percent that it increases the danger of nuclear attack.

5. According to the comparative Gallup survey reported in *Le Point*, West Germany remains the most pro-American and Atlanticist country in Europe. Surprisingly, the most neutralist and anti-American of the four countries surveyed (France, Britain, the FRG, and Italy) appears to be Great Britain.

and priorities of the French youth, of the French intellectuals, and of the influential media are strikingly different from those we have noticed among their West German counterparts. This is shown by their contrasting reactions to the two issues of American missiles and the Poland coup. In West Germany, demonstrations on the first issue gathered hundreds of thousands; on the second, hundreds at best. In France, the ratio was almost exactly the reverse. Both governments signed the gas deal (indeed the French, unlike the West Germans, did it after the Polish coup). But in France the decision was unanimously criticized by the noncommunist left, including unions and newspapers favorable to the socialists, while it was unanimously accepted in the Federal Republic except in almost perfunctory statements of the CDU/CSU opposition.

Yet, when all these distinctions are made, there are real differences between Europeans and Americans as such. They are found particularly on détente—with Americans more willing to resist aggression militarily, even in Europe, than the Europeans themselves, and the Europeans, particularly the West Germans, less willing to sacrifice détente. In a 1980 poll, 57 percent of Americans were putting firmness first, 52 percent of the French and 67 percent of the West Germans were giving priority to détente.[6]

The American result is all the more remarkable since, as another poll shows, while fear of war has increased in the United States, as in Europe, fear of communist aggression has decreased, and to a much greater degree than in the latter.[7] The only way I can see to reconcile all this is that the American public is more self-confident and wants to reassess America's role in the world in competition with the Soviet Union, while maintaining a dialogue with the latter to avoid nuclear war, and the West European public, particularly the German one, is more worried, less prone to take risks, and more anxious to save détente, both because of its positive gains and prospects and as a supplementary insurance against Soviet aggression.

This can be understood above all in terms of *comparative vulnerability*. The United States has become vulnerable both to a Soviet nuclear attack and to an Arab oil boycott, hence it is bound to look at its own interests as at those of the Western system, and to be more careful about the risks it takes or the sacrifices it accepts to protect the latter. On the other hand, the Europeans (as well as the Japanese) have always been vulnerable and still are, only more than before and still more than the Americans. It is the latter who hold the ultimate key to relations with the Soviet Union and with the oil producers, but it is the Europeans who, if things go wrong, will suffer the consequences even more than the

6. *Le Point*, March 9, 1981.
7. Cf. William Watts, "America's Hopes and Fears: The Future Can Fend for Itself," *Psychology Today*, September 1981, pp. 36–48. According to Watts, fear of communism or aggression by a communist power has declined steadily from 29 percent in 1964 to 13 percent in 1974, to 8 percent in 1981 (p. 43).

Americans, while having less control over events. This feeling of being potential victims of a situation they cannot control makes, if not necessarily for German angst, at least for a nervous and potentially distrustful watching of
American policies and crisis management, and for a predisposition to take
more insurances rather than undertake more commitments. In turn, this
creates understandable irritation and mistrust among Americans, who feel that
Europe's greater vulnerability should lead it to a greater commitment to the
containment (or even the punishment) of the Soviet Union or to the security of
the Gulf, whereas it is precisely because of this greater vulnerability that Europe
is less able to take risks. On the other hand, the Europeans' own recipe for
reducing their vulnerability may actually increase it: this may well be the case
for the gas deal with the Soviet Union. More generally, the positive achievements of détente and Ostpolitik create by definition a vested interest in maintaining them, and this vested interest entails, also by definition, an increased
vulnerability to blackmail from the Soviet Union or East Germany, and to
suspicion (leading to another form of blackmail) from the United States.

The result is what I call the mutual fear of decoupling. In a time of parity,
when local Soviet superiority is no longer balanced by American strategic superiority, Europeans worry (and are encouraged to do so by authoritative Americans)
about the future of extended deterrence, and they fear American strategic decoupling. On the other hand, in an age when conflicts have become global and
Europe's environment is no longer controlled by the United States, Europeans
try even harder to decouple intra-European détente from conflicts in other parts
of the world (including within Europe itself) and from Soviet-American relations. They want deterrence to remain indivisible but détente to become divisible, or they want their own détente without having their own defense—hence
they justify American fears of European political decoupling. Of course, the two
fears feed upon each other: the more that Europeans try to decouple their
détente from American policies, the more Americans wonder why they should
not decouple their defense from that of Europe; and the more the Americans do
that, the more the Europeans wonder whether under these conditions the
American connection does not increase the danger of war (limited in the eyes of
the United States but meaning total destruction for Europe) rather than diminishing it—whether they are being asked by the Americans to pay an increasing
political and economic price for decreasing protection. Hence the debate between the two establishments feeds the two unilateralist extremes who believe
neither in nuclear deterrence in Europe nor in common policies elsewhere.

"Hot Peace," Guns versus Butter, and Diverging Domestic Policies. While this
mutual fear of decoupling is made more acute than before by these new vulnerabilities (or by this new consciousness of old vulnerabilities), it is, in a sense,
nothing new. Europeans have been worrying about American protection and
Americans about Europeans dragging their feet since the beginning of the

alliance, and the most serious crises of the latter have been about conflicts out-side its geographical jurisdiction, in particular over the Middle East in 1956 and 1973. But what adds a new dimension to an old problem is the change in the domestic context due to the general character of the period and to the specific political situations in the various countries of the alliance.

Since 1973 we have been sliding into a period that I like to call by the name of "hot peace," and whose first phase between 1973 and 1979 could be seen as the decline of détente, whereas since 1979 it looks more like a new cold war. The point is precisely that it is more complex and more contradictory than either the old cold war or the old détente. It is characterized by the coincidence of renewed East-West tension and the rediscovery of the Soviet military danger on the one hand, and the general economic crisis on the other. Perhaps even more important, both crises are succeeding an easier period, characterized by both détente and economic growth, when the constraints of defense and those of scarcity were felt as becom-ing obsolete. This, in turn, led to other conflicts and crises, which were not caused by détente or by affluence but were made possible by them: they were linked to the search for the quality of life, for identity or meaning, and for self-fulfillment by various groups—national, ethnic, sexual, or generational.

Now that the old ghosts of war (cold or even hot) and poverty are again upon us, the first result is a fierce competition for limited resources, hence the rebirth of the old dilemma of guns versus butter, warfare versus welfare, military versus social expenditures, and, indirectly, defense versus détente—with arms control seen as an indirect way of maintaining the old priorities. Never has there been so little consensus on where the primary threat comes from. Naturally enough, the left in almost every country will give priority to social expenditures and the right to defense. Some countries, like France, where a consensus exists under the socialist-communist coalition for increasing defense expenditures, are trying to escape this dilemma; but even in France the growth of public spending for social purposes is bound at some point to make for hard choices or for economic disaster. Conversely, Mrs. Thatcher finds it increasingly hard to exempt defense from the general cut in public expenditures, and the priorities of the Reagan ad-ministration are increasingly challenged by its supporters themselves.

But if this is the most universal dilemma, it is not the only one. The genies let out of the bottle by the age of affluence and détente cannot just be put back in the name of the Soviet danger or of austerity. In some countries more than in others, the "cultural revolution" of the late 1960s and early 1970s is producing a delayed effect in a romantic and sometimes violent reaction against the new realism imposed by the return of the old constraints. Socialist and communist parties are often caught between the priorities imposed by a hardening of interna-tional politics, those of the working class and the welfare state which are their raison d'être, and those of a leftist, environmentalist, antinuclear, or pacifist youth whose disaffection may cost them the narrow margin that keeps them in power.

These priorities both collide with and reinforce each other: in Germany or Britain, economic insecurity among jobless youths seems to increase the feeling of insecurity linked to the danger of nuclear war. In the United States, the loss of confidence in President Reagan's ability to manage the economy seems to contribute to the loss of confidence in his ability to manage the arms race.

The only generalization one can make is that, faced with these multiple and contradictory crises, each government tends to have its freedom of action curtailed and its stability in power jeopardized. The almost inevitable quasi paralysis of governments, particularly in view of unmanageable economic issues, gives a premium to oppositions and to sometimes short-lived experiments with clear-cut alternatives whose actual content matters less than their contrast with policies or formulae of previous pragmatic, bureaucratic governments exhausted by their experience in office. Much more than the trends toward the left or the right that are advertised periodically, it is this search for change that explains the election of Mitterrand and Papandreou, as well as of Thatcher and Reagan. Rather than groundswells, then, one finds rather unpredictable and usually short-lived national changes whose accidental conjunction may nevertheless have long-range consequences. For instance, the parallel debates such as the guns-versus-butter one are unlikely to reach parallel conclusions in all major countries. This obviously makes any concerted policies, let alone any long-range planning, for a reform of alliance strategies or structures exceedingly difficult.

It is true that several examples—in particular the prolonged honeymoon between Reagan's America and Mitterrand's France—indicate that major domestic differences do not necessarily preclude major convergences in foreign policy. The clashes of 1982 over American sanctions related to the gas deal and French refusal to coordinate economic policies toward the East indicate how fragile this harmony may turn out to be. If economic failure brings about a radicalization of French domestic policy and a turn to protectionism, this may weigh more heavily than the support given to the United States on the military issue. Similarly, the French socialists may be happier with German CDU and FDP conservatives than with their SPD comrades on East-West and security matters but not on economic ones, and vice versa.

The United States and Germany: Parallel and Divergent. But the most serious prospect is that of the two countries whose relationship provides the structural basis of the alliance—the United States and the Federal Republic—being out of step with each other. Between them the issue of nuclear weapons and security is intrinsically divisive, and it can find no perfectly satisfactory solution in an age when parity makes protection doubtful and national identity makes it psychologically burdensome. But adjustments may be found and the very fact of running into parallel oppositions on both sides of the Atlantic may make mutual comprehension easier.

Where this mutual comprehension seems to be lacking is on the issue of the divisibility of détente, or of the long-range perspective of East-West relations. The question posed is whether détente can be divided according to issues (Can one have an understanding on arms control while pursuing political or even military confrontations? Can one combine structural cooperation with the Soviet Union, as in the gas deal, with a military-technological arms race?), according to regions (Can détente continue in Europe while conflict rages in Asia? Can one, conversely, oppose communism in Europe and accept it in Central America?), or according to partners (Can one have cooperation with smaller East European states and conflict with the Soviet Union? Or a return to the cold war between the superpowers and a continuation of détente between European small and middle powers, particularly between Central European states, and ever more between the two Germanies? Or can the West Europeans maintain their cooperation with the whole Soviet bloc, including the Soviet Union, while the United States stresses confrontation, according to the division of labor criticized by Kissinger by which defense would be left to the United States and détente to the Europeans?).

None of these questions should receive a yes or no answer. Yet to all of them this is what prevalent West German and American attitudes amount to, and in opposite directions. Increasingly, the prevalent aim of the West Germans seems to be to make Western and European policies on every subject—from Poland and East-West relations to strategy and arms control—safe for the pursuit of their increasingly dominant priority: the intra-German dialogue. Conversely, the aim of American foreign policy, under the Reagan administration, seems to be to subordinate any consideration to the overriding consideration of the military containment of the Soviet Union.

The Washington-Moscow-Bonn Triangle and the Struggle for Europe. Perhaps if Germany did not exist, a strictly defensive Atlantic policy might work; one could hope to stabilize Western Europe and the transatlantic relationship without having a policy for Eastern Europe and for the German problem. Perhaps if the Adenauer solution for the German problem (complete integration in a United Europe) had worked, this would still have been possible, even though the architects of postwar Western policy, from Churchill to Kennan, foresaw that one day the problem of some form of East European autonomy, all-European reunification, and unity of the German nation would reemerge. But certainly it has become clear since the 1960s that at least the problem and the aspiration have not died.

What has also become clearer, particularly since the invasion of Czechoslovakia, the reopening of the Soviet campaign for European security in the spring of 1969, the demise of de Gaulle, and the launching of Ostpolitik, is that the existence of the two alliances and the pan-European dimension are not two mutually exclusive alternatives, that a structural change of the European system (whether in the form of a collective security system or of a reunited and neutralized Germany, resulting from a German-Soviet deal or from a mutual withdrawal of superpowers) was unrealistic, and that under the cover of a confirmed status quo (or under the umbrella of the two alliances) a competition for mutual influence, or, as I called it at the time, a game of mutual "Finlandization," was becoming the most important dimension of European politics.

Many Americans—when looking at NATO essentially in terms of the military threat and at their allies essentially in terms of whether they adequately participate in the common defense, or when threatening to withdraw American troops in order to punish the Europeans for their misbehavior—seem to neglect the central fact that the political struggle for the orientation of Europe (and above all of Germany) is the ultimate purpose of the two alliances: Soviet policies toward Western Europe (particularly the FRG), and Western (particularly West German) policies toward Eastern Europe (particularly the GDR), are precisely the crucial variables to watch and to influence.

The Soviet Union is obviously trying to detach West Germany from Western Europe and Western Europe from the United States without losing control over Eastern Europe, including the GDR. It does not seem to be doing too badly. And any American reactions aimed at punishing either the Soviet Union or the West Europeans without due consideration of the consequences on the mutual relations of the two may well end up drawing them closer together, thus isolating the United States, which is precisely the Soviet objective.

Of course, much of the West German reaction will depend on which party is in government. While the constraints of space (its Central European location, its division, the vulnerability of Berlin) and of time (the passing of one generation since the war) are inescapable, the renewed national consciousness to which they lead takes at least four different forms. Two are relatively clear. At one extreme, there is a renewed emphasis on "German interests" (within the context of the European Community and of the Atlantic Alliance), which was stressed by Helmut Schmidt when he was chancellor, was made into an electoral slogan by Hans-Jochen Vogel as SPD candidate, and to which Helmut Kohl himself has, rather defensively, paid lip service. The two ambiguities connected with this emphasis (which certainly corresponds to the diffuse feeling of a majority of West Germans) are whether the notion of "German" interests concerns chiefly the Federal Republic, the German nation, or the German people, and whether these interests are more distinct from American ones (as parts of the SPD seem to believe) than from those of the GDR or even of the Soviet Union. At the other extreme, a small minority of "national-neutralists," chiefly from the Berlin "alternative" left but also from the right, believes in the two Germanies becoming nonaligned and ending both their division and that of Europe. In between, there are two ambiguous positions. There is that of the left-wing, Berlin, fraction of the SPD, represented by Willy Brandt and his advisers, Günter Gaus and Egon Bahr, whose influence has been growing inside the SPD and who seem bent, through various strategies and stratagems, on leading Germany from the first position toward the second without ever saying so. Finally, the political least powerful but historically and sociologically most intriguing position is that of the Greens, and, more generally, of important currents within German youth: while not focusing explicitly or even consciously on the national question, they exhibit a hostility to modern technology and society (which the United States and its missiles seem to incarnate), a nostalgia for the values of nature, community, and the inner soul, and a positive valuation of anxiety and despair, which remind their critics of traditional German romanticism. No Western policy can satisfy the aspirations of this fourth group; nor can the dreams of a neutralized Germany and/or Europe entertained by the more articulate and politicized "alternativists" be fulfilled in the foreseeable future, even though Soviet policy may be quite effective in playing upon them. On the other hand, whoever is in power in Bonn, the tendencies represented by Schmidt and by Bahr, of a reaffirmation of German interests and of a priority for maintaining contacts with the GDR, are likely not to vanish, even if, under a CDU/CSU government, they receive less emphasis and are compensated by a firmer commitment to Western solidarity. It is justified, then, to look upon the aspirations and policies of the SPD-led Ostpolitik of the last few years as representative of a certain West German consensus, even if they are likely, in the future, to be combined with either more conservative or more romantic trends.

The goal of the West Germans is almost certainly not to reach reunification at the price of neutralization; they know that this would be much too risky for both sides. But neither is their approach confined to security, whether through deterrence, defense, or appeasement. It consists in trying to influence East Germany directly and indirectly (via the Soviet Union and Eastern Europe) through economics and human and cultural communication, so as to maintain as much of an identity of the German nation as possible, to mitigate the human costs of the division, and to encourage a slow and discrete evolution of the regime in the GDR. In this mutual game of influence through interpenetration and interpenetration through interdependence, patience and continuity are of the essence. Any action that forgets that Eastern Europe and the GDR live under the shadow of Soviet power and that the Soviet Union has the means to block the process or set it back, or, conversely, any action that leaves the other half of Europe to its satellite fate and abandons any attempt to influence it, can only be considered harmful to this strategy. Hence we have the negative West German reactions to American-induced sanctions for Soviet misbehavior. Such sanctions, the West Germans fear, cannot undo Soviet misbehavior or prevent it in the future, but can make the desirable evolution more difficult.

American and other critics can reply just as validly that this West German policy gives the Soviet Union a permanent license to blackmail, and that the conquests of Ostpolitik are not real conquests if one has to live in permanent fear that the Soviets will overturn them. Thus the long-range, diffuse, or indirect political gains of increasing Soviet interdependence with the West are speculative at best; whereas the political costs of becoming too dependent on Moscow, in a crisis such as the Polish one, are immediate and tangible.

Although much of what disturbs Americans in West German and European attitudes—which they judge to be too soft on the East, too reluctant to take a stand on Poland or to sanction the Soviet Union—is indeed attributable to angst or greed, to fear of Soviet power, or to economic interests in deals with the East, the most important motive is less noticed. It lies in the fact that the Federal Republic is the only Western country that does deeply care about at least one part of Eastern Europe (namely the GDR), that does have an interest in challenging the division of Europe symbolized (wrongly) by the Yalta Agreement, and that does, moreover, have a strategy in this direction. But it so happens that this strategy is much the same as the old French principle of *revanche* after the lost war of 1870: "Y penser toujours, n'en parler jamais" (whereas the position of many others, particularly on Poland, may rightly be accused of being: "En parler toujours, n'y penser jamais").

A central element in this West German view is that no progress in intra-German relations will be made against the will of East German and Soviet rulers, hence they must be lulled or lured into relaxation through confidence and complacency; whereas protests and sanctions, and programs for liberation from the West or for revolution from below, can only shake them into repression and self-closure.

There is much, in my view, that is wrong with this strategy, both on moral and pragmatic grounds. This has been underlined in a particularly shocking way by the Polish crisis. In human terms it seems that the reaction of the FRG shows that the West German public puts its concern about not running any risk in its relations with East Germany well above any solidarity, grief, or indignation over the fate of the Polish people. Two of the most contemptible illustrations of this reaction were the editorials by Henry Nannen in *Der Stern* and Rudolf Augstein in *Der Spiegel* (December 21, 1981), in which the authors managed to convey both anti-American and anti-Polish feelings while avoiding any attack on the Soviets. Most disarmingly frank was the editorial by Theo Sommer, in *Die Zeit* (December 18, 1981), whose only concern was to save détente, and who was wishing for the success of Jaruzelski for this reason.[8] But even in relations with East Germany, the reaction of the Bonn government seems to lack the elementary feeling that there are times when one just must take a stand and say which side one is on. That Helmut Schmidt's first declaration about Poland's fate should have been uttered from East Germany in the way it was ("Mr. Honecker is as distressed as I am that this should have been necessary") is a black

8. For the German reactions to Poland, see Anne-Marie Le Gloannec, "Les réactions allemandes à la crise polonaise," *Documents*, March 1982, pp. 31–41.

mark on the record of one of the few Western statesmen who deserve respect and support.

Even on pragmatic grounds the West German strategy may suffer from being a fair-weather one that relies on the false hope of isolating relations with Eastern Europe from conflicts within other societies. One may argue that a certain amount of pressure and risk taking is indispensable in order to save arms control, détente, and Ostpolitik.

But American reactions were no more impressive on either grounds—moral or pragmatic. Some circles were almost looking forward to the Polish coup, or at least welcomed it when it happened (such as the *Wall Street Journal*), either because it would expose the bankruptcy of communism or because it would provide a strong government that would avoid the actual bankruptcy of Poland and thus of Western banks—or for both reasons. The same circles refused to do anything to help the Polish experiment while it lasted,[9] hence share some responsibility for the deterioration of economic conditions that made Jaruzelski's operation so much easier. But they turned around and expressed their moral indignation both at the coup (as if on *that* ground it was any different from other communist takeovers or from military coups, complete with states of emergency, arrests, and repression against trade unions and democratically elected officials) and at the lack of reaction of Europeans, which they interpreted as a betrayal against—of all people—the United States.

As for the Reagan administration, having already canceled the grain embargo and authorized the Caterpillar deal, is stressed for almost a week that the coup was an "internal affair" and the need was to avoid direct Soviet intervention. President Reagan even blamed (in his press conference on December 23, 1981) Solidarity's demand for free elections as having been the last straw that provoked the intervention. But then the administration hardened its tone. First it stopped food deliveries to Poland and then it embarked on the Carter road of a policy of sanctions against the Soviet Union, but under even worse conditions—without allied or Vatican support, of course, but also without doctrinal credibility and without the main instrument, a grain embargo, that would have made the policy effective and allayed the suspicions of Europeans that the proposed sanctions would hurt them more than the United States.

Last but not least, the Reagan sanctions did not distinguish clearly between what was to be stopped and what was to be prevented. The only thing that can be said in favor of the Reagan measures is that at least the United States did *something*, while France only talked and West Germany adopted a low profile in word and in deed (while intimating that there is more to its role, in terms of mediation or of a moderating influence in the East, than meets the eye). But at

---

9. See "The Poland Bailout," *Wall Street Journal*, August 27, 1981, and "To Some Bankers with Loans to Poland, Military Crackdown Isn't All Bad News," *Wall Street Journal*, December 21, 1981, compared with the editorials of December 15.

least the French and the West Germans have some kind of a vision (hidden or explicit, prophetic or misguided) of the future of Europe, whereas this is what the Reagan administration lacks most tragically and totally.

This analysis of the reactions to the Polish crisis only illustrates a general point. What may well be occurring is a further act in a play whose first act took place in the 1960s. At that time, both Zbigniew Brzezinski (in *Alternative to Partition*) and Henry Kissinger (in *The Troubled Partnership*) were writing that de Gaulle had a vision, but no policy, and the United States had a policy, but no vision. Today it is the German Social Democrats who seem to have taken the place of de Gaulle.

After the invasion of Afghanistan, many in the Federal Republic, including Schmidt, were so struck by the attachment of both West and East European governments to the preservation of détente—in spite of the hardening between the two superpowers—that they hailed this community of thought among the middle powers of Central Europe as the emergence of a new Europe. The illusions and false symmetries attached to this view were soon to be exploded by Gierek's fall, Honecker's tougher line, and the subsequent Soviet peace offensive. But even the Polish events (at least the breakdown of party authority) have been interpreted by the proponents of these notions as further proof that in Europe the ideological competition, hence the cold war, is over, and what is left are national realities forcing the two superpowers into global competition but drawing the two Europes together away from this global competition and toward "re-Europeanization."[10]

This view has been exposed in a particularly forceful and extreme way by Peter Bender in his book, *Das Ende des ideologischen Zeitalters: Die Europäisierung Europas* (Severin and Siedler, 1981). He pushed it to absurd lengths, in my opinion, both in terms of false symmetries between the two sides and in terms of policy recommendations. (In order to encourage Moscow to give up its rule over Eastern Europe, for instance, Western Europe should have neither missiles nor radio stations reaching the Soviet Union.) He cites the precedent of de Gaulle's ideas for a "Europe from the Atlantic to the Urals," and advocates Western Europe's detachment from the United States as a precondition for Eastern Europe's detachment from the Soviet Union. Clearly, the same reasons that provoked de Gaulle's failure (an overestimation of the leverage of a weak and disunited Western Europe and an underestimation of the Soviet Union's ideological character and its determination to keep what it has) are—as demonstrated once again by the Polish coup—even more valid today, since the Soviet Union is militarily much stronger and the need for Western Europe to reinforce its security link with the United States even more urgent. This is all the more so since the main thrust of these trends, particularly in West Germany,

10. For Günter Gaus, ideological considerations should be replaced above all by national ones: "Der West, Polen und der Kreml," *Die Zeit*, January 22, 1982. Bender and, more moderately, Richard Löwenthal put more emphasis on the European dimension.

is, much more than in de Gaulle's case, to make Western Europe weaker and more dependent—economically and militarily—upon Moscow's good will.

Yet who can deny that the secular trend is indeed in the direction foreseen by de Gaulle and rediscovered today: the increasing cost of empire, the increasing psychological gap between the two Europes and their respective superpowers, and the increasing human and economic ties between Eastern and Western Europe. Each of these trends has progressed spectacularly in the last fifteen years, especially in regard to West Germany, and can be expected to continue into the 1980s and 1990s.

I personally believe that the tragic course taken by the Polish affair represents a considerable setback for this evolution, whereas a successful continuation of the experiment would have considerably accelerated it. Yet earlier setbacks (such as the invasions of Hungary and Czechoslovakia) were unable to stop the trend; and this one may even favor it by promoting more disintegration in the West and more repression and thus, in the long run, an even less "organic" relationship in the East.

The two cardinal sins being committed by the new left-wing Gaullists are, on the one hand, jumping from social trends and perceptions to political conclusions and, on the other, confusing a long-range historical perspective with an immediately operational policy direction.

Some of the trends we have indicated may well look very different a few years from now. The reemergence of antinuclear and pacifist feelings in the United States, and the progress of the CDU in the Federal Republic, make it quite possible to envisage, by 1984, either a lessening in the West German–American divergence or a new turning of the tables, with the mutual suspicions resembling more those of the Kennedy-Adenauer days than those we have described. But while both American conservatism and globalism and West German and European pacifism and attachment to social priorities may produce their own counterreactions or correctives within their respective societies, the structural differences in vulnerability and attitudes toward risk on the one hand, and in priority for the GDR and Eastern Europe on the other, are not likely to go away. But the practical lessons to be drawn are far from simple. The Western policy goal must be to recognize trends and channel them in positive directions. This means combining unity and diversity within the West, firmness and openness toward the East, and attention to permanent requirements and changing conditions—that is, a simultaneous effort to strengthen present structures that are endangered but for which there is no substitute and to lay the groundwork for their transformation. Can one repair the present with an eye to the future? Can one act neither as if the long-range perspectives were never to materialize nor as if they were already here?

Each Western power has its own preferred way out of these dilemmas or around them. The French seem content to indicate a direction (to "get out of Yalta") and then to do nothing about it (in the name of the "slowness of history"). The West Germans apply the opposite combination. They are as discreet as possible about long-range goals and as active as possible about immediate "little steps." But they assume that these "little steps" can take place under the protective shadow of an East-West balance and of an American presence which may be challenged by isolationist trends in the United States and which they themselves may help to undermine by encouraging American suspicion and resentment. The Reagan administration tends to dream of a return to the (partly mythical) unity and simplicity of the past, yet when it cannot threaten or preach its allies into the same attitude, it makes sudden adjustments to their priorities.

Critics such as Brzezinski, who are more aware of the need for a comprehensive, differentiated, and evolutionary approach, nevertheless also tend to oscillate between the extremes of head-on collision (whether with Brezhnev or Schmidt) and imprudent encouragement of schemes, such as nuclear-free zones, that feed directly the most dangerous campaigns of the peace movement and of the Soviet Union and are more likely to undermine NATO and the necessary recoupling of European and American security in the short run than to contribute to the equally important long-run objectives of East-West reconciliation and all-European autonomy.[11]

But both the goal and the means are to be seen in this two-track or dialectical strategy. The goal of the West in East-West relations can only be, as Brzezinski points out, to encourage peaceful change in the communist world as a necessary precondition for peaceful accommodation between East and West. In the age of "hot peace" and of "competitive decadence" the name of the game is competition through mutual influence. The two sides share an interest both in weakening the other in the long run (or at least in avoiding being weakened by it) and in preventing its collapse in the short run. In a situation both dynamic and fragile, when the Soviet bloc is at the same time stronger militarily and weaker economically than before, when some of its members combine a dramatic economic crisis and a no less dramatic dependence on both the Soviet Union and the West, and when the road taken by the Soviet Union to handle these crises points more toward repression than reform, neither an unconditional cold war nor an unconditional détente is desirable, even if they were possible. As against the aim of breaking all contacts with the Soviet empire either in order to avoid being contaminated by it or to sharpen its crises and hasten its collapse, the West Germans and, more generally, the Europeans are right to believe that this gamble is too dangerous and uncertain to justify taking the risk of jeopardizing their own security and of worsening the fate of their East European brothers. But they are wrong to believe that either of the latter priorities is enhanced by unconditional economic help and by security concessions, no matter

11. See Brzezinski's "For a Broader Western Strategy," *Wall Street Journal*, February 19, 1982.

what the behavior of the Soviet and satellite rulers. The only policy that can influence the evolution of Central Europe favorably is an open-ended one that involves both sticks and carrots. The key word here is flexibility. Breaking up all economic ties would deprive the West of any economic leverage for political ends. Maintaining them unconditionally would have the same effect by making it the prisoner of these very ties, which should be its instruments.

In essence the West should demonstrate to the Soviet Union that the only way to remedy, if not to solve, the crisis of its empire is to accept a partial sharing of power over its more exposed parts with local forces and Western creditors. The only way to save détente, Ostpolitik, and the intra-German dialogue is to be willing to put them at risk if necessary. Otherwise the hardening of Soviet policy, the despair of East European populations, and the impatience of the United States have a greater chance of producing the very convulsions that West German policy rightly wants to avoid.

Conversely, the only way for the United States to carry its allies along, on a policy of balance and, if need be, resistance and denial toward the Soviet bloc, is to tie it to some form of positive vision that looks beyond the cold war. This is already painfully clear in arms control, where Kissinger's retrospective prophecy, "Six months of Cold War and we will be back to 'peace at any cost,'"[12] seems on the way to being confirmed. But it should also be clear that the same applies to relations with Eastern Europe. The German position, in a sense, has not changed for a generation. As Stephen Szabo so rightly reminds us, Karl Deutsch and Lewis Edinger were warning in 1959 that West Germany could be trusted as an Atlantic partner provided it was not faced with a stark choice between this partnership and its relations with East Germany and Eastern Europe. The Germans wanted to reconcile the advantages of the Western alliance with those of neutralism.[13]

Today, a deteriorating Atlantic Alliance and the emergence of both new links with Eastern Europe and new threats from the Soviet Union call for an updating of this warning. The West Germans still want to have their cake and eat it too. In a sense, this is only an expression of their unique situation, which makes it impossible for them to go all the way in any of the three possible directions—Atlantic, West European, and Central European. But in their attempt to combine them they need to be reminded of two things. First, some circumstances do impose definite priorities. The growing external power and internal crisis of the Soviet empire and the evolution of American society impose urgent priorities that cannot be sacrificed to the long-range one of the German

12. Henry Kissinger, *Years of Upheaval* (Boston: Little, Brown, 1982), p. 1030.
13. Karl W. Deutsch and Lewis J. Edinger, *Germany Rejoins the Powers* (Stanford: Stanford University Press, 1959), quoted by Stephen Szabo in "West Germany: Generations and Changing Security Perspectives," in Szabo, ed., *The Successor Generations* (London: Butterworth, 1982).

dialogue, even though that preoccupation can never be discarded. Second, to the extent that the West Germans engage alone in a dialogue with an East Germany ultimately controlled by the Soviet Union, they risk letting Moscow manipulate them into becoming the prisoners and the instruments of this triangular relationship. Only if Europe and the alliance provide them with a solid framework and an unequivocal—albeit not uncritical—backing can they continue to try to promote a discrete Finlandization of East Germany without becoming Finlandized themselves.

This presupposes that West Germany's partners understand that the original compact of the alliance—the FRG choosing the West but the West adopting the problem of Germany's division as its own—is still valid, even though in a changed form corresponding to the changed character of German national aspirations and of the European situation. This does not mean entrusting the Federal Republic with ultimate control over East-West relations. But it does mean, on the one hand, that the broader pan-European framework, which is that of West German concerns, must more than ever be adopted by the alliance itself, and, on the other hand, that within this collective framework the role of the different partners cannot help but be differentiated according to their respective vulnerabilities and aspirations.

Finally, the other West Europeans have an increasingly crucial role to play: given the centrifugal tendencies in both American and West German societies, they must provide the unifying cement, instead of indulging in the freedom of action they were able to enjoy when this cement was provided by the American-German entente. They must encourage both countries in the apparently contradictory directions of recoupling American and West European security now and of preparing for Europeanization in the long run. In the short run, the priority is both to restore a credible balance in the face of Soviet power (which means strengthening the Atlantic Alliance) and to try to influence the evolution of the Soviet empire, in particular through concerted, flexible, and discriminating trade and credit policies.

Both processes may eventually be channeled in the direction of a stronger Western Europe having a more autonomous dialogue with a weakened Soviet Union and encouraging a more autonomous Eastern Europe.[14] Of course, this is not likely to happen. But even among utopian policies it may be desirable to distinguish between those that rely on distorting simplifications (as may be the case for the new pacifists, the new gaullists, and the new cold warriors alike) and those that take into account a number of factors such as (1) the nature of the Soviet empire and of Moscow's strategy toward Western Europe, as it has been described in this book, (2) the complex relations within the Atlantic Alliance,

14. See my "American Policy towards the Soviet Union in the 1980s: Objectives and Uncertainties," in *America's Security in the 1980s*, Adelphi Paper no. 174 (London: International Institute for Strategic Studies, Spring 1982), pp. 35–52.

between universal, regional, and national concerns, which we have indicated in this chapter, and (3) the nature of the East-West problem as it emerges from the confrontation of these two series of factors.

In the last analysis, the East-West problem can be seen in terms of inevitable asymmetries and necessary symmetries. To put it more precisely, it consists in finding a tolerable combination of asymmetry and reciprocity, in recognizing the qualitative difference between East and West, yet finding enough of a common denominator to permit a stable military balance, meaningful arms control negotiations, mutually beneficial economic relations, and a minimum of common standards concerning relations between individuals and groups belonging to opposite political regimes.

To a very great extent, Soviet policy, in all these areas, consists in exploiting existing asymmetries and creating new ones in the name of a formal or apparent symmetry. Its military and arms control strategies seek to exploit both the geographical asymmetry between the two alliances (the lack of territorial contiguity between the United States—unlike the Soviet Union—and Europe) and the political one (the role of public opinion and mass movements in the West, the control over information and over political life in the East, the different degrees of integration of the two military alliances and of control of the two leaders over their allies).

The USSR's conception of East-West economic relations relies on encouraging interdependence when it suits its needs while maintaining the centralized structure it needs for political reasons and even exploiting it by creating an asymmetrical structure of interdependence, with more flexibility in the East and more irreversible vested interests in the West. In human and cultural relations the asymmetry between open and state or party-controlled societies is even more obvious. Finally the very conception of the structure and evolution of Europe (a "dynamic status quo" in Western Europe and a frozen one in Eastern Europe—a reversible one in one case, an irreversible one in the other) is fundamentally asymmetrical.

In the West, both yesterday's proponents of détente based on economic convergence and today's proponents of peace and disarmament based on disengagement and denuclearization naïvely assume a symmetry in the political effects of economic interdependence or of protest movements in the West and in the East. But their error does not remove the need for agreements, whether in the economic sphere or on arms control. The question is to what extent one can avoid that the asymmetry of political regimes (elections, mass protests, private business interests on one side, centralized control on the other) should produce an asymmetry of results (SS-20s on one side, no Pershing II and cruise missiles on the other) or, put differently, how much reciprocity and communication the West can expect from the East without hoping for convergence or demanding conversion.

Obviously the problem of a common language or code between different or opposed systems arises not only for the pursuit of agreements but just as much for the management of conflict, the appraisal of the military balance, or the calculus of deterrence and of influence. Two examples of difficulties in devising Western policies toward an opponent about whose intentions and reactions we still know very little, except that they can be neither similar nor unrelated to ours, are the military and economic arenas.

Whether on central nuclear war or on military conflict in Europe, Western controversies are based on unproven assumptions about Soviet strategy. In the debate on nuclear doctrine, a curious turnaround has taken place. From McNamara on, Americans had undertaken to teach the Soviets the "rational" doctrines of mutual assured destruction and arms control. Critics such as Richard Pipes and Colin Gray have emphasized that this approach was based on an illusion, since Soviet doctrines were rooted not in ignorance but in a different "strategic culture," itself based on both Russian tradition and Marxist ideology, emphasizing conflict and victory. But then, after having pointed out the structural differences between America and Russia, the same analysts and policy makers turn around and advise Americans to become the pupils of the Soviets instead of their educators and adopt a Soviet-type posture based on war-fighting and the search for victory—as if, by their own reasoning, a doctrine fit for a totalitarian empire was not unfit for an open democratic coalition.

To cap it all, the Soviets, once they have reached parity or superiority, start adopting a declaratory policy based on the language of American arms controllers; and the United States, while having trouble maintaining even a modest form of extended deterrence, starts adopting the earlier Soviet language, with unknown effects on Moscow but with known and rather disturbing effects on its own population and allies.

On the European theater, the new debate about NATO strategy seems either to ignore the "other side of the hill" or to rely on selective evidence attributing to the Soviets the strategic concept or posture that would fit the preferred Western response. Whether the proposals burgeoning on both sides of the Atlantic for a "no first use" of nuclear weapons, for a conventional posture based on defensive weapons only (or, on the contrary, on a conventional conteroffensive) or the banning of battlefield nuclear weapons (or, on the contrary, intermediate ones), are based to any significant degree on a serious evaluation of the likely nature of the Soviet military threat is doubtful. Conflicting claims have been made, however, going from the notion of a "surgical nuclear strike" enabling the Soviet Union, thanks to the SS-20s, to disarm NATO without fighting a war, to a new conventional emphasis enabling Moscow, through the newly created "operational maneuver groups," to destroy NATO's nuclear installations through conventional means.

In both the intercontinental and the European case, the political goals of the Soviet Union in peacetime are clearer than what would actually happen in case of war; countering them should probably be given first priority in Western strategy. It seems reasonable to assume that Moscow aims at keeping as many options for itself and closing as many options to the West as possible, so as to keep the political initiative and to induce paralysis and mutual suspicion and recrimination within NATO. Without wishing to fight and win a nuclear war, it thinks both deterrence of Western attack and political influence are enhanced by a known ability to do so if worst came to worst, coupled with a denial of any such intentions. In Europe, the central concept would still be one of "combined arms operations" in which distinctions between nuclear and conventional weapons and phases would be less sharp than in Western doctrines. But the greater feasibility of more extreme (nuclear only, or conventional only) scenarios serves to deprive the West of military escalatory options and to promote the "decoupling" of American and European defense.

Conversely, the Western priority should be to promote "recoupling" at both the military and the political levels: to maintain or regain a certain strategic flexibility necessary to the credibility of extended deterrence, but not at the cost of encouraging a European "political decoupling" that would endanger whatever would be gained in "military recoupling," or of sacrificing political "reassurance" (to use Michael Howard's expression) on the altar of operational effectiveness. Furthermore, just as the Soviet goal seems to be to reduce the American role and presence in Europe while avoiding its replacement by a strong autonomous West European defense, the Western objective must be to promote the latter without prematurely jeopardizing the former.

But to the extent that the Western alliance has any prospect (beyond defending its own independence) of affecting the evolution of the other side, this cannot be through military intimidation, in the manner of the Soviet Union; the main instrument has to be economic. But should one rely on the global positive effects of economic intercourse, or on the global negative effects of economic denial, or on a more discriminating policy based on both sticks and carrots and on using economic leverage for political aims? And should this leverage be explicit or implicit, specific or diffuse? Should it be applied by a united West to a united Soviet bloc, or should it start from the inevitable differentiation, if not divergence, of Western interests and encourage a similar differentiation in the East?

No clear answers exist to these questions in Western policy and public opinion—perhaps not even in this book. But the difficulty lies less in discerning Soviet aims and strategies, as in the military field, than in clarifying Western objectives and, even more, Western assumptions about the structural constraints and the margins for reform in the Soviet bloc, about its current crisis and its prospects of paralysis or collapse. Do we want to help them or to hurt them? Do we want, in the first case, to change communist leaders into peaceful consumers or to alleviate the fate of their victims? Do we want, in the second case, to hasten their collapse or simply weaken their power of hurting us? Or are helping them and hurting them, using carrots and sticks, two methods with the same goal—to redirect their allocation of resources from the military to the civilian sector?

Neither the successive American administrations nor the various European governments have stated these assumptions in a clear and coherent way. The rationale for American sanctions has seemed to oscillate between reversing Soviet actions (like the invasion of Afghanistan or the Polish coup), punishing Moscow in order to deter similar behavior in the future, reducing its military effectiveness, or transforming its regime. Europeans have oscillated between affirming a doctrinaire separation of economics and politics (belied by their insistence on embargos in other cases such as Argentina, Turkey, or South Africa) and a belief in their positive link through the beneficial effect of trade and help upon détente, upon the stability of communist regimes, and upon their liberalization.

The only certainty is that the assumptions behind the more extreme versions seem disproved or implausible. The structure and evolution of communist regimes, particularly the Soviet one, make it highly unlikely that interdependence with the West will solve their economic problems or promote their political transformation. The Brezhnevian economic opening to the outside world has rather been an alternative to reform, and has not decreased the priority of guns over butter; in Poland, Western credits have produced instability leading to repression rather than the harmonious progress expected by the Western promoters of economic détente.

Conversely, the worsening crisis of the Soviet bloc does not seem likely to lead to its collapse, even if a unanimous West were to practice a policy of general embargo and even if this total Western denial were possible and this abrupt Eastern collapse were desirable (two highly dubious propositions). Even less is the Soviet Union likely to change its priorities and risk military inferiority and domestic loss of control under Western pressure.

If both opposite extreme, global, and unconditional policies are unworkable and dangerous, and if abandoning any political considerations in favor of a purely economic approach in dealing with the most politicized economies on earth is equally so, there remains only a flexible, discriminating policy using both positive and negative sanctions, and distinguishing between different types of economic transactions in response to different types of foreign behavior and domestic evolution of the communist countries. But such concerted fine tuning may be the most unrealistic policy of all, not only because it aims at short-term effects and hence is compromised if they fail to materialize (unless one is dealing with global long-range policies that rely on an unverifiable gamble on future developments) but, above all, because the more flexible the policy the greater the necessary degree of cordination or control, hence the greater the incompatibility with the nature of capitalist economies and of the Atlantic Alliance.

The conclusion I draw is that no single coherent policy is possible, but that the West has to turn a liability (its own divergences of priorities if not of interests) into an asset. It must use its own diversity to encourage more diversity in the Soviet empire, by combining several policies or at least by applying different emphases to different targets.

With the Soviet Union, neither carrots nor sticks, neither short-term bargaining nor long-range gambles, are likely to change the nature of its regime or even its priorities. The only realistic goal is containment. This implies a much stricter control on "critical technology" (although not an excessively broadened definition of it that would imply a global embargo, for which there is no Western consensus), normal short-term trade, and an avoidance of grandiose long-term projects amounting to irreversible commitments or to disguised aid. These can be held in reserve for the unlikely prospect of a really significant change in Soviet behavior leading to a scaling down of the arms race. This hope cannot be excluded, but cannot be made the center of Western policy. With other communist countries, especially the new Soviet allies in the Third World, economic leverage has much more of a chance of producing political results: Angola or Mozambique, even Ethiopia or Nicaragua may be cases in point.

The communist countries of Eastern Europe represent an intermediate case: they are, as the events in Poland have demonstrated again, too vital for the Soviet Union to accept what would amount to a change in their political regime. But, on the other hand, they already have, more than the Soviet Union itself, a society whose life is *partly* resistant to party control; they are much more dependent on Western trade and credits; and while they are in some respects in deeper trouble than the Soviet Union, owing to their lack of raw materials as well as their greater indebtedness, the problems of at least some of them are more manageable because of their dimensions: decentralizing reforms have a better chance of working in Hungary than in the Soviet Union.

On the other hand, while the USSR has increased the sophistication of its control, both at home and in Eastern Europe, the economic crisis deprives it of an essential element of this control: economic compensations for political repression. It may, then, rather than running and subsidizing alone a re-Stalinized autarkic bloc, be willing to tolerate discrete compromises with local forces and Western creditors as long as the political evolution in these countries does not get out of hand. It may be too late or too early for that in Poland but not in Hungary. At any rate, whether it likes it or not, and whether through its actions or through its withdrawal, the West *is* involved in the management of the Soviet empire.

This is particularly true for Western Europe, and even more so for West Germany. No matter what Washington's policy on East-West relations is and no matter who is in power in Bonn, the intra-German trade will not lose its special status, which existed already in Adenauer's time and at the height of the cold war. The hopes, priority, and tactics of the policy of economic help to the GDR may change but not their substance. The problem is precisely that German, European, and Western aims will all be defeated if this policy is pursued by the Germans in isolation.

That is why the more complex policy, which takes into account the contradictory dimensions of the situation, may still be the most realistic, even if it is the most demanding one. To believe, like Peter Bender, that the ideological confrontation is over in Europe and relations between the two halves of Germany and of Europe can be dominated essentially by national interests and economic convergence is to forget the most important dimension: the nature of communist regimes and of the Soviet empire. The same illusion, shared by some of the same people, is at the root of the notion of "security partnership" with the East or of "common security interests of the two German states." But, conversely, to believe, as many influential members of the Reagan administration do, that the permanence of the East-West conflict can by itself dispose of the rebirth of national identities and of a Central European and pan-European consciousness leading to a special West European interest in Eastern Europe is equally misleading.

This is all the more so since, if properly understood, these apparently diverging priorities are more converging than contradictory. West German and West European solidarity is—or should be—directed at the people and societies of Eastern Europe, not at their governments and regimes, even if it leads to dealing with the latter. Conversely, the cause of the "free world" is served just as much as that of the cultural identity of the German nation and of European civilization by a greater autonomy for these societies and greater East-West contacts. Similarly, keeping the balance does serve peace as well as freedom better than unilateral disarmament or the dissolution of NATO.

Each country's and each continent's view of East-West relations is bound to be colored by its geographical situation and historical tradition. But if the West stands for something, it is for the idea that in the last analysis diversity and cooperation—or, put it differently, the three basic values of individual freedom, national independence, and a peaceful world order—stand or fall together.

Index

Western Europe (*continued*)
Czechoslovakia, 142; and Afghanistan crisis, 148–49, 184; and events in Poland, 152–53, 273; Soviet economic policy in, 159–208; economic relations with Eastern Europe, 160, 182; economic isolation from USSR during Berlin crisis, 162; encouraged by USSR to form alternative to NATO, 164; exports of machinery and transport equipment to USSR, 166; technology exports as political lever, 166–67; gas and oil imports from USSR, 172; bilateral trade agreements, 176; U.S. pressure on to restrict exports to USSR and Poland, 177, 273; industrial cooperation with Yugoslavia, 179; differences with U.S. on East-West trade, 184–88, 195, 199, 200, 201–3; and U.S. economic sanctions, 185–88; grain embargo, 187; and Olympic boycott, 188; and Soviet gas pipeline, 191–94, 263, 266; and CoCom, 194–98; reluctance to apply economic and political conditionality, 198–99; future trade policy, 205, 206; military planning, 230; Soviet studies of the Western alliance, 234–65; contradictions and cooperation in relations with U.S., 242–57; and Soviet proposal for security system, 246; and OPEC, 249; U.S. multinational corporations in, 253–54; U.S. military presence in, 254; analysis of relations with U.S., 266–99; nature of Soviet policy toward, 268–72; attitude to USSR, 272–74; roots of Western differences, 275–99; public opinion polls, 279–80; feeling of vulnerability, 280–81; economic priorities, 282–83; movement toward "re-Europeanization," 289–90; importance of economics in future of Western alliance, 296–97; and influence on Eastern Europe, 299. *See also* North Atlantic Treaty Organization

West Germany (Federal Republic of Germany, FRG): Ostpolitik, xv, 16, 19, 67, 142, 185–86, 244, 274, 275; economic and technological rise of, 11; powerful land army, 11, 19; SPD/FDP government, 13, 16, 67; relations with USSR, 16, 18–19, 23–24, 31–60, 154–55, 251, 268, 269, 274, 285; trade with the East, 19, 186; and peace movement, 22, 23, 42, 54, 59–60, 150, 154, 274; and military technology, 23; crucial to NATO and EC, 31; charged with "revanchism," 32, 64; cooperation sought by USSR, 32, 44, 57, 155; Soviet use of media for propaganda in, 33; threat of Soviet military posture to, 38; Soviet pressure on to reduce tension, 38–40; attitude to SALT

West Germany (*continued*)
II, 39; relations with East Germany, 39, 44–45, 186, 285, 286, 287, 298; Soviet strategic use of against the West, 40–42, 155; relations with France, 43–44, 64, 83, 266, 269–70; Basic Treaty (two Germanies), 44; and reunification, 44, 163, 269, 285, 286; and human rights policies, 46–47; and Soviet military intervention, 47–49; and Polish events, 48, 270, 280, 287; favors Eurostrategic arms buildup, 50, 54, 59, 278–79; urged by USSR to discourage NATO arms buildup, 56, 57; as intermediary in arms limitation talks, 57–59; endorses U.S. position on arms limitation, 59; criticism of Mitterrand, 75; and French security policy, 89; and invasion of Czechoslovakia, 142; and ecology movement, 154; and pipe embargo to USSR, 163; science and technology exchange agreement with USSR, 165; Gastarbeiter, 179; differences with U.S., 185–87, 193–94, 269; imports of natural gas and oil, 186; repatriation of ethnic Germans from USSR, 186; and Soviet gas pipeline, 191, 192, 193; and CoCom, 197; theory of spheres of commercial interest, 207; Finlandization of, 235; and Vietnam War, 243; and multilateral force, 243; relations with U.S., 246, 257, 269, 283–84; relations with Great Britain, 246; in triangle of power, 247, 284–88; accords with USSR and Poland (1970), 248; and nuclear sharing, 255; views of the public, 274, 278, 279–80; priorities, 283, 290, 292–93; renewed national consciousness, 285; political parties, 285–86; and Afghanistan crisis, 289; progress of CDU in, 290; mode of action, 291
Wharton Econometric Associates, 200
Wilson, Harold, 64, 164
World Bank, 162

Yakutia, 173
Yalta Agreement, 287
YANKEE-class SLBM, 223
"Year of Europe," 244
Yom Kippur War, 45, 272
Yugoslavia: early Soviet attitude to, xi; wartime resistance movement, xii; as alternative model of communist rule, xiv; participates in communist conference, 15; support of Eurocommunism, 25; and Tito's brand of communism, 95; Soviet concession to, 97; and pan-European conference, 120; and CoCom, 162; methods of financing trade with West, 179; industrial

Contributors

Herbert J. Ellison, formerly professor of history and chairman of the Center for Contemporary Chinese and Soviet Studies, University of Washington, is now secretary of the Kennan Institute for Advanced Russian Studies, Woodrow Wilson International Center for Scholars, Smithsonian Institution, Washington, D.C.

Trond Gilberg is director, Slavic and Soviet Language and Area Center, and professor of political science, Pennsylvania State University.

William E. Griffith is Ford Professor of Political Science, Massachusetts Institute of Technology.

John Hardt is associate director for senior specialists, Congressional Research Service, Library of Congress.

Pierre Hassner is senior research associate, Centre d'Etudes et de Recherches Internationales, University of Paris.

Benjamin S. Lambeth is a senior staff member of the Department of Political Science, Rand Corporation.

Robert Legvold is a senior fellow at the Council on Foreign Relations.

Michael J. Sodaro is assistant professor of international affairs and political science, George Washington University.

Kate Tomlinson is a research assistant, Congressional Research Service, Library of Congress.

Joan Barth Urban is associate professor, Department of Politics, The Catholic University of America.

Gerhard Wettig is section director, Bundesinstitut für ostwissenschaftliche und internationale Studien, Cologne.